P9-DXI-566

THE WATERGATE

THE WATERGATE

INSIDE AMERICA'S MOST INFAMOUS ADDRESS

JOSEPH RODOTA

WILLIAM MORROW
An Imprint of HarperCollins*Publishers*

THE WATERGATE. Copyright © 2018 by Joseph Rodota. All rights reserved. Printed in the United States of America. No part of this book may be used or reproduced in any manner whatsoever without written permission except in the case of brief quotations embodied in critical articles and reviews. For information, address HarperCollins Publishers, 195 Broadway, New York, NY 10007.

HarperCollins books may be purchased for educational, business, or sales promotional use. For information, please e-mail the Special Markets Department at SPsales@harpercollins.com.

FIRST EDITION

Designed by William Ruoto

Title page photo credit: AP/REX/Shutterstock

Library of Congress Cataloging-in-Publication Data

Names: Rodota, Joseph, author.
Title: The Watergate : inside America's most infamous address / Joseph Rodota.
Description: First tedition. | New York : William Morrow, 2018.
Identifiers: LCCN 2017038745 | ISBN 9780062476623 (hardback)
Subjects: LCSH: Watergate (Washington, D.C.)--History. |
   Celebrities—Washington (D.C.)—Biography. | Washington (D.C.)—Biography.
   | Washington (D.C.)--Buildings, structures, etc. | BISAC: HISTORY / United
   States / 21st Century. | POLITICAL SCIENCE / Government / National. |
   HISTORY / United States / State & Local / Middle Atlantic (DC, DE, MD, NJ,
   NY, PA).
Classification: LCC F204.W38 R63 2018 | DDC 647.09753—dc23 LC
record available at https://lccn.loc.gov/2017038745

ISBN 978-0-06-247662-3

18 19 20 21 22 LSC 10 9 8 7 6 5 4 3 2 1

To Erik.
For listening with a smile.
And for everything else.

We shape our buildings; thereafter they shape us.

—Winston Churchill

CONTENTS

THE WATERGATE

WITHDRAWN

SLAP.

A doorman dropped a copy of the *Washington Post* at the threshold of a Watergate apartment and continued down the long, curved hallway.

Slap.

He dropped a paper at the next doorstep, and the next, as he made his deliveries through the building.

Slap. Slap. Slap.

Watergate residents—some dressed for work, others still in bathrobes—opened their doors, grabbed their newspapers and stepped back inside their apartments. It was Friday, June 16, 1972. On the front page of the *Post*, a smiling President Richard Nixon embraced President Luis Echeverría of Mexico at the formal welcoming ceremony on the South Lawn of the White House. The United Nations had launched a new agency to promote international cooperation on the environment, to which the Nixon administration had already committed $100 million. The Soviet news agency Pravda said a thaw in relations with the United States was "both necessary and desirable." And Raymond Lee "Cadillac" Smith, a legendary figure among Washington's underworld of pimps, gamblers and hired killers, was finally captured at a Holiday Inn in Kingsport, Tennessee, ending a two-month spree of kidnapping, robbery and murder.

Early risers headed to the Watergate health club to swim in the indoor saltwater pool or use one of the new treadmills, which the club called "mechanical walkers." Each lap in the pool offered the comfort of routine in an era of unpredictability. Each mile on a treadmill measured progress in a city often frustrated by partisan or bureaucratic gridlock.

The Watergate comprised six buildings spread over ten immaculately landscaped acres: the 213-suite Watergate Hotel; the Watergate Office Building, adjacent to the hotel; a second office building at 600 New Hampshire Avenue, facing the Kennedy Center; and three cooperative apartment buildings, known as Watergate East, Watergate West and Watergate South. (There was no Watergate North.) There was underground parking for twelve hundred cars and a shopping arcade with a number of businesses bearing the Watergate name, including the Watergate Bakery, the Watergate Florist, the Watergate Gallery and the Watergate Beauty Salon. The Watergate had its own bank, a small post office, a Safeway supermarket, one dentist and three psychiatrists. A sophisticated security system, including fourteen cameras in Watergate East alone, recorded the comings and goings of members of Congress, cabinet secretaries, White House aides, journalists, judges and diplomats. Owners of Watergate apartments, from massive penthouses with Potomac River views to modest one-bedrooms overlooking the Howard Johnson Motor Lodge, had something in common: a desire to be close to the center of power in the capital city of the most powerful nation on earth.

Frank Wills, a guard with the Watergate Office Building's private security firm, wrote in his logbook "all levels" of the building "seemed secured" and ended his shift at 7:00 A.M. He turned in his keys and headed home, passing joggers as they returned to the Watergate from morning runs along the Potomac River or through Rock Creek Park. A small army of housekeepers arrived at the Watergate by bus. It was already in the mid-sixties. By late afternoon, Washington would be flirting with ninety degrees.

Rose Mary Woods stepped into the hall and locked the door to her two-bedroom apartment on the seventh floor of Watergate East. She had worked for Richard Nixon as his personal secretary since 1951, when he moved from the House to the Senate, but she was essentially a member of the family—"the Fifth Nixon," some said. She headed to the garage for her eight-minute commute to the White House.

At the other end of the Watergate, in a large seventh-floor duplex apartment with both city and river views, Martha Mitchell packed for California. She was still angry with her husband, John, who had resigned as attorney general four months earlier—against her wishes—to become chairman of Nixon's reelection committee, reprising the role he played during the 1968 campaign. Her unfiltered observations on virtually any topic, from the Vietnam War to the sexual revolution, had made her a national celebrity: Behind only the president and the first lady, Martha Mitchell was the top draw at Republican fund-raisers. Martha, however, was unenthusiastic about this trip to California. She hated to fly. She was overscheduled and exhausted. Besides, Mrs. Nixon was scheduled to attend the fund-raiser in Beverly Hills, which meant Martha would not be the center of attention. "You don't need me," she told Fred LaRue, her husband's top deputy. LaRue pleaded with her. He said his wife, Joyce, wouldn't go to California unless Martha was on the trip. "I felt sorry for her," Martha later recalled. "He lived in Washington at the Watergate, and she lived with the kids in Mississippi. She never got to go anyplace."

Upstairs in her two-story penthouse on the fourteenth floor of Watergate East, Anna Chennault opened the *Washington Post* and turned to the "Style" section, where she found her name—Mrs. Claire Lee Chennault—on the guest list for last night's state dinner at the White House, which included four members of Nixon's cabinet, three U.S. senators and two neighbors at the Watergate: Nixon's campaign finance chief Maurice Stans and his wife, Kathy, who lived on the tenth floor of Watergate East, and the dashing yachtsman Emil "Bud" Mosbacher, Jr., Nixon's chief of protocol, and his wife, Patty, who lived in a suite at the Watergate Hotel. Guests dined on scallops and beef with mushrooms. The Nixons served a Schloss Johannisberger Riesling, followed by a claret. After dinner, everyone moved to the East Room and listened to a performance by New Orleans jazz clarinetist Pete Fountain. President

Nixon turned to Jack Benny, who had flown in from Los Angeles for the evening, and said it was a tragedy that Benny had left his violin in California.

In his fourth-floor studio apartment, Walter Pforzheimer finished getting ready for work. Since 1956, he curated the CIA's Historical Intelligence Collection—the spy agency's in-house library. Pforzheimer owned two apartments at the Watergate: this studio, where he slept and dressed, and a one-bedroom duplex on the seventh floor, where he hosted visitors and displayed his personal collection of espionage literature and artifacts related to spies and spying, including the canceled passport of Mata Hari.

At 8:07 A.M., President Nixon arrived at the Oval Office, just a few steps from the office of Rose Mary Woods. At 8:34, he posed in the Rose Garden for a photo with Vice President Spiro T. Agnew and the entire cabinet, including John Volpe, the secretary of transportation, who lived with his wife, Jennie, in a Watergate East penthouse.

At 9:30, Anna Chennault arrived at the embassy of the Republic of Vietnam, to say goodbye in person to her friend Bùi Diem, on his final day as South Vietnam's ambassador to the United States.

At 10:17, Nixon adjourned the cabinet meeting and returned to the Oval Office to discuss with a few key aides the progress of welfare reform legislation on Capitol Hill. The day before, nineteen Republican senators had written Nixon urging him to work more closely with Senator Abraham A. Ribicoff, Democrat of Connecticut, to draft a "humane and decent" welfare reform compromise. Ribicoff and his wife, Ruth, lived in the Watergate, as did two GOP senators who signed the letter: Jacob K. Javits of New York and Edward W. Brooke of Massachusetts.

By 10:00, most of the shops at the Watergate were open. At 11:00, the morning mail was sorted and ready to be picked up at the front desk in each of the three apartment buildings.

At National Airport, just ten minutes and three traffic lights from the Watergate, Martha and John Mitchell boarded a Gulf-stream II jet provided to them by Gulf Oil. Martha's personal secretary, Lea Jablonsky, and the Mitchells' eleven-year-old daughter, Marty, joined them on the flight to California. Marty looked forward to visiting Disneyland. Martha looked forward to getting a few days' rest at the beach.

At noon, following a quick stop at the South Korean embassy to meet with Ambassador Kim Dong Jo, Anna Chennault met Ray Cline for lunch. Their friendship went back decades to her days as a reporter in China, before the Communists seized power. Cline, the former CIA station chief in Taipei, now directed intelligence gathering for the State Department.

Back at the Watergate, women gathered to swim, sunbathe and gossip at one of the three outdoor swimming pools. Each "regular" had her favorite spot. "If it only had a tennis court and a movie theatre," said Mrs. Herbert Saltzman, who lived next door to Senator and Mrs. Javits in Watergate West, "I don't think I'd ever have occasion to leave the place."

The Mitchells and their entourage arrived in Los Angeles and were whisked off to the Beverly Hills Hotel. It had been a long flight. After a room-service dinner, John retired early and Martha stayed up and had a few drinks.

Four men, using assumed names, arrived at National Airport and took a taxi to the Watergate Hotel. They checked into suites 214 and 314. At 8:30 P.M., they dined on lobster tails at the hotel restaurant.

At 10:50, a man signed the logbook in the lobby of the Watergate Office Building and took the elevator to the eighth floor, where the Federal Reserve kept an office. He taped open the stairwell locks on the eighth floor before continuing down to the sixth floor, taping its door as well as the doors on the B-2 and B-3 levels, and those leading to the underground garage.

On the sixth floor of the Watergate Office Building, in the offices of the Democratic National Committee, Bruce Givner, a twenty-one-year-old summer intern from UCLA, was making use of the committee's free long-distance telephone. He called friends and family back home in Lorain, Ohio, pausing only to step onto the balcony and relieve himself in one of the potted plants. He was observed by a man stationed in Room 723 of the Howard Johnson Motor Lodge, across the street, who passed word to the men in Room 314 of the Watergate Hotel that the DNC suite was still occupied.

At 11:51, Frank Wills returned to the Watergate Office Building to begin his midnight to 8:00 A.M. shift. He made his rounds and discovered tape on the door locks at levels B-2 and B-3. He removed the tape, returned to his desk in the lobby and documented his discovery in his logbook. He called the answering service for GSS, the private security firm for which he worked, and left a message for his supervisor to call him.

Shortly after one in the morning, on Saturday, June 17, 1972, five men took the elevator from the second and third floors of the Watergate Hotel down to the underground garage and made their way to the Watergate Office Building.

Within a few hours, the Watergate—and the nation—would never be the same.

PART I

Recognizing the outstanding possibilities of the site on the River; its strategic location to the Center of the City; the close proximity of significant developments (both actual and planned—The State Department, Lincoln Memorial, National Cultural Center . . .); the architects approached the problem by providing a "Garden City within a City" where people could live, work, shop, and play, with cultural opportunities within walking distance.

"The Watergate Development," February 28, 1962

IN 1946, THE WASHINGTON GAS LIGHT COMPANY BEGAN switching its customers in Maryland, Virginia and the District of Columbia to "natural" gas, which meant the West Station Works, where coal was converted to "mixed" gas, was no longer needed. The land beneath the plant, a six-and-a-half-acre parcel bordered by the Potomac River and Virginia and New Hampshire Avenues, was now for sale at $3 million. There was some flexibility in price—the company was "open to offers," subject to approval by the board of directors of the Washington Gas Light Company—but the property was only available in its entirety. Any "piecemeal" offers, the *Washington Post* reported, would be rejected.

John Nolen, Jr., the staff director of the National Capital Planning Commission, the federal agency formed in 1924 to oversee planning within the District of Columbia on behalf of the federal government, said he would support residential or other uses for the gas company site—as permitted under existing zoning—provided they were "harmonious" with the major federal buildings planned nearby, including the massive new State Department headquarters. The gas company printed up a brochure with illustrations of eight- and five-story apartment buildings that could potentially be constructed on the property. According to the brochure, a buyer would find support among city planners for closing streets and merging the lots spanning F, G, H, 26th and 27th Streets—on the same grid originally laid out by Charles L'Enfant—into a single buildable site, "thus adding materially to the value of the property." The gas company, however, retained an adjacent parcel where two massive gas storage tanks were located. "It could be the best residential area in town," observed the District of Columbia's top planning bureaucrat, "were it not for those tanks."

One week after Harry S. Truman surprised Thomas E. Dewey, the *Chicago Daily Tribune* and the nation by winning the 1948 presidential election, a crowd of two hundred "real estate men" gathered in the East Room of the Mayflower Hotel, a thirteen-minute walk from the White House. Local auctioneer Ralph Weschler, hired by the gas company to sell the property, called it the District's "most strategic" development opportunity, by virtue of its location overlooking the Potomac River, within a two-mile radius of the city's most important office buildings. Hotelier Conrad Hilton read the auction prospectus carefully, but decided not to bid. He could not figure out what to do with the oddly shaped site. Roy S. Thurman, a local developer with an uneven track record, was undeterred by the nearby gas storage tanks. He thought the waterfront parcel would make a good spot for apartments and a shopping center and opened the bidding at $750,000. Stanford Abel, treasurer of a local engineering firm, who told a reporter he had "nothing special" in mind for the land, raised his paddle. The two men bid against each other until Abel dropped out, leaving Thurman the high bidder at $935,000. Marcy L. Sperry, president of the gas company, promptly declared the bid unacceptable. Weschler then offered each of the six lots individually. He looked around the room, but was met only with stares. There were no bidders. Within a few minutes, the auction was over.

When the Washington Gas Light Company finally announced plans to dismantle its unsightly gas storage tanks, George Preston

Marshall, owner of the Washington Redskins football team, decided to pounce. With John W. Harris, developer of the Statler Hotel in New York, Marshall formed a syndicate and purchased an option to develop most of the gas company land in Foggy Bottom, about ten acres. In September 1953, they revealed plans for Potomac Plaza Center, a "high character" project, including a thousand-room hotel, a two-thousand-car garage, six office buildings, two apartment buildings, a shopping center, an ice rink and a yachting marina, at a total cost of $75 million. *Time* magazine called the proposed development "Rockefeller Center–like." The firm of Harrison & Abramovitz, architects of Rockefeller Center, had designed the project. In the summer of 1955, Harris brought in a new investor, American Securities Corp. of New York, which agreed to supply working capital for the project and help raise up to $100 million in financing for the Potomac Plaza Center project. American Securities made a "substantial cash deposit" with the Washington Gas Light Company, extending the option on the land another five years.

LA SOCIETÀ GENERALE IMMOBILIARE DI LAVORI DI UTILITÀ pubblica ed agricola (in English, "General Building Society of Works of Public and Agricultural Utility") was the largest real estate development and construction firm in Italy. To the company's employees, it was known as Immobiliare. In the media, the firm was usually identified as either Società Generale Immobiliare or by its initials, SGI. The company was as old as Italy itself: Founded in the northern city of Turin in 1862, SGI moved its headquarters to Rome in 1870, just as that city became the capital of the Kingdom of Italy. Over the decades, SGI cleared slums, enlarged plazas throughout Rome, and created large suburban developments outside the city. These subdivisions had all the amenities, from roads and utilities to churches and soccer fields. For the 1960 Olympic Games in Rome, SGI built the Olympic Village. In partnership with Hilton Hotels, the company built the Cavalieri Hilton on a hilltop overlooking Vatican City, beating back protestors who wanted the site preserved as a public park. Eugenio Gualdi, an engineer and former president of the Lazio soccer organization, was managing director and chairman of the board. But the key figure in transforming SGI into a "construction titan," according to *Time* magazine, was Aldo Samaritani.

Samaritani, trained as a banker, joined SGI in his late twenties and was now vice director of the firm, second only to Gualdi, with the understanding he would take control of SGI when Gualdi retired. With his neatly trimmed mustache and slicked-back hair, Samaritani appeared easygoing and modest, but he was shrewd, competitive and disciplined. Colleagues called him "a human computer" for his ability to juggle financial and other details for every SGI project. He worked twelve-hour days, which left him little time for his seven children and eleven grandchildren. He looked forward to retirement. "Many of my colleagues fear the vacuum that will be created in their lives when they stop working actively," he told a reporter. "But I will have more than enough to do—seeing hundreds of movies I have missed, reading hundreds of books that I have left unread, listening to phonograph records that others have heard."

Under Samaritani's direction, SGI had expanded into the rest of Europe and now looked to North America. "We once considered Italy's boundaries as our frontiers," he said. "Now we consider the whole Western world as our country." There were plans for a $25 million shopping mall on the Champs-Élysées in Paris, a $100 million office complex in Montreal and a $300 million housing project ten miles outside Mexico City. Geographical diversification served another purpose: Assets and revenues from abroad reduced the financial risks to the company from Italy's perennially unstable domestic political climate.

After earning his engineering degree from the University of Milan, Giuseppe Cecchi went to work at SGI's Milan office. He had a strong jaw, light brown hair and the physique of a wrestler.

While working in the project-planning department of SGI's head-quarters in Rome, Cecchi learned about the company's prospective New York office and volunteered for a position there. He listed his qualifications: He was young, single, and he had "a little knowledge of English." He was also the son of Antonio Cecchi, a senior executive at SGI. Samaritani signed off on the transfer and Giuseppe Cecchi set off for New York and reported to the office of Nicolas Salgo and Company.

Tall and distinguished, with a deep voice and prominent eyebrows, Nicolas Salgo was fluent in four languages—German, French, English and his native Hungarian. He was born in Budapest and lived in Geneva during World War II, working in various Swiss-run trading and investment firms. After the war, Salgo, married with two children, moved to New York and became a U.S. citizen in 1953. He managed U.S. investments, including a real estate portfolio, for a prominent Swiss family and went toe-to-toe with William Zeckendorf, head of Webb & Knapp and a legendary figure in New York real estate, over a deal. Zeckendorf was impressed and hired Salgo, sending him to Rome to manage Webb & Knapp's involvement in the EUR district, an industrial park south of the city. The lead developer on that massive project was SGI.

Shortly after Salgo returned to New York to start his own investment firm, Samaritani attempted to recruit him to lead SGI's expansion into the American market. But Salgo wasn't interested in working for someone else. He made a counterproposal: Within six months, he promised to bring SGI three potential development projects to consider. "You will have the liberty to refuse one, two, or all three," he told Samaritani. "If you refuse, you don't owe me a nickel. If you accept any one of these proposals, you don't owe me a commission—because I want to be your partner." Salgo also promised to help see any development through to completion. "But I will never be on your payroll. I will always be independent." Samaritani accepted.

Salgo let brokers and former colleagues know he was on the hunt for large-scale projects that could be built in or near urban centers, with a mix of offices, residences and other amenities. Within a few weeks, a friend called him from American Securities Corp. They did not have the funds to proceed with the Potomac Plaza Center, which had yet to win approval from federal and local agencies. Their option on the Washington Gas Light Company site was expiring in six months and they were ready to sell. When Salgo first saw the gas company site, he thought it looked "simply awful." Warehouses and other industrial structures had been demolished, leaving behind cracked foundations barely visible among the weeds. Homes in the area were selling for as little as $2,000. The noise of rush-hour traffic rose from a busy street just a few hundred feet away. "No one wanted to live there," he recalled later. Yet despite its flaws, the site was a rare opportunity to have a major footprint in America's capital city. Salgo presented three possible sites to SGI, two near New York City and the Washington Gas Light Company land in Foggy Bottom. Giuseppe Cecchi was keenly aware the local real estate community considered the site to be inferior. But it was on a river—and people were always attracted to live or work with a view of a river, he knew—and it was close to downtown and to the White House. Cecchi believed the locals were wrong.

On February 1, 1960, at the SGI board meeting in Rome, Chairman Gualdi announced the "Potomac deal." Two plots of land, "centrally located" at Virginia Avenue and New Hampshire Avenue, had been purchased at a total cost of $3.75 million. There were two separate contracts, including an outright purchase of one parcel from the Washington Gas Light Company and the purchase of an option from American Securities Corp. Salgo became a partner, with an 8 percent share, in a new subsidiary of SGI, to be named Island Vista, Inc., the sponsor of the as-yet-unnamed development.

Cecchi hoped to avoid the bureaucratic gridlock that had stalled the Potomac Plaza Center. He met informally with William E. Finley, known as Bill, the new executive director of the National Capital Planning Commission, to introduce himself and the project. Finley listened to Cecchi's tentative plans and recommended the design "harmonize" with plans for the National Cultural Center.

On September 4, 1958, while vacationing in Newport, Rhode Island, President Dwight D. Eisenhower had signed legislation to authorize a National Cultural Center, and the following June, the center's first board of trustees selected Edward Durell Stone to design the building. An Arkansas native, Stone had worked as a junior architect on Rockefeller Center with Harrison & Abramovitz—the same firm that designed Potomac Plaza Center—and went on to launch his own firm, winning a series of important commissions, including the U.S. embassy in New Delhi, India, and the U.S. pavilion at the 1958 international exposition in Brussels. In September 1959, Stone unveiled his plan for the National Cultural Center—a curved, concrete-and-glass structure, resembling a large clamshell, facing the Potomac. The center's executive committee endorsed the design unanimously and commended Stone and his team "for their exceptionally fine work." The *Washington Post* called it "little short of breath-taking." The estimated construction cost—up to $60 million—shocked Representative Frank Thompson, Jr., of New Jersey, an original sponsor of the bill to create the National Cultural Center. He called Stone's vision "beautiful but grandiose."

Cecchi forwarded images of Stone's dramatic design to the offices of Luigi Moretti, SGI's top consulting architect, in Rome. In his early fifties, Luigi Moretti was at the top of his game, a member of Rome's arts and business elite. He entered restaurants like a Renaissance prince and rode through town seated next to his chauffeur in a two-toned, black-and-white Chevrolet convertible with red upholstery. A former athlete, he was now overweight and diabetic. He had a bearlike presence, a powerful gaze and a legendary temper. But he also had a poetic and passionate soul, and sometimes displayed a sad, melancholic expression. He was fundamentally an introvert, his nephew would later recall.

Moretti was the illegitimate son of Luigi Rolland, a Belgian architect, and Maria Giuseppina Moretti. After graduating from Italy's Royal School of Architecture in 1929, Moretti, like many of his peers, found work designing buildings for the Fascists. He designed the headquarters of a Fascist youth organization and joined the team of architects working on the Foro Mussolini, a massive sports complex north of the Vatican. According to a Mussolini biographer, the dictator and the young architect often met early in the morning hours and walked the site, contemplating "the rapport between man and the city and between the city and the countryside." At Foro Mussolini, Moretti designed the public square extending from the Il Duce Obelisk to the main stadium, the headquarters of the national fencing academy and the interior of Mussolini's private gymnasium before World War II intervened and work on the site was halted.

After the Fascist government collapsed in July 1943, Mussolini fled north with his mistress. Moretti, like hundreds of other Fascist sympathizers, followed Mussolini across the border and joined him in exile. After Mussolini's execution in April 1945, Moretti was arrested and sent to San Vittore Prison in Milan, where he met and befriended another inmate, Count Adolfo Fossataro. Upon their release from prison—under a general postwar amnesty—the two men formed a business partnership to design and develop buildings in Rome. Moretti soon thereafter struck out on his own and established Studio Moretti in the vast Palazzo Colonna, property of one of Rome's most prominent families, with deep ties to the Vatican. Moretti's studio spanned three apartments: one for his personal office and administrative staff, a second for draftsmen and other support staff, and a third "design development office" for projects commissioned by the Vatican, including a cathedral to commemorate the Second Vatican Council. He founded *Spazio* magazine in

1950, devoted to a "Festival of Arts and Architecture," and published seven issues with the assistance of another survivor of the Fascist era, Felicia Abruzzese. Moretti was "the talent," an associate later recalled, but Abruzzese was "the connection"—to top officials in the Vatican and senior executives of SGI.

Moretti rejected boxy buildings with right angles, which he considered "extreme modernism." He drew inspiration from the Spanish architect Antoni Gaudí, who had transformed sections of Barcelona with his sweeping designs, and the Finnish architect and designer Alvar Aalto. Moretti considered the circle a Renaissance shape; the oval, baroque; and the "free unstructured shape," modern. He preferred to work in "the Roman way," a junior architect later recalled, which meant an "endless number of drawings, changes of ideas, going away for a long vacation, come back and start all over again." Moretti began each project with free sketches, which he then translated into paintings, through which he was able to express his "feeling for the site."

When SGI's new U.S. project arrived at his studio, Moretti had yet to visit Washington. For source material, he had only Edward Durell Stone's "clamshell" design for the National Cultural Center, with which the new project was expected to "harmonize," as well as maps and photographs of the site. After careful study of these materials, Moretti concluded the site was a "transition zone" between the natural environment of the Potomac River and Rock Creek Park, and the "man-made" city designed by Charles L'Enfant, whom he admired. Moretti told associates he saw himself as another European architect leaving his mark on America's capital. He recognized the new project from SGI as more than a typical commission. It was an opportunity to create an international symbol of Italian genius and creativity.

Moretti's first sketches for the new SGI development show three curved buildings parallel to the Potomac, rising behind a small cluster of waterfront villas inspired by the noble houses of Pompeii.

In subsequent sketches, the buildings were reshaped, curving around three separate open spaces facing the water. Moretti obsessed over the buildings' facades, likening them to walls surrounding gardens. The facades, he said, would make the buildings "sing." As his studio assistants translated these freehand sketches into architectural drawings, Moretti insisted every line be inspired by *"comme un police arrabiata"*—in English, "the action of an angry thumb." He vetoed any translations that were too mechanical or stiff.

Back in Washington, in the Connecticut Avenue offices of Island Vista, Cecchi and Salgo searched for an American architect who could translate Moretti's drawings into workable plans. A local developer put them in touch with Milton Fischer, an architect with the firm of Corning, Moore, Elmore and Fischer. Cecchi shared Moretti's design concepts for the "Foggy Bottom Development" with Fischer, who reacted to them in a detailed memo. Fischer carefully limited his comments to technical issues. Regarding floor-to-ceiling heights, Fischer noted eight feet was "considered satisfactory" and met local building code requirements, but nine feet, the typical ceiling height for "older apartments in town," was appropriate for an "ultra-luxury apartment." Fischer recommended setting the ceiling heights for typical units at eight feet six inches. He offered no comments about Moretti's overall design.

Antonio Cecchi visited the United States to check in on his son Giuseppe—who was now known as Joe to his American colleagues— and review progress on SGI's new project. The elder Cecchi met personally with Milton Fischer and reported back to Aldo Samaritani with his impressions. The American architect, Cecchi wrote, was "professional" and appeared to have an "in-depth understanding of the laws, regulations, and best practices in the construction field" and "in-depth knowledge of the local market," but was artistically "mediocre" and not particularly "assiduous when it comes to exercising his skills." In other words, Fischer was perfect for the job.

"It seems to me," Cecchi concluded, "that he would be particularly suited for collaborating with Architect Moretti."

THREE MONTHS INTO HIS NEW ADMINISTRATION, PRESIDENT John F. Kennedy appointed Elizabeth Ulman Rowe to the National Capital Planning Commission. Rowe, known as Libby to her friends and family, was born in Maryland but considered herself a third-generation Washingtonian. She attended Madeira School in Virginia before heading off to Bryn Mawr, on the Main Line outside of Philadelphia, a region she later recalled "as conservative and as Republican as any section of the country." She found politically like-minded friends while volunteering for Franklin D. Roosevelt's 1932 presidential campaign and, after graduating in 1935, returned to Washington and took a job with the United Mine Workers. Nearly all her coworkers were men, either retired miners or the sons of working miners. Her duties included writing articles for the *United Mine Workers Journal*, including the "Women's Page," which featured recipes, fashion tips (she modeled a "charming daytime frock of heavy silk" in the January 1936 issue) and profiles of notable women.

During the 1936 presidential campaign, Libby wrote speeches for Roosevelt supporters to deliver in mining communities. She also met a bright, handsome young lawyer with the Securities and Exchange Commission, James Rowe. Jim and Libby married in 1937, International Women's Year. Although the United Mine Workers was progressive on organizing black miners, it was less supportive of women in the workplace and did not employ married women. After Libby Ulman became Mrs. James Rowe, she was terminated.

Jim and Libby befriended a young couple from Texas, Lyndon Johnson and his wife, Lady Bird, and it was Johnson, Libby later said, who "made me into a planner." In 1955, then–Senate Majority Leader Johnson arranged for Libby to take one of the two Senate appointments on the D.C. Auditorium Committee, tasked with finding a home for the National Cultural Center. "You're my oldest

Washington friend," Johnson told her. "I need a real Washingtonian on that committee, and you're gonna do it."

Rowe worked closely with Jacqueline Kennedy during the 1960 presidential campaign and helped manage the inaugural parade. When Kennedy's staff asked Rowe where she would like to serve in the new administration, she suggested the National Capital Planning Commission. As a member of the Auditorium Committee, she had seen firsthand the planning commission's power to affect the physical layout of the federal city: Its refusal to support relocating a segment of the proposed Inner Loop freeway, for example, had helped doom the initial location for the National Cultural Center. The planning commission also appealed to her because the work was part-time, and she was raising three children: Betsy, Jimmy and Clarissa.

On May 18, 1961, Elizabeth Rowe was sworn in as a member of the planning commission, replacing Claude W. Owen. "We should have had a lady on the Commission a long time ago," Owen said. Her colleagues welcomed Rowe with a standing ovation and an orchid plant. Another Kennedy appointee soon joined her on the planning commission: Walter C. Louchheim, Jr., a Harvard philosophy graduate and a banker. He seemed to be from another time, a character from a Henry James novel, perhaps. He was a fastidious dresser. He read history, poetry and philosophy, but drew the line at novels. Although he never learned to play a musical instrument, he could whistle all the themes from Beethoven's quartets.

At the June meeting of the commission, Dr. Archibald M. Woodruff, a land economist and dean of the School of Government, Business, and International Affairs at George Washington University, became the commission's chairman, and Rowe was elevated to vice chairman.

The same day, Giuseppe Cecchi sent a memorandum to Rome, summarizing a recent meeting with representatives of the National Cultural Center. Cecchi, Milton Fischer and Royce Ward, an executive who had joined Island Vista after working on the Potomac Plaza Center, presented the "general trajectory" of their project to Jarold A. Kieffer, the center's executive director. Kieffer said he was "very concerned" about the "form and height" of any buildings near the center and was "definitely negative" when told that one of the buildings would be on the border of the parcel, "nearly at the front door" of the center. Fischer reassured Kieffer the final design for the development would be "harmonious" and would "conform with the Cultural Center's architectural forms."

The subject line of Cecchi's memorandum of June 8, 1961— "WATERGATE—CULTURAL CENTER"—is the earliest use of the word "Watergate" in the surviving files of SGI at the Central State Archives in Rome.

LIKE THE EVENTS THAT TOOK PLACE AT THE WATERGATE ON the evening of June 16, 1972, and the early-morning hours of June 17, 1972, the origin of the Watergate name remains in dispute.

Warren Adler, who would go on to become a major novelist, playwright and screenwriter, managed his own public relations firm in Washington. The new owners of the Washington Gas Light Company site asked him to come up with a name for their project. He recommended Watergate, drawing inspiration from the nearby Water Gate Inn, which had opened its doors in August 1942, serving Dutch-inspired dishes, such as pork tenderloin and red cabbage, to the thousands of new federal employees flooding into Washington in support of the war effort, and from the floating concert shell known as the "Potomac Watergate" or "Watergate Barge," the home of the summer music series of the National Symphony Orchestra since 1935.

According to Giuseppe Cecchi, the Watergate name was "obvious." Everyone was well aware of the Water Gate Inn and the Watergate concert barge, he said, and the development was "right by the water." Cecchi said he and Salgo, along with Royce Ward, recommended the name to SGI headquarters. "Everything had to be approved by Rome," Cecchi later recalled.

Marjory Hendricks, the owner of the Water Gate Inn, hoped the planned National Cultural Center would attract thousands more visitors—and potential diners—to Foggy Bottom. She asked Washington architect Donald H. Drayer to design an "Apartment Hotel" to replace her existing restaurant. Between October 1959 and January 1960, he completed detailed drawings for a modern seven-story building with ninety apartments, mostly studios, with a restaurant, cocktail lounge and gift shop on the ground floor. Across the top of the structure, in capital letters, was the proposed building's new name: WATERGATE.

According to Nicolas Salgo, he regularly ate lunch at the Water Gate Inn and was looking for someone to operate a restaurant in the new hotel planned for Island Vista's new development. He persuaded Marjory to bring her restaurant into the hotel, along with the name Watergate.

Several months later, Salgo was eating lunch at the Water Gate Inn when she came by his table with bad news.

"I'm sorry," she said, "but I have to welch on our deal."

"How can you do that?" he asked.

The National Cultural Center wanted the land, and her lawyers had advised that if she closed down, she would receive "millions more" for it than if she moved her restaurant to a new location. Salgo said he would let her out of her contract, but only if she gave up all rights to the name Watergate.

"That's how the Watergate name came over to us," Salgo later recalled.

Marjory Hendricks would never receive "millions more" for her property. The Kennedy Center trustees eventually offered her only $450,000. She took them to court and settled for a payment of just $650,000.

BILL FINLEY, THE STAFF DIRECTOR OF THE NATIONAL CAPITAL Planning Commission, circulated a glowing report to the commission on the "Proposed Watergate Towne Development," which concluded the project was "very sound" and predicted "the community will gain a great deal from the development as designed." The developers could, under existing zoning and without closing any streets, build "the typical cross-shaped apartment buildings found in Northern Virginia and parts of the District," which would result in "buildings tightly packed and without distinction." Instead, the Watergate architects had designed structures "with graceful curves and unusual elegance." To execute this design, the developer was asking for more flexibility under Article 75 of the District's zoning code, which directed the planning commission to make recommendations regarding the height, mass, parking and overall treatment of the project and allowed the District Zoning Commission to waive various zoning rules. The net effect of Article 75 was to enable "more creative use of land and more successful large scale developments."

At the September 1961 meeting of the planning commission, Milton Fischer said the Watergate was designed to "attract people to Washington" and "assist in reversing the suburban trend." The developers had set out to create not only an "income-producing" project but one that also "had beauty, that had a relationship to the city that would add to the character of the entire environment." He presented a design for the site, including three apartment buildings, an office and a hotel. The tallest of the buildings would reach 155 feet into the sky, measured from their foundations. Two levels of penthouses would sit atop each of the fourteen-story residential buildings. Two-story "Pompeiian villas" would be placed on the grounds between the buildings.

Finley explained to the commissioners that the Watergate developers were not requesting any action at this time, but only wanted to know if they were "on the right track."

"I think the apparent consensus is favorable," replied Dean Woodruff, the chairman.

Mrs. Rowe had no questions.

THE COMMISSION OF FINE ARTS, KNOWN BY ITS INITIALS, CFA, was established by Congress in 1910, with control at first only over the appearance of public buildings. In 1914, President Woodrow Wilson expanded this authority to include all major buildings in the District of Columbia, both public and private, with the exception of the U.S. Capitol grounds. While the CFA could not grant construction permits, it could veto any building on purely aesthetic grounds.

The chairman of the CFA, David E. Finley (no relation to Bill Finley, the planning commission staff director) was the only son of a Democratic congressman from South Carolina. Finley served in World War I and practiced law in Washington until 1921, when he joined the legal staff of the treasury department, headed by Secretary Andrew W. Mellon. Among other duties, Finley provided Mellon with legal assistance as he assembled his spectacular art collection, and in 1927, when Mellon started the National Gallery of Art, Finley became Mellon's special assistant. Following Mellon's death in 1937, Finley supervised the completion of the gallery and served as its first director. In 1943, President Roosevelt appointed Finley to the CFA. At the end of World War II, as vice chairman of the Roberts Commission, Finley played a key role, with the famous "Monuments Men," in saving the artistic treasures of Europe. When Jacqueline Kennedy undertook the renovation and restoration of the White House, she turned to Finley for guidance. There was no heavier hitter in Washington arts and culture than David Finley.

The day before Milton Fischer was scheduled to brief the CFA on the Watergate for the first time, commissioners met privately to examine Moretti's sketches and a scale model of the complex. They were uneasy about the height of the buildings and "the use of such unconventional architecture in an area of such importance," but agreed to withhold comments until they met with the architect and the development team.

The next day, in public session, the commissioners told Fischer they did not have enough information to reach any conclusions about the design, but praised the spacing of the buildings, which they said created "an impression of openness." They noted, however, that nearly all of the open areas were taken up by the proposed "Pompeiian villas." They had no objection to the buildings being as tall as 130 feet, but recommended that more of the land should be set aside as open space between buildings. On October 2, Finley wrote to the District of Columbia's chief of permits, Julian Greene, informing him the CFA would approve closing streets "in order to encourage the builders to plan these squares of land in a unified manner, and to avoid producing a series of separate and unrelated designs." Finley added the commissioners "would also not oppose a limited deviation from the planning and zoning standards that are followed in other areas of the city, if relaxing these standards would afford the designers the opportunity to achieve a character more consistent with the open park-like nature of this site." Finley's letter did not raise concerns about the height of the complex, but recommended the Watergate developers include more open space in their plan. The final judgment of the CFA, however, would have to wait "until such a time as a detailed study of the land usage, density of occupancy, and other planning matters have been fully explored."

Back in Rome, Samaritani read Finley's letter carefully. Despite its calls for more open space, Samaritani was encouraged. The CFA appeared open-minded about the Watergate. He wrote *"Molto bene!"*—"Very good!"—in red ink on his copy.

ON NOVEMBER 9, 1961, THE NATIONAL CAPITAL PLANNING Commission met to consider the Watergate. The commission was under new management: Libby Rowe was now chairman.

David Finley attended the meeting and spoke first. Over the past month, he had soured on the Watergate. He warned that the buildings would overpower both the Lincoln Memorial and the planned National Cultural Center. He suggested the entire parcel be set aside as a public park.

District Engineer Commissioner Frederick J. Clarke, a retired general and a member of the District Zoning Commission, said the developer had "a perfect right" to "build a series of apartment houses in this area." He estimated the unimproved land was now worth approximately $7 million. "Unless someone can write a check for the land," he said, "I think we have to let it go." A subcommittee of four commissioners, including Rowe and Louchheim, the two Kennedy appointees, was directed to delve further into the details of Watergate Towne and report back to the full planning commission the next month.

When the National Capital Planning Commission released its December meeting agenda, however, there was no mention of the Watergate. Cecchi sent an urgent telegram to Rome:

PLANNING COMMISSION IS TRYING TO PUT OFF DECISION UNTIL JANUARY STOP
FIGHTING TO GET THE COMMISSION TO LOOK AT OUR PROJECT ON THE 7TH SALGO WILL BE THERE STOP

Bill Finley called Cecchi and told him it would be "impossible" to place the Watergate on the December 7 agenda. Rowe, Finley confided, was working with an unnamed aide in the Kennedy White House, who was abroad at the time, to get the federal government to purchase the land and turn it into a public park. "Mrs. Rowe,"

Finley said, "does not want to make any decision or take any action before she consults with that person." He advised Cecchi to "put up a strong fight, at the same time acting in a respectful manner, at least for the moment."

A clerk in the District's zoning department told Royce Ward a park was "impractical" and offered to "go to the newspapers with a strong blast against the delaying tactics." Another member of the Watergate team urged Cecchi to send a telegram to each member of the planning commission "informing them of our frustration." Finley recommended patience. "Mrs. Rowe's visionary dream cannot come to fruition," he told Cecchi, and the Watergate developers "should not do anything that might make her feel antagonistic." Finley suggested instead that Cecchi and his colleagues consider preparation of a "conventional" design for the site, allowed under existing zoning, to use as leverage in future negotiations—"but without giving the impression it's some kind of shakedown."

Cecchi called Rowe at her home and offered to set up a meeting with Salgo on December 7. She put him off, saying she had been ill and could not meet that day, but agreed to meet another time, perhaps on Salgo's next trip to Washington.

Samaritani, who was closely monitoring events in Washington, weighed in: "I believe now is not the time to dramatize what has happened by undertaking a publicity campaign that might, in the end, place us at a disadvantage," he wrote Cecchi. It would be "a mistake," he added, to alienate anyone whose support would be useful, especially Mrs. Rowe, considering "her political point of view, and her influential contacts at the White House."

In an interview with the *Washington Post*, Rowe went public with her concerns. She said many of her fellow commissioners had a "substantial feeling" the Watergate site should be "reserved for public purposes." The *Washington Star* blasted her for "fuzzy thinking on several counts" and scoffed at any suggestion Congress would appropriate funds to condemn the land, seize it and compensate the developers. The Lincoln Memorial, the *Star* editorialized, was a half mile away and in no danger of being "overshadowed" by the Watergate.

OVER THE HOLIDAYS, A STORY APPEARED IN THE *WASHINGTON Post* with the headline: FOGGY BOTTOM PROJECT SPONSORS SAID TO HAVE VATICAN FINANCIAL TIES. According to the *Post*'s Rome bureau, "Loopholes in Italian law make it impossible to determine who controls the world-wide real estate organization that is sponsoring a proposed 50-million-dollar apartment project in Washington's Foggy Bottom. But the general consensus here is that the largest single shareholder in the Società Generale Immobiliare is the Vatican, through its several financial departments and agencies." As evidence, the *Post* noted four of twelve members of SGI's board "are known to be very close to the Vatican," including Count Enrico Pietro Galeazzi, vice president of the firm and head of the Vatican's technical and economic department; Prince Marcantonio Pacelli, a nephew of the late Pope Pius XII; Marquis Giovanni Battista Sacchetti, holder of a "high honorary office in the Vatican"; and Luigi Mennini, "an official of the Institute for Religious Works, which is one of the main arms of the Vatican's financial administration."

The story was read closely by Glenn Archer, executive director of Protestants and Other Americans United for Separation of Church and State, known by its initials, POAU. With 100,000 members and supporters nationwide, POAU was familiar to the Kennedy team. During the 1960 presidential campaign, POAU published at least three pamphlets raising questions about Senator Kennedy's Catholic faith. "The Church of the Catholic candidate asserts absolute control over its members in regard to what it defines as 'moral and spiritual' issues," Archer warned in one broadside. "These are frequently civil issues as well." If elected, POAU warned, Kennedy "would be subject to considerable clerical pressure."

The January 1962 issue of *Church and State*, POAU's monthly newsletter, carried an article with the headline: WORLD'S RICHEST CHURCH SEEKS GOVERNMENT SUBSIDY. "Watergate Towne, a project of the largest real estate company in Italy—a company owned by the Vatican—is working its way through the federal and local zoning agencies."

CECCHI MET WITH BILL FINLEY PRIVATELY AFTER THE FIRST of the year and gave him a book about Italian parks and cities. Finley assured Cecchi that Rowe's idea for a park on the Watergate site was going nowhere, although she "is still holding onto every hope." He told Cecchi not to "surrender" to his chairman's demands and predicted the Watergate would end up with the support of "a majority" of the planning commission votes. He advised Cecchi to request approval for a height of 180 feet "and allow them to do the cutting." The Watergate, Finley assured him, "is good for Washington." Finley pushed the commission's consideration of the Watergate off another month, until February, to give Cecchi and his colleagues more time to prepare.

When the National Capital Planning Commission met on February 1, 1962, Morton Hoppenfeld, a staff architect, declared "the proposed design is of high architectural quality." Although the relationship between the Watergate and the proposed National Cultural Center was "difficult to evaluate" because the center's plans were in flux, Luigi Moretti's "qualifications and previous work" should give the commission "every indication of a singular goal of good design quality."

Dean Woodruff, the commission's vice chairman, warned that failing to support the Watergate proposal might drive the developers away, as had happened with the team behind Potomac Plaza Center just a few years earlier. "It is costing these people a lot of money to stand still," he said. "Their taxes are coming along day by day." If these developers walked away, he said, more than twenty buildings might sprout on the existing streets. The choice was between the

Watergate's "very imaginative treatment" and a more conventional plan, which would "look exactly like so many lumps of sugar stacked neatly along the streets."

"As Chairman of this Commission," Rowe said, "I am always looking for public interest. It is a very ephemeral thing. . . . In this case I think I have found it. I may be wrong, but I am persuaded . . . that approval would not, in the way I understand it, be in the public interest."

Commissioner C. H. Bronn moved the planning commission approve "in principle . . . the land use and design concepts" of the Watergate Towne application, with a "maximum height of 130 feet," and direct the National Park Service to enter into negotiations with Island Vista, regarding the exchange of lands within and adjacent to the site. Rowe called the roll. The motion passed by a vote of seven to three, with Rowe, Louchheim, and Conrad L. Wirth, the National Park Service director, voting no.

Bruno Foa, an Italian economist based in New York, sat in on the planning commission hearing as an observer for SGI and sent Samaritani a report. The "marginalization of Mrs. Rowe, because of her opposition to the project," he wrote, was "conspicuous." He specifically praised Finley, the planning commission's staff director, whose "cooperation" enabled the meeting to be moved from January to February, which "allowed us to gain at least one more month." The vote was "a turning point," Foa wrote, which "gives us a psycho-logical edge" in the battles ahead. He predicted, however, that Rowe and the Commission of Fine Arts "will continue to set up barriers along the way."

Foa sent a second letter, this one to Antonio Cecchi. The planning commission vote was "a truly decisive step toward the realization of the project," Foa wrote. He praised Nicolas Salgo, who "conducted everything with great skill and diligence." Foa predicted the "battle with all of the bureaucrats is going to be played out over several months" and "might be won within the next two months." Anticipating a fatherly interest, he wrote that Giuseppe "like always, has been working around the clock."

As Foa had predicted, David Finley and the CFA took aim at the Watergate at its March 20 meeting. Commissioners approved a resolution with a detailed and wide-ranging case against the development, objecting to the proposed height; the "sweeping, curvilinear forms"; the "continuous arrangement of building masses," which would, "for all intents and purposes, shut off the important views of the Potomac River and Roosevelt Island"; and the "overpowering mass of the total composition." The CFA resolution mocked the Watergate's vision of itself as a "Garden City within a City," as set forth in its brochure. "The Commission adheres to the principle that large-scale developments should be subordinate to the city as a whole, especially in instances where the site is of such importance and in close proximity to important monumental areas."

The battle over the Watergate now shifted to a new venue, the District of Columbia Zoning Commission, composed of five members: District of Columbia Engineer Commissioner General F. J. Clarke and District Commissioners Walter N. Tobriner and John B. Duncan, each appointed by Congress; the head of the National Park Service, Conrad L. Wirth; and the Architect of the Capitol, J. George Stewart. Their first hearing on the Watergate, at 10:00 A.M. on Friday, April 13, began favorably for the developers when the zoning commission secretary read into the record an endorsement by the three-member Zoning Advisory Council, which found the development to be "in the public interest." Attorney William R. Lichtenberg, representing Island Vista, described the Watergate as "a well-planned development" that was both attractive and efficient. "The architectural design," he said, "is both creative and imaginative. A prime consideration in the design was that it would complement the unique area of the property involved and that, when completed, would add beauty to the city and the area, as well as enhance the values of surrounding areas." After

Lichtenberg returned to his seat, Chairman Clarke asked if any other supporters of the project were in the room. James C. Wilkes, Jr., a land-use attorney, introduced himself and submitted a letter of support for the record, signed by "Mrs. Marjory Hendricks, the owner of the Water Gate Inn, who favors the proposed project."

Clarke called forward the first speaker against the proposal, Mrs. Harold B. Hinton, chairman of the Planning and Zoning Committee of the Progressive Citizen's Association of Georgetown. "We don't oppose the Watergate," she began, but the developer's plans, models and drawings, she said, were deceptive. "It is not going to be a low thing," she said. "It is going to be a Trojan Wall." She pointed to the model. "It is just too tall. Aesthetics is not un-American. It was planned into this capital."

Charles Martin, the CFA's counsel, presented a four-page statement in opposition to the Watergate, indicating "disappointment with the preliminary plans and designs for the proposed Watergate Towne and office complex." The CFA was "greatly concerned" over the height and "character" of the Watergate, its size relative to the public monuments nearby and the inadequate amount of open space provided. The "strongly sculptural" and "sweeping" design was "overpowering." According to the *Washington Star*, the Commission of Fine Arts considered the Watergate to be "neither fine nor artful."

A week later, at the next public meeting of the CFA, District Engineer Commissioner Clarke acknowledged "several" of his fellow members of the District Zoning Commission had some "misgivings" about the Watergate's impact on the surrounding area. But he urged the CFA to endorse the project, observing "it is in the interest of the city to allow some development to go ahead there as rapidly as possible, simply for tax considerations." He presented a rendering of an alternative vision for development on the site—helpfully provided to him by the Watergate team, which got the idea from Bill Finley at the planning commission—showing a series of ordinary, cross-shaped apartment buildings that could be built on the site, using current zoning rules and regulations. "I am not here to sell anything," Clarke said, but the proposed design for the Watergate was "something a whole lot better" than forcing the developers to construct "routine" apartments on the site.

THE FOLLOWING WEEK, CFA MEMBERS RALPH THOMAS Walker and Douglas Orr, both architects, met with Milton Fischer, Nicolas Salgo and Giuseppe Cecchi in New York, at Walker's office on Park Avenue. The CFA had given up on converting the land to a park and was now willing to allow some sort of development on the property, Walker said. But if the Watergate wanted approval from the CFA, the buildings would need to be smaller and shorter. As currently conceived, the Watergate was a nonstarter.

None of the Watergate representatives at that meeting had the authority to change Luigi Moretti's design without his approval. Instead, they proposed bringing Moretti to the United States to discuss the matter in person, if the CFA would postpone its formal vote on the project. Walker and Orr agreed and a meeting was set for May 15. Fischer flew to Italy to brief Moretti.

"To those who oppose the project," the *New York Times* reported, "the meeting represents a step toward saving the capital from what might prove to be an architectural catastrophe on a scale so grand that the city's character would be irretrievably damaged."

WHITE HOUSE ACTS TO CUT HEIGHT OF HUGE WATERGATE DEVELOPMENT, read the headline in the May 5, 1962, edition of the *Washington Post*. "The White House has been thrust into the billowing controversy over the proposed $50 million Watergate Towne development along the Potomac shore at Foggy Bottom," the *Post* reported. "While it is not clear who on the White House staff notified District officials of the Administration's interest in the zoning dispute, it was understood that the President had been briefed."

Cecchi was aware, from his back-channel conversations with Bill Finley, that Rowe had sought support from a White House aide for her park proposal, but had made no progress. Finley called Lee White, an aide to Kennedy speechwriter Ted Sorensen, who said there was "no official White House position" on the project and the Watergate had "never become an issue" in the White House, and he suspected it would not be. The *Washington Star*, in an editorial titled WEAK IN THE KNEES, expressed skepticism about the *Post* report. "If this position has been taken by the President, which we doubt, it of course would carry considerable weight," the *Star* wrote. "If, however, it was expressed by some White House assistant who was persuaded to do so by the opponents of the project, it is not entitled to serious consideration."

Nerves were raw as the National Capital Planning Commission met in closed session on May 6. Commissioner C. McKim Norton charged Chairman Rowe and Commissioner Louchheim had "pulled the rug out from under us" by attending a meeting with the District Zoning Commission and the CFA without any representation from the majority of planning commission members who supported the Watergate. "The idea was, as the papers picked up apparently, the Commission votes one way and the chairman and somebody else didn't like it," fumed Commissioner Alexander C. Robinson. Woodruff, the vice chairman, said he was "greatly disturbed that an intimation could be made in the press that the Commission either had changed its mind without having formally done so or that you, Madam Chairman, were taking the reins in your own hands and speaking adversely to an opinion which had been expressed collectively by the Commission."

"Everyone there knew exactly what the Commission had done," Rowe objected. "I don't feel as indefensible as you make me sound."

General Clarke turned to Rowe. "I am not at all being critical of you expressing your personal views," he said. "I admire you for expressing them. But here, in the case of the Watergate, we have known as a Commission for a year that our staff was actively engaged in that work. I just don't feel that we can ever go back and say, 'Well, that was only the staff acting.' "

"Mr. Louchheim and I didn't know anything about this project until last fall," Rowe replied. "I don't know how informed the other members of the Commission were. You might have been well informed, but I did not know the staff was working closely with the developers."

"I thought we all knew it," said Clarke.

Louchheim proposed the planning commission release a statement as a placeholder, pending further developments, which read: *"The National Capital Planning Commission has no new position on the Watergate project, but its staff will, of course, cooperate with the Fine Arts Commission and the architects of the project toward working out a satisfactory solution."*

The motion passed. Rowe handed Louchheim's notes to a staff member. "Would you get this typed up," she asked, "so we can move on to something peaceful?"

The *Washington Post* reported the National Capital Planning Commission stuck by its support for the Watergate, despite "White House concerns about the impact of the massive development on the city's skyline." The *Post* added, however, at least two individuals "close to President Kennedy have said that he has expressed personal concern about the size of the project, but they differed as to how strongly he felt about it."

LUIGI MORETTI ARRIVED IN WASHINGTON. IT WAS HARD FOR him to travel outside Italy—he was extremely ill, with diabetes and a heart condition—yet he recognized that in order to defend his design, it was imperative he do so in person.

The CFA met on May 15. Chairman Finley said the Watergate failed to "harmonize" with nearby buildings and was too tall. Moretti, through an interpreter, said he was open to discussion of his design, but on the matter of height, there could be no compromise. If the CFA insisted on keeping the Watergate to a height of no more than ninety feet, he said, the developers would simply abandon the project and sell the land to whoever wanted it, presumably to erect more "conventional" buildings. The meeting ended with an agreement to hold one final session three days later in New York.

After the meeting with the CFA, Moretti paid a call on the district commissioners. Speaking through an interpreter, Moretti said he had studied Washington and discovered a "deep commitment" in the federal city, inspired by English landscape design, to link nature and architecture through gardens and greenery. He assured the commissioners his design for the Watergate was solidly in that tradition and his overall design—which he called "a petrified garden"—was simply a modern take on Washington's architectural heritage.

In New York, Moretti and three architect members of the CFA—Ralph Walker, Michael Rapuano and Douglas Orr—met for three hours and hammered out an agreement. According to the *Washington Post*, the developers agreed to "scale down" the square footage of the project and Moretti agreed to review his design "to create the impression of maximum space" between the buildings. Commissioners said they would "depend on Moretti's judgment in the scaling down of building heights and other proposed changes." SGI and the Commission of Fine Arts issued a joint statement that "expressed agreement in principle" with Moretti's design, but noted "the height of 130 feet of the buildings should not exceed 25% of the total of the building complex to be erected"—a poorly crafted sentence that would cause the entire agreement to unravel within a year.

Moretti returned to Rome. The trip to America had exhausted him. While he recovered, architects in the Studio Moretti offices at the Palazzo Colonna, working with SGI architects, developed new designs consistent with the agreement reached in New York. CFA chairman David Finley informed District Engineering Commissioner Clarke that agreement had been reached and "there would seem to be no reason for delaying action on the zoning request."

On July 13, 1962, the District Zoning Commission voted three to one to approve revised plans for the Watergate. The only opposing vote was Capitol architect J. George Stewart. The zoning commission added a condition requiring the height of the building closest to the planned National Cultural Center be subject to "a possible adjustment." An SGI representative told the *Washington Post* final plans would be submitted to District building officials in the fall, and construction would begin in the spring of 1963.

That prediction would prove to be optimistic.

MEMBERS OF THE NATIONAL CAPITAL PLANNING COMMISSION met in June for a private lunch at the Cosmos Club in Washington, to resolve the bitter conflicts between Libby Rowe and Bill Finley, which had spilled out into the press. "It has been an open secret that Planning Commission Chairman Elisabeth [*sic*] C. Rowe, a Kennedy administration appointee, and planning director William E. Finley have not seen eye-to-eye on some key city planning issues," including the Watergate, the *Washington Post* reported. Rowe could count on Walter Louchheim's support, but the rest of her colleagues were in Finley's camp. To avert a "potentially dangerous impasse," agreement was reached on a "stronger role" for Rowe and the commission on planning issues, while "administrative authority" was retained by Finley. Authority shifted clearly—and publicly—to Rowe. Within a few months, Finley would step down as staff director of the National Capital Planning Commission to head the planning and development of the new town of Columbia on fourteen thousand acres in Maryland.

IN MID-JULY, DREW PEARSON, WASHINGTON'S MOST FORMI-dable syndicated columnist, reignited the Watergate controversy, in a column headlined: VATICAN SEEKS IMPOSING EDIFICE ON POTOMAC.

"Some prominent Catholics in Washington," Pearson wrote, "are concerned over the battle staged by Vatican representatives to override Washington building codes in order to erect a massive, Italian-type apartment house on the banks of the Potomac not far from the Lincoln Memorial." Abigail McCarthy, wife of Senator Eugene McCarthy of Minnesota, a Catholic, had told her friends, "I feel certain that if some of us went to Rome and talked to the Pope, he would agree with us that the building ought not to be built."

Fueled by the attention Pearson's column generated, POAU kicked its anti-Watergate campaign into high gear. The Rev. Dr. C. Stanley Lowell, assistant director of the organization, urged supporters to protest the Watergate.

ROGER L. STEVENS, PRESIDENT KENNEDY'S PICK AS THE new head of the board of trustees of the National Cultural Center, discovered shortly after his appointment in September 1961 that the center's ambitious fund-raising plan was a flop: The center's bank account held just $13,425. Stevens, a successful New York real estate investor, sent Edward Durell Stone back to the drawing board to come up with a new design for the building—at half the cost of the concrete-and-glass "clamshell."

On September 11, 1962, Stone presented his revised plans for the National Cultural Center to the trustees and First Lady Jacqueline Kennedy, at a meeting held at The Elms in Newport, Rhode Island. Stone called the center's waterfront location "one of the most glamorous settings for a public building in the world," adding that America had "not made sufficient use of our rivers as settings for great buildings." He replaced his original "clamshell" design with a streamlined, rectangular structure housing a 1,200-seat theater, a 275-seat symphony hall and a 250-seat opera house, all under one roof. A "garden-like" area, for festivals, balls and other functions, included a retractable roof for year-round use. The center would be faced in white marble—following the Washington tradition of "white buildings in park-like settings." And, as requested by Stevens, the new design cut construction costs in half.

MORE THAN FIFTEEN HUNDRED LETTERS ARRIVED AT THE White House by mid-November 1962. Charles Horsky, Kennedy's aide for affairs in the capital, responded to every letter, assuring writers that "Watergate Towne" would be carefully vetted by the appropriate federal and local agencies; that "nothing will be done which will not enhance and improve the Nation's Capital"; and that developers "would of course pay taxes" on the property. Horsky's letters carefully avoided making reference to SGI, Italy or the Vatican. He described the Watergate developer only as "Island Vista, Inc., a District of Columbia Corporation" backed by financing from "a Boston insurance company."

On January 23, 1963, after more than three thousand letters protesting the Watergate had been received at the White House, Horsky sent Kennedy a three-page memo about the "Watergate Towne Project," alerting the president to the controversy. The developer, Horsky wrote, "is Island Vista Corporation (a DC corporation), which is a subsidiary most of whose stock (and perhaps all of it) is owned by Societa Generale Immobiliare." He explained "the Vatican" was one of SGI's principal stockholders, and "several Vatican officials" sat on the SGI board of directors. "It is this latter fact that has sparked the current protest against Watergate Towne."

Horsky enclosed for the president's information a copy of the response he had been using for months, expressing "confidence" in the judgment of the responsible agencies. "I propose to continue to respond this way," Horsky wrote. Kennedy instructed Horsky to handle the Watergate controversy as he saw fit—and to keep it away from the Oval Office.

Separately, Kennedy had asked Horsky what could be done in the year ahead to help make Washington "a more beautiful and functional city." The president had recently read an article in

Architectural Forum by Paul Rudolph, chairman of the Department of Architecture at Yale, bemoaning the federal city's "monumental dullness" and characterizing the new buildings in the District as "ridiculous." Horsky sent Kennedy a four-page memo outlining goals and actions for the administration, including an intense effort to improve Pennsylvania Avenue and the National Mall and steps to "lift, in a major way, the architectural and aesthetic quality of government architecture." Horsky also recommended Kennedy "rejuvenate" the Commission of Fine Arts "by appointing new blood of the highest caliber possible." Kennedy had an opportunity to replace six of the seven sitting CFA commissioners. Horsky reported that William Walton was already engaged in seeking out new members.

Sandy-haired and youthful, Walton looked "like a rugged representative of the New Frontier," according to a *Washington Post* profile. He was born in Jacksonville, Illinois, to a newspaper family, and received a journalism degree from the University of Wisconsin in 1931. Two years later, he was hired by the Associated Press and in July 1934 he covered the shooting of John Dillinger in Chicago. Walton went to work for *Time* in 1941 and reported on U.S. Air Force operations in England, where he jumped with the 82nd Airborne Division to cover the D-Day invasion of Normandy. Walton returned to the United States after the war and worked as the Washington editor of the *New Republic* until 1949, when he quit and devoted himself to painting full-time. Walton met young congressman John Kennedy and a beautiful photographer named Jacqueline Bouvier in Washington shortly thereafter. After the Kennedys married, they moved into the townhouse next door to Walton's in Georgetown.

During the 1960 presidential campaign, Walton volunteered for Kennedy in three states—Wisconsin and West Virginia in the primaries, and New York in the general. After the election, Walton served as an unpaid advisor to the White House on arts and culture. At Walton's recommendation, Kennedy had earlier appointed landscape architect Hideo Sasaki to the CFA, replacing a Republican appointee, Michael Rapuano. Sasaki—known as Hid to his friends and family—was born in Reedley, a small town in California's Central Valley. He studied planning at the University of California, Berkeley; when World War II erupted he was sent to an internment camp—along with five hundred of his fellow students. After the war, Sasaki received degrees from the University of Illinois and Harvard, where he became chair of the department of landscape architecture in 1958.

Walton suggested five more candidates, each of whom Kennedy approved: Gordon Bunshaft, architect of the twenty-four-story Lever House on New York's Park Avenue; Burnham Kelly, dean of the College of Architecture, Art and Planning at Cornell University; California architect and Stanford football star John Carl "Jack" Warnecke, a personal friend of President and Mrs. Kennedy; sculptor Theodore Roszak; and art critic Aline B. Saarinen, widow of the famed Finnish architect Eero Saarinen, who had died two years earlier.

All that remained was the selection of a new chairman: On March 30, 1963, the *Washington Post* reported CFA chairman David Finley intended to resign after twenty years. Kennedy already had a replacement in mind: William Walton. "I hope you are including your name on the list," Kennedy wrote Walton. "If you can't lick them, join them." Jacqueline Kennedy sent Walton a twelve-page letter. "I don't blame you for not wanting to be head," she wrote. "But if you aren't head—you are useless—as people only listen to the head—& it is all going to be involved with all the things we care about—when Jack is gone—so he won't be able to help you—& lovely buildings will be torn down—& cheesy skyscrapers go up."

Walton gave in, and on June 20, 1963, the president appointed him chairman of the Commission of Fine Arts.

For Washington to be a beautiful city, Walton told the *Washington Post*, the federal government must enlist the talents of good contemporary architects. "I hope we can influence good design in Federal buildings and also influence private buildings by setting a good example."

Before stepping down, David Finley sent General Clarke at the District Zoning Commission a list of continuing concerns with the Watergate: There was still not enough public space, the ends of some of the proposed buildings were "too sharp" and the buildings, at approximately 130 feet, were still too high. The CFA continued to object to the "overpowering mass of buildings" and recommended a "greater variation in the heights of the buildings . . . in order to avoid the dullness of a uniform skyline."

Back in Rome, however, the board of directors of SGI was informed the "Fine Arts Commission is favorable to the general project for the Watergate."

IN AUGUST 1963, MORETTI RETURNED TO WASHINGTON TO unveil the revised Watergate design. At a press conference, he said he had carefully studied Washington and set out to harmonize the three striking features of the Nation's capital: its monumental area defined by the National Mall and the Lincoln Memorial, the downtown business district and the waterfront. The location was "one of the best, if not the best, areas of Washington," he said. His revised design let the park areas "flow" into the monumental areas by allowing pedestrians an open view of the river: Four of the five buildings in the complex would be on columns, allowing an almost unobstructed view of the Potomac. He drew a diagram in the air with his hands as he explained the curves of the building would allow almost every residence to have a view of the water. His design was dramatic and modern. The Watergate, he said, would bring to Washington "a touch of Rome."

In the early 1960s, Americans were enthralled by anything Italian. Fellini's *La Dolce Vita* and *8½* filled American movie theaters and actresses Sophia Loren and Gina Lollobrigida captivated American audiences. Oleg Cassini designed gowns for Jacqueline Kennedy, and Gio Ponti designed silverware for Reed and Barton. Spumone ice cream was becoming a popular family dessert.

On September 17, 1963, the CFA met in closed session. It was William Walton's first meeting as chairman and David Finley's final meeting as a member. CFA staff briefed the new commissioners on the complicated history of the Watergate, including the May 1962 meeting in New York. Walton and the new commissioners were told the Watergate developers had agreed at that meeting to limit 25 percent of their buildings to a maximum height of 130 feet.

Moretti returned a month later to present his design to the CFA. Through an interpreter, he said the Watergate site "was a very particular one, because it is in fact where the utilitarian part of the city ends and where the romantic part starts." He showed his model and explained the key elements of the design. After Moretti concluded his presentation, Walton excused the Watergate representatives and asked his fellow commissioners what they thought.

"I was terribly impressed with the whole humanistic approach of this design," Ted Roszak said. "I think it was a healthy note in view of the fact that we're constantly viewing things that ignore these facts. I think it's important not only to have an example of it, but to set an example perhaps for other architects to study and maybe emulate."

"I like it," said David Finley. "There's no reason not to have them in Washington. But the mass and height is what bothers me."

"It is the details that frighten me to death," said Jack Warnecke.

"We can't go along with the exuberance of detail," said Burnham Kelly. "I'd like them to realize we would really blow the whistle on having Miami Beach come to Washington."

Kelly asked Charles Martin, the CFA attorney, about the relationship between the commission and District planning staff. "It's pretty bad," said Martin. "There is an underlying feeling of resentment of any referrals of Federal agencies on what they consider to be strictly district or local matters." Martin noted the CFA had shared its concerns about the Watergate with District planners, without impact. "What they are interested in is investment and tax returns," explained Finley. "That is what they really care about, not appearance."

With the possible exception of Roszak, the new members of the CFA were just as opposed to the Watergate as their predecessors. Walton sent a letter to Julian P. Green, assistant superintendent of District Licenses and Permits, outlining the CFA's lingering concerns and recommending "a substantial reduction" in the height of the Watergate.

Watergate planners were blindsided by Walton's letter, which they considered a violation of the agreement reached in New York in May 1962. According to the *Washington Post*, the developers, who were "used to fighting Italian city halls back home and unraveling red tape like spaghetti," were readying their formal application for a building permit and ran "smack dab into a new Fine Arts Commission, strong-minded and strong-willed," and "now manned by Kennedy appointees." Cecchi offered to meet with the commission to address their concerns, but Walton responded there was no point arguing about "old plans they already have found objectionable." In an editorial, the *Washington Post* denounced the CFA:

> The Watergate architects originally cooperated with the Planning Commission's staff to the point of collaboration, only to find themselves vehemently attacked when the management of the Commission passed into new hands. The builders thought they had reached an accommodation with the Fine Arts Commission, but now the membership of that Commission has also been changed and the new arrivals announce that there is no agreement. . . . Most builders, lacking the patience and the resources of Watergate's backers, will not risk good architecture until they are assured that innovation does not automatically subject them to delay and political attack.

The SGI board was told nothing about problems with the Commission of Fine Arts. According to the official minutes, the board was informed only that Moretti was scheduled to meet again with the CFA on November 19, which "will be decisive for getting the permit," and construction "will soon start as the procedures for obtaining the building permit have begun."

On November 19, 1963, the Commission of Fine Arts met in closed session. Walton urged his colleagues to hold nothing back. The Watergate team was then invited into the room. For the first time since the project began its long journey through the bureaucracy, the Watergate delegation included Aldo Samaritani.

Samaritani, through an interpreter, said his company's goal was to create a building that would "do credit to the standing and traditions" of SGI, a century-old company, and "contribute to the dignified image of the urban development of the City of Washington, and also would be worthy of the nation's capital." He introduced Moretti, who, also speaking through an interpreter, offered to take one floor off each of the two buildings nearest the water, while maintaining a consistent roofline across all five buildings in the complex. He also agreed to remove the villas between the main buildings, increasing usable open space.

"We tried very hard and could not find any other solutions than the ones which you see before you," said Nicolas Salgo. "This is the overall plan, the openness, etc.; and the forms were satisfactory, we have to assume, because nobody ever questioned it, nobody ever told us, 'Gentlemen, go back and come back with a completely different plan.'"

"I am just going to say what I think," Bunshaft said to Samaritani. "You have a problem, I know, as an architect, and a desire to get as many apartments in the project as you can. But you tried to just handle us. Well, we are not going to be handled."

Milton Fischer stepped up to the podium. If the offer to scale down the buildings by removing a floor was not acceptable to the CFA, "I think the best we can do, then, is to start from scratch."

Walton asked the Watergate developers to leave the room.

Bunshaft said the entire complex needed to have a unified height. Staggering the size of the buildings, he said, would be "awful."

Warnecke asked Walton to clarify the agreement reached between the Watergate and the CFA in May 1962. "What do the minutes say of that meeting?"

"The minutes of that meeting are shocking," said Walton. "They prove their point completely."

"We are sitting here in a rather difficult position," said Bunshaft. "I think he's telling the truth, from what the minutes say."

"So do I," said Walton.

"If we really cut it down, as we are talking," said Bunshaft, "they can't build it economically."

"We've been at it for years," said Walton. "It's a big civic issue which grows bigger all the time." He was keenly aware local planners, eager to see development on the ragged industrial site, wanted the Watergate built. "We can't ignore the fact that we live in a political situation."

He gave a signal to invite the Watergate delegation into the room.

"Well, gentlemen," Walton began, "we have considered it very deeply for a long, long time, as you have; and we want, as much as you, to reach an agreement and want this built as beautifully as you do. We want the same contribution to the civic landscape of Washington. We understand that you have very practical problems. We have weighed these all in. We would propose that the overall height be 140 feet with one penthouse." The height of 140 feet was to be measured from the shoreline of the Potomac River. All earlier discussions had focused on a height of 130 feet, measured from the base of each building—the equivalent, taking the contours of the site into account, of nearly 160 feet above the waterline.

Moretti described this proposed height limit a "surprise." Samaritani said the CFA's position was inconsistent with the May 1962 agreement.

Salgo addressed the CFA. "You must understand that we feel very discouraged to a certain degree, because it's less than we believe we can live with. We have to now go back home to do our homework to really find out what it means to us."

Walton adjourned the meeting. The Watergate team filed out of the room.

The next day, Walton sent a letter to General Clarke setting forth the CFA's position, "because the Watergate people have a marvelous facility for blurring issues to their own advantage and twisting the meanings of our Commission decisions." Walton said the CFA position was "very generous" to the developers. All that remained was to wait for the Watergate team to respond.

TWO DAYS LATER, PRESIDENT KENNEDY WAS SHOT AND killed in Dallas, Texas. Walton spent the next week absorbed in details related to the funeral and was present, with Kennedy's widow and immediate family, when the late president's coffin was closed. From their offices on Connecticut Avenue, Giuseppe Cecchi, Royce Ward and the Island Vista staff watched the slain president's funeral procession.

ON JANUARY 7, 1964, WALTER JENKINS, PRESIDENT JOHNson's chief assistant, reached out to William Walton and invited him and his fellow CFA commissioners to meet with the new president. The meeting was originally suggested to Jenkins by Fred Stanton, the president of CBS News, who wrote Jenkins to say a meeting would be "highly desirable, in view of the Kennedy interest in this area." The meeting was set for the Oval Office at 11:00 A.M. on January 9.

On January 8, CFA met in executive session and commissioners were informed by staff that the Watergate developers intended to go ahead with plans for the first building with no changes, and scale down other buildings to the height of 140 feet—measured from the base of each building, however, and not from the riverline—plus one penthouse.

"In other words, they haven't changed at all," said Aline Saarinen. "Boy!"

Walton told his colleagues not to expect help from the District government. General Clarke had called several times pressing him to approve the Watergate. The District's chief permit officer, Julian Green, was "very deeply sympathetic to this project, very deeply involved with developers, financier, and so forth." But Walton said the CFA had an important ally: Charles Horsky, who would be staying on in the Johnson White House and serving as the president's liaison for District affairs, had called two District commissioners to lobby against the Watergate as proposed. "He is going to back us 100%," Walton reported.

AT 9:35 A.M. ON THURSDAY, JANUARY 9, THE COMMISSION OF Fine Arts met in open session. Chairman Walton welcomed the Watergate delegation. "We have just one hour, alas!" he said. "Not because of our own wish, but the President has asked us to come and call on him." Walton was sending a signal: *You may have the ear of the District government, but we are about to have the ear of the president of the United States.*

Samaritani addressed the commission. "At the last moment yesterday we had a new conversation which led to a final possibility, which is in this last plan," he said. The revised plan removed additional floors on the balance of the complex, while retaining the first building with no changes, in order to address "the prescriptions of the Board of Zoning Adjustment."

"I am at a point which pleases me as an architect and I feel that this has realized the requirements of the Fine Arts Commission," Moretti said. "I feel the project can be saved."

Salgo asked Walton for the commission's reaction.

"You will know within the next hour," Walton replied. The Watergate delegation left the room.

"Does anyone have any new ideas?" Walton asked.

"I think we ought to stick by what we have done," said Bunshaft. "This thing is really ugly, and I think we shouldn't give another hair."

"We've gone as far as we can go," said Kelly.

"I propose to give them the answer that they have not conformed to the agreement we offered to them," said Walton. "Therefore, we have nothing more to say. This is the extent of our compromise."

"I just think this is going to look like Atlantic City 1920, within five years," said Warnecke.

"Sooner," said Walton.

Walton suggested they hammer one issue—the height of the complex relative to the Lincoln Memorial. "They're afraid of that Lincoln Memorial line." He summoned the Watergate team back into the room.

"Our position is unchanged," said Walton. "Thank you for coming."

In a briefing memo to President Johnson for his meeting with the Commission of Fine Arts, Arthur M. Schlesinger, Jr., a special assistant to the president, noted the CFA opposed the "so-called Watergate development" and "has refused to permit the construction of a new housing development which would be higher than the Lincoln Memorial." Walton and his fellow commissioners met with President Johnson over coffee for approximately half an hour. When they emerged from the Oval Office, Walton told reporters that Johnson was interested in obtaining "the best of modern architecture" while preserving the best of the past; and the CFA had Johnson's "full support" in carrying out the policies it had formulated on behalf of President Kennedy.

Within twenty-four hours, Samaritani surrendered.

The Watergate would be no higher than 140 feet, he wrote Walton, measured from the waterline—coming in ten inches below the Lincoln Memorial. Samaritani added that he regretted any impression by the Watergate team that the developers had not been "entirely frank with you." Walton told the *Washington Post* the CFA "would look favorably" on the revised plans at its next meeting.

On January 23, 1964, Congress officially changed the name of the National Cultural Center to the John F. Kennedy Center for the Performing Arts.

The next morning, construction crews arrived to excavate the foundation for the Watergate.

CHAPTER TWO: CITY WITHIN A CITY

Washington's new Watergate community represents more than a dramatic addition to the National Capital's skyline. It symbolizes the broad changes in character that have taken place in Washington in the last quarter century.

Since the beginning of World War II, Washington has grown tremendously in size, and at the same time has become a true "international capital." The gracefully curving buildings of Watergate rising from the banks of the Potomac embody the sophistication and dedication of the "new Washington."

Watergate press release, April 12, 1967

WHILE THE WATERGATE WAS STILL CUTTING THROUGH THE thicket of local and federal approvals, Giuseppe Cecchi and Royce Ward sat down in Washington with executives of the H.G. Smithy Company, a prominent local apartment leasing agency. After studying plans for the first Watergate apartment building, which included more than five hundred units offered for sale as cooperative apartments, the agents recommended reducing the number of luxury three-bedroom units and instead offering more two-bedroom and efficiency units that could be converted into three-bedroom apartments later, if demand warranted. Many potential residents of the Watergate were government employees with "modest" incomes who would be "more interested in the lower priced units." The agents also recommended half the building be offered as rental apartments and the other half offered as cooperative apartments available for purchase. Offering five hundred co-op apartments for sale at the same time, they warned, "might be too much for the market to absorb."

One other reason behind their recommendation was a regulation, then pending with the District government, "which will make it mandatory for all apartment and real estate developments to accept negroes." The proposed regulation was unlikely to affect rental projects, but "there would be resistance on the part of buyers in a project which must be integrated for fear that the resale value of their apartment would decrease if a colored family occupied an adjacent unit." Ward checked with another Washington real estate agent, who told him some owners in existing buildings might "become panicky and sell at a loss." Some purchasers of new apartments, however, would "understand the regulation and eventually accept it" but others "will refuse to buy." The agent said the effect on the Watergate, a large development operating as a cooperative, would be "small in view of the obvious costs," pointing to the recent experience of the River Park Cooperative apartment complex, in southwest Washington, which had "less than 8% colored buyers" due to the "large down payment," which, Ward noted, was negligible compared to the expected down payment for a Watergate apartment.

AS EXCAVATION BEGAN ON THE FIRST WATERGATE BUILDING, which would soon be named Watergate East, contractors struck "river rock" weakened by water pressure and shot through with cracks and fissures. They also encountered unstable subsoil, permeated with more than a century's worth of tar and oil from the former gas manufacturing plant. But Jim Roberts, project manager for Magazine Brothers Construction Corporation, the general contractor for the Watergate project, had a bigger problem to contend with: Luigi Moretti's design.

There were "no continuous straight lines anywhere—horizontally on the floors or vertically on the facade," Roberts said, and "no two floors had a facade exactly alike." Coordinates therefore had to be calculated separately for each segment of each curving wall on each floor, plus variations for unique balconies. One engineer spent more than six weeks working out the curves for the building's second floor alone. More than 2,200 exterior wall panels needed to be made in 100 different sizes and shapes. Another 80,000 square feet of "window walls" were needed, in 596 different configurations.

Roberts turned to Engineering Physics Co., a Rockville, Maryland, consulting firm that had an IBM 1620 computer, similar to the model displayed at the 1962 Seattle World's Fair and used at NASA headquarters to simulate orbits for the Gemini space capsule. Running a modified version of COGO, a civil engineering program, the 1620 recalculated curves for a floor of the Watergate in eight hours. Roberts was convinced. He added the 1620 and its programmers to his Watergate team. He later estimated the 1620 saved three thousand hours of manual computation time on just the windows in the first Watergate building alone.

Boris Timchenko was the most prominent landscape designer in the region when Cecchi tapped him to design the Watergate's public spaces. Timchenko was born in Lipetsk, Russia, and immigrated to France in 1920, where he studied landscape and design before arriving in the United States in 1926. Timchenko had designed the gardens of Hammersmith Farm in Newport, Rhode Island, where Jacqueline Bouvier and John F. Kennedy held their wedding reception, and went on to design the garden of the Georgetown home Senator and Mrs. Kennedy shared before moving into the White House in January 1961. He also designed the gardens at the new headquarters of the National Geographic Society and at Tompkins Hall at George Washington University, just a few blocks from the Watergate.

The Watergate presented Timchenko with two challenges: how to make the landscaping look attractive when viewed from apartment balconies or street level; and how to install everything on top of an underground parking garage. Timchenko placed clusters of trees throughout the grounds, connected by walkways and lawns in broad circular patterns echoing the shapes of the buildings. He covered the roof of the parking structure with two feet of sod. To support 150 trees, he designed concrete planters that sat directly on top of interior columns in the garage. A two-story colonnade at the entrance included several waterfalls. The total effect, the *Washington*

Star reported, was to create "the atmosphere of a formal Renaissance-style garden."

Luigi Moretti made several trips to Washington to monitor progress on the Watergate. He got along well with Timchenko and was pleased with the landscape design. But Moretti's relationship with Fischer, his American counterpart, was contentious. "I felt like a marriage counselor," said Cecchi, who was often forced to adjudicate their disputes. Moretti, Cecchi later recalled, would walk through the Watergate, inspecting every inch of the building and asking questions of the American architect and contractors. During one visit, Moretti noticed a seventh-floor window had been set back six inches. He had wanted it set back an entire foot. He threw his hat on the floor, stomped on it and screamed in rage.

RIVERVIEW REALTY, THE EXCLUSIVE SALES AGENT FOR THE Watergate, opened a sales center at 2700 Virginia Avenue NW, down the street from the construction site. Harold A. Lewis, CEO and founder of Riverview Realty, had worked with Nicolas Salgo at the Webb & Knapp construction firm. Lewis played golf and rowed varsity crew at Boston University before earning a business degree from Harvard. He was slim and tall, with "marble hair" and freckles. His clients and coworkers called him Hal.

The Watergate sales center included a dramatic thirty-by-thirty-foot reflecting pool surrounded by low-spraying fountains. Prospective owners could inspect a scale model of the 238-unit Watergate East; examine floor plans of various apartments, with suggested furniture arrangements; and imagine views from any apartment in the building, displayed on a cyclorama.

The press release announcing the new sales center called the Watergate "the Garden City Within a City." Newspaper advertisements invited prospective residents to visit and learn more about "Washington's consummate cooperative apartment residence." The ad showed the floor plan for Apartment 403-N, featuring two bedrooms ("one enormous, one large"), a "graciously proportioned" living room, a kitchen with "cabinet space by the acre" and "every work-saving appliance," two "luxuriously appointed" baths and five "mammoth closets." Bidets were standard in most apartments and every unit came with at least one "marble-topped" toilet. A heating and cooling plant on site, built by the Washington Gas Light Company at a cost of $1.65 million, provided steam for heat in the winter and cold water for cooling in the summer—offering year-round "climate control" and "no furnace to nurse, no air-conditioner to baby." Tranquility was also assured by extensive soundproofing between apartments: A layer of insulation underneath the floors in each unit promised "the ultimate in aural privacy."

As developers refined their plans and adjusted to the height limits insisted upon by the Commission of Fine Arts in January 1964, the number of apartments in the first building was cut in half—well below the level that might overwhelm the local market. Prices ranged from $17,500 for a studio to more than $200,000 for one of seven penthouses with river views. The IBM 1620 computer, deployed initially to develop layouts and the dimensions of windows and exterior panels, was programmed to calculate pricing for each of the apartments, taking into account views and square footage.

Riverview Realty's Lewis told the *Washington Star* that the Watergate embodied three principles of good urban design: mixed-use construction, "healthy" land use and "occupant ownership." At a luncheon meeting of the Cosmopals, a club for wives of members of the all-male Cosmopolitan Club, Lewis said women were the key to his marketing strategy for the Watergate. "Suburbia didn't answer the promises we looked for," he said. "The old Anglo Saxon concept of man's home with acres of rolling grounds around it we miniaturized into rows of monotonous little houses constructed on postage-stamp lots." A father now "fights his way through miles of traffic to the office" while his spouse is stuck at home all day "with just the television and the telephone for company." Women had forced their

families to move out to the suburbs after concluding "the congestion, noise and disorder of the cities could no longer be tolerated."
Now, he said, women would lead the flight from suburbia back to
urban settings.

The Watergate was also attractive to single women. It offered
three things they wanted in an urban residence: the possibility
of ownership, at a price within reach to an independent, working
woman; a stylish, high-quality environment; and security. Watergate East boasted fourteen security cameras, including one in each
elevator, monitored by a central facility in the building. Residents
could summon assistance simply by picking up their phones. "What
all of this means," the *Washington Star* reported, "is that intruders
will have difficulty getting onto the grounds undetected, and they
will find it almost impossible to get into the building itself without
being seen by the TV cameras."

By mid-February, with the opening of the building still nine
months away, two-thirds of the apartments in Watergate East were
already sold.

IN FEBRUARY 1965, LUIGI MORETTI, ON HIS WAY BACK FROM
Montreal, stopped in Washington to celebrate the "topping off" of
Watergate East. He stepped out of a champagne reception at the sales
center to pontificate on a range of topics to a *Washington Post* reporter.

Washington's public buildings, Moretti said, "are too many, they
are too massive, and they are too conformist." There was no evidence in the typical federal building, he said, of either the "spirit" of
the architect or the function of the government agency. As a result,
"the overall beauty of Washington suffered."

He said Stone's rectangular design for the Kennedy Center did
not conflict with the "delicately flowing" Watergate, but provided "a
welcome contrast."

Asked about the Watergate's progress, Moretti smiled. "Fine," he
said. "Fine."

Guests at the reception, including the Italian ambassador to the United States, Sergio Fenoaltea, admired a cake in the shape of Watergate East, from the Avignon Freres bakery. One guest would become one of the Watergate's most enduring—and controversial—residents: Anna Chennault.

Chennault was petite and elegant, of Chinese heritage, with dramatic eyebrows and perfectly manicured fingernails, which were often painted bright red. She had recently told her extraordinary life story in a 1962 biography, *A Thousand Springs: The Biography of a Marriage*, which, by 1965, was in its sixth printing. "I was a fortunate woman," she wrote, "for I was married to a great man who deeply loved me." General Claire Lee Chennault had retired from the U.S. Army in 1937 to accept an offer from Madame Chiang Kai-shek to serve as an "observer" with the Chinese Air Force at a salary of $1,000 per month, plus expenses. In July 1941, six months before the Japanese attack on Pearl Harbor, he formed the American Volunteer Group, known as the Flying Tigers, to defend China. When America declared war on Japan, he became commander of the U.S. 14th Air Force.

As a nineteen-year-old reporter for the Chinese Central News Agency, Anna covered a press conference at the headquarters of the U.S. 14th Air Force, in Kunming. She was the only woman in the room when General Chennault arrived for his press conference. "Good afternoon, gentlemen," he said before he saw Anna and added: "And lady!"

Anna told her sister later that day she had met a man who was simply "magnificent."

When Japanese troops pressed deeper into China, Anna's father asked General Chennault to send Anna and her five sisters to California for safety. Chennault made arrangements, but Anna decided to stay behind. She was secretly in love.

After the Japanese surrendered in 1945, an estimated 2 million Chinese turned out to cheer General Chennault's farewell parade through the streets of Chungking. Before he left for Louisiana to re-join his wife and eight children, according to Anna's memoir, he kissed her for the first time and assured her he would return. By Christmas, he was back in Shanghai. He asked Anna to dinner and told her he had divorced his wife and returned to China a free man. He asked Anna to marry him. The general had two requests of his young bride: "One, always remain a Chinese wife. Two, keep your beautiful, slim figure." As Anna explained in her memoir:

> A Chinese wife knows that by yielding on small issues, and exercising the subtle art of gentle persuasion in important matters, such as the care and welfare of the children, she can usually control the main pattern of family life. She is content to win while looking defeated, and to let her husband appear to win while actually losing. She is, in a word, a subtle, gentle being who strives unobtrusively to combine the tact of a diplomat with the tactics of a psychiatrist.

They married in 1947. She was twenty-two; the general was fifty-four. They bought property in Monroe, Louisiana, but spent most of the year in Taipei, Taiwan, where Chennault managed a cargo airline. On Christmas morning in 1957, he coughed up blood. Six months later, with Anna at his side, he died at Walter Reed Hospital. He left her $225,500—enough to be "well-off but not really rich," Anna wrote later—and asked his friend and longtime attorney Thomas Corcoran to look after her.

Corcoran, known as Tommy or Tommy the Cork, was Washington's first "super-lobbyist," according to his biographer David McKean. A graduate of Brown University and Harvard Law School, Corcoran became a key strategist in Franklin D. Roosevelt's White House, helping shape the Fair Labor Standards Act of 1938 and establish the Securities and Exchange Commission. He was an advocate within the White House for General Chennault's Flying Tigers and after the war served as Chennault's lawyer and business partner.

After the general's death, Anna moved to Washington with her two young daughters, Cynthia and Claire. Besides Corcoran, she knew political and business leaders who lived in the capital. And Washington, with a large Chinese local community, was more cosmopolitan than Monroe, Louisiana—a small town in a state that still had antimiscegenation laws on its books. She bought an apartment on Cathedral Avenue in northwest Washington and enrolled the girls in a nearby elementary school. Corcoran introduced her to the president of Georgetown University, where she landed a job writing Chinese-English dictionaries and helping to develop a machine that could print Chinese characters.

In 1960, Sylvia Hermon, chair of the Republican Women's Federation of Maryland, asked her to help organize ethnic minorities for the presidential campaign of Richard Nixon. Anna had met Nixon before—in 1954, when he was vice president and attended a banquet in Taiwan, given for him by President Chiang Kai-shek. Nixon had sent her a condolence note when her husband died. Anna worked in Nixon's Washington, DC, campaign office and gave speeches around the region. Although Nixon lost the race, she found the campaign environment "intoxicating," according to her biographer Catherine Forslund.

Chennault campaigned aggressively for Senator Barry Goldwater's 1964 presidential campaign, focusing on raising funds and reaching out to ethnic minorities, and hosted "strategy" sessions, attended by Republican members of Congress and their top aides, in her apartment on Cathedral Avenue, which became, she recalled later, "a popular watering hole for ranking Republicans." It was also a "sales room" on Sunday afternoons, reported Sarah McClendon, where she sold "beautiful Chinese art objects."

Anna Chennault visited the Watergate or its sales office twelve times before she finally settled on a 4,500-square-foot penthouse on the fourteenth floor.

ON DECEMBER 2, 1964, PRESIDENT JOHNSON TURNED THE first shovel of dirt at the groundbreaking ceremony for the John F. Kennedy Center for the Performing Arts. "This Center will brighten the life of Washington," Johnson said, "but it is not . . . just a Washington project. It is a national project." Among the dignitaries on the dais for the ceremony: William Walton, chairman of the Commission of Fine Arts.

Later that day, Roger Stevens briefed the Kennedy Center trustees on the Watergate. The fifth and final building in the development, he said, would rise forty-one feet above the main roof of the Kennedy Center. "It will be necessary to vigorously oppose the proposed height of this building," Stevens advised them.

At a meeting of the Kennedy Center's executive committee on March 12, 1965, Stevens and in-house counsel Ralph Becker reviewed the Watergate's "height problem." The executive committee unanimously adopted a resolution stating that the final Watergate building would "seriously impair the esthetic values of the Center."

Wolf Von Eckardt, the *Washington Post*'s architecture critic, weighed in. He accused the Watergate of "woefully crowding in" the Kennedy Center. "The southernmost, massive, sausage-like building of this wiggly complex," he wrote, "encroaches to within 300 feet upon what is to be a national shrine. The dignity of the John F. Kennedy Center demands more land, air around it."

William R. Lichtenberg, an attorney for Island Vista, offered a solution: If the Kennedy Center needed to be taller than the Watergate, then the trustees should add a few feet to the top of their own building.

Becker, the Kennedy Center lawyer, dismissed the suggestion outright. Raising the Kennedy Center just fifteen feet, Becker said, would require a complete redesign. The cost would also be prohibitive—far more than the $1 million back-of-the-envelope estimate provided by the Watergate—and the Kennedy Center would then be taller than the nearby Lincoln Memorial. Becker promised to appear before any "relevant official body" to oppose approval of the final Watergate building at a height greater than either the Kennedy Center or the Lincoln Memorial.

The District Board of Zoning Adjustment, under the terms of the original permit granted to the Watergate by the zoning commission in 1964, was empowered to "review" plans for the final building. At the board's June 16 meeting, Becker testified that Kennedy Center trustees had unanimously agreed to oppose the final Watergate building unless it was reduced by five floors.

Lichtenberg said the Kennedy Center was relying on outdated plans. The final building, he assured the board, would be built to a height of 140 feet above the waterline, a mere 5 feet above the roof of the Kennedy Center. The elimination of five floors would cost developers in excess of $5 million.

"My client has tried . . . to be a cooperative and interested direct neighbor of the center," Lichtenberg wrote the Board of Zoning Adjustment. "We expect to continue to do everything possible within reasonable limits to cooperate with the Center, but we expect in return fair and equitable consideration based on all the facts involved."

THAT WEEKEND, THE MODEL APARTMENT IN WATERGATE EAST opened to the public. Admission was fifty cents per person, with the proceeds donated to local charities. The apartment was designed by Duke Arturo Pini di San Miniato, a friend of the Duke and Duchess of Windsor (he designed their suite at the Waldorf-Astoria Hotel in New York), who was completing his term as president of the National Society of Interior Designers. He became an interior designer, he told the *Washington Star*, "via the route of restoring palazzos in his native Italy where he inherited the family title of duke."

His biography was somewhat less authentic than the antiques he placed in the model apartment.

According to a report in the *New York Times*, Pini di San Miniato was a former antiques dealer from Bologna who married a Canadian heiress and acquired his title in 1964 by purchasing it from the tiny Republic of San Marino, a "micro-state" completely surrounded by Italy, located about an hour south of Venice on the Adriatic Sea. The *Times* story infuriated Pini di San Miniato, who hired an attorney and demanded a retraction. "I'm the only American citizen who legally has the right to call himself duke," he insisted. An internal *Times* investigation could not find his title listed in *World Nobility and Peerage*, the *Almanach de Gotha* or the 1964 edition of the *Enciclopedia Araldico-Cavalleresca*. The rumor in Italy, according to the *Times*'s internal investigation, was that Pini di San Miniato arrived in the United States after World War II, "told everyone he was titled" and then proceeded to purchase the title from "an elderly, childless Italian."

"He's definitely not a Duke," said Princess Elvina Pallavicini.

"He would have made it without the title," added Princess Domitilla del Drago. "I wonder why he bothers. It's amusing." The *Times* eventually concluded Pini di San Miniato could call himself a duke, because the title had in fact been conferred by the Republic of San Marino, without claiming any noble lineage.

Pini di San Miniato's design for the model "contemporary home" at the 1964 New York World's Fair was praised by *Better Homes & Gardens* magazine for its "restrained but vibrant tone," but there was nothing restrained about his design in Watergate East. The apartment was furnished "in a Classic Continental style," the *Washington Post* reported, with French and Italian furnishings suggesting "Oriental Opulence and Italian Grandeur."

The *Post*'s Von Eckardt inspected the model apartment. His verdict: "Well, it's different."

"If the bare and square uniformity of modern apartment house slabs bothers you," he wrote, "be happy in the knowledge that the architects have provided here as much sculptural dressing as Baldassare Longhena, master of Baroque palazzos, ever dreamed of." He described the model apartment as a "miniature replica of a 17th century Parisian palace" with "wedding cake icing on the dining room ceiling, a miniature hall of mirrors, more mirrors around a somewhat bothersome structural column in the living room, a nonstructural Romeo and Juliet colonnade in the master bedroom, valences, scallops and all kinds of Louis This and That bric-a-brac." He called the layout "rambling" and "complex" and complained he couldn't "find a right angle anywhere." The apartment, he conceded, had ample closet space and "splendid" views.

The *Milwaukee Journal* described the apartment's eight-foot ceilings as a "necessity" after "zoning controversies" forced the building to be "squeezed down," forcing air-conditioning units, originally planned between floors, to be set under windows—taking eighteen inches off the width of the room. The Watergate's low ceilings, Pini di San Miniato acknowledged, presented some challenges—which he addressed by carefully selecting furniture and adopting "gimmicks of one sort or another in every room." He placed a triple-arched colonnade in the master bedroom, for example, to "give an effect of height" and also form "a pleasant lounging area."

On the evening of October 25, 1965, the grand opening of the Watergate was held for fifteen hundred invited guests. Aldo Samaritani and Luigi Moretti flew in from Rome. Nicolas Salgo came down from New York. Other guests came from Mexico, where SGI was planning a community outside Mexico City, and from Montreal, where the company was erecting the tallest concrete-and-steel skyscraper in Canada, designed by Luigi Moretti and Pier Luigi Nervi.

"From the inception of our task to build Watergate," Samaritani wrote in the dedication program, "we were conscious of the extraordinary opportunity we possessed, and the responsibility that we had accepted." He called Washington "the most important city of our age" and said his goal was to do more than simply "develop" the site but to give Washingtonians a "distinctive and valuable addition to their city . . . consistent with the beauty and spirit" of the nation's capital.

Samaritani thanked "the many District of Columbia officials whose assistance and cooperation have been invaluable in our work." He pointedly left out any mention of either the Commission of Fine Arts or the National Capital Planning Commission.

Clara Graff, whose husband, Bill, worked as an architect on the Watergate project for SGI, noticed Luigi Moretti hanging to the side of the room during the festivities. Moretti, "like many architects," was an introvert, she recalled later, and was self-conscious about his limited English. Clara sat with him during dinner and kept him company the entire evening.

The first Watergate East apartment was sold to Admiral Paul Dudley, a graduate of the U.S. Naval Academy and a veteran of World War II and the Korean War. The first residents to move into Watergate East were Mr. and Mrs. Louis Ratner—he founded the Louis Creative Hairdressers chain—who moved into their penthouse the morning of October 16. Admiral and Mrs. Dudley moved into their unit later the same day.

George Arnstein had recently accepted a job with the National Education Association and found the commute from Arlington, Virginia, to downtown Washington "a bit tedious." Life in Virginia, moreover, was not a match for the progressive politics of George and his wife, Sherry: The state still had a poll tax and their African-American friends could not join them for weekend swims in their local public pool. The Arnsteins stretched their finances and purchased a Watergate apartment off of a floor plan they saw at the sales center. They originally planned to move in over Thanksgiving weekend, but delayed a month because the building, Sherry thought, looked "unfinished." When they asked to see their assigned parking space, the sales associate replied awkwardly the building did not yet have an occupancy permit for the garage, but would provide valet parking in the interim. The Arnsteins celebrated the holidays with a party in their new apartment and gave guests a "punch list" to write down anything that needed to be fixed.

Margaret and Ralph Berlin moved into the Watergate from Bethesda, Maryland. He was the carpet buyer for Kann's, the first Washington department store to have black mannequins in its window displays. When Margaret first saw their apartment, which had no formal dining room, she asked her husband, "Where do we eat?" To make friends with their new neighbors, Margaret and Ralph organized weekly potluck dinners in their hallway. Ralph vacuumed the hall after each gathering.

Forrest Mars, Sr., an heir to the Mars candy fortune, and his wife, Audrey, bought a penthouse, merging a duplex with an adjacent apartment to form an urban mansion. They employed a full-time gardener for their terrace, with sweeping views of downtown Washington, the Potomac River and Georgetown. Forrest lived mostly in Nevada. According to a family biographer, he and Audrey were not companions "in any sense of the word."

Lillian and John E. Cannaday, Jr.—the *New York Times* listed his occupation as "investing in the stock market"—bought a penthouse and hired a decorator to pull the apartment together while they went on a world cruise. When they returned in December, "the paintings were hung, and the drapes were in place. All they had to do was to unpack their trunks and suitcases and enjoy their new home."

Congressional aide Robert McCord and his wife combined two penthouses. They installed a fountain in their entry, setting it low "so it wouldn't make a splash."

Another penthouse owner, Arthur Hill, paired a Van Gogh painting with a Spanish rug "bought on sale at Bloomingdale's."

New owners received a "welcome" letter from the Watergate, which read in part: "You have purchased the ultimate in luxury living—a purchase that can only grow and increase in living comfort as well as monetary value.

"Your future happiness is assured here. Nothing will be spared in keeping you surrounded with the same beauty and atmosphere that made you originally decide upon Watergate East."

All new residents also received a copy of the building's "Rules and Regulations," with forty-seven specific policies, including:

Mops, cloths and brooms shall not be dusted or shaken from apartment windows, balconies or in the halls or stairways.

The dictates of good taste and propriety in the matter of dress will be observed in the public areas of Watergate East.

Pets are permitted as long as they behave.

Barbecuing and cooking on the balconies is prohibited.

All persons using the pool from their individual apartments when in bathing attire, will wear robe and slippers, exit and enter pool area as directed by resident manager.

Anna Chennault sketched the layout for her new penthouse herself, designating spaces for two bedrooms, a maid's quarters, three bathrooms (plus a powder room), a study and a large combination living and dining room. An elevator connected the first floor of the duplex to a rooftop garden. As construction was wrapping up, she asked Vlastimil Koubek, a prominent Washington architect, to inspect the unit. He reported back to her on December 20, 1965, listing a number of "deficiencies and/or possible problems" including:

- Low ceiling heights;
- A "heatilator" in the living room, which should be replaced with a conventional fireplace;
- "Unfortunate" architectural features, including columns blocking windows;
- "Makeshift" placement of a rectangular heating/cooling unit against the curved wall in the foyer;
- A continuous crack along the top of the plaster walls; and
- Placement of the dryer exhaust in the kitchen, which could cause "lint flying all over the roof when you have guests enjoying a roof garden party."

Chennault presented the list to the Watergate sales team. She persuaded them to knock $75,000 off the purchase price of her penthouse, bringing it down to $250,000.

Walter Pforzheimer bought the last one-bedroom apartment in the initial offering of Watergate East. A Yale Law School graduate, he was practicing law in New York when the Japanese attacked Pearl Harbor. The next day, he joined the army's Senior Air Intelligence Staff and served under Colonel Lewis Powell, chief of operational intelligence and later a Supreme Court Justice. In what would later become known as the Yale Library Project, Pforzheimer distributed funds to various informants throughout Europe, under the pretext of buying books for Yale's libraries. After the war, he moved to Washington and helped write the legislation creating the Central Intelligence Agency.

A lifelong bachelor, Pforzheimer was the son and nephew of noted book collectors. His father's Molière collection was the finest outside of France and his uncle Carl owned a Gutenberg Bible. Bill McCarthy, a rare book dealer from New York and a Yale classmate, reached out to Pforzheimer one day to offer him an original intelligence report from the American Revolution, regarding fortifications in Brooklyn. Pforzheimer bought it for $35. As he was leaving, McCarthy said he had something else that might be of interest. Walter took a seat and McCarthy brought out a folder, with a handwritten letter, dated July 26, 1777, addressed to Colonel Elias Dayton. The letter read, "The necessity of procuring good intelligence is apparent and need not be further urged" and signed "G. Washington."

"I knew right away that this was my make or break point, my right of passage," Walter recalled years later. "If I bought this, I would be a real collector in the field of intelligence service. If I walked away, I would not be a serious collector." He paid in the "middle four figures" for the letter, which created something of a "cash flow problem." He kept the purchase secret from his father for nearly five years, fearing a negative reaction; when his father, near death, saw the letter, he congratulated his son on the purchase.

Pforzheimer persuaded Allen Dulles, the first civilian CIA director, to establish within the spy agency a library, which became the Historical Intelligence Collection. Pforzheimer became its first curator in 1956. The collection was in part a resource for checking what was public and what remained secret, to be used whenever former CIA personnel wrote memoirs and submitted them, as required under federal law, for review to ensure they contained no classified material. Pforzheimer also used the collection to help the CIA rebut any fabricated claims about the history of U.S. intelligence gathering abroad, a common Soviet disinformation tactic during the Cold War.

Pforzheimer often purchased two copies of any book that caught his eye—one for the CIA, one for his personal library. By the time he moved into Watergate East, his personal collection included three thousand volumes. He stored his most valuable items on the upper floor of his duplex, behind a locked steel gate. He received visitors for cocktails and cigars in his first-floor "sitting room," which also held his collection of Washington Redskins memorabilia. As his collection grew, he needed more room. Since neither apartment on either side of him was for sale, he bought a studio apartment on the fourth floor, where he slept and dressed—and stored hundreds more books, periodicals and newspaper clippings.

SGI EXECUTIVES IN ROME ORDERED A REPORT FROM WASH-ington on the extent of changes being made for new owners in Watergate East. The report showed customization had gotten out of hand. Three out of four bathrooms in Watergate East had been changed. Nine bidets had been added, but another thirteen had been removed. Five apartments had eliminated service entrances. Nearly three-quarters of apartments had changed their kitchens. "The more the client is prepared to spend," the Watergate's local team reported, "the more exacting he is." Only 13 percent of the efficiency apartments had been revised at the request of the owners, but 100 percent of penthouse owners had demanded changes.

Until there were enough residents to form a cooperative association, the Watergate development team had run the building. It was now time to turn over the reins to the owners. On April 18, 1966, in the auditorium of the Peoples Life Insurance building across the street from Watergate East, the developers called a meeting to organize the association.

Riverview Realty announced a slate of nominees for election to the board of directors of the new association. They included Joel Barlow, a partner at the Covington & Burling law firm and owner of a penthouse; Charlotte Smith Alford, a freelance illustrator and artist; Elizabeth Guhring, a prominent divorce lawyer; Walter Rosenberry, a paper and forest products executive; John Kern, a tax judge and a former mayor of Indianapolis; Charles Simpson, another tax judge; William Smith, a U.S. Army officer; Robert McCord, a congressional aide; William Simon, a Washington lawyer and former general counsel to the Senate Interstate and Foreign Commerce Committee; and Harold A. Kertz, a lawyer and vice chairman of the District of Columbia Public Service Commission. The nominees were approved by a vote of the owners.

In a "Report from Management," the developers thanked residents for their "patience and understanding" and expressed a shared goal of reaching a "normal" level of operations and an end to ongoing construction. The developers also announced they were hiring additional engineers and "porters" at no charge to the residents, in order to address "increased maintenance problems." They promised the lobby would be completed "in the near future"; the outdoor fountains would shortly resume operation; the swimming pool would be ready before summer; and the air-conditioning would be turned on no later than May 1.

Back in Rome, Samaritani reported to the SGI board that 206 of 240 apartments in Watergate East had been sold; 34 apartments and 54 garage spaces, some of which were being rented out, remained available for purchase. The external walls and balconies of the Watergate Hotel and Watergate Office Building were finished. Progress on the fourth building, Watergate West, was going ahead "with alacrity."

The Watergate Shopping Mall opened on October 27, 1966, with a tasting of Italian wines sponsored by the Italian Ministry of Foreign Trade. Over a thousand guests at the gala opening toured the new Peoples Drug Store and the Watergate Safeway store, serenaded by strolling musicians playing "popular tunes."

JOHN BAILEY, CHAIRMAN OF THE DEMOCRATIC NATIONAL Committee, learned from his landlord that the rent on their K Street offices was going to be hiked significantly. "We need to find another space," Bailey told his administrative assistant, R. Spencer Oliver, who began reaching out to real estate agents. One day, Oliver's phone rang. It was Giuseppe Cecchi.

"I understand you're looking for office space," said Cecchi. "Come to the Watergate."

Oliver was reluctant. At the time, taxi rates in Washington were determined by the number of zones crossed per ride. The Watergate was two taxi zones away. "That's pretty far from the center of town," he said. "I don't know." Cecchi pressed Oliver to come over and take a tour.

They stood in the center of the sixth floor of the office building. There were no walls, just support columns and a sweeping view of the Potomac River. "We'll design it for you however you want it to be," Cecchi promised. Oliver sensed Cecchi desperately needed tenants for the new office building.

"I'm in negotiations already with a couple other places," Oliver said.

"We can beat any offer you have," Cecchi insisted.

When Oliver got back to the office, he popped in to see Bailey. "I think they're gonna make us a deal," Oliver said.

Cecchi sent over a proposal. He offered the DNC the entire sixth floor of the Watergate Office Building, with the potential to expand into another floor during presidential campaigns, plus another suite on the basement level for the new DNC computers. Next door, in the Watergate Hotel, Cecchi included a three-bedroom hospitality suite upstairs in the hotel, overlooking the Potomac, for only $300 a month. (Separately he leased a dining room, kitchen and office on the B-2 level for the National Democratic Club.)

"We'll never raise the rent," Cecchi promised.

Bailey took the deal.

ON APRIL 1, 1967, THE WATERGATE HOTEL OPENED TO THE public. Hotel rooms—called "apartments" in the press release—could be rented by the month or by the day. Two-bedroom "presidential suites" were available for $900 per month.

The interiors of the 213-suite "apartment hotel" were designed by Ellen Lehman McCluskey of New York, a daughter of a Lehman Brothers partner and a debutante, presented at the Court of St. James's in London in 1932. She was an accomplished ice dancer and a pilot who trained men to fly during World War II. After the war, she opened her own firm in New York, designing interiors for the Plaza in New York and the Motor Lodge at Chatham Center, Pittsburgh.

According to a Watergate press release, she selected "period pieces" to "soften" the hotel's modern interiors. Her lobby design was "oriental in feeling," with leather sofas, antique Chinese chairs and a European commode. She placed abstract paintings throughout the public areas. "The architecture of the building has dictated a contemporary treatment of the interior design throughout," according to an article in the August 1967 issue of *Interior Design*. "The curvature of the exterior walls, the vast expanse of windows and the fact that all the supporting members of columns extend into the rooms posed a number of interior designing problems which Mrs. McCluskey has solved by presenting 89 different furniture arrangements to satisfy each irregularity of plan, and five different color schemes are interspersed throughout. In a way, this was an asset as it gave each apartment an individual look all its own." Cecchi sent a copy of the magazine to Samaritani in Rome, who was unimpressed. He found the design "awful." Any number of "top-notch" interior designers, Samaritani wrote, could have created interiors "of a very different design than that which has been created by the woman for Watergate."

The Watergate Office Building, marketed as "planned and constructed to meet the special needs of Washington's many trade associations, professional firms, and non-profit and charitable organizations," opened the same day as the Watergate Hotel. According to a press release, the office building was "more restrained in its design" than the hotel and apartments and was the only building "without sweeping balconies." The Watergate Office Building's only outdoor space was the terrace on the sixth floor—the new home of the Democratic National Committee.

ANNA CHENNAULT'S HOUSEWARMING PARTY WAS COVERED by *Washingtonian* magazine and the *Washington Star*. Guests included three of her "closest friends" in Washington: Senators John Tower of Texas, Karl Mundt of South Dakota and Jack Miller of Iowa, all Republicans for whom she had campaigned. She invited FBI director J. Edgar Hoover, but he sent his regrets. Chennault's guests admired her "oriental" living room and made their way up the spiral staircase to enjoy a view of the Capitol, the Washington Monument and the Potomac. Someone produced a "wiggly substance" called "super stuff"—"the newest thing in children's toys." Senator Tower kept rubbing his hand along the side of his dinner jacket to get rid of the "sleek feeling." Another guest produced a "super ball." No bigger than a marble, the rubber ball, when thrown properly, bounced back—no matter where it was thrown.

IN JULY 1967, PRESIDENT AND MRS. JOHNSON ATTENDED THE open house at the DNC's new Watergate offices. Bailey showed the president the computer room. Upstairs, Lady Bird Johnson admired the view, but expressed concerns about the 220-foot-high smokestacks that marred the otherwise picture-postcard view of Georgetown from DNC vice chairman Margaret Price's office. The first lady was in the midst of a national beautification initiative and was happy to learn the unsightly structures were about to come down. Nobody told her a freeway would replace them.

Some of the party faithful were "uneasy, even sheepish," as they tried to reconcile the new offices—with their wall-to-wall carpeting, art-and-tapestry-lined walls, pastel push-button telephones and "VIP Room" with a built-in sink and refrigerator—with the "Common Man image of the New Deal, the Fair Deal and the Great Society," the *Washington Star* reported. "It looks like Republican headquarters," observed Johnson's labor secretary Willard Wirtz, only half in jest. "Nothing's too good for the party of the people," said Associate Supreme Court Justice Thurgood Marshall. According to the *Miami Herald*, "The music is soft and piped. The girls looked like they escaped from a James Bond movie. There's a great view of the Potomac, too. Real or contrived, happiness pervades the sixth-floor ultra-modern suite."

One unnamed official said the DNC was able to get the "plush" suite at a good rate because building management had failed to anticipate the robust demand for office space in the new building. Committee staff members had numbers at the ready to defend the move: The new offices contained 20 percent more floor space (5,000 to 6,000 feet) and cost $7,000 a month—$100 less than the monthly rent on their previous digs. "By taking a whole floor in a new building, we got our space custom-designed for our needs," said Al Mark, the DNC's public affairs director. "The air conditioning has especially installed ducts" to accommodate the committee's "data-processing equipment," he added. Another attendee at the VIP opening reception pointed out to a reporter the curtains were fiberglass and "quite inexpensive."

Party chairman John Bailey said the move would help the Democrats get a "smooth start" on the 1968 campaign. The Johnson organization reserved space for the reelection campaign next door, in the Watergate Hotel.

AT ITS SEPTEMBER 1967 MEETING, THE KENNEDY CENTER board of trustees voted unanimously to oppose construction of the final Watergate building. They had tried to work with the developers to reduce the height and had been unsuccessful. Now they wanted the building nixed entirely.

The Commission of Fine Arts took up the matter in a closed session later that month. In the eyes of the CFA, protectors of the aesthetic quality of Washington, the Watergate was no longer an issue. The problem was Edward Durell Stone's design for the Kennedy Center.

"Frankly," said Gordon Bunshaft, the Watergate fit the site "much better than this thing that Stone is doing." The Watergate, he added, was designed before the Kennedy Center—and therefore was one of the "problems" Stone had to work with, "which he ignored."

The next day, in a public session, Edward Durell Stone appeared before the CFA. "It is my belief that this building should not be built," Stone said, gesturing to an illustration of the final piece of the Watergate.

Commissioner Roszak asked Stone what he would do if someone came to him and suggested one of his designs should be cut in half. "Now, you may not agree with Mr. Moretti," Roszak said, "but this man has a right to his expression, and I think it is tremendously presumptuous to tell an artist what to do."

"I have a compassion for fellow creative workers," Stone sniffed. "I haven't said the buildings were ugly."

Nicolas Salgo read from a *Washington Post* report five years earlier in which Stone said the Watergate would not "crowd in" on the National Cultural Center. "I think it will look wonderful together with the Center," Stone had reportedly said.

"I have no recollection of making such a statement," Stone asserted. "Certainly, I never made it formally. It is a suicidal statement, and I doubt under any circumstances that I would be that foolish."

Stone failed to persuade the Commission of Fine Arts to stop construction. The CFA approved the final Watergate building, at the same height as the rest of the complex. The CFA added, however, that their action "should in no way affect" any efforts by the Kennedy Center to acquire the site from the developers.

The *Washington Post* published an editorial slamming the "unattractive arrogance" of the Kennedy Center trustees. "Maybe the Kennedy Center would look a little better if the White House were moved slightly to the left," the *Post* sneered. "Maybe the lily of culture could be gilded a trifle by moving the Watergate Development to the other side of the Potomac."

The fate of the final Watergate building was now in the hands of the District Board of Zoning Adjustment, which took up the question on October 18, 1967. Charles M. Nes, Jr., of Baltimore, a former president of the American Institute of Architects, testified against the Watergate. He said he did not "know of any country in the world that would permit a speculative building within 300 feet" of a national performing arts center. John R. Immer, a local activist, urged the Kennedy Center to be relocated to Pennsylvania Avenue—"where it belongs." The board voted four to one to approve the final building as designed—allowing it to rise four feet above the Kennedy Center.

The Kennedy Center trustees, however, refused to surrender. Their lawyer promised to file a lawsuit to prevent the District from issuing a building permit. They turned to the Department of Justice and the Department of the Interior to request for purchase of a "scenic easement" for the Watergate property. In January 1964, the interior department paid Jacqueline Kennedy's stepfather, Hugh D. Auchincloss, $500,000 to stop construction of a proposed seventeen-story apartment building at the Merrywood estate, on the Potomac River. The interior department told the Kennedy Center this option was not available, as the department had no funds with which to purchase an easement and did not believe Congress would make an appropriation. Interior secretary Stewart Udall agreed to step in and attempt to mediate the dispute over the final Watergate building.

At the December 1967 meeting of the National Capital Planning Commission, Chairman Rowe cited language in the original permit that promised the final Watergate building would be subject to further review by federal and local planners. The building closest to the Kennedy Center, she said, "didn't have final Commission approval," and should be "stepped down . . . as a way of fitting it into the Kennedy Center."

ON APRIL 4, 1968, DR. MARTIN LUTHER KING, JR., WAS ASSAS-
sinated and riots swept through Washington. George Arnstein and a
few neighbors went up to the roof of Watergate East. "We could see
the fires in the distance," he recalled years later. "And there were . . .
police vehicles in our garage, presumably as a precaution."

R. Spencer Oliver and his colleagues at the DNC offices at the
Watergate stood at the windows of their suite, looking out at the
smoke rising over the city. The staff went down to the lobby bar in
the Watergate Hotel. The doors suddenly burst open and soldiers,
wearing riot gear and gas masks, flooded into the lobby and announced the city was shutting down.

The hotel closed the bar. Oliver and his coworkers headed home.

ON APRIL 22, 1968, INTERIOR SECRETARY UDALL ANNOUNCED
a compromise: The final Watergate building, originally planned for
apartments, would instead become a second office building and be
turned slightly, adding 380 feet between the two structures and creating 600 additional parking spaces. The trustees of the Kennedy
Center unanimously endorsed the revised design.

Later that evening, however, the directors of the Watergate East
co-op voted unanimously against the agreement. As reported in the
Watergate Post, the community newsletter, residents attacked the revised plan, which they said would change the character of the entire complex, introduce traffic congestion and "bright fluorescent
lights," and undermine "enjoyment of the pool." Board member
William Simon said the owners of Watergate East were "never consulted" during the mediation process and the agreement "gave very
little to the Center, a greater deal to the developer, and was at the
great expense of Watergate East owners." Simon denounced the col-
laboration of the developers and the Kennedy Center as an "unholy
alliance."

On May 1, 1968, Watergate attorney William R. Lichtenberg told the owners of Watergate East the developers did not "promise" an apartment building would be built adjacent to them, and only said the final Watergate building was "planned" for apartments. One owner asked Lichtenberg why the developers changed their minds. "Because the United States Government asked us to," Lichtenberg replied. An unnamed federal official who was present at the meeting was asked directly if that was the case. The official said no.

Two weeks later, Simon wrote an eight-page letter to Pope Paul VI—"the controlling stockholder in SGI"—asking him to investigate the situation at the Watergate. "Your Holiness," Simon wrote, "in all commercial dealings I believe we are entitled to expect integrity from those with whom we do business. I urge you to require that standard from SGI." Simon sent copies of the letter to the Apostolic Delegate in Washington and to Samaritani back in Rome.

On June 19, 1968, Simon wrote to District mayor Walter E. Washington, city council members John W. Heckinger and Walter E. Fauntroy, and the Architect of the Capitol J. George Stewart, to oppose the rezoning of the final Watergate building from residential to office use. "In my view," Simon wrote, "such a change would go clearly against the interests of the people of the District of Columbia. It would permit a small group of foreign businessmen, whose recent practices have flouted conventional business ethics, to profit at the expense of causing financial loss and psychological discomfort to the residents of Watergate East, compromising the integrity of the District of Columbia Zoning Commission and depriving the District of an attractive view as well as an opportunity to attract new taxpaying residents which Mayor Washington has recognized that it so desperately needs." The proposed office building, Simon continued, would bring at least 3,500 daily workers, not including visitors and vendors. The traffic congestion "will be intolerable." The park areas among the Watergate buildings would be filled with "office workers and their litter" during lunch hours. And security would be much more challenging with the many people passing through the office building. "This is not the exotic beauty we were sold," Simon wrote. He sent a copy of his thirteen-page letter to Roger Stevens, Aldo Samaritani and Interior Secretary Udall.

On June 26, 1968, more than 150 residents of Watergate East testified before the District Zoning Commission against the proposal to rotate the final building and convert it from residential to commercial use. A *Washington Post* city reporter named Carl Bernstein sat in on the hearing and reported on the dispute.

"The developers took our money on the representation . . . that this was an apartment development, not an office building area," said Democratic senator Wayne Morse of Washington, a Watergate East resident. "We should not have our property values decreased . . . by an office building." Thomas Corcoran—identified incorrectly in Bernstein's report as a resident of the Watergate—also testified against the proposal. "God knows, as an Irishman of New England, I'm for the Kennedy Center and for the memory of the Kennedys," he said. But the construction of an office building was "an affront to the owners of the Watergate," who collectively had invested $20 million in their units. Corcoran charged developers were attempting to "blackmail" residents of Watergate East into supporting the plan by offering to repair a leaky roof, at a cost of $400,000, under the condition that they drop opposition to the fifth building. William Lichtenberg scoffed at any suggestion the offer was an attempt at blackmail. "If they have any claims" for repairs, he said, "they obviously have to be taken care of." Corcoran questioned the timing of the offer; a request for these repairs had been pending for months.

THE SAME DAY CORCORAN WAS TESTIFYING IN WASHINGton against the final Watergate building, Anna Chennault was in New York. She stopped by the Nixon for President campaign headquarters to see the Republican candidate. He wasn't in the office, so Chennault left a message with a secretary and followed up two days later with a note. "In my humble opinion," she wrote, the Johnson administration should explain to the American public "what to expect of the Paris peace talks and what position the Administration plans to take if the peace talks should fail."

She offered to arrange a meeting between the Republican presidential candidate and the president of South Vietnam. "President Thieu of South Vietnam's visit to Washington was canceled after Senator Bob Kennedy's assassination but now it has been rescheduled," she continued. "He will be in Washington for two days. . . . If you should decide to meet with President Thieu, please let me know and I will work out the detail and make the arrangement."

Chennault's letter was forwarded to Nixon with the annotation "NO! NO!" and a message: "Allen"—referring to Richard Allen, the campaign's national security advisor—"recommends this not be done for any reason and under no circumstances. Proposal dangerous in the extreme and injurious to our V.N. [Vietnam] position—i.e., to U.S. national interests."

ON JULY 11, 1968, ELIZABETH ROWE ATTENDED HER FINAL meeting of the National Capital Planning Commission. She had earlier informed President Johnson she was stretched thin by her responsibilities as commission chairman and as a mother, and had asked him not to reappoint her. The new chairman was Philip Hammer, a Harvard-trained urban economist and city planner. "I won't even try to fill your petite shoes with my size-11 feet," he told Rowe. "You had the glamour," he said to the commission and its staff, "now you get the 'Hammer.'"

It was also the final meeting for Walter Louchheim. He and Rowe had formed an alliance against the Watergate. Six years later, the Watergate was back on the agenda.

The commission's zoning committee studied the compromise and concluded conversion from residential to office use was "inappropriate and inconsistent with the Commission's previously stated land use objectives for Watergate." Commission staff director Charles Conrad said he thought the proposal, which would add 700,000 square feet of office space for 3,500 employees, "changes the complete nature of the project." The planning commission, he said, has worked to get a "24-hour type of population in this section of the city." The proposal for another office building would make the Watergate a "predominately commercial area."

The planning commission, by a unanimous vote, urged the District Zoning Commission to delay approval of the final Watergate building as proposed, and directed its staff to continue discussions with the developers, the Kennedy Center, the interior department and the owners of Watergate East, in order to find a compromise that improved the "height-distance relationship" between the Kennedy Center and the Watergate, while keeping the area "predominantly residential."

ACCORDING TO NICOLAS SALGO, THE "TROUBLES" WITH THE final Watergate building began when the "Kennedy family" got involved. An executive at John Hancock, which had provided construction financing for the Watergate, invited Senator Edward M. Kennedy and Salgo to lunch. "We discussed the situation but weren't able to get anywhere," Salgo said. He called their initial negotiations "shadowboxing."

Salgo then called upon Roger Stevens. They had known each other since the 1950s, when Salgo was with Webb & Knapp in New York and Stevens was a major figure in New York real estate. "Look," Salgo said to Stevens, "let's stop the nonsense." The two men had several meetings, mostly in New York so as not to become part of the Washington rumor mill, and Salgo offered a solution: Shrink the final Watergate building slightly and cut it in two. The new building closest to Watergate East would hold apartments, satisfying concerns of the Watergate East owners; the building closest to the Kennedy Center would hold offices. Stevens liked the idea. The question: How to get it done? Salgo suggested Stevens tell Senator Kennedy and other family members the solution came from him, not the Watergate team; Salgo in turn told "the Italians" the solution was his idea.

Watergate East owners were satisfied with the compromise and backed down. The National Capital Planning Commission voted in favor of this revised plan and transmitted it to the zoning commission on August 9, 1968. The compromise, according to the planning commission, improved the setting of the Kennedy Center, and protected the "residential setting" and "improved the views" of Watergate East.

ON OCTOBER 16, 1968, NIXON JOINED A CONFERENCE CALL with President Johnson; Vice President Hubert Humphrey, the Democratic presidential nominee; and independent candidate George Wallace. LBJ told them there had been "some movement" by the North Vietnamese in the Paris Peace Talks, but "anything might jeopardize it."

At 7:30 A.M. on October 30, FBI agents monitoring the South Vietnamese embassy learned that Ambassador Bùi Diem "was contacted by a woman who did not identify herself, but whom he recognized by voice." Agents identified the caller as "possibly Mrs. Anna Chennault." The woman apologized for not having called the day before, "inasmuch as there were so many people around," but thought "perhaps the Ambassador would have some more information this morning." The caller then "asked what the situation is." Ambassador Diem said he could not go into specifics, but something was "cooking" and suggested the caller drop by later that day. The caller said she would drop by "after the luncheon for Mrs. Agnew."

At 3:26 that afternoon, Chennault entered the South Vietnamese embassy. More than an hour later, FBI agents watched her leave the embassy in her 1968 maroon Lincoln Continental and stop by her office on K Street before proceeding to a party hosted by Robert Mc-

Cormick, the editor and publisher of the *Chicago Tribune*. National Security Advisor Walt Rostow forwarded the information to LBJ at 6:50 P.M. on October 31, 1968—Halloween—with a note: "The latest on the lady."

That night, President Johnson invited Nixon, Humphrey and Wallace to join another call just minutes before he planned to announce, in a televised address from the Oval Office, a halt to the bombing of North Vietnam. "Some of the old China Lobbyists—they are going around and implying to some of the Embassies . . . that they might get a better deal out of somebody that was not involved in this," Johnson told them. "Now that's made it difficult and it's held up things a bit, and I know that none of you candidates are aware of it or responsible for it." According to Chennault's biographer, Johnson was warning Nixon that he knew about the backchannel communication between Chennault and Diem, and wanted it to stop. According to Chennault, John Mitchell called her with a message on behalf of Nixon. "It's very important that our Vietnamese friends understand our Republican position, and I hope you have made that clear to them." He asked Chennault to stay in touch.

The next morning, Anna Chennault left a message for Ambassador Bùi Diem asking him to "make certain he notified her in the event he leaves town." The call was reported to the White House Situation Room and Rostow, who forwarded the information to President Johnson.

Shortly after 6:30 P.M., FBI agents observed Anna Chennault and Tommy Corcoran leave Watergate East and head over to the Sheraton Park Hotel, where they attended a reception hosted by socialite Perle Mesta on the seventh floor. From there they went to the nearby Ontario Theatre for a private showing of *Funny Girl*, after which they attended another party at the Shoreham Hotel, hosted by Columbia Pictures executive Raymond Bell. Chennault dropped Corcoran off at his residence shortly after midnight and her driver took her home to Watergate East.

The next morning, Rostow updated President Johnson and attached a "significant intelligence report" from that morning's *Washington Post* society section: an article headlined A WEALTH OF TALENT, describing the forty-two-year-old widow of General Claire Chennault as "the most titled woman in the Nixon campaign and one most likely to be offered a post in his administration if he wins."

On November 2, FBI wiretaps picked up a telephone conversation between Chennault and Diem. Chennault told the ambassador she had received a message from her "boss," which "her boss wanted her to give personally to the ambassador." Her message: "Hold on, we are gonna win." According to a summary of the call, transmitted to the White House Situation Room within hours, Chennault told Ambassador Diem "her boss had just called from New Mexico." Vice presidential nominee Spiro T. Agnew was in New Mexico that day on a campaign swing. That afternoon, FBI agents observed Chennault as she got into her car at 1:45 P.M. and headed north on the Baltimore-Washington Parkway, with her chauffeur at the wheel. Agents assumed she was headed to New York, but later observed her returning to the Watergate for the evening.

On November 3, FBI agents observed Chennault leave Watergate East. She drove herself to the Apex Theatre on Massachusetts Avenue to see the movie *Finian's Rainbow* with "an unidentified male companion."

On the morning of November 4, Chennault paid another visit to the South Vietnamese embassy, where she remained for approximately thirty minutes before continuing to Nixon's campaign office at 1701 Pennsylvania Avenue, a block from the White House. An embassy aide called her there, and asked her to return for a meeting with Ambassador Diem; Chennault hopped in a taxi.

On Tuesday, November 5—Election Day—Anna visited her voting precinct and stopped by briefly at her offices on K Street before heading to New York. At 7:45 P.M., FBI agents confirmed she was in the Nixon suite at the Waldorf-Astoria Hotel in New York, waiting to go down to the ballroom for the victory celebration.

At 12:30 A.M., NBC News reported Humphrey was ahead by 600,000 votes. Nixon remained in his suite. At 6:00 A.M., Humphrey's lead had shrunk to 5,000 votes, with 94 percent of the nation's precincts reporting. At 8:00 A.M., the networks called California and Ohio for Nixon. Finally, at 8:30 A.M., ABC projected a Nixon victory in Illinois and declared Nixon the newly elected thirty-seventh president of the United States.

The next day, LBJ bundled up a week's worth of intelligence reports and handed them to an aide, with the notation: "Put that with the other stuff on that woman." He was not yet finished with Anna Chennault.

JOHN MITCHELL SAID HE TURNED DOWN THE POST OF ATTORney general twenty-six times before relenting. "I'm a fat and prosperous Wall Street lawyer, which is just what I always wanted to be," he said. The real reason Mitchell hesitated was his concern that his wife, Martha, could not survive in the Washington fishbowl. She had "very real psychological problems," recalled Nixon aide Leonard Garment. Bringing Martha to Washington, he said, was "sort of like carrying an explosive substance into a very hot area."

Mitchell sold Martha on the move to Washington by telling her he needed her help putting together the new administration. As she was checking out of Craig House, a psychiatric hospital on sixty acres in Beacon, New York, overlooking the Hudson River— the same facility where Zelda Fitzgerald sought treatment—she told hospital staff to pick up the pace and stop "holding up the selection of Nixon's Cabinet."

According to Chennault, John Mitchell had been to her penthouse on several occasions and liked the Watergate, so Anna put him in touch with the management and within a few weeks he bought a three-bedroom duplex at Watergate East boasting "one of the most impressive views in the Nation's Capital." Martha Mitchell told the *Washington Post* she selected the apartment personally, although John liked it when he finally saw it. According to a report in the *Washington Post*, the Mitchells paid $325,000 for apartment 712-N, but building records show the sale closed on December 16, 1968, for price of $151,880. Maintenance charges, including property taxes, were reportedly $1,000 per month.

Anna Chennault met Martha Mitchell for the first time only after they moved into the Watergate, in an elevator on the way to a reception.

"Martha, this is Anna Chennault," Mitchell said. "You've heard me talk about her."

Martha looked her over, in what Anna later called "the most blatantly curious way."

"Well, well," Martha said. "If I had only known what a beautiful woman my husband's been working with, I would have been so jealous."

Anna recalled later that Martha was "uninhibited about the rivalry, so honestly competitive."

"I liked her instantly," Chennault wrote.

CHAPTER THREE: *TITANIC* ON THE POTOMAC

Views that never lose their appeal. Peaceful. Quiet. Or alive with night lights. The splash of a summer sunset. The flash of fall. Winter white. The Potomac with its graceful bridges. A misty sunrise. Or a glorious one that lights up a row of barges gently moving with the flow of the river.

Watergate South marketing brochure

ON JANUARY 20, 1969, PRESIDENT AND MRS. JOHNSON RE-turned to Texas, the Nixon family moved into the White House, and Edith and Lee Burchinal received a golden key to their new apartment in Watergate West.

By the time the Burchinals moved in, 87 percent of Watergate West's 143 cooperative apartments, priced from $28,000 to $186,000, had been sold. There were 33 different floor plans, including 8 penthouses with roof terraces and 14 townhouses. The average apartment cost around $70,000 and the typical down payment was more than $25,000. When Aldo Samaritani visited the Watergate from Rome, he learned sales had already reached $19 million. "It takes a heap of selling to move a shelter project with that price tag," the *Washington Post* reported.

As a student at George Washington University, Mike Brenneman had parked his "clunker" on the site of the abandoned Washington Gas Light Company plant to attend classes. At age thirty-seven, he now parked his car at about the same location—but in the underground garage of the Watergate. He was now president of Riverview Realty, the exclusive sales agent for the complex.

From his office in Watergate East (the original sales center, with its flags and fountains, had been torn down to make way for construction of the Watergate Hotel and the Watergate Office Building), Brenneman, tall and handsome with a perpetual tan and graying sideburns, briefed a reporter on his sales strategy. "All of us in this office," said Brenneman, "stress the obvious blessings of our location, the striking architecture of Luigi Moretti, the concept that includes shops, the Watergate Hotel, the office building, health club, the restaurant and the environment of open acres around the building." The *Post* gushed, "Watergate statistics sing from the Brenneman tongue that has been trained by its owner to relate the luxury-living aspects of the town within the city concept."

Riverview also had the contract to manage the operations of Watergate West on behalf of the residents. The company had a similar contract to manage the affairs of Watergate East, the *Post* reported, until owners there "had construction gripes" and "wanted a change." Brenneman acknowledged it was "something of a conflict to represent both the developers and apartment owners." But he predicted those problems would be avoided in Watergate West, because he had set up "an advisory group of owners" and planned to consult with them on contracts for insurance and maintenance.

The two-story model townhouse apartment in Watergate West was furnished by members of the local chapter of the American Institute of Interior Design. They used "subtle, earthly colors" to "create a restful mood"—in sharp contrast to the "Oriental Opulence and Italianate Grandeur" of Duke Arturo Pini di San Miniato's design for the model apartment in Watergate East. Sixteen design students in Washington and Baltimore entered a contest to design the new Watergate West apartment of Howard Mitchell, conductor of the National Symphony Orchestra, which had performed summer concerts on the nearby Watergate Barge until noise from nearby National Airport closed the venue in 1965.

The Italian influence found its way into the public spaces of Watergate West. A local designer, Don D. McAfee, selected Pietro Lazzari to design a sculptured frieze for the lobby. Lazzari was born in Rome, apprenticed to a local sculptor at the age of fifteen and earned a degree from the Ornamental School of Rome in 1922. He immigrated to the United States in 1929, exhibited his work in New York galleries, made courtroom sketches of the Lindbergh kidnapping trial for a New York newspaper and designed post office murals for the U.S. Section of Fine Arts of the Works Progress Administration. Since 1942, he had lived in Washington with his second wife, Evelyn, and taught painting and sculpture.

When Lazzari initially balked at the $5,000 commission for a hundred-foot sculptural frieze, which he felt was too low, McAfee suggested he prepare a small section that could be "mechanically repeated" to cover the entire lobby. Lazzari was appalled at that idea, however, and accepted the original budget. He designed a series of figures on horseback, surrounded by flowers and trees, and produced panels in his studio in sections, framed in white, with anchoring devices on the backs to allow workmen to attach each piece to the lobby's masonry walls. Cecchi inspected the frieze and asked that one panel, which had been touched up by the artist after installation in darker shades, be repainted to match the others. McAfee praised the design, telling Lazzari the frieze provided "some real 'guts' " in the lobby and the developers were "quite pleased."

"TO GO FORWARD AT ALL IS TO GO FORWARD TOGETHER," read one applause line in Nixon's Inaugural Address. So many new members of the Republican administration were making the Watergate their home, the *Washington Post* quipped, "much of his Cabinet and other aides and officials took it literally."

Rose Mary Woods, Nixon's "confidential secretary," rented a two-bedroom duplex on the seventh floor of Watergate East, with a "verbal" option to buy. She selected the apartment because it was an eight-minute drive from the White House—even in traffic—and it was a duplex. "I bring a lot of paperwork home on weekends," Woods told the *Post*. "If friends stop by, I can leave all that work out upstairs in the den, and the downstairs won't be disturbed."

Another Nixon secretary, Shelley Ann Scarney, a petite blonde with a broad smile, ran into Elizabeth Hanford at a party in New York, soon after the election. Hanford, a graduate of Duke University and Harvard Law School, was working in the White House Office of Consumer Affairs and had been asked to stay on by the incoming Nixon administration. Hanford lived in Watergate East and recommended the building to Scarney, who called the leasing office and learned a one-bedroom apartment would be available soon, on the sixth floor. Scarney took the apartment, at a monthly rent that was only a few dollars more than what she was paying in Manhattan. While waiting for the current tenants to move out, she rented a room at the Watergate Hotel for $17 a night. The hotel had been open more than a year, but was nearly empty. Her boyfriend, a young Nixon speechwriter named Pat Buchanan, rented an apartment nearby.

Nixon press aide Nancy Lammerding took a one-bedroom apartment in Watergate West because the building had a swimming pool and was close to the White House, where she sometimes worked long hours. "It's easier for the White House limousine to drop me off there late at night than it would be if I lived in the suburbs," she told the *Washington Star.*

Maurice Stans, the incoming secretary of commerce, read Horatio Alger stories as a young man, following the prototypical young hero as he struggled valiantly against poverty and adversity and traveled the road from "rags to riches," fulfilling the American dream. Stans's own life followed the Alger formula. He was born in Shakopee, Minnesota, to Belgian immigrants. After high school, he moved to Chicago and worked as a stenographer by day while earning his business degree from Northwestern University at night. He moved to Washington in 1953 and within two years was recruited into the U.S. Postal Service as deputy postmaster general. President Eisenhower tapped Stans in March 1958 to head the Bureau of the Budget, the predecessor of today's Office of Management and Budget. After Eisenhower left office, Stans became a banker. He raised funds for

Nixon's failed 1960 presidential and 1962 gubernatorial campaigns and served as finance chairman for the 1968 Nixon-Agnew presidential campaign, whose $36.5 million in expenditures set a new record.

The Stanses paid $130,000 for a Watergate East apartment on the twelfth floor, only belatedly realizing Watergate South would eventually block their prime view of the Potomac. Kathy Stans, a tall, glamorous brunette, was delighted that nearly all the furniture from their New York apartment fit into their new home, which had three bedrooms, a library and a working fireplace in the massive living room. She installed yellow-and-white wallpaper in the foyer and hung her husband's collection of African ceremonial knives in the master bedroom—on his side of the bed, next to his exercise bike—and had curtains made from the same fabric used for the dresses of African tribeswomen. In the library, with its grass-cloth wall coverings, seven-foot-tall elephant tusks joined a coffee table with an elephant-leg base and a rug made from the skin of a Bengal tiger shot by Maurice on one of his many international hunting expeditions. They called it their "Africana room." A combination den/ TV room/guest room was turned into a "patriotic suite," with blue carpeting, three white walls and one wall covered in red felt. "Isn't it mad?" Kathy giggled.

Martin Anderson, an MIT-trained economist and author of *The Federal Bulldozer*, in which he recommended the repeal of the federal urban renewal program, was named a special assistant to Nixon. Annelise Anderson was finishing her Ph.D. at Columbia University and followed her husband, Martin, to Washington. She went to the Watergate office to inquire about renting an apartment. "They were rather snobbish," she recalled, "until I told them my husband would be working at the White House." Martin and Annelise rented a two-bedroom, two-bath apartment on the second floor of Watergate West, facing Virginia Avenue and the Howard Johnson Motor Lodge. "Everything was well-equipped," she said, "and seemed to be very secure." Martin worked long hours at the White House for Arthur Burns, another Watergate resident, until Burns left the White House staff to become chairman of the Federal Reserve Board. Annelise worked at the justice department and finished her dissertation on organized crime in America. Their apartment was a seventeen-minute walk to the White House, although Martin purchased a used car to make the trip home safely at night.

Transportation Secretary John Volpe and his wife, Jennie, bought a three-bedroom penthouse in Watergate East for $130,000. Their apartment had two working fireplaces, one of which Nicolas Salgo found in a demolished mansion in Europe. Mrs. Volpe removed the bright lemon-yellow-and-white wallpaper in the foyer and painted the living room blue, to show off her collection of French provincial furniture upholstered in blues and golds. "I like my old things," she told a reporter.

Martha Mitchell was slow to acclimate to her duplex, which spanned the seventh and eighth floors of Watergate East and came with four parking spaces. She missed her massive house on a golf course in Rye, New York. "Twenty rooms that I had worked so hard on," she lamented. "It took three years to decorate. I had no idea of ever leaving. I'm going to have to do so much consolidating. I guess I'll have to store a lot of things."

Martha said their new apartment lacked "the woman's touch" and immediately began personalizing it. "I hate to walk into a decorator-decorated place," she said. "It looks like a hotel room." She replaced the parquet floor in the foyer with marble, painted most of the walls her favorite "Wedgwood blue" and brought in a "more traditional" stairway to replace the "contemporary one" that came with the apartment. Surrounded by sawdust, she complained to a reporter about the shortage of local suppliers. "I have to go to New York and get wallpaper, that's how desperate I am," she fretted. If the perfect wallpaper could not be found right away, "I'll just have to paint." She bought a new wardrobe as well—"with special attention paid to clothes suitable for a Cabinet wife to wear during the Inaugural festivities," according to her biographer Winzola McLendon—and proudly showed off her bulging closets to an old friend who had come to visit.

In March, Sidney James, a lobbyist for Time Inc., hosted the first stop of a black-tie "progressive party" in his Watergate East apartment for some of his new neighbors, including the Mitchells, the Volpes and the Stanses. After cocktails at the James apartment, the group moved to the apartment of Laurence Wood, Washington vice president of General Electric Co., for dinner. From there, they went to the apartment of Joseph Farland, former ambassador to Panama and now a Washington lawyer, for coffee. The hosts told the *Wall Street Journal* their goal wasn't to build relations with the Nixon crowd, but to allow their wives to "exchange decorating ideas."

Other Nixon appointees who moved into the Watergate included Postmaster General Winton M. Blount; the incoming U.S. chief of protocol Bus Mosbacher; Frank Shakespeare, chief of the U.S. Information Agency; H. Dale Grubb, a Nixon liaison to Congress; White House aide James Keogh, managing editor of presidential messages; Mary T. Brooks, director of the U.S. Mint; two assistant secretaries of commerce, Kenneth David and Robert Podesta; Deputy Postmaster General E. T. Klassen; and "a smattering of unofficial Republican heavyweights."

A Watergate sales executive said all the residents in the complex were "delightful people," but the Republicans were "the icing on the cake."

ANNA CHENNAULT HAD CAMPAIGNED AGGRESSIVELY FOR THE Nixon-Agnew ticket. She attended the GOP convention in Miami as a delegate from the District of Columbia, served as executive secretary to the GOP Platform Committee and raised $250,000 for the party. Shortly after the election, she received a letter from the president-elect, asking her to recommend "exceptional individuals" to serve in his new administration and enclosing the initial application form. It was a form letter, with an auto-pen signature, incorrectly addressed to "Mr. A. Chennault."

A week before Nixon's swearing-in, Anna Chennault threw a lavish buffet supper for one hundred guests, prepared by her long-time Chinese chef, in her Watergate East penthouse, followed by a screening at the MacArthur Theatre of the movie *Oliver!* Chennault's guests included the legendary Washington hostess Perle Mesta, prompting *Washington Post* society reporter Maxine Cheshire to wonder if she was witnessing the passing of a torch. Cheshire's story about the party carried the headline NEXT PERLE MESTA?

The *Cleveland Plain Dealer* called Chennault the "hostess with the mostess" and a "Party Queen." The *Washington Sunday News* called her "The Tiger Lady." *Palm Beach Life* referred to her as "Madame Chennault," the "unofficial ambassador-at-large for the Nixon Administration."

Chennault was certainly "a figure of glamour and mystery" in the capital, Cheshire wrote. "If she were to become known primarily as a party-giver, Nixon's foreign affairs advisers will probably breathe a sigh of relief."

Ten days earlier, the *St. Louis Post-Dispatch* reported Chennault had made "secret" contact with the South Vietnamese just before the election, at the request of the Nixon campaign. Several anonymous sources—including foreign diplomats, Johnson aides, "and a number of Republicans, including some within Nixon's own organization"—corroborated the report. "Who told you that?" Chennault asked the *Post-Dispatch* reporter, with a half-smile, as she toyed with the collar of her Chinese silk dress. "You're going to get me into a lot of trouble. I can't say anything . . . come back and ask me that after the inauguration. We're at a very sensitive time. . . . I know so much and can say so little."

At the party, Cheshire asked Chennault directly if she had any current or prior ties to the CIA. Chennault responded with a stony-faced "no comment."

Senator Tower told the *Washington Star* "any story that Mrs. Chennault tried to stall peace talks is manifestly untrue." John Mitchell, however, was reportedly "unavailable for comment."

As the controversy grew, Anna Chennault acquired a new nickname: the Dragon Lady.

TWO MONTHS INTO THE NEW ADMINISTRATION, ROSE MARY Woods returned late at night from an eight-day international trip with President Nixon and discovered her apartment in Watergate East had been burglarized. Thieves took a suitcase containing jewelry from a bedroom closet, Nixon's press secretary Ron Ziegler confirmed, as well as personal gifts from Nixon. The FBI was called in to investigate.

"It's really a tragic thing," said Ziegler. "This brings the whole problem of crime close to home. It demonstrates the need for action against the criminal elements that have gotten out of control."

The front-door lock to Woods's apartment was neither forced nor damaged, suggesting someone had entered using either a duplicate or a master key. Woods had her locks changed and refused to allow the front desk to have a copy of the new key. She kept a duplicate key in her office and her remaining jewelry in a White House safe.

"What a way to live," she lamented.

BACK IN ROME, SGI ENGINEER PIERLUIGI BORLENGHI RE-turned from Washington to brief Luigi Moretti on modifications to the residential and commercial buildings of Watergate South, necessitated by the compromise reached among the developers, the Kennedy Center and the residents of Watergate East. The briefing did not go well. Outraged at the changes to his original design, Moretti fired off a letter to Aldo Samaritani. The "penny-pinching attitude" of the Watergate team in Washington, Moretti wrote, had resulted in an unattractive facade of the office building facing the Kennedy Center, and a lobby design of which he was "ashamed." (Similar cost cutting, he added, had resulted in the "ruin of the hotel.") "Nothing is accomplished by trying to save money when it comes to small details," he wrote. "It displeases me to have to say it, but it seems to me that it has come about because of the team of Giuseppe Cecchi and Salgo."

"Because of your friendship," Moretti concluded, "I know that you will forgive me for all of this venting."

Samaritani, however, had more on his plate than the complaints of his temperamental friend.

In 1967, the leftist press in Italy published a series of articles calling the Church "the biggest tax evader in postwar Italy." The finance minister of Italy's center-left coalition government, headed by Aldo Moro, wanted to force the Vatican to pay taxes on its dividend income from Italian companies. The Moro government asked the Church for a list of its holdings in the Italian stock markets. The Vatican refused to share the information. Pope Paul VI turned for help to a lawyer named Michele Sindona.

Sindona was of average height, trim, with close-cropped gray hair, a high forehead and dark eyes. First-time visitors to his office sometimes found him humorless and stern. Others considered him relaxed and unpretentious. He illustrated his speech with vigorous gesticulations, a stereotypical Italian trait, but he did not dress the part of the Italian banker. He wore dark suits, white shirts and conservative ties.

He was born in Patti, a small town in Sicily, where his father worked for a farm cooperative. Sindona worked his way through law school at the University of Messina, managing his dormitory in exchange for free room and board. He also worked for a local government tax office, a bank and a citrus company that was the largest company in Sicily at the time. Lemons, because they prevented scurvy, were deemed "an essential war product" by the Italian government during World War II, and Sindona leveraged his employment with the citrus company to secure an exemption from military service. When Sicily fell to the Allies in 1943, Sindona got a job driving fruit from the coast into the Sicilian interior and returning with grain. It was a grueling schedule. Sindona later recalled working nearly fifteen days straight, stopping only to nap briefly and take a quick shower.

After the war, Sindona moved to Milan and established a law firm specializing in tax issues. He added an auditing department and worked for some of the most important firms in Italy, as well as top foreign companies doing business in Italy. Some of his clients gave him stock, stock options or board seats in lieu of, or in addition to, legal and auditing fees. Within a few years, Sindona was a listed director of over fifty companies. His small office in Milan looked out over the roof of the Church of San Giuseppe, near the Opera House, in the center of Milan's banking establishment. A life-size wooden statue of a young Italian nobleman, by Antonio del Pollaiuolo, an important fifteenth-century Italian painter and sculptor, stood in the corner. He used a heavy sixteenth-century table as a desk and gave visitors a choice of two eighteenth-century armchairs, which a reporter described as "sufficiently uncomfortable to discourage any lengthy conferences."

Sindona persuaded the Moro government to slow down the repeal of the Church's tax exemption, earning a few more years during which the Vatican continued to avoid paying taxes on its dividends from Italian companies, including SGI.

In 1969, the Italian parliament voted to require the Vatican to pay taxes on its dividends. Paul VI again summoned Michele Sindona for a visit. According to author Luigi DiFonzo:

Only one light was burning in the pope's chambers as Michele Sindona entered late on that spring night in 1969. Paul was seated in one of the satin-covered chairs. His body bent forward and his face distorted by shadows, he appeared tired and ill.

Sindona wore a navy blue suit, a white shirt with gold cuff links, and a blue tie. He appeared fresh and confident. He approached the Holy Father with respect and a strong, warm smile. Paul did not offer his hand for Michele to kiss; instead, they greeted each other with the handshake of old friends.

This is a terrible problem, Paul told him. . . . If the Vatican allowed Italy to tax its investments, it would be a signal for other countries to do the same.

Sindona proposed the Vatican move its investments out of Italy and into the "more profitable, tax-free Eurodollar market." This would protect the confidentiality of the Church's investments, he promised, and demonstrate to other countries the Vatican's willingness to play hardball. The Pope agreed. Sindona transferred the Vatican's Italian stock portfolio to a series of holding companies in Luxembourg and Liechtenstein; from there, he sold shares and reinvested the proceeds in European and American companies.

On June 19, 1969, the *Washington Post* reported the Vatican was interested in selling its holdings in the development firm SGI, perhaps to "Rockefeller interests in New York." Aldo Samaritani flew to the United States "for an extended stay," the purpose of which SGI refused to confirm.

If Samaritani's goal was to find an American buyer for the Vatican's shares in Società Generale Immobiliare, his trip was a failure. Michele Sindona had already found a buyer: himself.

Sindona arranged for the Church's shares in SGI to be first transferred to Paribas Transcontinental of Luxembourg, and then to Fasco AG, his personal holding company. Italian newspapers learned of the transaction and asked the Vatican for a response. "Our policy is to avoid maintaining control of companies as in the past," said the pope through a spokesman. "We want to improve investment performance, balanced, of course, against what must be a fundamentally conservative investment philosophy." Sindona, reached in his Milan office, refused to answer press questions.

Pietro Vacchelli, a lawyer, and Antonio Cecchi, whose son, Giuseppe, had left Rome nine years earlier to help launch the North American expansion of SGI, resigned from the board. According to their letters of resignation, they were "motivated by the desire to facilitate the potential admission onto the Board of a wider representation of the shareholders." The board elected two new members, Sindona and Dr. Raffaele Politi, an educator. Among the first votes Michele Sindona cast as a member of the board of SGI was in support of a resolution giving Aldo Samaritani special powers as *consigliere delegato*, or "delegate board member." These powers gave Samaritani near-complete control over company activities, with minimal board supervision, including the ability to mortgage properties; hire and fire managers, and set their salaries; and assign "extraordinary powers" to any SGI executive as required. It was an unprecedented expression of trust.

These powers would eventually also be placed in the hands of Michele Sindona, with disastrous results.

ON DECEMBER 10, 1968, ANNA CHENNAULT WROTE THE NIXON transition team to seek a position with the new administration. She suggested a White House appointment as "an advisor-diplomatic messenger in Asiatic affairs" or perhaps as assistant secretary of state for cultural affairs. A State Department post, she wrote, would not interfere with her ability "inconspicuously to be consulted [by the White House] and used on the political affairs with which I am particularly familiar, i.e., the problems and attitudes of the governments of Southeast Asia."

Anna waited patiently for a response. Weeks went by, but she heard nothing from anyone with either the Nixon transition team or, following Nixon's swearing-in, the White House staff. Eventually, she got tired of waiting.

She took the elevator from the fourteenth to the seventh floor of Watergate East, rang the doorbell of Apartment 712-N and told her story to Martha Mitchell. As a result of her labors, Anna said, the peace talks in Paris had been delayed. She showed Martha a large folder containing letters and other documents, which she said confirmed that Nixon had met with Ambassador Bùi Diem in his Fifth Avenue apartment in July 1968. When John Mitchell returned home from work that day, Martha told him Anna Chennault had stopped by and was angry. Martha handed him the folder. "Stay out of it," he told her.

On July 11 and 18, 1969, *Life* ran lengthy excerpts from Theodore "Teddy" White's new book, *The Making of the President 1968*. The excerpt added new details to the events first reported by the *St. Louis Post-Dispatch* six months earlier:

> There is no way of clarifying what had happened except by introducing, at this point, the name of a beautiful Oriental lady Anna Chan Chennault, the Chinese widow of World War II hero General Claire Chennault. Mrs. Chennault, an American citizen since 1950, comes of a long line that begins with Madame Chiang Kai-shek and runs through Madame Nhu, the Dragon Lady of South Vietnam, a line of Oriental ladies of high purpose and authoritarian manners whose pieties and iron righteousness have frequently outrun their brains and acknowledged beauty.

Chennault, White wrote, had "undertaken most energetically" to sabotage the Paris Peace Talks. "In contact with the Formosan, the South Korean and the South Vietnamese governments, she had begun early, by cable and telephone, to mobilize their resistance" to the emerging settlement agreement—"apparently implying, as she went, that she spoke for the Nixon campaign."

Chennault, however, "neglected to take the most elementary precautions of an intriguer." Her communications with Asia "had been tapped by the American government and brought directly to the perusal of President Johnson." According to White:

> At first report, Nixon's headquarters had begun to investigate the story, had discovered Mrs. Chennault's activities, and were appalled. The fury and dismay of the Nixon staff were so intense they could not have been feigned. Their feeling on Monday morning before the election was simply that if they lost the election, Mrs. Chennault might have lost it for them. She had taken their name and authority in vain; if the Democrats now chose to air the story, no rebuttal by the Nixon camp could possibly be convincing. They were at the mercy of Humphrey's goodwill.

Chennault, who was on a business trip to Saigon when the excerpt appeared in print, refused to comment. "The public must wait for my book about Vietnam which is coming out soon," she said. "If I tell all, I won't find my way back to Washington. We can't kiss and tell."

A Humphrey aide confirmed the former vice president knew of Chennault's activities at the time. "We suspect that she was doing this as part of a plan with the encouragement or at least the knowledge of the Nixon people," said Ted Van Dyk, chief policy advisor to Humphrey's 1968 campaign. "The reason we did not use the issue in the closing days of the campaign was not because we thought Mr. Nixon was innocent. Rather we thought the American people shouldn't learn that sort of thing about the man who might turn out to be their president."

A week later, at a press conference at the President Hotel in Saigon, Chennault said White's account was "an insult to my intellect and the integrity of the South Vietnamese government."

"Mr. White is an excellent writer, but sometimes good writers make mistakes," she said. "Some day when the time comes, all the facts will be made known."

Sarah McClendon, an independent reporter covering the White House, pounced on the story. In a scathing *Washington Examiner* profile titled "The Mysterious Anna Chennault," McClendon wrote Chennault failed to register as a foreign agent with the justice department, as required by law; delivered paid speeches that amounted to little more than "unconnected phrases"; and overcharged "wealthy socialites" for Chinese art objects. "For whom does Anna Chennault work?" McClendon asked. "Where does she get all her money? And for what?"

Chennault said either John Mitchell or Senator John Tower would defend her role in the 1968 campaign. But Tower offered only a terse "no comment." Mitchell told McClendon he ran into Chennault only occasionally in the lobby of the Watergate. Martha Mitchell, however, directly contradicted her husband's account. "She is down here a lot," she said about their upstairs neighbor. "We visit and play bridge."

Chennault returned to the United States and released a statement that raised more questions than it answered. "I deny the accusations as false," her statement read. "Presumptively, they are politically inspired to find a scapegoat for inaccurate political calculations in high places by those who presumably had all instrumentalities of intelligence at their disposal." She said the allegations "had not the flimsiest evidence to sustain them except hearsay references to mysterious undisclosed wiretap evidence allegedly by sources close to the Democratic Party." She challenged White to produce "any hard evidence" in his possession.

Chennault confirmed only that she was a "consultant" to the "Key Issues Committee" chaired by Senator Tower, "and under his orders I acted along with others as 'eyes and ears' for information from which the Committee could form judgments as to the likelihood of a political resolution of the Vietnamese conflict prior to the election and report to him, among others, my every action and all my information. I am a soldier's wife, and I try to act as a soldier should pursuant to his orders and in channels." She referred all further inquiries to Senator Tower, whose staff told reporters he was unavailable for comment.

On the heels of White's book came a scathing exposé in *Washingtonian* by Judith Viorst titled "Anna Chennault: Washington's Own Fortune Cookie."

"The many mysteries of Anna Chennault extend to her family life, her finances, and her backbreaking schedule," Viorst wrote.

A close friend said Chennault liked men more than children, and would be "delighted" to get her daughters "settled and out of her hair."

Chennault "adores being newsworthy," Viorst wrote, "even if she has to prepare the press releases herself."

"Skeptics" in Washington "insist that Anna sometimes allows people to carry away the impression that she is far more of an international operator than, in truth, she is."

Some of Anna's anonymous detractors described her as "a clever but not terribly extraordinary lady who has gone a long, long way on an exotic background, the Chennault legend, good looks, and a great flair for publicity."

Chennault, Viorst wrote, maintained a "feverish pace" because she needed the money.

Not even Chennault's marriage was spared:

Anna, in rapturous prose . . . unfolds her story of the great romance between the innocent young reporter and the imposing general. There are, however, variations on this story which rather dim the luster of the love theme. In one, Anna is featured not as the innocent young reporter, but as an employee of Chinese intelligence in charge of keeping an eye on the general. In another, Anna's attraction to Chennault is attributed less to passion than to the appeal of his exalted status in Asia. And while everyone agrees that Claire Chennault did indeed care for the lady, there are some doubts about the mushy dialogue attributed to him in *A Thousand Springs.* "He would never have talked that way," insists an old friend of Chennault. "After I finished that book I went upstairs and threw up."

Robert Gray, a former Eisenhower aide, awkwardly compared his friend Anna Chennault to a geisha, "in the old, complimentary sense of the word—very solicitous, very gracious, and quite capable of providing anything from the right conversation to the right neck massage."

Tommy Corcoran also rose to her defense. "Anna's power and influence are greater than any woman in Washington," he said.

But Viorst questioned how—and to what end—Chennault exercised this power. To her critics, Viorst wrote, Chennault was a woman "of fierce ambition, whose self-control and self-discipline have been enlisted in the cause of winning for herself attention, recognition and what in this city passes for glory." Anna said her frenetic life—writing books, giving lectures, throwing parties and raising money for the Republican Party and the General Claire Lee Chennault Foundation, which brought medical and aviation students from non-Communist Asian countries to the United States to meet Americans and "absorb knowledge of . . . America's free society"— was solely to help others. "I have no ambitions to join the Administration," she told Viorst. "If I wanted a job, every Republican would have recommended me."

Peter Flanigan, Mitchell's deputy at the campaign and now a White House aide known as Mr. Fixit, sent a memo to Mitchell regarding rumors Anna Chenault was "unhappy because she has not been recognized by the Administration."

"Since you had the liaison (if it could be called that) with this good lady," Flanigan wrote, "I'd like your suggestions as to whether we should take some action to recognize her. If the answer is 'yes' should this be in terms of invitation to dinner at the White House or something more important?"

On November 19, 1969, as the Apollo 12 astronauts prepared for their second walk on the moon, President Nixon hosted a state dinner honoring Prime Minister Eisaku Satō of Japan and his wife, Hiroko. Nixon toasted the character of the people of Japan and called the country "a modern miracle of economic progress." Guests enjoyed dances from "Fancy Free," a new ballet choreographed by Jerome Robbins, set to the music of Leonard Bernstein and performed by the American Ballet Theatre, the resident ballet company of the Kennedy Center. Guests at the dinner included Watergate residents Kathy and Maurice Stans, Patty and Bus Mosbacher, Johnson's former defense secretary Robert S. McNamara—and Anna Chennault.

According to White House chief of staff H. R. Haldeman's notes, Nixon asked his aides to give Chennault a "high-level title"—but insisted it "can't be in government." More than a year into the Nixon administration, Anna Chennault finally got her presidential appointment. She was named to the Kennedy Center Advisory Committee on the Arts, a ceremonial body with 108 members.

THE AUGUST 8, 1969, COVER OF *LIFE* SHOWED THE FOOTprints of Neil Armstrong and Edwin Aldrin on the surface of the moon. Inside, life at the Watergate was documented in an eight-page, full-color spread. Georgetown was "the right address" during the Kennedy era. Under Nixon, the "toothy structure" of the Watergate was the place to be.

Photographs by Michael Rougier showed residents enjoying the amenities of the development some called "White House West." Lifeguard Linda Fox watched over the swimming pool. Bus Mosbacher, Nixon's chief of protocol, slipped into a limousine with his wife, Patty, and headed off to a dinner at the White House. Anna Chennault inspected place settings for "a 13-course dinner she prepared herself" and chatted with Senator Tower and Attorney General Mitchell. The Mitchells, reflected in a gold-framed mirror, chatted in their Wedgwood blue foyer. Transportation secretary John Volpe read briefing papers in his penthouse study. Walter Pforzheimer admired a signed photograph of Mata Hari. Kathy and Maurice Stans relaxed in their "Africana room," decorated by trophies from nine safaris. Mary Brooks, director of the U.S. Mint, dictated a memo in her kitchen, which doubled as a home office. Martha Mitchell and Kathy Stans gossiped in the Watergate Salon, while Martha's eight-year-old daughter, Marty, cradled her puppy. New York senator Jacob Javits leapt from a diving board into the outdoor pool.

Life compared Watergate West to a cruise ship—"with curved decks and rooftop smokestacks"—and listed the Watergate's "luxury" appointments: a lobby "resplendent with fake Chou Dynasty lamps," curtains "handwoven in Swaziland," elevators "flooded with Muzak" and bathrooms "paved with marble and equipped with bidets and golden faucets." A total of twenty-three closed-circuit cameras watched over residents in Watergate East and West.

"Any American who comes under the heading of 'forgotten' may as well not apply," *Life* continued. "Membership in Watergate . . . is sharply restricted both socially and financially."

IN WASHINGTON IT USED TO BE GEORGETOWN—NOW IT'S WATERGATE, read the headline. JUST EVERYBODY LIVES THERE.

ON SUNDAY, JUNE 13, 1971, MUCH OF THE FRONT PAGE OF the *Washington Post* was dedicated to the Rose Garden wedding of Tricia Nixon and Edward Finch Cox. About four hundred guests watched President Nixon give his oldest daughter away, braving a light rain; Alice Roosevelt said she felt as if she had been sitting on a "wet sponge" during the ceremony. Several guests used their white satin programs to shield themselves from the rain. Martha Mitchell, however, was "sitting snugly protected by her yellow parasol," reported the *Post*, ignoring instructions to check her umbrella.

More than a dozen Watergate residents were among the guests at the wedding ceremony and reception, including the Mitchells; Shelley and Pat Buchanan (the Nixons had attended their wedding a few months earlier, and Pat had moved into Shelley's apartment); Mary Brooks; Helen and Arthur Burns; Patricia and Victor Lasky, a White House speechwriter; the Mosbachers; Fred J. Russell, the undersecretary of the Interior; and Rose Mary Woods. Kathy and Maurice Stans were unable to attend, as their son was getting married the same day in New York. Anna Chennault was not invited to the wedding, the *Post* reported, and "was diplomatically out of town."

That day, the *New York Times* ran the Nixon-Cox wedding on its front page, which also included the first of several stories about a three-thousand-page study of America's involvement in Indochina over the past three decades. The leaked documents would become known as the Pentagon Papers.

AS THE FINAL BUILDINGS IN THE WATERGATE—THE WATER-gate 600 offices and the adjacent Watergate South apartment building—prepared to open, Washington's commercial real estate market began to sputter. The General Services Administration reduced its standard rate to $5.40 per square foot, down nearly 10 percent from a year earlier. Some luxury buildings in the District had leased to the government at that rate, just to have rent coming in.

Over a weekend in mid-August, President Nixon met with fifteen advisors, including Federal Reserve chairman Burns and treasury secretary John Connally, to plan a response to two crises: Great

Britain's demand for $3 billion in gold from the United States and an inflation rate that was running three times above recent levels. In a nationally televised address on August 15, 1971, President Nixon ordered a freeze on "all prices and wages throughout the United States" for ninety days and disconnected the dollar from the price of gold. In a poll conducted shortly after Nixon's speech, 75 percent of Americans backed his "New Economic Policy." At the Watergate South sales office, however, prospective tenants, uncertain about the economy, began to delay their lease negotiations or back out of them entirely.

Nicolas Salgo, Royce Ward and the Watergate leasing team desperately needed a full-floor tenant to reassure Samaritani and other jittery SGI executives back in Rome. Ward stepped up marketing efforts, sending a mailer to local trade associations; a select group of New York law firms; professionals in the District, Maryland and Northern Virginia; embassies, unions and nonprofits. A veteran in local real estate who had survived other recessions, he deployed a tactic that had worked before: His team inspected older buildings in Washington, discovered their flaws and wrote to their tenants. "Not criticizing their buildings," a sales associate explained in a memo that was shared with SGI officials back in Rome, "but if their elevators are slow, we emphasize our high-speed elevators; if their building is dark, we emphasize our light airiness."

Salgo and Ward explored other ways to fill the new office building, like putting a Watergate Club on the seventh floor, which might include sixty small furnished offices that could be rented out monthly, an idea that was being tried out in other cities. To capitalize on the excitement surrounding the Kennedy Center, scheduled to open in September, the sales team drew up a new brochure which read: "People who appreciate the beauty and the excitement of our glamorous new neighbor, The Kennedy Center for the Performing Arts, are people who would enjoy the Watergate, where living is an art, too."

"We are trying everything that is possible to bring in every inquiry we can," a Watergate salesman assured Ward. "To lease, we have to find the individual who is willing to pay more for the Watergate atmosphere."

The law firm of Fried, Frank, Harris, Shriver & Jacobson had represented the Watergate developers in many transactions, including the original arrangement of financing with the John Hancock insurance company and the mortgage on Watergate 600. The firm was looking to expand and signed a lease for space at 18th and K Streets downtown when Nicolas Salgo reached out to Hans Frank, a named partner with the firm, to ask him to consider the Watergate's new office building. They had already signed a lease elsewhere, but Salgo was insistent and offered a very favorable lease—including payment of all penalties that would be incurred by dropping plans to move into the building downtown. Not wanting to disappoint a good client and risk losing future business, Fried, Frank, Harris, Shriver & Jacobson took over the entire sixth floor of Watergate 600, with a sweeping terrace overlooking the Potomac.

The firm's partners loved the building, another partner of the firm, Daniel M. Singer recalled, because it was convenient to the neighborhoods of northern Virginia, Maryland and northwest Washington, where most of them lived. But the staff "hated" the building, he said, in part because there was no "cheap place" to eat or shop anywhere on the Watergate grounds.

Luchino Villarosa, a Watergate leasing associate, pitched the Italian ambassador to the United States, Egidio Ortona, to relocate the Italian embassy to Watergate South. The embassy's current address, above Adams Morgan, was "no longer one of the best," Ortona acknowledged, but the convenience of having the embassy, chancery and official residence all in one spot would be difficult to replicate, unless something could be built from scratch. Besides, he said, the Italian parliament would have to approve the cost, which was highly unlikely.

Villarosa next called on the Italian embassy's Commercial Minister Alberto Rossi and gave him a list of diplomatic outposts the Watergate was exploring as potential tenants for their final office building, including the embassies of Korea, Mexico and the Philippines. Villarosa considered Rossi an important part of the Watergate marketing strategy. "Being in contact socially with so many eminent people," Villarosa wrote Aldo Samaritani back in Rome, the minister could publicize "our leasing advantages." Morever, Rossi was a Watergate resident.

Villarosa next met with Guillermo Sevilla Sacasa, the Nicaraguan ambassador to the United States since 1943 and dean of the diplomatic corps. Villarosa reported back to Rome that Sevilla Sacasa was "most receptive and provided a number of excellent ideas" regarding diplomatic tenants, including some of the 120 different chanceries and missions currently renting space all over the city. The Watergate was attractive, Sevilla Sacasa suggested, because of its proximity to the State Department, the on-site hotel, shopping and restaurant facilities, and its "prestigious name."

Sweden opened a new chancery spanning the entire twelfth floor of Watergate 600 in November. The old chancery, at 2249 R Street NW, had become so packed that bathrooms were being remodeled into offices. The new suite covered 24,000 square feet, roughly double the size of its former quarters. Architect Björn Hultén of Göteborg adapted the new interiors to the Watergate's kidney shape, filling offices and conference rooms with Swedish furniture and contemporary art. The blue-and-white color scheme matched the Swedish flag. Every office had a view. "The military section chief can literally wave at his counterpart at the Pentagon," the *Washington Post* reported. Chancery personnel had access to the rooftop terrace, with its panoramic view, and reserved spaces in the garage. The only concern was the city bus lines did not conveniently link the Swedish embassy with the Watergate, so a private bus was put into service to shuttle employees between the two locations.

Don McAfee designed the interiors of three Watergate South model apartments, including fully furnished one- and two-bedroom apartments and a partially furnished three-bedroom unit. McAfee used "a whole range of warm neutrals" with "a few dashes of black." In one living room, everything was ivory—furniture, walls, draperies and carpet—to put "more emphasis" on the vivid paintings of artist Tom Woodard. McAfee placed white furniture against modern wallpaper with pastel flowers or white geometrics against backgrounds of brown or black. "The effect is striking," noted a local reporter.

A brochure for the Watergate South apartments listed the building's amenities:

> Magnificence. Flair. Saunas.
> An outdoor café.
> Parking. Restaurant. Wining. Dining.
> A sinfully good pastry shop.
> A marvelous little hairdresser.
> Security. Intercoms.
> And, a bidet.

Over the past six years, real estate prices had climbed throughout the Watergate. One owner of a three-bedroom apartment in Watergate East sold it two years later for a $14,000 profit. When Watergate East was first built, the least expensive unit was a studio priced at $17,500. Units in Watergate South now started at $32,000. On the tenth floor, the least expensive unit was a one-bedroom apartment with a view of the courtyard, priced at $70,000.

Despite the slow pace of leases for the Watergate 600 office building, optimism permeated SGI headquarters back in Rome. Negotiations were under way for the purchase of six acres on New Mexico Avenue, close to Glover-Archbold Park, for another cooperative apartment, and a lot on the corner of Virginia Avenue and

25th Street, facing Watergate East, for the construction of a ten-story apartment building. Across the Potomac River, the company was ready to purchase land, some private and some public, within the city limits of Alexandria, Virginia. That location, Samaritani said, was the perfect site for a new residential community of *buon tono* ("good tone"), with buildings of about fifty meters in height, with commercial spaces, where residences could be sold, like the Watergate, as cooperative apartments. The price of the land—about $1.5 million—was "most favorable, given the property's attractive location."

Many Alexandria officials wanted to bring a "Watergate-type" development to their side of the Potomac; a year earlier, the Alexandria board of trade endorsed a thirty-to-forty-story hotel for an area known as "Watergate north." In May, the city council approved a new zoning ordinance that permitted construction of high-rise buildings along the waterfront. Some residents of Old Town Alexandria were alarmed. But Royce Ward, who was both a Watergate executive and an Old Town resident, said many of his friends supported the idea. He assured the *Post* any new development would be as architecturally distinctive as the Watergate, whose developers had no tolerance for "pedestrian buildings."

Henry Winston became president of Watergate Management Company and Watergate Improvement Associates, the two entities responsible for sales, leases and operations throughout the complex, and began planning a new shopping arcade for the ground floor of Watergate 600. The arcade would be called Les Champs, patterned after a similar "boutique mall" of eighty shops built by SGI on the ground floor of the Pan American building on the Champs-Élysées in Paris, and would draw suburban shoppers with valet parking, a shuttle service to downtown Washington and on-site babysitting.

"IN LITTLE MORE THAN A YEAR," *NEWSWEEK* GUSHED, "THE Watergate has blossomed from just another ostentatious housing development into the *ne plus ultra*, the *sine qua non*, the *honi soit qui mal y pense* of gracious Washington living." (The last of these phrases, in French, "Shame on him who thinks evil of the place," is the motto of England's Royal Order of the Garter.)

On warm evenings, Maurice Stans took his projector down to the Watergate East outdoor pool and set up a screen, inviting neighbors to watch home movies of his adventures on safari. (The films might not have had "overtones of racism," neighbor George Arnstein commented, but they were at least "patronizing.") Another movie director who lived at the Watergate showed films that had not yet been released, or something starring Rock Hudson and Doris Day. A waiter from the Watergate Hotel served caviar while residents sipped champagne and watched the movie under the stars.

According to *Newsweek*, the center of the social life at the Watergate was the penthouse of Anna Chennault, who was fond of serving guests her special dish "Concubine Chicken," and was careful to invite some of her Democratic neighbors, including Senators Russell Long of Louisiana and Alan Cranston of California. "You learn you can disagree but not be disagreeable," she said.

One evening, a small dinner party in Anna Chennault's apartment was interrupted several times by calls from the White House. One by one, Chennault's guests—including John Mitchell, H. R. Haldeman and John Ehrlichman—were called away from the table to speak with President Nixon. As each aide got up to take his call, she observed Henry Kissinger become agitated. She thought he was wondering when—or if—his turn would come.

When dinner was over, Kissinger turned to her. "Well, I didn't get any calls from the White House," he said, smiling, "but the next time I come to dinner at your place I'll make arrangements with the White House operator to call me so I don't feel left out."

Martha and John Mitchell hosted a cocktail buffet to celebrate the engagement of Nancy Hardin, daughter of the secretary of agriculture, and Douglas Rogers, son of the secretary of state. Vice

President Agnew sat down at the piano and played "a romantic piece for the couple as they stood over his shoulder, then he switched to a jazzy beat and really swung it." He played one song on Martha's Hammond organ and guests thought they were about to be treated to a duet. But Martha got "cold feet," *Washington Star* columnist Betty Beale wrote, "because the vice president can play by ear and she can't."

Chennault and the Mitchells began to see more and more of each other. According to Chennault, John Mitchell would call her up in the evening and ask if he could come up to her penthouse "to discuss an issue," or Martha would invite her down "to have a drink or play bridge." They often attended the same parties and functions and, upon returning home to the Watergate, would stop at either the Mitchells' or Anna's for a nightcap.

"I love it," said director of the mint Mary Brooks about the Watergate. "Everything you want is here," said Hobart Taylor, Jr., a former director of the Export-Import Bank and one of the Watergate's few black residents, "post office, bank, florist, grocery, travel agency. Last night, I wanted some ginger ale. I used the phone. It was up in ten minutes. I didn't need money, just signed for it."

"The view is glorious," said another resident. "My wife and I sit there and hold hands like a couple of kids. It could be Florence or any romantic city."

According to the *Washington Post*, the Watergate was "a glittering Potomac Titanic," as glamorous as the doomed ocean liner, but "with no icebergs or steerage class."

CHAPTER FOUR: NOT QUITE PERFECT

WATERGATE EAST. By appt. today. "You bring the dollars—we have the quarters!" This grand upper floor apt. even includes quarters for the maid (room and bath) plus two large bedrooms, 2 baths (the 3rd Bedrm. has been added to the spacious living room to effect a magnificent sweep of about 38 feet). Large dining room, kitchen with a window, impressive foyer and powder room. We haven't done it justice; it must be seen.

Washington Post classified advertisement

NICOLAS SALGO TOOK A CALL FROM AN SGI EXECUTIVE IN Rome. "You have a new boss," the caller said. "His name is Signore Michele Sindona."

"How?" Salgo asked.

"He's bought Immobiliare."

Salgo didn't know what to think of the news.

"You've got to meet Sindona," the caller said. "He's brilliant. He's nice. He's . . . *agreeable.*"

Salgo met Sindona for the first time at the Monaco Grand Prix. SGI had a major development in the Mediterranean kingdom and Sindona invited Salgo and his wife, Josseline, to attend as his guests. They had dinner with Sindona and his wife, Caterina.

"What do you think of the Sindonas?" Salgo asked Josseline after the dinner.

She paused.

"He will never put his foot in my home as long as I am there," she said.

"Why do you tell me that?" Salgo asked. "What did he do?"

"He didn't do anything," she said. "But I don't like him. It's your business if you want to work with him. Socially, he is not acceptable."

ON FEBRUARY 20, 1970, FIVE OF THE "CHICAGO SEVEN" WERE sentenced to five years in prison and fined $5,000 each for crossing state lines with the intention of causing a riot at the 1968 Democratic National Convention. Within hours, nearly six hundred protesters marched on the Watergate. "Two, four, six, eight—liberate the Watergate!" they chanted. Demonstrators shouted epithets at District police and threw rocks, paint and hot water. According to flyers handed out on the streets, protesters targeted the Watergate because it "symbolizes the ruling class." It was also, of course, the home of Attorney General John Mitchell. Antiwar activists had another name for the Watergate: the "Republican Bastille."

O. P. Easterwood, president of Watergate East, sent around a memo instructing residents to stay in their apartments and not attempt to watch "the proceedings" from either the lobby or outside. "If you try to come down," he wrote, "it will only hamper the efforts of the police and furnish material for the news media."

Walter Pforzheimer, chairman of the Watergate East security committee, surveyed the scene as he smoked his pipe. He wore an American flag pin in his lapel and a walkie-talkie strapped to his hip. He told a resident he was "in charge of this thing for Watergate" and ordered her to go up to her apartment. She refused to budge. "When the police tell me to go, I'll go," she snapped.

One Watergate resident, in slacks and a bandanna, stood in an island in the middle of Virginia Avenue and sketched the scene. Another removed wooden items from her ground-floor balcony "in case they threw firebombs." Some residents stocked up on food and other necessities at the Watergate Safeway, afraid the store would be looted by the rioters. The maître d' of the Watergate Hotel attempted to escort three guests to the Watergate Pastry Shop and was trapped for twenty minutes in a locked passageway.

Six busloads of police officers kept protesters a block away from the Watergate, while other officers guarded the roofs and lobbies of each building. "I sure wish we had all this protection the night my suit was stolen out of my car in the parking lot," said one resident, sipping a cocktail at the Watergate Hotel bar.

By late afternoon, the situation was under control. District police, armed with clubs and tear gas, arrested 145 protesters. Mary Brooks returned to the Watergate around 5:15 P.M. to walk her toy poodles, instructing them to "say hello" to District policemen.

The next day was peaceful, though at least a dozen officers remained scattered around the Watergate in case protesters decided to return. Building management set up a coffee urn and a tray of Fig Newtons and lemon wafers in the lobby to serve to District police officers on duty. The Watergate Hotel sent over ham sandwiches.

Martha Mitchell was home the entire time. She told *Washington Star* columnist Betty Beale it was "absurd" for protesters to target the Watergate. The Chicago Seven trial centered on events at the Democratic National Convention in Chicago, Martha fumed, "which had nothing to do with us."

A few weeks later, Jerry Rubin, one of the Chicago Seven, posed in front of the Watergate, flipping his middle finger for photographers. He stopped by the Saville-Watergate Book Shop to sign copies of his new book, *Do It!*, and inscribed a copy "Fuck John Mitchell" and sent it up to the Mitchells' apartment.

"HELLO, GORGEOUS!" JOHN MITCHELL SHOUTED, AS HE stepped into the foyer of the apartment and greeted his wife with a kiss, in the presence of two reporters, Vera Glaser and Malvina Stephenson, who were writing a profile of Martha.

"Hi, honey!" Martha bubbled.

Martha said she was initially "dead set" against moving to Washington and giving up her house and friends in New York, "but she adjusted fast" to life in Washington. She initiated "study visits" by cabinet wives at their husbands' agencies and functioned as "leading lady" and "unpaid assistant" to her husband. "We think just alike on everything," she said. "Yes, he's tough. I wouldn't want him any other way." Asked if his wife was an efficient aide, John Mitchell laughed. "She's tremendous," he said. "She knows how to fib."

"Incredible as it seems today," wrote Martha Mitchell's biographer, Winzola McLendon, "Martha lived a relatively private life the first ten months her husband was Attorney General." That changed on November 21, 1969, when Martha appeared on *CBS Morning News* and took a question on recent antiwar protests in the capital. "My husband made the comment to me, looking out the Justice Department it looked like the Russian revolution going on," she told correspondent Marya McLaughlin. "As my husband has said many times, some of the liberals in this country, he'd like to take them and change them for the Russian Communists."

Following the broadcast, Martha recalled, "Holy hell broke loose."

Her remarks became instant fodder for national and local television news broadcasts and newspaper columns and letters to the editor all over the country. Nixon White House communications chief Herb Klein called and told her the comments were reminiscent of Senator Joseph McCarthy. He asked her to consider the impression she was making as "the wife of a Cabinet officer." Worse, according to her biographer, Martha believed her own husband "seemed to side against her." He told reporters he would have preferred she had used "violence-prone militant radicals" rather than "liberals." Martha took refuge in her apartment for days until the president sent her a supportive note. "Don't let the critics get you down," Nixon wrote. "Just remember they are not after you—or John—but me." He assured her, "We'll come out on top at the end."

"That letter is what gave me the courage to go on," Martha told McLendon.

According to McLendon, the CBS interview made Martha Mitchell "a national celebrity" and set her on course to become "eventually something of a folk heroine." According to John Mitchell's biographer, James Rosen, "hordes of reporters began flocking to the Watergate East, eager to exploit the new source of snappy comment." Unfortunately, Rosen wrote, "Martha seldom thought before she spoke."

"My family worked for everything," she told *Time*. "We even have a deed from the King of England for property in North Carolina. Now these jerks come along and try to give it to the Communists."

In an interview with *Women's Wear Daily*, she lamented living conditions at the Watergate. "We're not living on the same means that we had in Rye," she complained. "I had to sell my stock, and now we are having to dip into the till."

"I think the government should give us free housing," she pouted.

Mail flooded into the Mitchell apartment—up to four hundred letters a day, overwhelmingly supportive, although there were hate letters and even threats of violence, which were turned over to federal authorities. Martha had one secretary, provided by the justice department, to help answer the letters, but could not keep up. When she asked her husband for another secretary, he suggested she throw the mail in the garbage. "His answer infuriated me," she told McLendon. "I felt that if the public wanted something of me, if there were questions they wanted me to answer, I was going to answer them—that's why I was in Washington."

Then, with a single phone call placed from their Watergate apartment, Tropical Storm Martha Mitchell was upgraded to a hurricane.

Early on the morning of April 10, 1970, while her husband slept, Martha Mitchell woke up, downed a few drinks and placed a call from the green phone in her bathroom to the *Arkansas Gazette*. She launched into a tirade against Senator J. William Fulbright, a fellow Arkansan, who had recently voted against Nixon's nomination of G. Harrold Carswell to the U.S. Supreme Court. "I want you to crucify Fulbright and that's it," she told reporter John Woodruff, who was recording their conversation. "He is not representing the people of Arkansas." She hung up the phone, walked down the hall and rejoined her husband in bed.

The next morning, John Mitchell got up, turned on the radio "and heard the sound of his world turning upside down." Martha's comments in the morning's edition of the *Arkansas Gazette* were national news.

John Mitchell told Nan Robertson of the *New York Times*, "What else can I do, but let her speak? She has no inclination to be quiet. She's not politically motivated, she's just saying what she feels." He was fully aware, of course, of his wife's unstable condition. He felt responsible for placing her in the public eye, despite the risks to her emotional well-being, by having accepted the job of attorney general. There was another reason, however, why he stood by his vivacious, exasperating bride. "I love her, that's all I have to say."

Over the next forty-eight hours, Martha received more than a hundred requests for media interviews. At his personal expense, John Mitchell hired Kay Woestendiek, the former women's editor at the *Houston Post*, to serve as his wife's press secretary. Woestendiek compared working in Martha's "command post"—the turquoise-blue breakfast room in the apartment, with a Formica table, fish tank and potted plants—to a stint at the U.S. Post Office after a mail strike.

Martha became "the darling of the press; among all those drab, button-down Nixonians she provided a gaudy splash of color." She kept up a steady pace of outrageous commentary. "I think I'm going to join the Women's liberation movement," she proclaimed. She criticized the *Brown v. Board of Education* ruling and challenged a reporter: "Are you going to be prejudiced against me because my grandparents had slaves?" She appeared on CBS's *60 Minutes* and told Mike Wallace, "I love the Democrats." She complained about a heating plant she said was polluting the air outside her Watergate apartment, lobbied for a woman on the Supreme Court and declared "the Vietnam war stinks!"

Martha was "compulsive," "emotionally volatile" and "totally unprepared" for her life in Washington, Woestendiek recalled. "Hardly a week passed, when Martha was scheduled to be at a social event, that she didn't first have a feeling of great depression. She wouldn't want to go. She might actually be in tears. The dread was almost overwhelming. Once she got there, it was like a shot of adrenaline. She would turn on."

Martha, she said, reacted to the public "like others react to hard liquor."

Woestendiek lasted only two months in the job. Her husband, Bill, found a new editorial post with the *Colorado Springs Sun* and the family moved to the Rockies. "Those two months Kay was with Martha were probably the best of Martha's Washington experience," McLendon wrote.

A Gallup poll showed Martha Mitchell had 76 percent name identification. "No woman in public life has achieved so quickly the national awareness of Martha Mitchell," concluded the American Institute of Public Opinion. She became the first-ever cabinet wife to be named one of the ten most-admired women in the world. "Thousands of admirers thought of her as a national heroine," McLendon wrote. "Middle America loved her." According to McLendon:

The Silent Majority embraced her as its own. Martha had struck a chord with all these people by saying in public the same thing she and John had been saying for years, in the den before dinner over those glasses of Scotch. Liberal permissiveness—in the courts, the schools, the Congress, and especially in the press— was selling the United States down the drain to Communists. Every time she took off after justices, educators, senators and representatives, reporters and newscasters, her mail increased a hundredfold.

Within the District of Columbia, however, the reception was less enthusiastic. A Washington socialite called her "grotesque." "She's quite an unstable one, isn't she, calling a newspaper long distance at two or three in the morning?" said Mrs. J. William Fulbright.

Nixon's top aides H. R. Haldeman and John Ehrlichman, however, thought Martha could be useful as an "unofficial spokesman" for the administration. As a woman, she could make statements that would be attacked if they were made by a man. They treated her as a "prize product" and "packaged" her for the public. Her code name—"The Account"—was an advertising term for "client."

"Why would John Mitchell join in this scheme to exploit his wife?" McLendon asked later. He thought of himself as Martha's protector, and was worried she was in over her head. "John Mitchell knew his wife was totally unprepared for the rough and tumble life of a controversial Washington celebrity," McLendon wrote. "He was aware of her feelings of insecurity and that she was high-strung and had a drinking problem. It was obvious she was a poor risk for overexposure to the limelight."

Herb Klein said Mitchell went along because he thought Martha was enjoying the attention, and because he felt guilty working long hours at the justice department. Klein also thought putting Martha on the campaign trail might keep her busy, and make things at home "more peaceful" for the attorney general.

Martha moved from her breakfast room to an office at Nixon campaign headquarters—a cubicle so small, she sarcastically complained to the *Washington Star*, that she and her secretaries nearly drowned when she spilled a cup of coffee. She was eventually moved to a two-room suite on the eleventh floor. She filled it with paintings and objets d'art from her Watergate apartment, original cartoons of herself, and a red, white and blue French telephone she received after appearing on *The Dinah Shore Show*.

An unnamed Nixon aide later confessed to McLendon there was another reason Martha Mitchell was given an office: "She has to be watched."

SPRINKLED THROUGHOUT THE *LIFE* MAGAZINE STORY IN August 1969 about life at the Watergate were indications everything was not quite picture-perfect. "Watergate has been gradually revealing its imperfections," *Life* wrote. Despite twenty-three closed-circuit TV cameras on the property, there had been several "spectacular" jewelry thefts. Some residents felt "dwarfed and entombed" by the concrete-and-glass buildings. Jets from nearby National Airport interfered with conversations on the balconies. The Potomac River was so polluted, "on some hot summer evenings you can hardly smell the honeysuckle." John Mitchell said their apartment was "convenient but that's about all."

Martha showed a reporter the seventh-floor hallway carpet, which had stripes of blue tape covering rips at regular intervals. "It's a disgrace," she said. "I have been trying to get them to fix it ever since we have been here." Plaster walls in her duplex were cracking. "The noise is terrible," she told *Newsweek*. "The balconies are so close together everyone can hear you talking—you feel like a monkey in the zoo." (A neighbor suggested Mrs. Mitchell was responsible for much of the noise, as she "talks to her maids at the top of her voice.") "It's not a good place to live," Martha said. "I've had better apartments in New York for $120 a month."

Kathy and Maurice Stans returned from a weekend trip to discover water had seeped into their apartment from leaks in windows in two of the rooms, damaging art objects and important papers. They asked the building's engineer to check immediately with the apartment above theirs, as previous leaks had been caused by planters in that unit's balcony. But the owner refused to let the engineer enter his apartment and check the situation. "I am now out of patience," Stans informed Arthur Weld, chairman of the Watergate East building committee, and Robert R. Mullen, president of the board. Stans demanded the building take steps to force his upstairs neighbors to reimburse him for the loss. Mullen wrote back, sympathizing with Stans and promising only, "we will do our best."

E. F. Hamm, president of Traffic Service Corp., which published trade magazines, noticed leaks in his $150,000 Watergate East penthouse. "Once we noticed in the morning that water had come down near the fireplace and buckled the parquet floor in the living room," he told the *Wall Street Journal.* "Another time, before a cocktail party, we had a leak in the hall. We had to mop it up just before everybody arrived." Additional leaks appeared in the penthouses of Joel Barlow and Anna Chennault. To fix leaks in his penthouse, John Cannaday's rooftop garden had to be uprooted completely. He was able to move his fruit trees to safety, but his vegetable garden was interrupted until repairs were completed.

In some apartments, the air-conditioning system malfunctioned—cooling a room from the waist down, but emitting hot air from the waist up. The air-conditioning in the Stanses' apartment gave out completely. "We couldn't breathe at all," lamented Kathy Stans. Humidity caused her parquet floors to buckle and wall-to-wall carpeting to shrink in seven different rooms. The tiger skins, elephant tusks and other mementos of her husband's safaris were at risk of damage.

The basement of Watergate West flooded during a summer rainstorm. Residents were urged to hurry downstairs and remove snow tires, heavy furniture and other possessions from their storage lockers. "I thought I had seen a lot of water in the submarine service," said one resident, "but nothing like this!"

A prominent stockbroker said he could hear his neighbor in Watergate West take a bath. His ice maker also "went berserk," he said. "Cubes spill all over the floor."

There were "cubbyholes" outside the apartments in Watergate West where laundry could be left and picked up, and packages delivered while residents were away. When White House aide Martin Anderson tried on his shirts, they didn't fit at all—the sleeves hung way below his fingertips. Annelise figured out her husband's laundry must have been switched with Tennessee congressman William Anderson's and called the lobby to report the error. "It's computerized," the attendant sniffed, "and the computer never makes a mistake."

Television reception was spotty, despite two years of work on the rooftop antenna. "You'd get ghosts and many times you couldn't get any picture at all," said retired admiral Paul Dudley. The *Watergate Post* resident newsletter advised that channel 26 could be found on channel 6, and channel 20 could be found on channel 12—"we hope."

"The Watergate is not what it's cracked up to be," said Nancy Lammerding.

What most unnerved Watergate residents, however, was a rash of burglaries that demolished their sense of personal security.

Shortly after Nixon's secretary Rose Mary Woods was burglarized, thieves stole a fur coat and $6,000 worth of jewelry from the Watergate apartment of Laurence Wood, General Electric's Washington vice president. In April 1969, the Mosbachers' suite in the Watergate Hotel was burglarized and $3,500 in valuables taken. Thieves broke into four Cadillacs parked in the underground garage.

Apartment maids told reporters it was possible to enter the Watergate through unlocked service elevators open to the parking garage. "There used to be hotel policemen patrolling the halls," one maid said, "but I haven't seen them in quite a while." Irone Shah, resident manager of Watergate East, declined to comment on security, except to note the closed-circuit television units were monitored by front-desk staff twenty-four hours a day. But residents said desk clerks often ended up watching "elevator scenes of women hiking up their skirts to fix their stockings or wriggling around to straighten their girdles." Security patrol and "listening devices" installed in the parking garages and laundry rooms were there to deter violent crimes, the *Wall Street Journal* reported, but were not useful in preventing burglaries of apartments.

O. P. Easterwood, chairman of the Watergate East board, said the thefts were most likely perpetrated by "somebody on the inside with a key." Residents suspected the thefts were mostly "inside jobs." The apartment key rack was located alongside a key-making machine just off the lobby, behind the front desk—with easy access for maintenance staff.

Carolyn Blount, wife of the postmaster general, reported $2,000 in jewelry was missing. Although she wasn't 100 percent sure the theft took place at the Watergate, the Blounts surrendered their Watergate apartment and moved to Georgetown.

"USUALLY AT DINNER PARTIES YOU END UP SITTING NEXT TO someone, and you don't have any idea who he is, much less his politics or religion," Anna Chennault, in a coral-colored mini-dress, told her guests as they arrived at her penthouse. "So let me introduce you to each other once again."

The occasion was a farewell dinner for the departing ambassador of Ceylon, Oliver Weerasinghe, and his wife, Cristobel. Chennault's guests included the ambassadors of Burma and Saudi Arabia; Watergate residents Laurence Wood and Walter Pforzheimer; the State Department's Ray Cline; James Holcombe, a vice president of Northrop Corporation; and the president of the Export-Import Bank, Henry Kearns. "Don't eat too much shrimp," she warned her guests. "We have an eight-course dinner." Guests climbed the spiral staircase to see Chennault's new "dancing room"—an enclosed pavilion on her rooftop terrace. She had built it "because it's windy up here," she said, "and also because I like to dance." Downstairs, seating charts were adorned with different-colored flowers, matching the flower arrangements on each table. Before dinner, guests stood as Chennault spoke about each person, and sat down to applause.

Anna's party that night was covered by a *Washington Post* reporter named Sally Quinn. Sally's parents, Bette and Bill Quinn, were friendly with Chennault. They met through Arizona senator Barry Goldwater. Bill Quinn retired from the U.S. Army with the rank of lieutenant general—the same rank as Anna's late husband—and Chennault sometimes came to dinner at the Quinns' home in

Chevy Chase, Maryland. Bette and Bill also went to Chennault's Watergate penthouse or joined her for dinner around town.

Washington Post executive editor Ben Bradlee had just started the "Style" section in March and put Quinn to work covering parties. Washington hostesses would call the *Post*'s social editor and tell her about a party coming up, and the *Post* would send out a reporter. "They all wanted their parties covered," recalled Quinn. "And generally, in those days, the coverage was all benign."

Chennault was "a pistol," Quinn said. "She took no prisoners. She was extremely aggressive socially, and ambitious, and she wanted to be the queen, she wanted to be on the top of the social heap, and she worked it." Quinn added, "People were kind of afraid of her."

Chennault was "worshipped" by the conservatives in Washington, Quinn said, but never "cracked" the liberal, Democratic, Georgetown elite. "That was not her crowd."

Quinn remembered Chennault's long red fingernails, her tightly wound hair on the top of her head and her perfect, dramatic makeup. "I loved watching her."

Quinn covered Anna's party for producer M. J. Frankovich (*Bob & Carol & Ted & Alice*) and his wife, actress Binnie Barnes. "Richard Nixon missed a good party last night," Quinn wrote. "In fact, it could have been a Cabinet meeting in the corner by the buffet for a while." David Kennedy, the secretary of the treasury, chatted with White House aide John Ehrlichman. Rose Mary Woods was there, as was Jack Valenti, head of the Motion Picture Association of America. Chennault introduced Vlastimil Koubek, the architect who had earlier examined her penthouse while it was under construction and produced a long list of defects needing attention, to Robert Finch, secretary of health, education and welfare. Another guest, John Lear, inventor of the Lear jet, was in town "to do something about air pollution." Kathy and Maurice Stans joked they had walked the length of the building "for a plate of food to take back to our apartment."

"As far as the social life of the Nixon Administration goes," a source told the *New York Times*, "the Watergate is where it's happening, and the hot center of it all is Anna Chennault's apartment." The Associated Press reported Chennault go-go danced every night to rock music for fifteen minutes for exercise and guests at her parties sometimes did "silly things like throwing cards into a hat on the floor."

Nancy Reagan, wife of the California governor, came to Anna's apartment for lunch. Martha Mitchell joined them. "Your apartment is lovely," Mrs. Reagan wrote Anna later, "and it was fun to have girl talk with you and Martha."

In June 1970, Chennault made the cover of the *Parade* magazine insert in Sunday newspapers around the country. The article, written by Lloyd Shearer, was headlined: ANNA CHENNAULT: HER ENEMIES CALL HER THE DRAGON LADY OF WATERGATE EAST.

"For years diminutive Anna Chennault has been regarded as one of the most intriguing and controversial personalities in Washington," Shearer wrote. "Referred to by others of her sex as a little Chinese scorpion stinging her way through life," Chennault's "icy and imperious beauty has earned her the name of 'The Dragon Lady.'"

"Most of the stuff written about me is lies, especially what was written about me in Theodore White's book," she said. "About that I am really sensitive." She continued:

Of course, I campaigned for Richard Nixon. And of course I talked to the representatives of the South Vietnamese government. I talk to them all the time. But I did not advise them not to send peace representatives to Paris until after the election so that Richard Nixon could win.

This is just stupid for anyone to believe. I discussed the South Vietnamese issue with Richard Nixon during the campaign. He regards my knowledge on Southeast Asia very highly. I gave information to Sen. John Tower and the Republican campaign committee. But to say that I tried to influence the South Vietnamese government, that's to underestimate my intelligence. To have Teddy White not even check with me and to write about that kind of thing—that the government tapped my telephone line. I don't know if they did—it was so unfair.

Lots of people came to me after Teddy White's book and said, "Anna, you must make a statement." Now, if I were a smaller person, I would have come out and said, "You are terrible, Teddy White," and so forth. But I felt the country had enough problems. So I said nothing. But I am going to write a book about this and it's going to be very, very interesting.

Shearer reported Anna was "unabashedly in love" with Tommy Corcoran. "As a woman I am more interested in love than power," Chennault said.

ON THE NIGHT OF NOVEMBER 23, 1971, RICHARD NIXON picked up his phone. "Miss Woods, please," he said to the White House operator.

After a moment, the operator got back on the line. "Mr. President, I find Miss Woods has gone to a reception at Mrs. Chennault's."

The party was a salute to the U.S. Air Force, at which Anna presented $63,000 in checks to various charities—proceeds raised the year before at the annual Air Force Ball, which she had chaired.

"Would you like me to reach her there?" the operator asked.

"No, no, skip it, thank you."

"All right."

After a few moments, Nixon picked up his phone again. "Mr. MacGregor, please," he said. Clark MacGregor, a Republican former member of Congress from Minnesota, was one of Nixon's liaisons to Capitol Hill.

"Mr. MacGregor is at Mrs. Chennault's reception. Did you want me to reach him?"

"Yeah," Nixon said.

"That was a great vote," Nixon said once MacGregor got on the line. The president was referring to a key Senate vote that evening on a defense bill. MacGregor agreed. "This is a darn good development," he said.

"Give my best to Anna Chennault," Nixon said. "Is she there?"

"Yes, she's right here," MacGregor replied. "You want to . . ."

"I'll talk to her, yeah."

MacGregor handed the phone to Chennault.

"Mr. President?"

"Yes."

"Oh, we are raising money for the air force. You know, we do need some defense."

"That's great."

"That's so very kind of you to say hello to me."

"Well, you've been a great friend."

Chennault promised to "keep on fighting."

"Well, you're a great lady," Nixon said. "We appreciate it."

Nixon hung up. Chennault handed the phone to MacGregor and rejoined her guests. Dorothy McCardle was covering Anna's party for the *Washington Post*. According to McCardle's story in the *Post* the following day, President Nixon "personally telephoned Mrs. Chennault during the party to congratulate her on her 'hard work' for the Air Force."

"Anna Chennault has beauty, lots of political clout and umpteen million dollars," an anonymous source told the *Los Angeles Times*. "But charm? No. Besides, she over-invites and under-feeds." *Washington Post* columnist Barbara Howar wrote: "Anna Chennault is like a woman with a small bosom, but at least she's holding it out there."

"If the war in Vietnam were to end tomorrow," said one anonymous critic, "Anna Chennault would be finished socially in Washington. Mainly, she runs a salon for the Vietnam hawks."

MARTHA MITCHELL MADE THE COVER OF *LIFE* MAGAZINE'S October 2, 1970, issue. "She still relishes her role as a public figure," *Life* wrote. "But she is becoming increasingly uncomfortable."

Largely as a result of her own doing, Martha was under siege. The telephones rang constantly in her Watergate East apartment. When she went out to shop, she drew crowds of supporters—as well as detractors. Her outspokenness turned off many Nixon aides and made their wives wince. She had no close friends in Washington. The Mitchells began to withdraw from the Washington social circuit. Their normal routine was to stay home—and drink heavily. John could hold his liquor; Martha could not. When John retired for the evening, Martha would "get on the phone, a lonely, frustrated woman who would pour out her soul to a secretary or a wire-service reporter or virtually anyone who would listen to her."

One night at dinner in Anna Chennault's penthouse, Martha became drunk and threatened to toss her shoe across the table at John.

"Just you try," he said.

"Martha reached down, pulled one spike-heeled, sling-back shoe off her foot, and hurled it at Mitchell who, either from frequent practice or excellent reflexes, neatly ducked the flying object," Chennault wrote.

"It's time to go home," John Mitchell said.

"I don't want to go home," Martha protested.

She reluctantly grabbed her purse and the Mitchells said good night.

THE BOARD OF DIRECTORS OF WATERGATE EAST GREW frustrated with the deterioration of day-to-day operations and fired the building manager. His replacement soon discovered the building's records were "vastly inadequate." Deliveries and repairs to apartments could not be made because the staff did not know which residents lived in which apartments. No records documented who was authorized to use which parking spaces in the underground garage. The association's finances were also in disarray. The board discovered "inherited annual operating budget deficiencies" and a debt of $370,000 that had accumulated over the past several years.

In November 1971, the Watergate East board voted to impose a 10 percent increase in co-op assessments and an additional "special assessment" of $370,000 to retire the debt. Residents were outraged. Many questioned the board's decision to retire this debt over two years, rather than over a longer period, and petitioned the president of the co-op board to call a general membership meeting, at which residents voted to direct the co-op board to explore refinancing the original mortgage for the land, still held by John Hancock Mutual Life Insurance, and stabilize the co-op's finances—while at the same time reducing future "special assessment" surcharges.

At the next Watergate East annual membership meeting, the board of directors presented a plan for refinancing the mortgage with John Hancock. Residents overwhelmingly supported the plan, but because the board did not have ballots identifying owners' voting shares, based on the relative size of each apartment, a formal vote was not possible. Instead, residents instructed the board of directors to issue a referendum within two weeks that, if passed by 75 percent of the voting shares, would empower the board to move forward with the refinancing.

The board also engaged the architectural and engineering firm of Nelson, Dollar and Blitz to conduct a structural, mechanical and electrical analysis of the building to identify and confirm all construction defects and project the costs to repair them. The board recommended this independent, professional assessment rather than continuing to rely simply on owners' complaints—"a practice followed for the past six years," board president Robert M. Caldwell informed the residents, "which failed to identify and correct deficiencies by either the Developer or owners."

ON JANUARY 7, 1972, PRESIDENT NIXON DECLARED HIS IN-
tention to seek a second term. In mid-February, Maurice Stans
resigned as Nixon's secretary of commerce to chair the finance committee of the Committee for the Re-Election of the President (also
known as the Committee to Re-elect the President), the same role
he had in 1968. He had resisted a return to campaign fund-raising
because he enjoyed being secretary of commerce, but Nixon attorney
Herbert Kalmbach recruited him aggressively—even suggesting an
appointment in Nixon's second term to head the World Bank. When
word leaked out, Robert McNamara, a Watergate neighbor and the
incumbent president of the World Bank, was quickly reelected to
another five-year term—a full year ahead of schedule.

John Mitchell resigned as attorney general on March 1 to chair
Nixon's campaign. Martha had fought the move for weeks. She
thought it was a demotion for her husband—a loss of cabinet rank,
along with its perks and social invitations. "They can't do this," she
ranted. "What will our friends think? We gave up everything to
come here to help Mr. President and the country; now they want
to cut us off. I won't stand for it!" When he finally stepped down,
Martha was so upset, her secretaries had to come stay with her in
the apartment.

According to one of John's former aides at the justice department,
neither First Lady Pat Nixon nor Adele Rogers, wife of the secretary of
state, could stand Martha Mitchell. As Martha predicted, once John
Mitchell left the cabinet, "Pat and Adele cut them off of every list."

Within days of John Mitchell's departure from the justice department, the White House telephone was removed from their
Watergate apartment.

WILLIAM D. LEE RENTED AN APARTMENT IN WATERGATE WEST
for approximately six months before purchasing it—"as is"—at a
$10,000 discount. Lee, an electrical engineer, submitted an exten-

sive list of "latent defects," many of which related to the electrical and air-conditioning systems. His list was ignored. This would turn out to be a mistake. Lee was a deputy assistant secretary for the U.S. Department of Commerce and executive director of the President's Commission on Consumer Affairs, and therefore knowledgeable about and professionally committed to the emerging field of consumer protection. He was also president of the Watergate West co-op board.

In 1969, the first summer at Watergate West, the building's cooling system malfunctioned. Engineers working for the developers assured residents the problem was temporary and could be easily corrected, no later than the fall of 1969. The next winter, Watergate West experienced problems with its heating system, and the board retained an engineer to investigate and document his findings. According to the owners, Giuseppe Cecchi dismissed the engineer as inexperienced and hired another consultant, who prepared a report stating there was nothing seriously wrong with the Watergate West heating system, and that all it needed was "corrective work," which was already under way. Cecchi assured residents the developers would "do everything reasonably required" to solve the problems with the heating and cooling system, and "stand behind their product."

According to the board of Watergate West, the "corrections" performed by the developers proved to be "temporary and basically ineffective." Cecchi claimed all the defects had been fixed.

The board then retained new engineers, who prepared a detailed report of problems, which was shared with Cecchi in December 1971. Around this time, Watergate West also terminated the management contract with Riverview Realty, just as Watergate East had done. With a new building manager in tow, Lee and his fellow board members inspected Watergate West from top to bottom, including the mechanical room. They met with Cecchi's engineers to review problems with the heating and cooling system in early January 1972. Those conversations went nowhere as well. Lee and the board made an offer to Cecchi: Open up the utility column in the building. If an investigation disclosed that no repairs were needed, all repair costs would afterward be paid by the co-op board. But if defects were visible, then the developers would pay all the costs of repair. At this point, according to the owners, Cecchi terminated negotiations. Decades later, Cecchi could not recall the specifics of the dispute.

The board opened up the utility column anyway, and discovered the entire heating, cooling and ventilating system needed to be replaced. Within days, the Watergate West owners association and ninety-six individual residents—including Edith and Lee Burchinal, who had received a golden key to their new apartment the day the building opened—filed a $1.5 million lawsuit against Watergate Improvement Associates, the sponsor of the development; Watergate Construction Corp., the general contractor; Riverview Realty Corporation, the exclusive sales representative for the complex; Milton Fischer; Maurice P. Foley, Inc., the electrical contractor; Cotton & Harris, the engineers; and The Whalen Company, the manufacturer of parts of the heating and cooling system. Two weeks later, additional defendants were named, including the Washington Gas Light Company, which managed the on-site heating and cooling plant; the Tappan Company; and General Electric Company's appliance division. (On November 18, 1972, two weeks after the election, Watergate West residents Geneva and Alan Cranston and Ruth and Abe Ribicoff joined the suit as plaintiffs.)

According to the suit, Watergate West was advertised as "the ultimate in luxury in cooperative living," but was plagued with a variety of defects, including:

- Inadequate air-conditioning in 70 percent of the apartments;
- Water damage in 40 percent of the apartments;
- Defective kitchen appliances in 45 percent of the apartments; and
- Plumbing deficiencies in 22 percent of the units.

Each of the residents who signed on to the suit contended their apartments were "defective in the heating, cooling and ventilating systems" and "the kitchen appliances and the plumbing fixtures were not of the high standard promised." The lawsuit claimed repairs would exceed $60,000 per apartment, an astonishing sum—in many cases, exceeding the purchase price of the apartments themselves—based on an estimate prepared by Fred J. Maynard, an employee of the George A. Fuller Company, which was engaged in repair work throughout Watergate West.

Developers had tried to correct the problem of water damage during rainstorms, but the problems continued, the residents charged. "Our position is that if there is something wrong and it's our responsibility, we'll take care of it," said Cecchi, but he said the residents' claims were unsubstantiated. "Our consulting engineers met with their consulting engineers," he told a reporter for the *Washington Post*. "They weren't able to document anything. They couldn't even show us in which apartments were the defects. In a deluxe cooperative, everybody thinks he's entitled to everything, so the complaints are always there. But we have taken care of the complaints." If the problems with the building were so bad, Cecchi asked, why did Watergate values keep rising?

Three weeks later, the developers fired back. They charged the Watergate West lawsuit was an attempt to cause "malicious embarrassment" and interfere with sales at the new Watergate at Landmark complex they planned to build in Arlington, Virginia, across the Potomac River. The developers sought $4 million in damages. They also contended the owners' complaints were "grossly exaggerated." There was "some" water damage, the developers acknowledged, but said it had been corrected or, if it existed, was beyond their control and therefore they were not liable for any damages.

IN MARCH 1970, ROBERT S. STRAUSS WAS ELECTED TREA-surer of the Democratic National Committee and began dealing with a flood of creditors. "I would be less than candid," Strauss wrote one creditor, "if I did not say to you that the Committee has absolutely no funds on hand for debt payment right now." The DNC's total debt in 1970 was $9.5 million, including $7 million from the Humphrey primary and general campaigns, and $1 million of the late senator Robert F. Kennedy's primary campaign debt.

As the Democrats headed into the 1972 election, they fell behind on their rent at the Watergate Office Building.

Giuseppe Cecchi was Italian by birth, but he considered himself "fully Americanized" and wanted to send the DNC an eviction notice. "Are you crazy?" a colleague asked him. "McGovern may be the next president of the United States. You don't want to do that."

According to the Harris Survey released March 2, 1972, Nixon's approval rating had risen to 55 percent. In late April, the Harris Survey gave Nixon a strong lead over his Democratic rivals, by margins of 6 to 18 percentage points if Alabama governor George Wallace entered the race.

Cecchi was overruled by Rome. The DNC could stay, and any past-due rent could be collected after the election.

No eviction proceedings were begun.

On June 8, 1972, Strauss and Larry O'Brien established the Democratic National Committee Telethon Trust to retire all outstanding debts of the DNC and distribute any excess funds to the committee and to state party committees. The telethon netted just $2 million. Strauss was able to pay some bills. He asked other creditors to accept 25 cents on the dollar. A check for $2,500 was eventually sent to Watergate Improvements out of the telethon account on July 18, 1973.

ON MONDAY, MAY 22, SIX MEN ARRIVED IN WASHINGTON from Miami: Bernard Barker, Eugenio Martinez, Felipe de Diego, Frank Sturgis, Virgilio Gonzalez and Reinaldo Pico. They checked into the Manger Hamilton Hotel at 14th and K Streets. Four days later, on the afternoon of Friday, May 26—the start of the Memorial Day weekend—the men transferred to the Watergate Hotel under rooms reserved by Ameritas, a Miami-based corporation. Dorothy Hunt, wife of E. Howard Hunt, Jr., identified herself as a secretary with the firm and spoke directly with the Watergate Hotel staff to plan a "small banquet" in the Continental Room in the basement of the Watergate Office Building. The room was equipped with a bar, but lacked a working kitchen. Events in the Continental Room were catered by the staff of the Watergate Hotel. According to hotel records, cocktails would be served at eight, followed by a dinner of filet mignon. The reservation was for ten guests, at a charge of $14.95 per person, plus taxes and gratuity.

According to the plan, when the dinner meeting ended, hotel staff would clear the table and the bogus Ameritas "executives" would watch a film Hunt had rented for the occasion. The screening gave the meeting "an air of authenticity." It also gave the men a reason to remain in the Watergate Office Building as they waited for the last staffer to leave the offices of the Democratic National Committee on the sixth floor.

The FBI later interviewed Franco Rovere, the waiter who took care of the Ameritas party. He told agents "the main topic of conversation in the room was night clubs in the Miami area and women." When he checked in on the group around ten-thirty to ask if they needed anything more, he was told he was not needed and he returned to the Watergate Hotel.

According to Hunt's account of the evening, while the movie was under way and the room was dark, six men left the Continental Room, exiting through a door that led to an internal hallway to wait for word from James McCord and Alfred Baldwin, monitoring the office building from a room across the street at the Howard Johnson Motor Lodge, that the DNC was unoccupied. Virgilio Gonzalez and Howard Hunt stayed behind in the Continental Room.

At eleven, the lights were still on at the DNC. The six men in the corridor outside the Continental Room aborted their mission and returned to the Watergate Hotel.

Between 1:00 and 2:00 A.M., Frank Wills, the Government Security Services guard, locked the front door of the Continental Room. He wrote in his logbook:

> *CONTINEAL ROAM OPEN*
> *HAVING MEETING CONT*
> *ROOM CLOSE AT 2:10 AM*

Hunt and Gonzalez, however, were still hiding inside the Continental Room's closet. When nature called, Hunt, fearful he might be discovered were he to seek out a proper restroom, urinated in an empty bottle of Johnnie Walker Red. They emerged at six the next morning and returned to the Watergate Hotel.

The next night—at twelve-thirty on Sunday, May 28—seven men in business suits signed the visitors log in the lobby of the Watergate Office Building. They used aliases—one man signed in as "John Smith"—and gave their destination as the Federal Reserve Board, which had offices on the eighth floor. Frank Wills, the security guard on duty, sent them up in the elevator to the eighth floor. The men walked down the stairwell to the sixth floor and entered the lobby outside the entrance to the DNC office. Gonzalez tried and failed to pick the lock to the DNC door. McCord called Gordon Liddy, who came over from his room in the Watergate Hotel to take a look. Liddy feared the lock might have been damaged enough to show DNC officials that a break-in had been attempted, which would prompt them to notify the police. Liddy signed into the visitors log downstairs at 2:55, using an alias, and listed the Federal Reserve Board as his destination. He inspected the lock and was satisfied the damage was minimal. He returned to the lobby, signed out and returned to the Watergate Hotel.

On Monday—Memorial Day—Gonzalez flew to Miami to pick

up additional lock-picking tools and returned to Washington that afternoon. McCord taped open the locks of the door that led from the underground garage to the basement stairwell in the Watergate Office Building. Around 11:00 P.M., McCord and four men entered the building from the garage and made their way up the stairwell to the sixth floor. This time, Gonzalez was able to pick the lock.

They placed eavesdropping devices in the suite and took photographs of correspondence on DNC chief Larry O'Brien's desk. Liddy later claimed he and Hunt were "delighted" by the operation.

ON JUNE 15, 1972, THE FIRM OF NELSON, DOLLAR AND BLITZ submitted its "Structural Analysis of Watergate East," as requested by the board of directors.

The firm identified fifteen different problems in the building that required correction, including cracks in the underground garage; leaking balconies, windows and penthouse planters; and various mechanical and ventilation defects. The total cost to address these items came to $580,000, with annual maintenance costs of $65,000 thereafter.

AT AROUND 12:30 A.M. ON SATURDAY, JUNE 17, FRANK WILLS took a call from his supervisor, Bobby Jackson. Wills explained he had discovered and removed tape on the stairwell doors and Jackson directed him to check other doors in the building and report back. Wills hung up and finished his cheeseburger and fries.

At around 1:10 A.M., the five-man "entry team"—Sturgis, Barker, Martinez, Gonzalez and McCord—arrived at the door on the B-2 level of the underground garage and discovered the tape was missing and the door was locked. Three of the men returned to the Watergate Hotel to consult with Liddy and Hunt; Sturgis and Gonzalez picked the lock, taped it open and proceeded to the sixth floor.

Frank Wills finished dinner and made his rounds, checking for tape on other locks, as he had been instructed. At the B-2 level he found the doors had been re-taped. He left the tape in place and returned to the lobby, where he met Walter Hellams, a security guard working for the Federal Reserve Board, who had just arrived to conduct a routine check on the board's suite on the eighth floor. Wills asked Hellams whether he should call the police; Hellams said he should, as it was clear a burglary was under way. Wills first called Bobby Jackson, and then, at 1:47, the Washington Police Department.

Officer Carl Shoffler, Sergeant Paul Leeper and Officer John Barrett were undercover near the Bayou nightclub on K Street NW, less than two blocks from the Watergate. Shoffler was in disguise, wearing shoulder-length hair and "hippie clothes." A radio call came at 1:52 from a police dispatcher to head over to the Watergate. Leeper and Barrett suspected a typewriter heist. Thefts of IBM electric typewriters had been a recent problem throughout the city's commercial district.

Wills met the officers and showed them the tape he had discovered on the B-2 basement door. Hellams told them about a burglary that had taken place recently in the eighth-floor suite of the Federal Reserve Board. Together, they climbed the stairs to the eighth floor, where they discovered the tape on the door.

They made their way down to the sixth floor and found another taped door. Entering the hallway, Shoffler noticed an open window onto a balcony. "It was our experience these guys will hide anywhere," he later recalled. "They are like roaches." He crawled out onto the narrow balcony, expecting to bump into one of the burglars, but instead he saw a man across the street observing the scene through binoculars from a room at the Howard Johnson. Just as Shoffler crawled back into the building, he heard Barrett shout, "Freeze! Police! You are under arrest!"

Shoffler watched from behind a pillar as five men stood, raising their arms above their heads. "We're expecting thieves," he recalled, "and I got five guys with sport coats." The men were speaking to each other in Spanish as the officers directed them to speak English, to no avail. It was only at that moment the officers looked around the room and realized they were in the offices of the Democratic National Committee.

CHAPTER FIVE: THE MAELSTROM

Only after crossing an elevated threshold of income and maturity can life be transformed into an art of living.

At Watergate, in its apartments, its hotel, its office buildings, you'll find this art. And you'll find residents, professionals, visitors, employees unified by an appreciation of the uniqueness that is Watergate.

Art, and the willingness to invest in the refinement of that art of living. This is the essence of Watergate people.

People who love privacy as much as luxury.

"Les Champs at Watergate" marketing brochure

SHELLEY AND PAT BUCHANAN MARRIED IN MAY 1971 AT Blessed Sacrament in northwest Washington and Pat moved into Shelley's apartment in Watergate East. The Nixons and the Mitchells attended the wedding—Martha was "a sensation" at the parish and both Mitchells stayed late at the reception—and the Buchanans and the Mitchells became good friends. The Mitchells gave the newlyweds a silver bell engraved "from The Attorney General and Mrs. Mitchell." Martha and Shelley chaperoned students from the District's public schools for boat rides, with hot dog lunches, on the presidential yacht *Sequoia*.

On Saturday morning, June 17, Shelley and Pat were at his parents' home on Utah Street. The phone rang, and Pat was summoned to take the call. It was another White House aide, Ken Khachigian. "His voice was low," Pat recalled, "like someone relating news of a bad turn in the medical condition of a friend." Ken told him five men were caught breaking into the DNC at the Watergate. "Instantly, I knew it was us," Pat recalled.

Buchanan had earlier received photographs of documents from the Edmund S. Muskie campaign and passed them along, in blind envelopes, to sympathetic reporters. He had understood the photos had come to him via a "spy in the Muskie camp," but suddenly feared he had been misled—and that the photos had been taken by the same people who had broken into the Watergate. If his hunch was true, they had committed a felony. "I felt ill," Pat recalled.

BRUCE GIVNER, THE TWENTY-ONE-YEAR-OLD UCLA INTERN who had been the last to leave the DNC offices the night of Friday, June 16, 1972, returned to the Watergate around ten Saturday morning to help open mail. He arrived to find a crime scene.

"Holy crap!" he said as he emerged from the elevator on the sixth floor. "What's going on?"

"There was a break-in last night," a coworker told him.

JOHN MITCHELL AND HIS DAUGHTER, MARTY, ATE BREAKFAST in their suite at the Beverly Hills Hotel while Martha slept in. Downstairs in the Polo Lounge, Joyce and Fred LaRue were having breakfast with Gail and Jeb Magruder. A waiter brought a telephone to the table for Magruder. The caller was Gordon Liddy. He told Magruder about the arrests the night before.

Magruder whispered the news to LaRue, who left the table and headed upstairs to brief Mitchell. "That is just incredible," John Mitchell said when he heard the news.

When Martha finally emerged from her bedroom, John told her he was heading back to Washington. He suggested she get some rest and spend the weekend in Newport Beach. Martha agreed and, with her assistant Lea Jablonsky and Marty, plus a security detail, left the Beverly Hills Hotel and headed to the Newporter Inn.

Spencer Oliver was on the Outer Banks of North Carolina that weekend, vacationing with his family. He heard on the Sunday evening news there had been a break-in at the DNC. "I thought that was strange," he recalled. "Why would anybody break into the Democratic National Committee? I mean, we don't have any money; the convention's coming up and everybody's moved to Miami; the delegates have been picked and the primaries are over. So why would anybody be in there?"

JUNE 18, 1972, BEGAN LIKE ANY OTHER SUNDAY AT THE Watergate, Maurice Stans later recalled. He slept in one additional hour, as he often did on the weekend. He performed his morning exercise routine, including about twenty minutes on his electric bicycle. He showered and put on a robe.

Slap.

The *Washington Post* landed at the front door of his apartment and the doorman continued down the hall.

Slap. Slap. Slap.

Stans opened the door, picked up the *Post* and stepped back inside his apartment. He went into the kitchen to fix a breakfast of dry cereal, toast and tea, and turned on the morning news. Not much was going on. The war situation in Vietnam was unchanged and the economy was "doing fine." A headline on the front page, however, caught his eye: FIVE HELD IN PLOT TO BUG DEMOCRATIC PARTY OFFICE.

Who in the world could have been up to that? he asked himself. He wondered if the intruders might also have targeted the Nixon campaign headquarters.

He did not recognize any of the names of the five men arrested at the DNC. "For that matter," he recalled, "I did not even know that the Democratic Party headquarters were in the Watergate office building, although my Watergate apartment was only two hundred feet away."

AT THE NEWPORTER INN, MARTHA FOUND A COPY OF THE Monday *Los Angeles Times* and took it upstairs to her bedroom, where she first read the news of the Watergate break-in and arrests. "Jesus Christ!" she exclaimed. She jumped out of bed and tried to reach her husband by phone, but he was in the air on his way to Washington.

She became agitated and began drinking gin—straight, with no ice. "Those bastards left me out here without telling me anything," she snarled at Steve King, the ex–FBI agent who served as her security detail. She burned her hand when a pack of matches exploded as she was trying to light a Salem Long; a doctor came to the hotel to bandage the wound and prescribe the painkiller Phenaphen.

On Tuesday, LaRue and Robert Mardian met with Gordon Liddy in LaRue's Watergate West apartment. Liddy asked LaRue to turn up the radio, so that the conversation couldn't be recorded, then told of his activities, including the hiring of the Cuban burglars, with their CIA and Bay of Pigs backgrounds, and a prior wiretapping of the DNC offices in the Watergate Office Building.

On Wednesday, John Mitchell arranged for friends to fly with Martha to New York, on the red-eye, and moved her into the Westchester Country Club. A frustrated and unhinged Martha once more turned to the telephone. "I'm not going to stand for all those dirty things that go on," she told UPI reporter Helen Thomas. Mitchell flew to New York and brought his wife back to the Watergate on June 28. The next day, Mitchell confided to Haldeman that Martha was despondent and drinking heavily. "He feels she's suicidal as well as a little cracked," Haldeman wrote in his diary, "and that there's nothing he can do to cure it."

ANNA CHENNAULT ATTENDED A WHITE HOUSE BRIEFING IN advance of the upcoming GOP convention in Miami. As the briefing concluded, White House aide John Ehrlichman stood and asked if there were any questions. Chennault raised her hand.

"I wondered if you could tell me any more about the break-in at the Watergate?" she asked. "I live there, so I'm interested in knowing what it's all about."

Chennault recalled laughter rippling through the audience. "Nothing like starting with the really important questions," someone said.

"Who cares?" said another.

Ehrlichman smiled. "Anna," he said, "by the time we get to Miami for the convention, this will all be water under the bridge. All of this will be cleared up. So don't worry about it."

Anna felt foolish for having asked the question. Whatever went on at the DNC, she thought, couldn't be worse than the burglary at Rose Mary Woods's apartment.

A week after the Watergate break-in, Maurice Stans was informed that Gordon Liddy, general counsel to the campaign's finance division for the past three months, had refused to answer questions from the FBI. Stans fired Liddy immediately. "I did not know what the questions were that he did not answer," Stans later wrote, "or what his complicity was, but clearly I could not support his failure to cooperate with the investigative agency."

Because he was outside the "narrow orbit" of Nixon's inner circle, Stans was kept in the dark about the "frantic meetings" taking place to deal with the growing scandal. His job was to make sure money kept coming into the campaign.

On June 29, Anna Chennault brought Ernesto Lagdameo—a member of one of the wealthiest families in the Philippines, whom Chennault had feted with a party in her penthouse upon his appointment as ambassador to the United States—to meet Maurice Stans at the headquarters of the Committee for the Re-election of the President. Lagdameo presented $30,000 in cash, which he said was contributed in equal amounts by three donors, including himself. Because White House counsel John Dean had recently raised a red flag about accepting foreign contributions, Stans accepted the cash only on the understanding that he would check with counsel to be sure the contributions were legal to receive.

The following day, Chennault escorted Ambassador Lagdameo

and his wife into the Oval Office, for a photograph with Nixon. "Chennault, you're a real, real tiger—flying tiger," Nixon joked. "I really oughta get going to all these nice parties you people give. You give a real, real good ball."

A Nixon campaign attorney, Stanley Ebner, informed Stans the contribution could not be accepted legally, and Stans arranged for the money to be returned to Chennault, who then returned the funds to Lagdameo.

Stans considered the transaction "aborted" and, as he had returned the funds during the same reporting period in which they had been offered, did not disclose the funds as having been received by the Nixon campaign on the next campaign finance report.

AFTER MARTHA MITCHELL LEFT THE WESTCHESTER COUNTRY Club and returned to the Watergate, she became a virtual recluse. She told Winzola McLendon she was ashamed to see anyone, as she was distraught over the possibility her husband was involved in "something like Watergate." She soon realized her "self-imposed exile" was a mistake. Rumors flew around Washington that she had a "severe personal problem" and was "cracking up." "I played right into their hands," Martha lamented.

Martha reached out to a woman known in Washington social circles for her ability to sell household items discreetly, raising cash for her clients without drawing attention. This broker then contacted Mary Gore Dean, co-owner of the Jockey Club and widow of Gordon Dean, the first chairman of the U.S. Atomic Energy Commission. The two women met at a Watergate apartment. Dean hadn't been told whose it was, but within a few minutes realized she was in the home of Martha and John Mitchell.

Dean admired a blue corduroy sofa. They agreed on a price and the broker went downstairs to coordinate with the driver of a small moving van while Dean waited upstairs. A few minutes passed. Then Dean heard a man's voice outside the door and the jingle of keys. She raced into an adjoining study and hid in a closet just as a man entered the apartment. She listened as he wandered around the apartment, entered his study, fixed "a few drinks" and made phone calls laced with profanity. Eventually, he went upstairs, changed for dinner and left the apartment.

After a few minutes of silence, the front door opened and the furniture broker called out Dean's name. She gingerly stepped out of the closet. Furniture movers entered the apartment. They placed the sofa on a dolly and headed to the service elevator.

Years later, after John Mitchell finished his prison sentence and returned to Washington, he began a long-term romantic relationship with Mary Dean. By this time, the blue corduroy sofa had long been re-covered and was now in the apartment of her daughter, Deborah Gore Dean. One day, John and Mary were at Deborah's apartment. He sat on the sofa and, after a few minutes, paused. "I used to have a couch just like this," he said.

On July 1, John Mitchell stepped down as campaign manager of the Nixon reelection campaign. In his resignation letter, Mitchell wrote he was unable to serve the campaign full-time "and still meet the one obligation that must come first: the happiness and welfare of my wife and daughter." An unnamed Nixon campaign source confirmed Martha had failed to keep all of her campaign commitments in recent weeks. In response to the rumors that Martha had "a severe personal problem," Kay Woestendiek, Martha's former press secretary, denied Martha was an alcoholic, but speculated the pressures of the campaign "may have been too much."

"My bride was tired of traveling, of making speeches, nervous about flying, and I wasn't around much to help," John Mitchell told a reporter. "It was as simple as that."

On August 5, the *Washington Daily News* reported Martha and John Mitchell had sold their "swank" Watergate duplex to Senator Russell B. Long and his wife of two years, Carolyn. The Longs were giving up their two-bedroom unit on the sixth floor of Watergate

East to move into the "plush, spacious duplex with its magnificent views" on the seventh and eighth floors. Carolyn Long said she had set her sights on the apartment for some time. The Mitchells were reportedly relieved to keep the sale in-house, thereby avoiding the need to list the apartment and open it up to curiosity seekers. Martha told McLendon she was "upset" about the sale price, which she said was "ridiculously low."

Long told reporters she would make major changes to Martha Mitchell's décor. "Everybody's taste is different," she said.

Martha was delighted to leave Washington for New York. "I woke up at five this morning and said, 'Goodie, goodie, I'm leaving!' " she told McLendon. As she packed up her Watergate apartment, Marty Mitchell was downstairs saying goodbye to the staff of the Watergate bookstore. Martha dropped hints about getting involved in local politics in order to rattle John Lindsay, the mayor of New York, whom she detested, and promised to write her own book. "You bet!" she grinned. "I'm going to tell it all."

At a luncheon honoring Lola Aiken, wife of Senator George Aiken, a Republican from Vermont, Anna Chennault was seated near Carolyn Long. "We'll have to vote on whether to let you into our building," Anna teased, apparently forgetting the Longs already owned a unit in Watergate East, and could therefore skip both the co-op board interview and vote.

UNDER ITS LONGTIME CEO ARTHUR T. ROTH, FRANKLIN National Bank introduced many innovations to the banking business, including junior savings accounts, bank credit cards and the drive-up teller window. The Long Island–based bank opened its first branch in New York City in 1961; in 1967, Franklin merged with another institution, picking up thirteen new branches in Manhattan. To remain competitive in the New York market, Franklin gave loans to companies with low credit ratings who had been turned down by the major New York banks, charging these borrowers the same interest rates as prime customers and offering other incentives. In 1964, Franklin had assets of $1.5 billion; by 1972, it had $3.5 billion in assets, making it the twentieth-largest bank in the United States.

In July 1972, Michele Sindona paid $40 million in cash—at a premium of 25 percent above market value—for a 21.6 percent controlling interest in the common stock of Franklin New York Corporation, the holding company of Franklin National Bank. At the time of his investment in Franklin National Bank, *Forbes* magazine reported Sindona had a personal net worth of $100 million, including his one-third stake in Società Generale Immobiliare. "I am going to make Franklin National a great international bank," he told a reporter. "You must believe me. I only tell the truth."

"Sindona's reasons for buying into the bank remain an enigma," reported *Fortune* magazine. "What exactly has he got up his immaculately tailored sleeve?"

Sindona refused to comment. "In Italy I would go to jail if I disclosed any information about my clients," he said.

His secrecy inevitably provoked suspicion, in Europe and in the United States. "Some people say he is a financial genius of our century, but then others say he is a financial gangster," said one Swiss banker. "Probably the truth lies somewhere in between."

ON OCTOBER 9, 1972, THE LES CHAMPS AT WATERGATE shopping arcade opened for business. Built at a cost of $1 million, the "final touch" on the entire Watergate complex was the street-level collection of high-end retailers, including Yves St. Laurent, Gucci and Pierre Cardin, selling ready-to-wear clothing and accessories for men and women, and two dozen "international shops" including a Tunisian embroidery merchant; Batik Walla, which sold women's clothing from India and Pakistan; Midnight Sun (Scandinavian glass, china and gifts); William Miller (English gifts); a Uruguayan vendor selling rugs and leather goods; and "an oriental gift shop."

According to the *Washington Post*, the arcade had an "airport bazaar flavor." The Colette boutique sold "California sportswear," Red Balloon sold children's clothes and toys and Charles Schwartz carried china and fine crystal. There was a record store, a wig shop, an art gallery, a parfumerie and an optician "dealing primarily in fanciful sunglasses," as well as barometers and telescopes.

Les Champs was "very unique—very exclusive—different from any other mall in town," said Cecchi.

According to Henry Winston, general manager of the Watergate's retail operations, Les Champs was designed to attract Kennedy Center tourists and patrons, Watergate residents and office workers, and shoppers from the District and its suburbs.

To design the interiors, Cecchi hired Carlo Natale, who had designed the Les Champs mall in Paris, and George Lawson, a local designer familiar with the Watergate. Lawson designed the mall's main restaurant to look "like a French storage depot"—different sections of the restaurant resembled a storehouse with "imports from the colonies spilling over into each other," including rugs from the Orient and tiles from Morocco. An antique elevator cage served as a salad bar. Lawson told the *Washington Post* his goal was to create "something that will remind you of Humphrey Bogart in *Casablanca*."

In addition to the shops and restaurant, Les Champs boasted a cocktail lounge and an "espresso bar Italiano," targeting patrons of the adjacent Kennedy Center. "If necessary, I'll drink enough cups to keep it going," said Cecchi.

ON AUGUST 4, ROBERT M. CALDWELL, PRESIDENT OF THE Watergate East cooperative, sent a final report to residents regarding the pending proposal to refinance the Watergate East mortgage. "The serious financial and structural correction problems confronting the Board of Directors and Members of Watergate East, Inc.," Caldwell wrote, "have reached the most critical stage in this Corporation's six-year history.

"It is important to recognize," he continued, "that Watergate East is now an aging building, which has not been operated or maintained with an optimum of management supervision and direction.

"The initial high hopes of many owners that Watergate East represented a prestigious facility, constructed with the highest quality of materials and workmanship which would be trouble free and economical to operate," he added, "have repeatedly proven to be a constant and expensive disappointment."

He went on to itemize the problems, including leaks in the main roof; leaking windows and balconies; and the deterioration of the entrance marquee, requiring $60,000 to repair. Despite the developers' assurances, he said, repairs were only partially made and, moreover, "neither were all major defects realistically identified" and fully calculated. In addition, management had failed to build up cash reserves sufficient for addressing normal wear and tear to either the structure itself or its electrical and mechanical systems. As a result of this neglect, parts of the building were breaking down and residents were hit with unpredictable "Special Assessments."

The proposal to refinance the building's mortgage required a 75 percent affirmative vote of the owners, based on shares. As of August 4, the proposal was stuck at 70 percent support. Some residents questioned the repair estimates as "extravagantly high." Other residents said they had no interest in spending any new funds on the building, or at least suggested any repairs should be the responsibility of the developers, but Caldwell noted that the building was now six years old. "Your present Board," he said, "is not in as favorable a position as past administrations" in extracting payments from developers as a result of "the passage of time."

Maurice Stans was initially skeptical, but after careful review of Caldwell's memorandum and supporting documentation, signed the referendum, helping to meet the 75 percent vote requirement. He thanked Caldwell for his leadership but added two requests: Could the management address the absence of humidity control in the heating and cooling system, and heat the outdoor swimming pool?

ELIZABETH HANFORD AND HER BOSS, VIRGINIA KNAUER, director of the White House Office of Consumer Affairs, pitched Senator Bob Dole, a Kansas Republican and chairman of the Republican National Committee, to add a pro-consumer plank to the 1972 GOP platform. "It was the first time I met Bob," Elizabeth recalled later. "When a side door of his office opened to reveal a tall, dark stranger, I thought he was awfully attractive."

Dole noticed the Harvard-trained lawyer from North Carolina as well, and wrote her name on his blotter.

"Maybe so," Elizabeth said later. "But I didn't hear from him for several months."

Hanford and Dole crossed paths again at the Republican convention in Miami, when they ended up at the same party, thrown by GOP donor and insurance executive Clement Stone. Bob called her shortly thereafter and they talked for about forty minutes— "long enough to discover how many interests and friends we had in common," Elizabeth said. He called her again a few weeks later and suggested it might be nice to go out to dinner sometime. "It certainly would," she replied.

She waited for him to suggest a time and place, but Bob never followed up.

"Third time never fails," she wrote later. After another long telephone conversation, he invited her to dinner at the Watergate Hotel restaurant. He told her later he had hesitated because he was self-conscious about the thirteen-year difference in their ages. "He was a little shy," she said. "I liked that. It contrasted nicely with the image some have of Washington as a town full of ladies' men."

IN AUGUST, MICHELE SINDONA AND CARLO BORDONI WERE elected to the board of directors of Franklin New York Corporation.

The Bank of England had before it an application from Franklin to open a London branch and was uncertain about Sindona's resources and intentions. The bank was also concerned about Bordoni, a foreign exchange trader with a "poor reputation" in international banking circles. Bordoni had been asked to leave an Italian bank because he had concealed foreign trades; he was asked to leave the Milan branch of an American bank after he was accused of speculation and falsely reporting profits. The Bank of England delayed approval of the application and reached out to American regulators for more information.

Sindona recruited Peter Shaddick to manage the international division of Franklin National Bank. Shaddick was known to the Bank of England, which welcomed news of his appointment. In November, the international division of the U.S. Comptroller of the Currency assured the Bank of England that Franklin was under sound management. Franklin's London branch was authorized shortly thereafter. According to Shaddick, Sindona directed him to be aggressive and generate profits. According to the masterful and detailed history of the Franklin collapse by Joan Edelman Spero, profits from Shaddick's unit were intended to compensate for losses in other divisions. Franklin's foreign exchange trading, however, would "push the bank over the brink into disaster."

AS THE SCANDAL UNFOLDED THAT SUMMER AND FALL, Watergate residents turned on the evening news to see their complex as the backdrop to a criminal investigation. SGI executives in Rome asked Cecchi to keep them informed of any new developments, although there was nothing to be done. All Cecchi could do was pass along reports from the American press.

Nicolas Salgo observed the unfolding events from New York. He knew immediately the incident would become a burden for the hotel. Watergate didn't need the publicity. It was already known as the top luxury hotel in Washington. Hotel staff told him guests were taking anything that had the Watergate name on it and wasn't nailed down. A maid entered a room just as its occupant, a senior executive with a major American corporation, was packing his bags. The room had been stripped bare. Even the bedspread was missing. Towels were disappearing at a rate of $4,000 per month, recalled a hotel employee. "We had to go with anonymous towels," Cecchi recalled.

The Watergate complex was the subject of a cover story in the Sunday *New York Times* three weeks before Election Day. "There is only one place in the world, outside of fiction," Sherwood D. Kohn wrote, "where such a pretentious pot-au-feu of newsworthy people could simmer so richly and continuously in such a compact vessel."

Kohn called the complex "unsettling" and likened it to the decrepit Marienbad spa, depicted in the 1961 French-Italian film *Last Year at Marienbad*, directed by Alain Resnais. "Once disgorged into an empty hallway, visitors are likely to feel a little desperate," he wrote. "In the curving beige corridors that run through the south and east buildings of the 10-acre development, you can see little more than four doors at a time, and if you're looking for the elevator, there is nothing to tell you which way it lies. And of course you've forgotten which way you came from. Is that what it's like to be eaten by a snail?"

Kohn noted the constant presence of TV monitors throughout the complex. He wondered if it would be possible to knock on the doors of the apartments and "find out what kind of people" can make a dinner without producing "odors" that might seep into the hallways. That would be "gauche," he concluded. "These are private people, very private."

Privacy was the first casualty of the Watergate scandal.

Tourists gaped at the Watergate through glass-roofed buses and posed for pictures in front of the Watergate sign. Airline pilots approaching National Airport pointed out the Watergate to passengers, along with the Pentagon and the national monuments. The *New York Times* published a map of "The Watergate Tour," with stops at 2600

Virginia Avenue, home of the Democratic National Committee, and at Watergate Wine & Spirits for souvenir bottles of Scotch ($5.99 a bottle) or gin ($3.79). The map also suggested souvenir hunters stop at the Watergate Hotel and pick up, for 50 cents, a plastic black widow spider with a silver *W* on its back.

Cassie Mackin, an NBC Capitol Hill correspondent, was reading the Sunday edition of the *New York Times* in her Watergate West apartment. "All of a sudden," she said, "I had the feeling that someone was looking at me. I told myself that was ridiculous, but finally, I got up and looked out the window and on one of the top floors of the Howard Johnson's Motor Lodge across the street, a lady with a pair of binoculars was looking at me."

A WEEK BEFORE ELECTION DAY, MICHELE SINDONA AND PAUL Luftig, president of Franklin National Bank, met with Maurice Stans in New York. Stans had been informed that Sindona was willing to support Nixon "in a large way" and came right to the point.

"I understand you are convinced that Nixon's re-election is important and are willing to help us out financially in the campaign," Stans said.

"I believe it is important to the United States and the world and for all of us that he continue in office," Sindona replied, "and I am ready to give a million dollars."

Stans smiled and said he was delighted.

"There is only one condition," Sindona continued. "Because I am well known, I do not want any publicity or public recognition. And I am not asking any favors." Sindona later revealed he wished to conceal the source of the funds "so as not to subject the donors, including myself, to persecution by Italian leftists."

Stans explained that federal law required full disclosure of campaign contributions. Sindona expressed regret and told Stans that if he could find a way to proceed, the offer was still on the table. "I just turned down a million dollars," Stans confided to an aide. A few days later, he sent a letter "regretfully declining" the contribution. Stans's letter soon found its way to the leftist Italian press ("certainly not by me," Sindona later claimed), which accused Sindona of "exporting capital" from Italy "to support a capitalist, an enemy of the people."

ON NOVEMBER 7, 1972, RICHARD NIXON WAS REELECTED IN A landslide. Anna Chennault drafted a letter of congratulations. "I am not looking for a job," she wrote, but she reminded him others, including Defense Secretary Melvin Laird and Senator John Tower, had "independently" pushed her for a post in Nixon's first term. "However, due to some complications at that time," she wrote, "I decided not to approach this matter further." Now, however, she wanted to "be in some position where I could really help with the difficult Asiatic problems that lie ahead and about which I have some knowledge."

Chennault asked to be named "consul or goodwill ambassador to Asia." She recited her long résumé of Republican activism and business activities throughout the region, suggested there was "something to be gained politically by an appointment of a first woman of Oriental descent to a significant national job" and asked the president for a personal appointment to discuss the matter.

On January 8, 1973, Rose Mary Woods told President Nixon that Chennault had sent him a letter. "I didn't bother you with it," Woods said. "And I don't know whether it should see daylight. She sent it down to my desk saying she'd be appointed your special ambassador to the Far East, because nobody else understands the Far— you know, the Oriental mind."

Woods suggested forwarding Chennault's letter to the White House personnel director for handling. "And then he'll just brush it off," Nixon agreed. "It'll never reach the light of day."

A week after Nixon was sworn in to a second term, Transportation Secretary John Volpe, Anna's neighbor in the Watergate, appointed her to a three-year term on the Federal Aviation Administration's women's advisory committee. Chennault was unsatisfied with the token appointment and kept up the pressure for something more significant.

Tommy Corcoran met with Nixon one-on-one in the Oval Office on March 6. "You know, I have a protégé," Corcoran said. "Her name's Anna Chennault."

"Yeah, sure," said Nixon.

"She is one of the best and loyalest friends you've ever had."

"I know, I know."

"Mr. President, I have never written a book. I don't kiss and tell."

"Yeah."

"I am amazed at some of the people in your administration that break under pressure and talk too much."

"Yeah, yeah."

Corcoran told Nixon he knew what was "going on" in the 1968 campaign, "when Anna kept her mouth shut" at the request of Nixon's top aides.

"I know," said Nixon.

Anna Chennault "wrote you a letter not so long ago and she wonders whether you ever got it," Corcoran said. "She's asked you if she may have an interview with you alone by herself." Corcoran handed Nixon another copy of the letter. "That's her own writing," he said. "She's worth her weight in gold."

Anna Chennault never got her private meeting with Nixon.

AFTER THE DEMOCRATS' DISASTROUS 1972 ELECTION, IN which Richard Nixon carried forty-nine of fifty states, Robert Strauss was elected chairman of the Democratic National Committee. He asked former party treasurer Pat O'Connor to find new office space for the DNC. A commercial agent investigated the District's rental market and reported back, "You have the best deal in town."

Spencer Oliver advised Strauss to stay put in the Watergate indefinitely, as "a constant reminder of what the Republicans did." Oliver saw the political value of having every news story about the DNC, every press release the party issued, connected to the now-infamous word "Watergate." But Strauss, Oliver suspected, wanted to "turn the page" and erase any connection to the Watergate, perhaps to aid a future presidential bid by his friend John Connally, a former Democrat who was now Nixon's treasury secretary.

On April 15, 1973, the Democratic National Committee moved out of their sixteen-thousand-square-foot suite in the Watergate to a building near Dupont Circle. "It's more sensibly located," Strauss told the committee. "It's easier for people to come to town. It's two blocks from the hotels."

"It's a little more than we need, but less than we have."

DNC staffers were unhappy with the move. The new suite was smaller and darker than the Watergate office, and it was only a mile and a half closer to Capitol Hill.

As the Democrats were moving out, the *Post* reported, "Washington's most notorious piece of commercial property is also its most valuable," with a market value in excess of $50 million. Efficiency apartments in Watergate East, which sold originally for about $20,000, were now worth nearly $40,000. All but three units in Watergate South had been sold. Donald H. Richardson, a mortgage broker with John Hancock Life Insurance and owner of a three-bedroom apartment in Watergate West with a river view, told the *Post* he still regarded the Watergate as "a premier place to live."

"If that imposing complex called Watergate is bothered by all the publicity," observed Renata Smith Byrne, the "Woman's World" columnist for the *San Antonio Light*, "it isn't evident." Byrne had arrived in Washington to interview Anna Chennault, who was unexpectedly called away to New York, but was given a private tour of Chennault's apartment by her new social secretary, Lou Tower, wife of Senator John Tower. Anna's private cook, Miss Shun Tang Ying, prepared dumplings while the two women toured the apartment, which Byrne described as "deceptively fragile, with a happy mixture of antique Chinese and French furnishings." Security in the building, she noted, had been upgraded since the break-in at the DNC. Every apartment in Watergate East appeared to have been wired to an alarm system, which could be set off "by merely touching a door that has not been programmed for your opening."

As the DNC break-in approached its second anniversary, many retailers who had offered Watergate-themed souvenirs had moved out. "We're down to the more solid stores," Henry Winston told the *Washington Post*. "Most are not playing it up at all now." The Watergate Men's Shop, however, still offered $20 red silk ties embroidered with Watergate bugs. Melvin Norwood, owner of the shop, sold them to everyone from singer Tom Jones to the son of Saudi Arabia's King Faisal. "I couldn't have bought this kind of publicity for a million dollars," Norwood said. At the Watergate liquor store, Rip Packman continued to sell Watergate Scotch, gin, vodka and bourbon. "After the break-in, *everybody* wanted Watergate booze," he said. "Our sales shot up 35% to 50% and I've increased the sales staff from two to eight."

A political memorabilia show was held in the carpeted halls of Les Champs. "Out of respect for the Watergate," said the show's organizer, "we have left out anything that would be derogatory to either the present administration or the Watergate." Items related to Martha Mitchell, including a "Free Martha" campaign button, were banned.

After more than a year on the market, however, the DNC suite in the Watergate Office Building remained vacant. Watergate sales manager Lee Elsen turned to a local advertising firm for help. Don Vogel, the firm's creative director, concluded his client needed to embrace the space's history. He designed advertisements, placing them in the *Washington Post*, the *New York Times* and the *Wall Street Journal*, which read: "Don't be bugged with the commonplace. Locate your office at the Watergate . . . the prestige location in Washington that is *ne plus ultra*." Elsen sent a thousand executives around the nation a mailing about the suite, accompanied by a bug-shaped tie clasp.

The ad campaign, however, failed to generate a viable tenant.

"FRANK WILLS IS A BLACK MAN WHO ALWAYS HAS BEEN jinxed by one thing or another," *Jet* Washington bureau chief Simeon Booker reported in May 1973, in a six-page profile of the former Watergate Office Building security guard.

Wills only made it as far as eleventh grade in Savannah, Georgia. He enrolled in the Job Corps and studied heavy machine operation in Battle Creek, Michigan, "only to be barred from union membership and not allowed to work." He finally landed a job on a Ford assembly line in Detroit, but his asthma forced him to quit. He arrived in Washington in 1971 and worked at a few hotels before getting work as a guard with the private security firm GSS.

"It was a deadbeat job," *Jet* reported. And because Wills had no seniority, he was working the "lonely midnight-to-dawn shift" when he discovered tape on a door in the stairwell of the Watergate Office Building on the morning of June 17, 1972.

After the break-in, GSS promoted him to the rank of sergeant and gave him a small raise—about 40 cents a week, after taxes. "They said I did a pretty good job," he said, "but they seemed more interested in plugging the firm than in trying to help me." He left GSS for another security job paying $5 more a week, and with better working hours—4:00 P.M. to midnight.

"Everybody tells me I'm some kind of hero," he said, "but I certainly don't have any hard evidence."

He received awards from the Democratic Party and the Southern Christian Leadership Conference, and played himself in the movie version of *All the President's Men*.

Mills eventually moved to South Carolina to live with his mother, and was arrested in a discount store for stealing a $17 pair of sneakers in 1982. At the time of his arrest, he had been unemployed for at least a year. He was convicted and sentenced to one year in prison. When his mother died in 1993, he donated her body to medical science because he did not have enough money to bury her. Wills died of a brain tumor in Augusta, Georgia, at the age of fifty-two.

AS AN AUDIENCE OF 80 MILLION WATCHED GAVEL-TO-GAVEL coverage of the Senate Select Committee on Presidential Campaign Activities, chaired by Democrat Sam J. Ervin of North Carolina, Nixon aide Pat Buchanan made a new friend at the pool in the Watergate Hotel: *Rolling Stone* columnist Hunter S. Thompson. "Your work is hilarious," Buchanan said, and invited him over to meet Shelley and have a beer at their Watergate East apartment. "She thought he might show up stoned," Buchanan recalled years later, but when Thompson appeared at their door he was "neatly dressed" and, as far as either of them could tell, perfectly sober.

In late September, *Rolling Stone* published "Fear and Loathing at the Watergate," in which Thompson wrote of swimming laps in the hotel pool the night of the break-in, before joining Tom Quinn, a sportswriter for the *Washington Daily News*, at the hotel bar for shots of Sauza Gold Tequila and general disparagement of the National Football League's management.

At Watergate East, Pat Buchanan was awakened every morning at six by the sound of the *Washington Post* landing on the carpet outside their apartment. Before he reached the door, their Persian cat Cratchit "had bounded out of bed and was there, anticipating this daily run the length of the building and back as I scanned the Watergate headlines," Pat wrote later. "The arrival of the *Post* was the alarm that awakened us both."

One evening, Watergate East resident George Arnstein went down to the pool for a dip. When he got back to the apartment, his wife asked, "Who else was there?" "Oh," he replied, "only three or four people. But I was the only one who wasn't under indictment."

IN 1968, AT AGE SIXTY-ONE, LUIGI MORETTI MARRIED MARIA Teresa Albani, a secretary in the offices of Studio Moretti. She had arrived in the office earlier that year, and junior architects and other staff considered her to be "very aggressive." Adrian Sheppard, a young Canadian architect who worked briefly in Moretti's studio at the Palazzo Colonna, visited the couple when he returned to Italy after a long absence. Their relationship, he thought, appeared to be "not particularly cordial."

Moretti's diabetes had gravely affected his heart and liver, and he suffered a major heart attack. He convinced his doctors to allow him to cruise the Tyrrhenian Sea, off the western coast of Tuscany, telling them it would be good for his recovery. In fact, according to his nephew Tommaso Magnifico, a young architecture student and Moretti's surrogate son, Moretti knew he was fading.

Maria Teresa chartered a boat and invited several close friends, including Moretti's personal physician, to join them. A few days into the voyage, a storm approached and they were forced to drop anchor a few hundred yards off the island of Capraia, a penal colony. In the middle of the storm, Moretti died.

According to Italian law, Moretti's body could remain on the boat only seventy-two hours. Under no circumstances did Maria Teresa want her husband buried on a prison island. She managed to get word to Tommaso to come at once and bring his uncle's body back to Rome.

Tommaso hurried to Piombino, on the mainland, and convinced a local fisherman to take him out to the boat. Together they lifted Moretti's rapidly decomposing body into a coffin and returned to shore—all in the middle of a raging storm. More than fifty years later, as Tommaso told the story to a visitor, his eyes filled with tears. "It was one of the most horrible experiences of my life," he said.

Back in Canada, Adrian Sheppard, like millions of people all over the world, was glued to his television set watching the Watergate Committee hearings in Washington, DC. Suddenly, on the bottom of the television screen, scrolled a news flash: *Luigi Moretti . . . architect of the Watergate . . . has died in Italy. . . .*

There had long been friction between Maria Teresa and the architects who had worked for her husband. After he died, she became *"molto, molto, molto volitiva"* ("very, very, very volatile"). Under the name Studio "Moretti"—the quotation marks were intentional—junior architects who had worked for Luigi Moretti finished whatever jobs could be completed. Other projects were simply abandoned, including a villa commissioned by Moretti's longtime friend and client Aldo Samaritani. The young architects salvaged whatever files, drawings and models they could. Maria Teresa threw out everything else and closed the studio.

In his hospital room in Rome, before he died, Moretti confided to his nephew that the Watergate scandal in America had caused him great anguish. How could something he had created to be so positive, Moretti asked, be associated with something so negative?

"It is a cruel joke of destiny," he lamented.

AT THE AUGUST 1973 SGI BOARD MEETING IN ROME, DIREC-tors were informed that all 260 apartments in Watergate South had been sold; of the 241 garage spaces available, only four remained on the market.

In September, Watergate Improvements Inc. formed a new company, named West Alexandria Properties, to develop the Watergate Landmark. The proposed project would include four sixteen-story towers, each with four hundred residential units, in "a completely closed community with attended gate houses and private security guards." "Why live next door to Watergate at Landmark when you can live in it?" asked a full-page ad in the *Washington Post*:

Live in the most exciting condominium community on the East Coast. A 90 million dollar, 37 acre residential park totally enclosed with gatehouse entrances and private streets. A quiet, secure community with 22 acres reserved as private parkland. A 2 million dollar recreation meadow with indoor-outdoor everything: golf, tennis, swimming. A fabulous water complex, party island, sand beaches, clubhouse, and too many other features to list.

Security would be "tight" in the new development, a *Washington Post* real estate writer predicted.

IN OCTOBER, SALLY QUINN MOVED INTO THE WATERGATE apartment of Ben Bradlee, the executive editor of the *Washington Post*. He had left his wife of twenty-two years for Sally, he wrote later, "spang in the middle of Watergate, the most important story of a generation."

Bradlee and Quinn had started seeing each other secretly in June, and he knew he was at risk of blackmail by "the Nixon people," whom he assumed were following him around town. He did not want to compromise the paper, so he moved out of his house and into the Georgetown Inn briefly, before renting a Watergate South apartment in mid-September. Sally started as an on-air correspondent for *CBS Morning News* in the beginning of August, but when they emerged as a couple, she quit CBS and moved into the apartment.

"It was wild," she recalled of her brief stay at the Watergate. Ben and Sally would run into Bob Dole in the elevator or in the lobby, she recalled, "and it would be, 'Hey, Ben.' 'How are you, Bob?' or 'Hi, good to see you'—as if nothing was going on, as though the country wasn't falling apart." Dole and Bradlee were both veterans of World War II and shared a mutual respect. Seemingly every day, however, brought another Watergate story in the *Washington Post*, followed by a denunciation by Dole, who was then chairman of the Republican National Committee. But within the Watergate, "it was all very congenial."

Ben and Sally kept a log cabin in West Virginia as a weekend escape from around-the-clock pressure at the *Post*. "Ben was a woodsman," she recalled, "and he had an axe and a chainsaw. That was his way of dealing with Watergate—just disappear into the woods for eight hours a day and chop wood." In preparation for a weekend project, Bradlee purchased a gigantic chain to attach to his Jeep tractor. He stepped into the Watergate elevator with Sally; she was in jeans, he was in jeans and a workshirt, with the huge chain hanging over his shoulder. Nixon aide Victor Lasky stepped into the elevator. He looked first at Sally, and then at Ben. "Jesus, Bradlee," Lasky asked, "are you into *that*?"

ON OCTOBER 17, 1973, ANNA CHENNAULT THREW ANOTHER party at her Watergate East penthouse and presented $50,000 raised at the National Air Force Salute to three charities. Guests included her Watergate neighbor Arthur Burns of the Federal Reserve. Tommy Corcoran identified himself to a reporter as "the butler." It was a windy evening, but guests still climbed the marble spiral staircase to the roof, where her "dancing room" was filled with blooming chrysanthemums and geraniums.

Anna was introduced to her guests as the "queen of the Watergate." That may be true, she said, smiling, but "we're still taking orders from a man." Women at the party cheered.

The guest of honor was Senator Barry Goldwater of Arizona, and Vice President Spiro Agnew's recent resignation hung in the air. "This is the first time a Republican has been welcomed back to the Watergate," Goldwater joked.

AFTER WATERGATE SPECIAL PROSECUTOR ARCHIBALD COX issued a subpoena to the Nixon White House for taped conversations, Nixon offered to allow Senator John C. Stennis, a Republican from Mississippi who was notoriously hard of hearing, to listen to the tapes and summarize them. Cox rejected the offer, and on Saturday, October 20, 1973, Nixon ordered U.S. Attorney General Elliot Richardson to fire Cox. Richardson refused, as did his deputy, William Ruckelshaus, and both men resigned. Solicitor General Robert Bork was summoned to the White House, sworn in as acting attorney general, and fired Cox. The events of that evening became known as the Saturday Night Massacre.

On November 4, Republican senator Edward W. Brooke of Massachusetts appeared on ABC's *Issues and Answers* program. Brooke said he hoped Nixon had not committed an impeachable offense, but in the wake of the Saturday Night Massacre the president was "too crippled to lead" and should resign. Nine days later, Brooke was summoned to the family quarters of the White House, with a handful of other Republican senators, to meet with Nixon. "This Watergate thing has gotten out of hand," Nixon said, and asked them for advice. "Mr. President," Brooke said, "I think you have lost the trust and faith of the American people. For the good of yourself and your family, for the good of the Republican Party, and more important, for the good of the American people, I think you should resign." The president stared straight into Brooke's eyes. "That would be taking the easy way out, the cowardly thing to do," Nixon said.

With one exception, the other senators present jumped to Nixon's defense. "Stick it out, Mr. President," said one. "Don't listen to Ed," said another.

After Brooke returned to his Watergate East apartment late that evening, he heard a knock on the door. It was his neighbor from down the hall, Rose Mary Woods. She was livid and unleashed a "profanity-laced tirade."

"You don't understand," he protested. "I don't have anything against the president personally. I only said what I believed, and I only gave him advice I would give myself. It was not mean-spirited." Woods continued "to take vehement exception," Brooke later recalled.

"I'm sorry you feel this way," he said. "I hope you will understand." She gave him what he called "one last choice epithet" and walked away.

The next morning in the Watergate garage, Brooke found a long, deep scratch on the door of his prized 1973 Mercedes-Benz convertible.

That Christmas, Shelley and Pat Buchanan attended a party at Rose Mary Woods's apartment, one floor above theirs in the Watergate. Pat told his fellow White House aides he felt the president had made "a grave mistake" in not releasing the transcripts of his conversations with former White House counsel John Dean. The situation was now terminal, Pat said.

A former White House speechwriter who was at the party leaked Pat's conversation to the *Washington Post* and the *St. Louis Post-Dispatch*, which quoted an unnamed "speechwriter" as saying, "It's like the *Titanic* . . . when the iceberg hit, passengers up on deck barely felt the ship shudder. But down below, the damage control men computed the flooding rate, consulted their charts, and told the captain, 'Never mind how things look now—she's going down.'"

"Unfortunately," Pat wrote later, "the quote was accurate. Nixon could not have missed it."

PETER SHADDICK'S TRADERS AT FRANKLIN NATIONAL BANK were inexperienced in dealing with floating exchange rates and in January 1973, expecting the U.S. dollar to continue to rise, took short positions in various currencies. By November 1973, Franklin had bet $62.6 million shorting other currencies; by May 1974, the bank's net short position was over $230 million. Shaddick and Bordoni concealed trading losses in part by entering into fictitious contracts with two Sindona-owned banks, Banca Unione of Milan and Amincor Bank, A.G., of Zurich. In September 1973, for example, Franklin's international division lost $244,000, but reported $1.5 million in foreign exchange profits. In the first five months of 1974, as the U.S. dollar fell against other major currencies, Franklin's traders lost $33 million.

On May 1, 1974, the Federal Reserve rejected an application by Franklin National Bank's parent company to acquire Talcott National Corporation, another financial entity in which Sindona held a 53 percent stake. "In rejecting the bid," *Business Week* reported, "the Fed dropped a trail of hints suggesting it had little confidence in Franklin's management." On Friday, May 10, Franklin National Bank canceled its second-quarter dividend—the first time since the Depression that a major bank had skipped a dividend—and announced losses of approximately $40 million in its foreign exchange unit. On Monday, May 13, Peter Shaddick resigned from Franklin, and the Securities and Exchange Commission halted trading in Franklin's stock.

On May 14, Italian newspapers reported Franklin's staggering losses in foreign trading, which led to rumors that Edilcentro Sviluppo, the SGI subsidiary reporting to Carlo Bordoni, was involved in the losses. SGI's stock price began to fall.

A reporter who visited Michele Sindona in his Milan office described him as "nervous" and "high strung." As Sindona sat for the interview, he folded multicolored squares of paper into little boats, which he stacked meticulously on his desk. By June, his stake in Franklin National Bank, for which he had paid $40 million in 1972, was worth less than $9 million.

Customers of Sindona's Italian banks began withdrawing funds and Sindona was forced to inform Italian regulators that his banks faced a liquidity crisis. At the direction of the Bank of Italy, the Banca di Roma extended $100 million in credit to Sindona, who put up his shares in SGI as collateral.

ON JUNE 21, 1974, WALTER PFORZHEIMER RETIRED FROM THE
CIA. When the Historical Intelligence Collection at the CIA had
been established eighteen years earlier, it had 1,190 books. Now, the
collection had grown to 22,000 volumes. Pforzheimer's worldwide
scavenger hunt had brought to the CIA at least 150 different books
about the Dreyfus affair; more than fifty books about intelligence
failures on the eve of the Japanese attack on Pearl Harbor; and a
small, privately printed book on the Boer War, written by an eight-
year-old named Allen Dulles, who would grow up to become director of the CIA.

The same day, the *New York Times*, citing "well-informed
sources," reported Republican officials in 1972 drew up a list of
companies and individuals who had "problems" with the government and targeted them for campaign contributions.

THE JULY 1974 BOARD MEETING OF SGI WAS HELD IN MILAN
rather than Rome. The chairman, Count Enrico Pietro Galeazzi, informed his colleagues that Carlo Bordoni had resigned as a director
and delegate board member, a post he had held only since March,
as well as from all other offices held in SGI affiliates, in Italy and
abroad. In his letter of resignation, Bordoni assured the board his
decision "was motivated by the desire to have the greatest freedom
to defend himself from tendentious and defamatory insinuations
published in recent days in the national press in connection with
the well-known events." Michele Sindona reassured the board that
Bordoni was "extraneous" to the "problems" with Franklin National
Bank, which he said were limited to *"operazioni non registrate"* ("un-
recorded activities") which were completely the fault of *"funzionari"*
("certain executives") who had either been fired or resigned already,
possibly referring to Peter Shaddick. Sindona confidently said he expected Bordoni to mount a vigorous attack on newspapers that had
spread "calumnious" reports.

Sindona then proposed as a new board member Giovanni Battista Fignon, the central manager of Banca di Roma. Fignon lasted only a few weeks on the board before resigning; he was replaced by a more senior executive from Banca di Roma, Danilo Ciulli, the bank's vice chairman, who was immediately elevated to delegate board member and vice chairman, giving him the same rank and powers as Aldo Samaritani.

ON AUGUST 5, 1974, THE "SMOKING GUN" TAPE WAS REvealed. Three days later, President Nixon addressed the nation a final time from the Oval Office and announced his intention to resign the presidency. "By taking this action," he said, "I hope that I will have hastened the start of that process of healing which is so desperately needed in America." He resigned on August 9 at noon, and said goodbye to his closest staff in the East Room of the White House, before boarding a marine helicopter and beginning the long flight to California.

As President Gerald Ford moved into the Oval Office, Nixon's personal effects were removed to his former hideaway office in the Old Executive Office Building next door, under the watchful eye of Rose Mary Woods. The office was exactly as he had left it. His glasses rested on his desk. His ashtray held a half-smoked cigar.

Robert Gray, the executive vice president of Hill & Knowlton and former secretary to the Eisenhower cabinet, escorted Rose to parties and dinners around town, even when she said she was too tired to go out. They went out two or three nights a week. She seemed more comfortable at large parties, friends said, because it was easier for her to make small talk and avoid discussing Watergate. Gray told a reporter he had no idea how long Rose would remain in Washington. "When your mother comes to visit, do you ask her how long she's going to stay?" he said. "She's living one day at a time. She loves her apartment, and all of her friends are here in Washington. But a year from now, who knows?" In February 1975, the contents of Nixon's hideaway office were finally crated and sent to the former president's home in San Clemente. Rose, however, did not follow the boxes to California. She sold her Watergate East apartment and returned to Ohio.

The youngest member of the Nixon administration to appear in the August 1969 issue of *Life* magazine was White House press aide Nancy Lammerding, who was photographed at the time wearing a cast—the result of a fall—which kept her out of the Watergate swimming pool. During the 1968 Nixon campaign, Nick Ruwe was known as one of the top advance men—staffers who traveled ahead of the candidate, making logistical arrangements for political rallies and other events—in Republican circles and Nancy was considered "the best-dressed girl in the Nixon campaign." Before the cloud of Watergate descended on the Nixon White House, Nick recruited Nancy to work with him at the State Department's protocol office, hiring her away from White House press secretary Ron Ziegler's staff. After Nixon resigned, Nancy went back to the White House to become First Lady Betty Ford's social secretary and Nick stayed at the State Department. Nick proposed to Nancy over dinner at the Sans Souci restaurant and the couple planned a formal engagement announcement in the *New York Times*. In the steam room of the Watergate health club, however, Nick told a friend he and Nancy were getting married. Their conversation was overheard by a reporter from the New York *Daily News*, who phoned Nancy for confirmation, thereby scooping the *Times*.

IN SEPTEMBER 1974, MARIO BARONE, PRESIDENT OF BANCA di Roma, disclosed that Sindona's entire $200 million line of credit had been used up and future losses from "unrecorded speculation and transactions" by Sindona could be "major." Italian regulators discovered an additional $50 million in foreign exchange losses at SGI and prosecutors in Milan issued a warrant for Sindona's arrest. Italian newspapers called the collapse *il caso Sindona*—"the Sindona case." *Business Week* had another name for the scandal: "Italy's Watergate."

Back in Rome, at the September meeting of the SGI board, Danilo Ciulli, the vice chairman of Banca di Roma, revealed that an investigation into SGI's finances, made difficult by "imperfect accounting and, above all, by the incompleteness of information," had confirmed heavy losses in the financial division—as much as 40 billion lira, or about $64 million. Despite several attempts to find him, Carlo Bordoni could not be located. The board voted unanimously to abolish the ill-fated financial division and extend a "formal invitation to Bordoni" to appear before them and explain his actions in full.

Samaritani informed his colleagues the company could absorb these losses and honor its debts, including $23 million owed to the Banca di Roma. But all foreign activity of the company—including the Watergate-style complex planned in Alexandria, Virginia, and the massive development planned for outside Mexico City, an original part of Samaritani's grand plan for North America—would have to be abandoned.

In September, Michele Sindona resigned from the board of Franklin National Bank. On October 3, he resigned from the board of SGI. Franklin National Bank was declared insolvent a week later, the largest bank failure in U.S. history. On October 9, Frank Willie, chairman of the FDIC, announced Franklin had been taken over by the European-American Bank & Trust Company, owned by six of Europe's largest banks. As Willie announced the bank's new owners, Italian authorities issued a warrant for the arrest of Michele Sindona in connection with irregularities on the balance sheets of one of his Italian banks.

ON OCTOBER 24, 1974, CBS AND THE *NEW YORK TIMES* BOTH reported Maurice Stans was under investigation on five possible charges, including bribery, extortion, knowingly accepting illegal contributions, sale of ambassadorships and failure to disclose campaign contributions.

Through his attorneys, Stans maintained his complete innocence and refused to engage in plea bargaining. The prosecutors, a team of "eager-beaver" lawyers led by Tom McBride, forty-four, a former assistant district attorney in New York and a veteran of the Organized Crime Section of the U.S. Department of Justice, made it equally clear that unless Stans submitted to questioning under oath, they would indict him on a multitude of charges.

Following the break-in at the DNC, Stans had been sued by the Democratic National Committee and its chairman, Larry O'Brien, for conspiring to disrupt the 1972 election, for $6.4 million; the Association of State Democratic Chairmen and its director, R. Spencer Oliver, sued Stans for another $10 million. A federal grand jury indicted him on ten counts of conspiracy, obstruction of justice and perjury, carrying potential sentences of fifty years in prison and a fine of $100,000. His successful defense against those charges lasted a year, but cost him hundreds of thousands of dollars in legal fees. He was sued in various civil actions for a total of more than $95 million, nearly a hundred times his net worth. And since August 1972, when his wife, Kathy, collapsed at their Watergate apartment early one morning, she had been in and out of hospitals, battling a rare blood disease.

Stans gave in to the prosecutors' demands. Without legal immunity, he answered questions from McBride and his staff for 110 hours. "When we finished, I was sure that everything had been fully covered and resolved to their satisfaction," Stans wrote later.

He could not have been more wrong.

McBride insisted Stans was not being forthcoming and was shielding "guilty people." He threatened to indict Stans on six counts.

"It was a no-win situation," Stans wrote later. His legal fees had already topped $700,000—some of which was reimbursed by the

1972 Campaign Liquidation Trust—and another trial might cost $250,000 or more. "Our analysis of the chances of fairness in a trial was not reassuring. I gave up, reluctantly, and in anguish."

Stans pleaded guilty to non-willful receipt of two illegal campaign contributions, including $30,000 from the 3-M Company and $40,000 from Goodyear, and three violations of campaign reporting laws, including one count involving a $30,000 cash contribution from Ernesto Lagdameo, arranged by Anna Chennault.

After checking with counsel, who concluded foreign contributions to the campaign were illegal, Stans had returned the funds to Chennault, who then returned the money to Lagdameo. But Stans did not disclose the contribution at the time. "No purpose would have been served by reporting a transaction that was never completed," he wrote later. The Nixon campaign in fact reported the contribution on June 10, 1973, following an internal audit. For the late reporting of that transaction, and for each of the other four misdemeanor charges, Stans was fined $1,000.

AT THE OCTOBER 22 BOARD MEETING OF SGI, DIRECTORS confronted more bad news. Debts totaling 58.8 billion lira—about $86 million—were owed to various banks. The company owed dividends to shareholders. Revenues were lower than expected. With the company's credit in tatters, there were no options for short-term borrowing. Samaritani informed his colleagues that they would need to consider selling "important properties," including the galleria Les Champs in Paris, the hotel Le Mirabeau in Monte Carlo, the Port Royal building in Montreal and two buildings designed by the late Luigi Moretti: SGI's own headquarters in Rome's EUR district, and Moretti's masterpiece on the shores of the Potomac River, the Watergate.

In November 1974, the board of Società Generale Immobiliare was informed Banca di Roma had sold its controlling interest in the firm to "a group of noted and qualified exponents of the construction industry." The new shareholders were members of a class of builders known in Rome as *palazzinari*.

A *palazzina* is a small building. A *palazzinaro*, Giuseppe Cecchi explained to a visitor years later, was a "displeasurative term" used within Rome's real estate circles to describe a "builder of small buildings." *La Repubblica* described the heyday of the *palazzinari* as "a huge feast: of bogus contracts, but above all of buying and selling under a shadow of ill repute." The future of SGI was now in their hands.

After more than thirty years as a member of the SGI board, including six years as chairman, Count Galeazzi announced his resignation. "The unexpected cyclone that has fallen upon the Company," he said, "makes even more pressing my desire to make room for someone better adapted for the special needs of the moment and less handicapped by age."

Aldo Samaritani spoke next. He asked his colleagues not to reelect him vice chairman of the board. At the conclusion of his term, he would leave the company and surrender all responsibilities he held in its subsidiaries. He said he had arrived at his decision carefully, motivated by "his strong desire to dedicate himself to his family" and by the "necessity of looking after his health." After forty-two years with SGI, Samaritani "considered his mandate concluded, although with profound bitterness and disappointment caused him by the events which had lately troubled the Company."

IN MARCH 1980, MICHELE SINDONA WAS CONVICTED ON sixty-eight counts of fraud, perjury and misappropriation of bank funds. He was sentenced to twenty-five years in the federal prison at Otisville, New York, but was extradited to Italy in 1984 to stand trial for his role in the collapse of Banca Privata Finanziaria and for illegally diverting funds from Italy to banks he owned abroad. On March 22, 1986, four days after an Italian court convicted him of arranging the assassination of Giorgio Ambrosoli, the liquidator of his bank holdings, Sindona was found dead in his prison cell after drinking coffee laced with cyanide. "They have poisoned me," he told a prison guard, just before collapsing into a coma.

The board of Società Generale Immobiliare dissolved the company and liquidated its assets in 1988. At the time of its demise, the company was 126 years old.

ON AUGUST 12, 1975, KATHY AND MAURICE STANS SPENT their last night in their Watergate apartment. Kathy served dinner in their Africana room, among the artifacts from various safaris and other adventures. More than three years had passed since the Sunday morning Maurice Stans picked up the *Washington Post* and first learned of the break-in at the DNC.

"The maelstrom was over," Maurice Stans wrote. "Its sheer revolving force would draw no more bodies and souls into the depths of its destruction, spewing out their shattered remains."

As the sun set over the Potomac, they reflected on the disasters that had engulfed so many friends. Some had admitted guilt; others had been convicted after lengthy, humiliating trials. Kathy and Maurice considered themselves fortunate. They were older than most of their friends, and had lived rich and full lives before it all happened.

The next morning, movers came and packed up their belongings. Everything went into storage. Kathy and Maurice decided to become nomads and travel a bit.

Their next home? They had no idea.

PART II

CHAPTER SIX: A LITTLE BLOOD

Does your dog need "a meaningful walk"? Is your old chess set worn from overuse and do you crave a $500 "hand-carved solid walnut Renaissance style" substitute? Are your scattered curios orphans and would a $250 lighted curio cabinet of solid fruitwood provide them with a decent home?

The various bulletin boards at the various Watergates take care of all these basic needs and much more. No cheapie post-Christmas sales are offered here. The bulletin boards are the gleaming reflections of the gleaming incomes of the gleaming residents, after all.

Washington Post, January 18, 1975

IN OCTOBER 1974, IN A COURTROOM IN BORDEAUX, PROSE-cutors presented their opening arguments in the trial of eight wine dealers for charges of fraud.

Since 1819, the Cruse family had been at the center of Bordeaux's commercial and social life. They had cellars on the Quai des Char-trons and a magnificent chateau in the Médoc. "The wine trade is to France what the automobile business is to the United States," observed *New York Times* wine columnist Frank J. Prial, "and the Cruse concern is easily the General Motors of the French wine world."

In June 1973, French tax inspectors, acting on a tip from an informer, entered the Cruse offices and demanded to review records. The owners tossed the inspectors out onto the street and denounced their "Gestapo methods." But the government's inquiry continued, culminating in a wide range of charges against the Cruse empire and a number of smaller vintners and exporters, including: up-grading cheap Midi wines to expensive Bordeaux by falsifying documents; sending lower-quality wines to the American market and labeling them Puligny-Montrachet or Meursault; and selling German consumers inexpensive 1970 white Bordeaux, misrepre-

sented as the prized—and costly—1969 white Graves. French authorities also charged some undrinkable wines were "recovered" by the
use of chemicals, including 84,000 gallons of wine that were "de-
odorized" by passing through charcoal filters. The legitimacy of
two million bottles of red Bordeaux Superior was in doubt.

After a ten-day trial, Lionel Cruse and his cousin Yvan were convicted of fraud and each fined 27,000 francs—about $6,000. The
New York Times reported the verdicts were "little more than wrist-
slapping," considering the damage the two men had done to the
reputation of the French wine trade. Pierre Bert, a wine broker, was
sentenced to a year in jail. Five smaller wine merchants received
suspended sentences and paid fines and back taxes.

According to Benoît Lecat, head of the wine and viticulture
department of California Polytechnic State University in San Luis
Obispo, California, the scandal damaged the reputation of Bordeaux wine merchants and resulted in a loss of trust between wine
consumers and vintners. In the aftermath of the scandal, French
authorities imposed strict new regulations on the industry. Although
wine merchants in Bordeaux bounced back from the scandal quickly
and resumed exports, an entire class of wine merchants in nearby
Burgundy was wiped out and local vintners were forced to bottle
their own wines and sell directly to consumers.

On the eve of the trial, Lionel Cruse dismissed the charges
against him as a "pseudo scandal" and defiantly proclaimed, "I
will be the Nixon of Bordeaux." According to Cruse, Nixon was
the victim of "a campaign of calumny orchestrated by the leftist, Washington press." The Paris newspaper *Le Monde*, however,
suggested the vintner's analogy was "an imprudent parallel," as
the former president had resigned in disgrace. The *Times*'s Prial
noted similarities between the Bordeaux and Watergate scandals,
including the disappearance and possible destruction of records.
The French named the affair "Winegate."

New York Times columnist and former Nixon speechwriter

William Safire, in his *New Political Dictionary*, defined the "-gate construction" as "a device to provide a sinister label to a possible scandal." According to Safire, the Bordeaux "winegate" affair was the first post-Nixon scandal to earn the "-gate" suffix.

NICOLAS SALGO ANSWERED HIS PHONE.

"May I talk to you?" asked Mario Barone, chairman of Banca di Roma.

"Sure," said Salgo. "What's on your mind?"

Banca di Roma, as one of Michele Sindona's largest creditors, had inherited his sizable stake in Società Generale Immobiliare and its real estate portfolio, including the Watergate. On paper, day-to-day operations at the Watergate appeared to be losing money. "We need somebody to clean it out," Barone said. "Would you be interested?"

Salgo had left the Watergate under less than ideal circumstances: Shortly after acquiring the Vatican's shares in SGI, Sindona fired him. The only reason the dismissal didn't sting was the last Watergate building had opened by then and there wasn't much more for Salgo to do.

"It so happens I don't have much to do right now, so I'm interested," Salgo replied. He had recently sold his interest in Bangor Punta, a conglomerate whose holdings included the Smith & Wesson firearms manufacturer and Piper Aircraft. "What are you proposing?"

"You write your own ticket," Barone said. "Just clean out the mess."

Nicolas Salgo returned to the Watergate and quickly discovered the payroll had nearly doubled in his absence. The Watergate's property management office, responsible for overseeing the hotel, two office buildings and the common areas—the three Watergate apartment buildings were managed by their respective cooperative associations—now employed thirty-two people.

"Where in the hell do you put thirty-two people here?" Salgo asked, looking around the cramped offices in Watergate East.

"There are only eighteen of us," shrugged the office manager. "The others never show up, ever."

Salgo demanded a letter of resignation from every employee by the end of the day. He received letters from eighteen and rehired each of them on the spot. He declared the other fourteen "absent without leave" and dismissed them.

"Overnight," Salgo recalled later, "I created a positive cash flow. I've never had an easier clean-up job."

There was one other casualty of the transition of power from Sindona to the new owners of SGI, the *palazzinari*. As SGI shut down its international operations, it abandoned the Watergate Landmark project in Alexandria, Virginia, and eliminated Giuseppe Cecchi's job managing the development. He was offered another job with SGI, but only if he returned to Rome. Fifteen years after he first arrived in America, "Joe" Cecchi now had a wife and family to consider. He had no interest in uprooting his family. Besides, SGI was no longer the company his father, Antonio, had helped to build, working side by side with Aldo Samaritani.

Cecchi submitted his letter of resignation. He decided to stay in America and go into the real estate development business for himself.

Watergate at Landmark was completed by another developer. Among its first residents: FBI associate director Mark Felt, later known by the pseudonym "Deep Throat," who was a member of the condominium association board of directors and helped draft its bylaws.

BOB DOLE FACED A TOUGH REELECTION RACE IN KANSAS IN 1974, like many Republicans running in the immediate aftermath of Richard Nixon's resignation. A Labor Day poll showed Dole losing by six points to his opponent, Democratic congressman Bill Roy. From the campaign trail, Bob would often call Elizabeth Hanford at her Watergate East apartment, sometimes as late as one or two in the morning. Hearing her voice, he said, gave him something to look forward to each day.

Bob called Elizabeth on election night and gave her the good news: He had just won reelection by the razor-thin margin of 13,532 out of 794,434 votes cast. He looked forward to celebrating with her when he returned to Washington. "Don't you remember?" she asked. "I'm leaving for Japan tomorrow!" She had previously committed to a three-week trip to Japan, as part of a delegation of young political leaders.

When Elizabeth returned to her apartment, she was greeted by a bottle of champagne from the Watergate Wine Shop and a dozen red roses from the Watergate Florist. "I knew that things were getting serious," she recalled.

Bob told her he wanted to be sure he had a job before he popped the question. "He never got down on his knees," Elizabeth wrote later. "Come to think of it, I don't even remember a formal proposal."

They were married in Washington Cathedral's Bethlehem Chapel on December 6, 1974. Elizabeth moved into Bob's "townhouse" duplex with an outdoor patio, Apartment 114, Watergate South.

ANNA CHENNAULT'S FRIENDSHIP WITH GERALD FORD DATED to their first meeting in 1949, when Ford was a first-term Republican congressman from Michigan. As House minority leader and later as vice president, Ford was a frequent guest at Anna's round dining table in her Watergate apartment. At one dinner covered by the *Washington Post*, Congressman Ford joined in a chorus of "Old MacDonald" with the former director of South Korea's intelligence agency, the former prime minister of Korea and retired general William Westmoreland. Senator John Tower read lines from *Hamlet* and Secretary of Transportation John Volpe sang a tarantella—in Italian. "I always resent it when they say Republicans give a dull party," Anna said, toasting her guests, to laughter and applause. In

September 1974, a few weeks after Nixon's resignation, Anna Chennault threw a dinner party in her penthouse and invited some of the new aides to President Gerald Ford. After dinner, Congressman Bob Michel, a Republican from Illinois, led guests in a sing-along as Tommy Corcoran played the piano. The last guest left around 2:00 A.M. Chennault invited the *Washington Star* to report on the evening, but insisted the article identify her as a "business executive, not hostess."

Ford invited Corcoran to "come in and talk about things" whenever he wished, but Corcoran waited until August 1975, more than a year into Ford's presidency, to accept the invitation. "It's about Anna Chennault," Corcoran wrote.

Anna has quietly told me that she has been deeply disappointed when in your Administration—as distinguished from its Kennedy-Johnson-Nixon predecessors—no invitation has been extended to her when leaders from Asia were dinner guests at your White House. This especially concerned her when White House guests were Prime Minister Lee Kuan Yew of Singapore whom she knows well and Minister Miki from Japan and many other of her V.I.P. friends from the Orient.

Lee Kuan Yew visited the White House on May 8, 1975, and the President and Mrs. Ford hosted a state dinner that evening. President Ford's black-tie dinner for Prime Minister Takeo Miki on August 5 was "stag"—there were no women among the thirty-five guests at the "working dinner."

Anna has "wondered" to me whether this is an oversight or deliberate policy on the part of the State Department—or some functionaries in the White House and the National Security Council—to exclude anyone who had relationships with the previous Administration.

It's hard to believe but I have long well known how
functionaries arrange for themselves matters within their
jurisdiction. I am sure and she is sure any "discrimination"
against her is not your or Mrs. Ford's personal intention.
  But as a friend may I alert you that the "wonder" exists.

Two weeks later, Robert T. Hartmann, counselor to President Ford, reviewed a list of potential guests for the forthcoming state dinner honoring the emperor of Japan. The list included Seiji Ozawa, conductor of the Boston Symphony; John D. Rockefeller III, president of the Japan Society; *CBS Evening News* anchor Walter Cronkite; the actor Peter Falk, star of *Columbo*, the "most popular TV show in Japan"; and Watergate residents Marian and Jacob Javits. Hartmann sent the list back to the White House Social Office, headed by Nancy Ruwe, and added a cover note. "The President requested," he wrote, "that I also remind you that Mrs. Anna Chennault should be given consideration for this or future State Dinners involving Asian leaders by virtue of her role as Vice Chairman of the National Republican Heritage Group Council," a GOP entity charged with reaching out to ethnic and national minorities.

Within weeks, Anna received an engraved invitation to attend the state dinner in honor of the emperor and empress of Japan.

Peter Gruenstein, a lawyer and former congressional aide and editor of the Capitol Hill News Service, which provided investigative reporting on Congress for small papers and other media outlets that did not have the budgets to operate major national bureaus, spotted a reference to "entertainment" in a document filed by Northrop Corporation with the Securities and Exchange Commission and decided to dig around for more information. He unearthed a draft report by the Defense Contract Auditing Agency, which found that up to $11,000 was spent by Northrop in 1972 for parties, attended by company executives, foreign officials and top Pentagon officials, to promote sales of Northrop's F-5 fighter jets to Asian nations. Northrop had submitted the expenses to the defense department for reimbursement; the auditing agency had ruled they were "unallowable."

On September 15, 1975, the Capitol Hill News Service reported Northrop Corporation improperly billed the federal government $11,000 for parties hosted by Anna Chennault in her Watergate penthouse. Senator William Proxmire, a Wisconsin Democrat with a national reputation for finding and exposing government waste, said Chennault's parties amounted to "a Defense Department subsidy of the Washington cocktail circuit. Every time the Pentagon buys a weapons system from Northrop, the taxpayer shares the cost of these parties." Gruenstein's discovery made the *Washington Post* the next day, as part of a larger story about the payment of "finder's fees" to middlemen who assist in landing defense contracts, and appeared a week later in the "Ear" gossip column in the *Washington Star*:

> You probably read that Northrop, the jet folks, billed the government for $11,000 of your taxes for Dragon Lady Anna Chennault's penthouse wingdings. Do you think it matters, Earwigs, that Mrs. John Tower works right there in Anna's office with her? You know Sen. John Tower of Texas, of the Armed Services Committee and Joint Committee on Defense Production?

On October 2, 1975, the President and Mrs. Ford hosted the state dinner for the emperor and empress of Japan. Sally Quinn covered the evening for the *Washington Post*. The royal couple were "so tiny and sweet-looking and so frail they almost look like little dolls on top of a wedding cake," Quinn wrote. After dinner and a performance by pianist Van Cliburn, the seventy-four-year-old emperor and his wife said good night; the Fords stayed behind for another hour and a half, "doing the Charleston and generally stirring things up." The guest list included the Milwaukee Brewers' Hank Aaron, who had broken Babe Ruth's RBI record five months earlier; the fashion designer Halston; the dancer and choreographer Martha Graham and the movie star Ginger Rogers, who danced with the president. "He's a lovely dancer," Rogers told Quinn. "Perfect rhythm. He talks while he's dancing, too." For the first time since June 15, 1972—the night before the Watergate break-in—Anna Chennault attended a state dinner. She brought Tommy Corcoran as her escort.

Four days later, the *Washington Post* reported defense department auditors had discovered Northrop had paid Chennault $160,000 in "consultant" fees since 1971 and billed those costs against their federal contracts. "In view of entertainment, which appears to be a significant part of her duties," auditors concluded, "and in the absence of activity reports to establish that (her) services are bona fide," Chennault's fees could not be billed to the government.

On October 12, the *Philadelphia Inquirer* reported Chennault was "secretly" paid more than $1,000 a month by Northrop, beginning in 1971, "to entertain political and military brass in a position to influence defense contracts." Among those she "wined and dined in her Watergate penthouse" was the House Republican leader at the time, Congressman Gerald Ford, the *Inquirer* reported. "The Fords, perhaps for other reasons, reciprocated recently by inviting Mrs. Chennault to the White House state dinner for Japanese Emperor Hirohito." Chennault flatly denied any impropriety. "Nobody pays for my parties," she snapped.

Two influential members of Congress took note. Congressman Les Aspin, a Wisconsin Democrat and chair of the House Armed Services Committee, asked the comptroller general to investigate Northrop and eleven other defense contractors for illegally billing costs to the federal government. "There is a distinct possibility that Northrop employees may be guilty of some kind of criminal fraud," he said. Senator Proxmire wrote defense secretary James R. Schlesinger and questioned the slow pace of Pentagon investigations into Northrop's activities. The purpose of these parties, Proxmire said, was to create "a network of obligations." The practice, he warned, had become "widespread, systematic, carefully planned and costly."

The Pentagon launched audits into eleven major defense contractors and opened informal inquiries into the activities of another thirty-three firms. Chennault told investigators she carefully complied with instructions from John R. Alison, former general and the manager of her Northrop contract, any time she submitted entertainment expenses for reimbursement. Alison, she said, suggested her parties be described in her expense reports as "conferences" at which "matters pertaining to the use of Northrop products now being operated in Southeast Asia" were discussed.

Northrop eventually reimbursed the air force $564,013 for expenses improperly billed against the company's federal contracts.

According to an Ernst & Ernst audit, Chennault's contract with Northrop ended in April 30, 1974. Six months later, the *Inquirer* reported it was "not known" whether the contract had been renewed. In fact, Chennault continued as a Northrop consultant for at least another decade. Her duties included advising Northrop executives "on matters relating to national and international sales" and putting them "in personal touch with representatives of foreign governments who are potential Northrop customers." Alison reminded her in 1980 to provide "as much detail as is consistent with confidentiality" in her monthly reports. "Unless your services are fully described and accurately recorded," he wrote, "your fees may be challenged by the Company's Government auditors or the Internal Revenue Service."

A PISTACHIO PUDDING SHORTAGE GRIPPED WASHINGTON IN late 1975, beginning around Thanksgiving, and became especially acute at Christmas. Grocery stores throughout the capital were stripped of Standard Brands' pistachio pudding mix the same day it arrived. Frank Gagan, a product manager with Standard Brands, suspected some people were buying more mix than they would ever need and were stockpiling it. "We're going at maximum speed to catch up," he said. A poor pistachio crop was partly to blame for the shortage, but Barry Scher, a spokesman for Giant Foods, identified another culprit: the popularity of Watergate Cake.

The key ingredients of Watergate Cake were pistachio instant pudding, white cake mix and chopped nuts. The recipe's "cover-up icing" was made from pistachio instant pudding, cold milk and Cool Whip topping. (One version of the Watergate Cake recipe called for 7UP soda and shredded coconut.) Watergate Cake was not to be confused with Watergate Salad, which was prepared in a mold using pistachio pudding mix, Cool Whip, miniature marshmallows, walnuts and a can of crushed pineapple, and placed in a refrigerator for at least an hour to set. Watergate Salad could be served either as a side dish or as a dessert.

The origins of both recipes remain a mystery. "There are several urban myths," according to the Kraft Foods website, "but we can't substantiate any of them."

"Perhaps to alleviate the sour taste of certain political events," according to "Anne's Reader Exchange" column published in the *Washington Post* on November 13, 1975, "some wag invented the Watergate Cake, a pistachio-flavored dessert that seems to delight all who have tried it." *Post* contributor Alexander Sullivan attempted in February 1976 to find out who named Watergate Cake. He reached out to Harold Giesinger, proprietor of the Watergate Pastry Shop, who said the recipe did not originate with him. "We haven't invented anything to which we'd attach a name like that," he said, and furthermore the Watergate Pastry Shop did not feature pistachios in any of its desserts. No one could explain how the cake got its name or why pistachio was the main flavoring, Sullivan concluded. "One current explanation leans on the presence of crushed walnuts in the cake—'bugs' in the parlance of kids."

Kraft's version of the story behind Watergate Salad goes something like this: General Foods released Jell-O Pistachio Flavor Instant Pudding and Pie Filling in 1976 and circulated a recipe for Pistachio Pineapple Delight. A food editor in Chicago renamed this recipe Watergate Salad and printed it in her column. In 1985 or 1986, General Foods put the recipe for Pistachio Pineapple Delight on packages of Jell-O Pistachio Flavor Pudding. In 1993, Kraft Foods, the new owner of the Jell-O brand, added marshmallows to the recipe and changed the name on the box to Watergate Salad.

But an investigation by the *Richmond Times-Dispatch* in 1996 failed to identify the Chicago-based food editor who allegedly renamed the recipe. Camille Stagg, a food editor at the *Chicago Sun-Times* around that period, said the Watergate Salad recipe was "rather unappealing" and therefore unlikely to have been picked up by any of the top food editors in the city at the time, who were generally focused on covering the growing interest in healthful eating—cutting sugar and salt, eliminating preservatives and cooking with natural, organic ingredients.

In early 1977, a reader sent the recipe for Watergate Salad to Hazel Geissler, a staff writer with the St. Petersburg *Evening Independent*, and asserted it came from "a restaurant in the now well-known complex." A radio station in Nashville, Illinois, reported the sous chef at the Watergate Hotel created the Watergate Salad "while in a hurry to create something for the buffet."

A spokesman for the California Pistachio Commission was unable to settle the controversy. The recipe for Watergate Salad, he said, didn't even require real pistachios—just pistachio pudding mix, "which doesn't always contain real pistachios."

Anton Obernberger, the current owner of Watergate Pastry, says he and his staff still get asked if they played a role in the invention of Watergate Cake. "We tell them we had nothing to do with it," he said. "As far as we know, Nixon liked pistachios, and that's where it got the name."

The recipe for Watergate Salad remains popular, according to Kraft Foods. During a typical holiday season, more than fifty thousand people search online for it. Cooks in North Carolina search for the recipe more than any other state.

"BURGLARS ARE AT IT AGAIN," THE *WASHINGTON POST* RE-ported on July 15, 1976. A few days earlier, a burglar had entered the Watergate South apartment of Mr. and Mrs. James E. Meredith while they were out of town and stole diamond rings, necklaces, bracelets and cash, with a total value of about $7,300. Then someone took a string of pearls, some rings and gold cuff links, worth about $1,300, from the apartment of Stephen S. Gardner. The two incidents brought to about forty the total number of burglaries at the Watergate apartments, hotel and office buildings since May 1974. Total losses were approximately $200,000.

The "phantom burglar," as District police named the thief—investigators assumed it was one burglar, working alone—was able to slip past desk clerks, porters and engineers working in the Watergate complex, avoid the elaborate closed-circuit television system monitoring all entrances to the apartment buildings, leave no fingerprints or other traces and enter apartments protected by dead bolt locks. The only clue District officers had to go on was the experience of a resident at Columbia Plaza, an apartment complex across the street from the Watergate, which had suffered a wave of burglaries the year before. She had been in her apartment when her front door opened and a "well-dressed black man" appeared. He excused himself and "quickly ran away."

Watergate managers vigorously defended their security precautions. They said master keys to apartments had long since been destroyed and most residents had changed their locks over the years. All visitors were required to sign in at the downstairs lobbies. Without express permission, no one was allowed into an apartment unless the owner or tenant was present. "I think we're giving people the maximum security possible," said the building manager at Watergate West. "They want security when they come here and they pay for it."

But Abu Forna, a desk clerk at Watergate West, suggested some of his colleagues in the complex might be reluctant to stop "official-looking people" from wandering through the halls. The Watergate, he said, had plenty of residents who were "official-looking"— including lawyers, lobbyists and members of Congress. "Sometimes you don't like to stop people because they might think you are insulting them. Then a tenant will say to you, 'Why did you bother my friend?'"

IN EARLY 1969, AT THE HOME OF A SOUTH KOREAN DIPLOMAT, who Anna Chennault later identified as "Dr. Chang Yang," she met a young man with a chubby face, wearing oversize glasses and an expensive suit. "Meet an able young Korean," the ambassador said, smiling. "He is anxious to do something for our country."

The young man was Tongsun Park.

"We had much in common," Chennault later recalled. She had worked at Georgetown University on a Chinese-English dictionary and he had studied there. "He was a personable young man," she wrote, "and I was happy to introduce him to those among my friends who wielded power of one sort or another. They all found him impressive. He was obviously very smart, very ambitious, in possession of all the tools necessary to realize his ambitions: cultured, socially alert, and utterly charming."

Tongsun's older brother, Ken Park, had inherited their father's shipping business, and Tongsun told Chennault he had grown tired of representing his brother's "interests" in the United States. He wanted to "branch out," he added, and promote Korean "culture" and "foster cultural and economic ties" between the two countries. "It all sounded very wholesome and harmless," Chennault recalled.

Tongsun Park was "Anna Chennault's protégé in the early days," a former associate of Park told the *New York Times*. She invited him to her parties at the Watergate and "introduced him to many in the elite of Washington and generally provided him a model of how to exert influence." Corcoran also introduced Park around town, as did Chennault's daughter Cindy, who lived in Watergate South. "A Cindy-Tongsun marriage was mentioned, even," according to *Washington Star* columnist Diana McLellan. Corcoran waved off any suggestion he and Park had any sort of business relationship. "I'm not Tongsun's lawyer, I'm his piano player," Corcoran quipped. "He had the best piano in Washington."

Park earned the nickname the "Oriental Gatsby" in media reports by working his way into Washington circles, dispensing gifts of Korean art and artifacts, and entertaining at his townhouse in Dupont Circle or at the top restaurants in the city. "His generosity seemed authentic," Chennault wrote later.

In 1961, Park acquired the lease to a building in Georgetown, believed to be at or near the former site of Suter's Tavern, where George Washington negotiated with nineteen local landowners to create the District of Columbia as the seat of the new federal government—including Robert Peter, owner of the Mexico plantation, which included the land now occupied by the Watergate. Park asked the Korean Central Intelligence Agency for funds to launch a new members-only club for lobbyists, politicians and other Washington VIPs, as part of a major lobbying campaign aimed at Congress. With $3 million in funding from South Korea's government, Park purchased the building in 1965. According to Chennault, when Park informed her about his plan to open a club, she assumed it was part of a "cultural exchange." In 1966, Tongsun Park and fourteen "founding members," including Anna Chennault and Tommy Corcoran, opened the George Town Club.

Tandy Dickinson, a "taffy-haired" debutante from Lynchburg, Virginia, "with expensive tastes and a studied air of wide-eyed naivete," according to *People* magazine, was living in a one-bedroom apartment in Watergate South when she first met Tongsun Park. She had the flu and had to break their first date—a birthday party for House Speaker Tip O'Neill. On their second attempt, Park took her to a gala at the Kennedy Center. He frowned in disapproval when he saw her backless gown. Park was "a very conservative gentleman," she explained, although he was only seven years older. They shared a villa in the Dominican Republic and traveled to Europe, Asia and the Middle East. Park always had "the best food, the best wine, the best champagne, the best music, the best people." "People would change their plans to make sure they'd be there" whenever an invitation arrived from Park, said Tandy.

"The name Tongsun Park meant a good party," Tandy added.

The party ended in 1976.

The justice department and congressional investigators began asking questions about Park's lobbying and business activities and he fled the country. On November 29, 1976, *Time* gave the scandal a name: Koreagate.

Kim Hyung Wook, the former director of the South Korean intelligence agency, appeared before the House Subcommittee on International Organizations the following summer. His testimony contained one bombshell after another. He told the committee Park said he needed to "do favors" for up to twenty congressmen, at a cost of $200,000 each. Wook also testified the South Korean government, at the request of two members of Congress, engaged Park as "an exclusive rice broker," in exchange for support of U.S. weapons sales to South Korea.

On September 6, 1977, the justice department unsealed an indictment charging Tongsun Park with thirty-six felonies, including conspiracy, bribery, mail fraud, racketeering, making illegal campaign contributions and failure to register as a foreign agent. The charges carried maximum penalties of up to 202 years in prison and $114,000 in fines. "I wasn't terribly surprised," Chennault wrote later, "for it did not seem inconsistent with his freewheeling generosity. But it did surprise me that he had covered so much ground within so short a time."

Griffin Bell, Jimmy Carter's attorney general—and a resident of Watergate South—urged the South Korean government, with which the United States had no extradition treaty, to facilitate Park's return to stand trial. "South Korea is a friendly power and an ally of the United States, and I wouldn't want to tell them how to return Tongsun Park," Bell said. "I'm sure they know how."

Under a grant of immunity, Park finally returned to the United States in April 1978 and testified before the House Ethics Committee. He admitted steering funds to more than thirty members of Congress. "Washington is a marvelous city for someone like me," he said. "Where else could a foreigner, an outsider like myself, do the things I was able to do?"

Just three members of Congress were censured and reprimanded for accepting gifts and campaign contributions from Tongsun Park and only one congressman, Democrat Richard Hanna of California, went to prison for his role in Koreagate.

After the Watergate scandal cost the GOP forty-nine seats in the House of Representatives, congressional Republicans saw an opportunity in Koreagate. "It's tailor-made," said Congressman Guy Vander Jagt of Michigan. "It's a high, hard one right over the center of the plate. We ought to be able to hit it for a homer." Added Republican Jim Leach of Iowa: "There are still people who think of us as the party of Watergate and cover-up. Now we can show them that it is our party that's anxious to investigate corruption in government."

Republicans picked up a net fifteen seats in the House of Representatives at the next election, depriving the Democrats of their two-thirds majority, although the election results had more to do with the energy crisis and inflation than political scandal. Republican candidates elected to Congress for the first time in that cycle included Dick Cheney, who captured the lone congressional seat in Wyoming. In Texas, a thirty-two-year-old oilman named George W. Bush ran for Congress. He lost to his Democratic opponent.

IN NOVEMBER 1976, SHORTLY AFTER GERALD FORD LOST TO Jimmy Carter, Anna Chennault posed for a photo shoot in her Watergate penthouse, to accompany a profile in the *Honolulu Star-Bulletin*. Anna was trying out a new look: slacks. It was time to turn the page on the Nixon-era version of Anna Chennault, the consummate hostess in the tight-fitting, custom-made embroidered silk mini-dress. The new Anna Chennault was a working woman.

"The day before my first child was born, I was at the office," she said. "Women who have nothing else to do but entertain are 'hostesses.' I would rather be identified as a woman in industry, rather than a woman in luxury."

"And don't call me Madame," she insisted.

She described her seven-day workweek, handling international negotiations for Flying Tiger Airlines and identifying opportunities in the United States for foreign investors. She had chosen to work in an especially challenging field for a woman. "If you are honest with yourself," she continued, "there is no question that aviation is a man's world. Women are thought of as stewardesses, but we are trying to recondition their thinking."

A new project was taking up a lot of her time, she added. "I am writing my memoirs. I've sent 10 chapters to Doubleday and they love it."

ON BEHALF OF BANCA DI ROMA, NICOLAS SALGO SOLICITED offers on the Watergate. Buyers sensed a fire sale and submitted very low bids. "All of them were sharks," Salgo said. "Your price is ridiculous," Salgo told one. "I am doing a favor for Banca di Roma because I got bored. But now I represent their interests. And your price is so ridiculous, I won't even transmit it. If you want, you can send it to Rome yourself." According to Salgo, a large number of buyers circled around the Watergate, including two or three "big names"— such as the Reichmanns of Canada, at one time the fourth-richest family in the world.

Salgo called up Mario Barone at Banca di Roma. "I'm tired of this nonsense," Salgo said. "Tell me what you want for the Watergate. If I think that it is worth it, then I want to have an exclusive option on it for six months and I will try to buy it myself."

"Fine," Barone replied. "Ten million." Salgo would also need to assume the first mortgage on the complex, which stood at $39 million.

Salgo didn't hesitate. He immediately took a six-month option on the property. He had a million dollars of his own and went looking for the rest. "I couldn't get a loan anywhere," Salgo soon discovered. "No bank would lend me money. Real estate wasn't hot."

Bob Page, with whom Salgo had worked on a previous deal with Bangor Punta, introduced him to Continental Illinois Bank.

The Continental & Commercial National Bank of Chicago was especially hard hit in the economic depression that followed the 1929 stock market crash and narrowly escaped insolvency, thanks to an investment from the Reconstruction Finance Corporation. Renamed the Continental Illinois National Bank & Trust Company in 1932, the bank pursued a conservative investment strategy over the next four decades, with a heavy emphasis on government securities. David M. Kennedy, a Mormon who had served as assistant secretary of the treasury during the Eisenhower administration and was now chairman of Continental's board, saw that many of the bank's domestic clients were doing business abroad. He launched the bank's international operations to keep pace.

Kennedy's strong preference was generally to open a foreign branch of the U.S. bank, but after the Italian government refused Continental's application, he looked for an Italian bank in which he could invest. The head of Italy's central bank introduced Kennedy to Banca Privata Finanziaria and its owner, Michele Sindona. Both came highly recommended, Kennedy later recalled, by the Bank of Italy and by unnamed Vatican officials. Continental bought 20 percent of Sindona's bank in 1965. "In retrospect," Kennedy's biographer wrote later, in a stunning understatement, "there was far more to Sindona than appeared on the surface."

In 1969, Nixon tapped Kennedy to become secretary of the treasury. As of June 1971, Continental was the largest bank in Illinois and the eighth-largest commercial bank, as measured by deposits, in the country. In a $100 million public offering managed by Lehman Brothers, Continental launched a real estate investment trust, or REIT, Continental Illinois Properties, in November 1971. James D. Harper, Jr., known as Jim, the president of Continental Illinois Properties, ran its operations out of Los Angeles. One of the REIT's trustees, Frank DeMarco, Jr., was a real estate lawyer with the firm of Kalmbach, DeMarco, Knapp & Chillingsworth, whose founding partner, Herbert W. Kalmbach, was President Nixon's personal lawyer.

Salgo presented the Watergate opportunity to Continental's executives. The Watergate, he explained, was an absolutely sure thing. The income it generated was already "substantial" and the hotel was being improved. Two weeks later, an executive from Continental Illinois called Salgo. The bank was interested in the Watergate, but had no interest in loaning Salgo money to buy it. They wanted instead to form a partnership. Continental offered to cover 90 percent of the purchase price if Salgo would put in 10 percent. They would then become fifty-fifty equity partners.

"Please repeat that," Salgo said.

The banker repeated the terms. Salgo accepted them on the spot.

The proposed partnership agreement between Salgo and Continental Illinois Properties, however, included a section that stated neither party could sell or otherwise transfer its interest in the Watergate without the prior consent of the other. Continental was not just making a real estate investment, it was backing Salgo's personal vision for reviving the Watergate after the scandal of the break-in and the collapse of SGI. "What they really wanted was to tie down every hair of my head so I couldn't walk out on them," Salgo recalled later. "Continental Illinois didn't look at the real estate, they looked at me."

Salgo's lawyer read the proposed agreement and advised him not to sign. "They are asking for impossible conditions," the lawyer said. Salgo rejected the advice. He was fine with Continental's agreement, he said, as long as it was reciprocal.

There was one possible obstacle to closing the sale. The residents of Watergate West were still locked in a legal fight with the Watergate developers. Since March 2, 1972, at least eight different law firms, representing the Watergate West owners, developers or other defendants, made at least fifty motions, and deposed more than twenty witnesses. The lawsuits—the suit filed by Watergate West against the developer, and the countersuit filed by the developer—needed to be cleared away before Continental Illinois Properties could invest.

In July 1977, the Watergate developers agreed to a $600,000 out-of-court settlement with the residents of Watergate West. Neither party shared details with reporters. The developers continued to publicly deny liability for heating and ventilation failures. "Both sides realized they were spending more in legal fees than they wanted," said Henry Winston, representing the Watergate. "It involved only money, no principles," said Mark Friedlander, Sr., attorney for the Watergate West owners.

The Watergate was sold to Nicolas Salgo and Continental Illinois Properties on November 2, 1977. Salgo put in $500,000 and Continental Illinois Properties provided $9.5 million. The sale included the Watergate Hotel, two office buildings, a shopping mall and the Les Champs arcade. The purchase price of $49 million included $10 million in cash and the assumption of an existing first mortgage of $39 million. In the *Wall Street Journal* report about the transaction, a Continental Illinois spokesman declined to reveal the seller by name.

Seventeen years earlier, Nicolas Salgo announced ten acres on the shore of the Potomac River had been bought by Società Generale Immobiliare for a new development that would become known worldwide as the Watergate. At age sixty-three, he now owned half of it. His new title: chairman of the Watergate Companies.

THE NATIONAL COAL BOARD, OVERSEERS OF GREAT BRITain's nationalized coal industry, represented 625,000 coal workers and retirees and managed pension funds with combined assets of $5 billion. There were two separate funds: the Mineworker's Pension Scheme, representing the blue-collar workforce, and the National Coal Board Staff Superannuation Scheme, representing white-collar employees. Hugh Jenkins was in charge of investments for both funds and wanted to diversify their portfolios by adding assets in the United States. For nearly a year, he looked for someone to lead the U.S. expansion, ideally an "English-trained" real estate professional with a working knowledge of the American market.

Wendy Luscombe was the only woman in her starting class in the estate management program at the Oxford School of Architecture. When she graduated and took her examination to become a professional appraiser, she was the only woman in a room of 350 men. While working as an appraiser with a London property consulting firm, she wrote an article for a London real estate magazine comparing the U.K. and U.S. appraisal methodologies and suggesting British firms could benefit from the in-depth research behind the American technique. Her article caused "a few ripples," she recalled. Her colleagues didn't appreciate being told they could learn something from the Americans. Jenkins, however, liked what he read. He tracked her down.

Luscombe confessed she had spent only a few weeks in the United States and knew "very little" about the market, but Jenkins decided she was perfect for the job and hired her away, at age twenty-seven, to scout U.S. real estate opportunities on behalf of the National Coal Board pension funds.

In her first month on the job, Luscombe visited eighteen American cities in a "windshield" tour, driving around the country and looking at properties. Taking time changes into account, she sometimes worked a thirty-hour day, taking morning calls from London through the following day, into the late-evening hours in Los Angeles. At her offices on Fifth Avenue in New York, callers sometimes asked if she was "Mr. Luscombe's secretary." Nonetheless, she considered New York an easier place for a woman in real estate than London. "People are less surprised here that you are young and female," she said.

To test the waters, she made an investment in a small office building in Florida and quickly turned a profit. The deal convinced Jenkins the U.S. market was worthwhile, but Luscombe thought it would be difficult to build a substantial portfolio by acquiring properties one at a time. Her fear was a British firm might be easily "ripped off" by unscrupulous players in the U.S. real estate market. A better course, she advised Jenkins, was to purchase an existing REIT with a strong portfolio. She already had in mind a possible takeover target: Continental Illinois Properties, one of the most successful real estate trusts in the country. It traded at $15 a share—$10 below its share price in 1971, the year Lehman Brothers took it public. Luscombe thought Continental was worth much more. One of its assets seemed to be significantly undervalued: the Watergate.

SALGO HAD BEEN UNHAPPY FOR YEARS WITH THE DEAL Giuseppe Cecchi had negotiated with the Democratic club, giving them the restaurant space in the lower level of the Watergate Hotel "for peanuts." Now that he was back at the Watergate, Salgo was delighted the Democrats had moved out. It was time, he decided, to put a "first class" restaurant into the Watergate Hotel.

Salgo's initial idea was to rotate six different three-star chefs through the hotel annually, giving each chef a two-month contract. He flew to France to pitch his idea to every three-star chef he could find. There were no takers. But one chef told Salgo about the youngest French chef in history to earn two Michelin stars. He was unhappy with his current business partner and might be available. His name was Jean-Louis Palladin.

Nic and Josseline Salgo knew Palladin's restaurant, La Table des Cordeliers, in the city of Condom in southwestern France. They dined there often and Jean-Louis had catered events for Josseline's family. In addition to the two Michelin stars, Palladin had been awarded seventeen of twenty possible points in the *Gault et Millau* guide and his restaurant was listed in the influential *Guide to the 50 Best Restaurants in France* by Nicolas de Rabaudy.

Salgo met up with Palladin in Paris. "I will pay your trip to the United States," Salgo offered. "Don't bring anything with you. Absolutely nothing. Don't even bring salt in your pocket. My people—including Josseline—will go with you to the market in New York and you will cook for us and for some of our friends there. Then we will take you to Washington, DC, and you will cook for a big crowd. If you like what you see—and if we like what we are getting—you have a job."

Salgo had abandoned his idea of rotating chefs through the restaurant below the Watergate Hotel. He wanted Palladin full-time.

Palladin arrived in New York and prepared a dinner in Salgo's Manhattan apartment for chefs and friends, including the architect I. M. Pei. After the dinner, Salgo handed Jean-Louis a legal pad and said, "Write down what it will take to get you to come to America." Palladin wrote his demands: a salary of $90,000 a year, an apartment at the Watergate for his family, and a full month of vacation every August—at full salary, plus all travel expenses. Salgo looked at the list. "When can you start?" he asked.

"I was fed up with problems," Palladin said. "I had spent 31 years in my region, in the same town. It was a grand experience, but very hard. I thought perhaps it was time to see something else, to take my work somewhere else." Salgo said he found Palladin at "a good moment."

Salgo was "very intimidating," recalled Jean-Louis's wife, Regine, but he spoke French beautifully and was a bit "mischievous." Looking back, she thought this mischievousness was one of the reasons Salgo and Palladin were "well-matched."

Salgo also agreed to hire Palladin's three top assistants from France: Sylvain Portay, Jean-François Taquet and Larbi Dahrouch. They arrived in Washington on August 10, 1979, and met Salgo at the Watergate Hotel the following day. The men had heard of the Watergate scandal, but had no idea there was a complex of buildings with that name, Dahrouch later recalled. With Salgo behind the wheel of his Bentley, Palladin and his team headed to Maryland to sample the local crab.

Regine joined her husband in their new Watergate South apartment. Her first impression was the building was "a little strange." With its sweeping curves and massive scale, the Watergate was "not like anything we had seen in France."

Salgo gathered a group of Washington diners, including local restaurant critics and food writers. Jean-Louis prepared a spectacular meal, using only what he found locally in Washington markets. "He met the challenge," Salgo said.

To design the interior of the new restaurant, Salgo hired George Lang, who had transformed Café des Artistes into one of Manhattan's most successful and romantic spots. Lang and Salgo were both Hungarians, but their wartime experiences were vastly different. Salgo spent World War II working in Switzerland. Lang survived a forced-labor camp on the Czechoslovakian border. His parents were murdered in Auschwitz. In the chaos of the closing days of World War II, Lang joined the Fascist Arrow Cross militia; assisted Jews in hiding, for which he was arrested and sentenced to death; was tortured and put on trial by the Soviet occupying army, only to be finally acquitted when several Jews testified in his defense; and escaped to Austria hidden in a coffin, before making his way to New York.

Lang started as a busboy at the landmark Reuben's Restaurant and Delicatessen in Murray Hill, sold wedding banquets at a converted Greek Orthodox church on Houston Street and the Waldorf-Astoria, and directed food operations for a dozen restaurants at the 1964 New York World's Fair. He formed his own restaurant consulting business, George Lang Corporation, in 1970.

Lang furnished the subterranean, barrel-shaped dining room with modern furniture and "stylish table appointments." There were fourteen tables, limiting the space to forty diners per seating, although more diners could be accommodated—as was often the case, as Jean-Louis sometimes invited friends to dine, even on nights when the restaurant was fully booked. Because the room lacked a river view, Lang created a curtained wall, lighting it from behind. The interior was "an orange cave," wrote the *Washington Post*'s Phyllis Richman, "with mirror tricks turning the curving walls into more unorthodox shapes."

While Lang tackled the new restaurant, Salgo launched a number of improvements throughout the Watergate complex. He ordered a $3 million refurbishment of the Watergate Hotel interiors. He brought in Elizabeth Siber, who had previously launched the restaurants at the World Trade Center in New York, to become general manager of the Watergate's restaurants. Siber reviewed Palladin's ideas for menus and prodded him to increase portion size and reduce the number of kidneys and sweetbreads. She also told him to lay off the purees. "Americans like to chew things," she told him.

In October 1979, Jean-Louis at the Watergate opened for business with a series of private parties and test dinners. The grand opening was low-key—just a small OPEN sign posted in the doorway—but the restaurant represented a "major gastronomic coup," according to

Washington Post food writer William Rice. "Never before—in the memory of contemporary observers," Rice wrote, "has a French chef of such stature come to the United States to direct a restaurant."

IN MARCH 1979, THE BOARD OF CONTINENTAL ILLINOIS PROP-erties received an offer of $25 a share for all outstanding stock, valu-ing the trust at $120 million. The offer came from Brabant NV, a company based in the Netherlands Antilles and owned by Saudi Arabian interests. Brabant announced it planned to serve as "passive investors" and form a management group that would include at least three current directors or executives. Continental called a special shareholder meeting to accept the offer and close the deal within ninety days.

Wendy Luscombe preferred to avoid bidding wars by making her first bid her last. But she was also an astute, conservative investor. She shared with the *New York Times* her motto: "We demand a little blood."

Luscombe bid $30 a share—$5 more per share than Brabant had put on the table—and in July 1979, the shareholders of Continental Illinois Properties accepted the offer.

DURING THE 1976 PRESIDENTIAL PRIMARY, REPORTERS pressed incumbent President Gerald Ford and his challenger, former California governor Ronald Reagan, to release their personal tax returns.

The Reagan campaign at first released only a four-paragraph statement referring reporters to a Statement of Economic Interest filed in 1975, covering the last year of Reagan's second term as gov-ernor. "Since leaving office," Reagan said in a written statement, "I have placed such assets as I have in a blind trust. The trust will continue at least for the duration of the time I am a candidate and under its terms I can neither inquire of the trustee's action, nor can they inform me of their actions. The trustees may deal with these assets as they see fit without my permission." After the Ford campaign released a table showing the President and Mrs. Ford's sources of income and taxes paid each year since 1966, the Reagan campaign released a table showing their candidate's "adjusted gross income"— net income, after all deductions, per his federal tax return—and "total taxes paid," which included federal and state income taxes, local property taxes, sales taxes and other "misc. taxes" for the period 1970 to 1975. That table showed Reagan had an adjusted gross income of $111,585 in 1974 and paid $50,429 in various taxes. In April, the campaign disclosed the Reagans paid $65,000 in federal income taxes in 1975, on an adjusted gross income of $252,000.

A *New York Times* analysis concluded Reagan "almost certainly paid no Federal income tax in 1970," despite earning at least $73,000 that year. The *Times* reached this conclusion by deducting property taxes—which were public record—from the total taxes of all kinds Reagan reported to have paid. The *Times* asked the Reagans to disclose additional information about taxes paid each year, but they refused. "Ronald Reagan has an unusual tax problem," the *Washington Star* editorialized. "The tax laws possibly operated too much in his favor in recent years." In an appearance on *Meet the Press*, Senator Paul Laxalt of Nevada, the national chairman of Citizens for Reagan, asserted the information provided by the campaign had settled the question. The *Star* disagreed. "We see nothing unreasonable about the public curiosity as to what a would-be President contributes to the national till," the *Star* wrote. "He is full of opinions about the uses of federal money, and the inadequacy of the country's $100 billion defense effort. And whether or not his tax contributions are seen as paltry in his years of $100,000-plus earnings, Mr. Reagan owes it to himself to have the judgment made on the basis of fact rather than the present mixture of fact and speculation."

In April 1980, President Jimmy Carter released his 1979 federal tax return. Reagan, the presumptive Republican nominee for president, at first told reporters he would make "any and all disclosures required by law"—noting the law did not require tax returns be released—but reporters continued to press the matter. During the GOP convention in July, Reagan promised to make "a comprehensive disclosure" and on July 31, Ronald Reagan made public his 1979 federal tax return, abandoning a long-standing practice of treating his financial affairs as "a private matter," according to the *Washington Post*. "Governor Reagan still has strong feelings about his privacy," a Reagan campaign aide said, "but he and his advisers felt he had nothing to hide, so he did it."

The tax return showed the Reagans earned $515,878 and paid $230,146 in taxes in 1979. The return also showed income of $234,455 in capital gains from the sale of stocks, most of which the Reagans purchased after he completed two terms as governor of California. William French Smith, Reagan's personal attorney, said a decision was made eight to ten months earlier to sell all of Reagan's stock "because it was good from an investment standpoint and because he was declaring his candidacy." By far the best-performing stock in the Reagans' portfolio was Continental Illinois Properties, half-owner of the Watergate. The Reagans purchased 11,000 shares in 1975, paying $11.53 per share; the stock was sold to the National Coal Board pension funds on July 11, 1979, at $30 per share, netting the future president and first lady a profit of $203,099.

NICOLAS SALGO HAD A NEW BUSINESS PARTNER: WENDY Luscombe. When the *Washington Post* reached him for comment about the sale of Continental's share in the Watergate, he played down the transaction. He had yet to meet Luscombe or anyone else at the National Coal Board. "Operationally there is no change here," he said.

Wendy Luscombe had other plans.

The Watergate is to Washington what the presence of a beautiful and charming lady is to a dull cocktail reception.

—Gabor Olah de Garab

General Manager, the Watergate Hotel

WHILE HIS NEW RESTAURANT WAS BEING BUILT OUT, JEAN-Louis Palladin and his team worked upstairs in the Watergate Hotel kitchen, developing dishes and scouting local sources for ingredients. Back in France, Palladin had driven from Condom to Bordeaux weekly to purchase fresh fish. In Washington, he prowled the markets of Georgetown. The local vegetables lacked flavor, he said, but they were fresh and "handsome enough to be useful." He did not put escargot on his menu because he could not find any fresh snails. He refused to serve canned snails. "The only good thing about them was the garlic butter!" he fumed. When he tried to buy fresh peas, a supplier instead handed him a can of Le Sueur *petit pois* and assured him these were the same peas served at the Carter White House. According to a profile in the *Washington Post*, Jean-Louis was "less pleased with chicken, still experimenting with ducks and is downright unhappy about cheese."

Palladin and his team went to work and built their network of suppliers. They headed up to Maine to source lobsters and other fresh seafood. Palladin sourced live scallops that could be flown in from Europe. He sourced a vendor to raise rabbits and another to forage mushrooms. "Doug the Egg Guy" delivered eggs that were one hour old.

One day, Richard Ober arrived at the door of Palladin's restaurant at the Watergate, carrying the renowned Louise de Vilmorin seed catalog tucked under his arm. Ober said he worked at the nearby State

Department but felt stifled. He had bet a friend he could grow herbs and vegetables and sell them to the best restaurant in Washington. He handed Jean-Louis a sprig of mint he had grown himself.

Ober was more than a state department bureaucrat with a mid-life crisis. He attended Harvard at the same time as *Washington Post* executive editor Ben Bradlee, graduated in 1943 at the height of World War II and went into the OSS. After the war, Ober joined the CIA, where he worked for counterintelligence chief James Angleton. Beginning in 1967, Ober managed a domestic "intelligence collection program" under the code name Operation CHAOS, reporting directly to CIA director Richard Helms. According to *New York Times* investigative reporter Seymour Hersh, the operation amassed files on ten thousand Americans before shutting down in 1968.

Deborah Davis, in *Katharine the Great*, her 1979 biography of Katharine Graham, publisher of the *Washington Post*, speculated Richard Ober was "Deep Throat." Her reasoning: Ober and Bradlee had known each other for three decades, since they were both members of the Hasty Pudding social club as Harvard undergraduates; Ober had "a small office in the basement of the White House," which offered "unlimited access" to Nixon; Ober was present "during Nixon's mental deterioration, as his obsession with his enemies began to push him to the limits of rational thought"; and Ober had a motive to bring down Nixon: to protect the secrecy of Operation CHAOS and other CIA covert operations. After the first edition of her book appeared in 1979, Ober told Davis he never had "any personal contact" with Nixon. She included his denial in the second edition of her book, which came out in 1987, but noted Ober "never denied being Deep Throat."

Ober's past was unknown to Palladin, who twisted the mint between his thumb and forefinger, inhaled its scent and pulled off a leaf to taste. "Did God send you to me?" he exclaimed. "You are exactly what I've been looking for!"

Richard Ober won his bet.

Three of the six buildings in the iconic Watergate complex. From left to right: Watergate West, the Watergate Hotel and Watergate South. *(Giuseppe Cecchi)*

Watergate architect Luigi Moretti in his studio at Palazzo Colonna in Rome, Italy. *(Archivio di Stato di Roma, Fondo Moretti)*

Luigi Moretti presents his design to a skeptical Commission of Fine Arts, in a cartoon by Joaquín de Alba for the *Washington Daily News. (Tommaso Magnifico/Joaquín de Alba Carmona)*

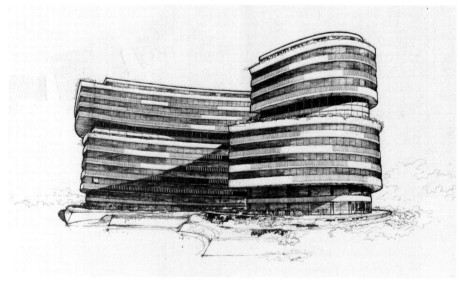

Studio Moretti drawing for the first Watergate building, 1961–63. *(Archivio di Stato di Roma, Fondo Moretti)*

A rendering of a Watergate swimming pool, Studio Moretti, 1961–63. *(Archivio di Stato di Roma, Fondo Moretti)*

The builders of the Watergate. Left to right: Luigi Moretti, architect; Royce Ward, a development executive with Island Vista, Inc.; Milton Fischer, the American architect hired to translate Moretti's designs into working drawings; Don Richardson, the John Hancock executive who arranged financing; Hal Lewis, president of Riverview Realty, the exclusive sales agency for Watergate co-op apartments; and Giuseppe Cecchi, the on-site manager of the project for Società Generale Immobiliare. *(Milton Fischer family)*

An early model of the Watergate, with the "Pompeiian villas" on the grounds between buildings, which were later eliminated from the plan. *(Archivio di Stato di Roma, Fondo Moretti)*

The Watergate site, prior to construction. The Washington Gas Light Company attempted to sell the land at auction in 1948, but rejected the final bid as too low. The Howard Johnson Motor Lodge looms in the distance. *(National Archives)*

Luigi Moretti visits the Watergate construction site, 1965. *(Archivio di Stato di Roma, Fondo Moretti)*

Watergate East under construction, April 1965. *(Warren K. Leffler/Library of Congress)*

President Lyndon Johnson tours the newly opened Democratic National Committee computer room in the Watergate Office Building, July 20, 1967. *(LBJ Presidential Library/ Yoichi Okamoto.*

Anna Chennault, the glamorous widow of General Claire Lee Chennault , in her fourteenth-floor Watergate East penthouse, 1969. She would become known as the "Dragon Lady" of the Watergate. *(Milwaukee Journal Sentinel, February 1969/George P. Koshollek, © 2015 Journal Sentinel Inc., reproduced with permission.)*

Nixon's commerce department secretary and campaign finance chair Maurice Stans reviews scrapbooks in his "Africana Room" on the twelfth floor of Watergate East with his wife, Kathy, 1969. *(Michael Rougier/The LIFE Picture Collection/Getty Images)*

Lifeguard Linda Fox watches over one of the Watergate's three outdoor pools, 1969. *(Michael Rougier/The LIFE Picture Collection/Getty Images)*

Martha Mitchell, controversial wife of Nixon's attorney general John Mitchell, and Kathy Stans, wife of commerce secretary Maurice Stans, in the Watergate Salon, 1969. Martha's daughter Marty holds their dog. *(Michael Rougier/The LIFE Picture Collection/Getty Images)*

Democratic U.S. Senator Jacob Javits dives into a Watergate swimming pool, 1969. *(Michael Rougier/The LIFE Picture Collection/Getty Images)*

CIA librarian Walter Pforzheimer in his Watergate East duplex apartment, 1969. By the time he gave his collection to Yale in 2000, he owned more than nine thousand books on espionage. *(Michael Rougier/The LIFE Picture Collection/ Getty Images)*

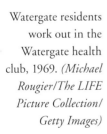

Watergate residents work out in the Watergate health club, 1969. *(Michael Rougier/The LIFE Picture Collection/ Getty Images)*

A glamorous night out at the Watergate, as depicted in a Watergate South sales brochure, circa 1971. *(Tina and Gigi Winston)*

An "antiwar demonstrator" is arrested near the Watergate during the Chicago Seven protests, February 1970. Protestors marched on the Watergate, known as the "Republican Bastille" because it was home to so many Nixon appointees. *(Photo by Wally McNamee/Corbis Historical/Corbis via Getty Images)*

ABOVE: Washington undercover officer Carl M. Shoffler, wearing long hair and a "hippie vest," reviews evidence in the Watergate Hotel during the early morning hours of June 17, 1972, following the arrest of five men in the Democratic National Committee suite next door at the Watergate Office Building. *(Paul Leeper)*

BELOW: The front door of the Democratic National Committee headquarters on the sixth floor of the Watergate Office Building, June 17, 1972. *(Photograph by Ken Feil/Washington Post/Getty Images)*

ABOVE: The six buildings that comprise the Watergate, from left to right: Watergate West, the Watergate Office Building, the Watergate Hotel, Watergate East, Watergate South and the Watergate 600 office building. *(Carol M. Highsmith/Library of Congress)*

BELOW: A Watergate residence with a view of the Kennedy Center and the Potomac River. *(Carol M. Highsmith/Library of Congress)*

ABOVE: Nicolas Salgo at Watergate South, 1980. Salgo identified the original Potomac River site and recommended it to Società Generale Immobiliare, which purchased the property and made Salgo an equity partner in the development. Salgo purchased the Watergate in 1977, with the backing of Continental Illinois Properties. *(Salgo Trust for Education)*

BELOW: Jean-Louis Palladin, 1991. Salgo recruited Palladin from France to open a restaurant at the Watergate Hotel. Ronald Reagan celebrated his seventieth birthday at Jean-Louis in February 1981. *(Laura Patterson/Library of Congress)*

Elizabeth and Bob Dole in their Watergate South apartment, 1982. Their first date was at the Watergate Hotel. *(Robert H. Phillips/Image courtesy Jenny Phillips)*

The Countess of Romanones poses for *Town & Country* magazine in her Watergate apartment, 1982. As Aline Griffith, from Pearl River, New York, she moved to Madrid during World War II and married a Spanish count. She later wrote three best-selling memoirs about her career as a spy, the details of which were questioned by *Women's Wear Daily. (Robert H. Phillips/Image courtesy Jenny Phillips)*

Mary Jane and Charles Wick in their Watergate South apartment, 1982. The Wicks were among President and Mrs. Reagan's California friends who moved into the Watergate during the early years of the new GOP administration. *(Robert H. Phillips/Image courtesy Jenny Phillips)*

ABOVE: Monica Lewinsky leaves the Watergate, on the way to a meeting with her lawyer, William Ginsburg, February 1998. Lewinsky lived with her mother in Watergate South, next door to Elizabeth and Bob Dole. *(Ron Sachs/AdMedia)*

BELOW: Reporters and photographers outside the entrance to the Watergate South parking garage, hoping to get a view of Monica Lewinsky, January 1998. A Watergate resident said it was "like the old Westerns, when the Indians went around the covered wagons." *(James M. Thresher/The Washington Post/Getty Images)*

The contents of the Watergate Hotel were sold as developers prepared to convert the building into co-op apartments, September 2007. *(Chip Somodevilla/Getty Images)*

Furniture and souvenirs are staged in a Watergate Hotel suite during the liquidation sale, September 2007. Over three days, more than twenty thousand items were sold to the public. *(Kristoffer Tripplaar/Sipa Press)*

The Watergate Hotel, June 2012. With the collapse of Lehman Brothers investment bank, plans to convert the Watergate Hotel to apartments stalled. The hotel remained closed for nearly a decade. *(Jim Watson/AFP/Getty Images)*

At age ninety-one, Anna Chennault in her Watergate penthouse, where she has lived for more than fifty years, surrounded by Chinese antiques and photographs of her encounters with politicians and diplomats, September 2016. (© *Stephen Voss*)

EVER SINCE THEODORE WHITE'S *THE MAKING OF THE PRES-
ident 1968*, Anna Chennault had been threatening to write another
memoir. Over six days in November 1979, Chennault's twenty-
first book, *The Education of Anna*, was excerpted in the *Washington
Star*, and it landed on bookshelves in January 1980, the start of a
presidential campaign year. "From Exotic Peking to the Corridors
of Power," read an advertisement for the book, "this stunningly
beautiful woman, Anna Chennault, was friend to six presidents, a
correspondent in World War II, a mother, writer, the confidante of
world leaders who also played a secret role in the Vietnam peace
talks. . . . Anna's life reads like a romantic novel and an international
thriller."

Chennault dedicated her book "to all my teachers, and to the
best teacher of them all, Thomas G. Corcoran." But the inspiration
for writing, she said, came from "a very dear friend." She did not
identify him by name but dropped a few clues. "We have been close
since we first met," she wrote, "though we knew from the beginning
there would never be marriage. Perhaps that is what has made the
stolen moments over the years so precious, the moments when it is
enough to be alone with each other, just to say, 'I miss you.'" She
had known this man only ten years, which ruled out her longtime
friend Tommy Corcoran. The anonymous "very dear friend" sometimes flew "ten or fifteen thousand miles just to spend a day with
me." Each time they met, he asked only one thing: "Please write
your book."

Anna may have had other reasons for writing her memoir. She
was still upset with Nixon for denying her role in his successful 1968
campaign. Chennault's recurring failure to earn a top appointment in
a Republican administration, one Washington insider observed, had
made her bitter. "What she really wanted was undersecretary of state
for far eastern affairs and was very upset when she didn't get it." Chennault told the *Washington Star* she turned down several jobs under

Nixon, and declined an offer to become U.S. treasurer in the Ford administration. "Politics is a very cruel game," she said. "After twenty years in Washington you learn to have a pretty strong stomach."

"If I were not an Asian, I would have been in the Nixon White House, but there was no one to speak for me," she told a reporter from *W* magazine. "The blacks have members in Congress, the Jews have a strong lobby, but who do the Chinese have? We don't have anyone in Congress to talk for us."

"What Anna fails to realize," said an unnamed source, "is that her contacts are perishing. A lot of them are no longer around."

Chennault's memoir gave her side of the 1968 "October surprise." At the height of the campaign, she wrote, she spoke with Nixon's campaign manager John Mitchell at least once a day. This "close contact" generated "considerable discontent" among other campaign aides, whom she dismissed as "the ranks of the frustrated." She could no longer recall whether it was Nixon or Mitchell who first suggested a meeting with Bùi Diem, the South Vietnamese ambassador to the United States, but the meeting took place at Nixon's Manhattan apartment. "Anna is my good friend," Nixon told Diem at that meeting. "If you have any messages for me, please give it to Anna and she will relay it to me and I will do the same in the future." Mitchell nodded "like a school teacher pleased by a pupil's performance."

A week after Election Day, on Wednesday, November 13, she flew to New York to meet with Maurice Stans in the morning and John Mitchell in the afternoon. "Mitchell was quick to the point," she wrote.

> Nixon, he said, had agreed with Johnson to come out with a joint statement announcing a Vietnam policy. And so, "We need to do something about our friends in Saigon."
>
> "Do what about our friends in Saigon?" I asked, not yet understanding.

"Well, persuade them to go to Paris," he said.

"You must be joking," I said, flabbergasted. "Two weeks ago, Nixon and you are worried that they might succumb to pressure to go to Paris. What makes you change your mind all of a sudden?"

Mitchell just shook his head. "Anna, you're no newcomer to politics. This, whether you like it or not, is politics."

I gathered up my coat. "I don't play that kind of politics. You go and tell them yourself," I said, and left in a rage.

"The election had been a bitter lesson," she wrote, "leaving me with no desire to serve in the new administration."

Elsewhere in her book, she criticized Jimmy Carter for relations with China. He acted with "high-handed secrecy and unnecessary haste," she wrote, and the recognition of the Beijing government was a "betrayal of a loyal ally"—Taiwan. In a note to Chennault's publisher, Senator Barry Goldwater praised the book for shedding important light on the "abrogation of our treaty responsibilities with Taiwan . . . and what the results are liable to be." Goldwater also sent a note to his friend Anna, congratulating her for making "a great contribution."

Anna's readers also learned that she once saw black-and-blue marks on Martha Mitchell's arms; that Henry Kissinger had an "immature and threatened ego," a "compulsion to impress" and committed the sartorial sin of wearing socks that were too short, exposing his bare shins whenever he sat down; and that legendary Washington hostess Perle Mesta once looked her over and sneered: "So what's a Chinese woman going to do in Washington?"

Chennault also wrote about life at the Watergate. When she bought her penthouse in early 1966, "the strange riverfront structure with its toothy balconies already bore the stamp of elitism in Washington." After the Nixon crowd arrived, "Watergate came into its own as the residential seat of power, becoming to the Nixon era what Georgetown had been in the Kennedy years." At the Watergate, Chennault began to entertain "in earnest," even though formal entertaining—"as the Merriweather Post generation had known it"—was on the decline, "a casualty of recession." Anna's formula rarely varied: she invited more men than women; served Chinese food that was "pleasing to the eye, fragrant to the nose, and appealing to the palate"; and provided after-dinner entertainment, including "parlor games" or "dancing lessons given by an instructor hired for the evening." And she limited "cocktail hour" to exactly sixty minutes. It was simply fair, she wrote, because she believed guests who arrived on time should not be penalized. It was also sensible, "because it minimizes premature drunkenness."

"There have been other distractions," began one review, "so we tend to forget that people actually live in that jagged heap of cement called Watergate, and one of the grandest dwellings there is the penthouse occupied by a mysteriously powerful woman named Anna Chennault." The reviewer called the book "intriguing" and "startlingly skillful" in light of Chennault's "bashful claims that she has difficulty speaking English."

Not all reviewers were enthusiastic. "She emerges as a somewhat naïve Dragon Lady, a socially bent Republican survivor," wrote Robert Shaplen in the *New York Times*. He found the book "sometimes disarming but often strident and self-serving" and "readable but rather shallow."

The Education of Anna failed to be the last word on Chennault's role in Nixon's 1968 campaign. In 1987, former South Vietnamese ambassador Bùi Diem released his memoir, *In the Jaws of History*, and gave his version of the events.

One night in June 1968, he wrote, "when I was having dinner at the Georgetown Club with Corcoran, Senator John Tower, and Chennault, Anna suggested I get together with the Republican presidential candidate.

". . . I told her I would think it over," he continued. "That was an enticing prospect, but also a dangerous one. Any meeting with Nixon would carry the inevitable implication that I was somehow dealing behind the Democrats' back." Diem decided to meet with Nixon, but only "independently, without reporting to Saigon," so that President Thieu could later repudiate him if necessary. Diem met with Nixon and John Mitchell in New York on July 12 at the Hotel Pierre; Anna Chennault met Diem in the lobby before the meeting. Diem did not inform Chennault that prior to the meeting, he had reached out to McGeorge Bundy, President Johnson's national security advisor, and promised not to discuss the Paris Peace Talks in anything but the most general terms.

At the end of the meeting, Diem wrote, Nixon thanked him "and added that his staff would be in touch with me through John Mitchell and Anna Chennault. I left the hotel quite pleased with the encounter, happy to have made contact with the Republicans and happy, too, that I have been candid about it with the Democrats."

After the election, and the reporting by Teddy White and others about Chennault's role in the Nixon campaign, Diem felt there were "uncomfortable ambiguities" about her role. "My impression was that she may have played her own game" by encouraging both the South Vietnamese and the Republicans.

Anna reviewed Diem's draft chapter and offered suggestions, many of which Diem appears to have accepted, including deleting a promise "to tell the whole story." "I don't think anyone really has the knowledge to tell the whole story," she wrote Diem, "because so many people were involved."

"What messages went to what people during that hectic and confused time are certainly beyond recovery at this point," Diem wrote in his memoir, "and the so-called Anna Chennault affair will doubtless remain a mysterious footnote to history, although one that could easily have had greater consequences."

Chennault also asked Diem to drop a reference to her as the "Dragon Lady." "That name was given to me by people who dislike the Asians," she wrote. "Since you are a friend, I don't think you want to use that name in reference to me." He deleted the phrase from his book.

DAVID BRADLEY RETURNED TO WASHINGTON AFTER A YEAR in the Philippines as a Fulbright scholar, teaching economics and exploring the fringes of political life under the Marcos regime. Funded by a modest grant, he interviewed political prisoners in Quezon City and Marxist guerrillas in the mountains of central Luzon and studied whether multinational corporations preferred martial-law governments over democracies (the answer was yes). It was an unusual way to spend one's first year after graduation from Harvard Business School—most of his peers from the Class of 1978 went immediately into finance or consulting.

Terry Bradley, David's mother, lived at 301 Watergate West. David's father, Gene, lived in Watergate East. The couple had divorced fifteen years after moving into the Watergate. Terry enjoyed buying, remodeling and selling apartments in the Watergate. In fact, she had found Gene's apartment for him: 705-S, the former apartment of Rose Mary Woods.

David narrowly escaped being tarred personally with the Watergate brush. At age sixteen, he was an intern with a White House conference on children and youth, and met White House aides John Ehrlichman and Egil "Bud" Krogh through church. As a student at Swarthmore in 1973, Bradley was offered a summer internship at the Nixon White House Office of Political Affairs, reporting to Charles "Chuck" Colson. David's father discouraged him from taking *any* job at a White House under siege. Father and son negotiated a compromise. David took a job in the White House Visitors Office in the East Wing, a world away from the tsunami that would eventually swamp the West Wing and the Executive Office Building next door, where Nixon kept his hideaway office.

Five years after Nixon's resignation, David was living in the spare bedroom of his parents' Watergate West apartment. Tourists were still dropping by the Watergate to look around and pose for pictures, which gave him an idea: Why not buy one of the stairwell doors that had been taped open the night of June 16, 1972, carve it into squares, and sell pieces to tourists and other history buffs? He reached out to the building management and asked to buy a door, but they turned him down.

David thought his future was in politics, not business. He wanted to be a United States senator from the time he was fourteen years old and planned to run as a moderate Republican—from Maryland, now one of the bluest states in the Union—so he enrolled at Georgetown Law School. He took a summer job working for a lawyer named Kenneth Starr. David liked and admired Starr—the two would remain lifelong friends—but decided three years of law school, on top of two years he had just spent at Harvard Business School, was impractical. David cut his legal education short after a year.

After Gene Bradley retired from General Electric, he started a nonprofit think tank, run out of the Watergate Office Building, hosting conferences on international trade and finance for high-level executives from the federal government and the private sector. David remembers his father as "a terrifically elegant man—and perfect for convening high-end dignitaries." David thought he would enjoy doing similar work, but as part of a for-profit company. Washington was packed with information, he thought. If that information could be found, packaged and distributed, it could be a decent business.

David persuaded his mother to allow him to convert the den in her Watergate West apartment into the offices of his new company: Research Counsel of Washington. Companies hired the firm to answer questions such as: Who makes uniforms for the National Football League? His first employee, Bonnie Williams, sometimes arrived at the "office" in the morning while David was still ironing his shirt. After David hired his fifth employee, the team spilled out of the den and into the dining room. The table groaned with books, papers and reports. A few hires later, David and his team were spread all over Terry's living room, with its chintz-covered sofas. Terry wanted her apartment back and ordered Research Counsel of Washington to find a real office.

"We had it coming, of course," David recalled.

ACCORDING TO NICOLAS SALGO, HIS NEW PARTNERS IN THE Watergate—Wendy Luscombe and the National Coal Board pension funds—left him alone for about a year. After that, they started to "meddle."

Luscombe had a different take: She and Salgo simply had "very different ways of doing things."

Shortly after acquiring Continental Illinois Properties and its entire portfolio, Luscombe brought her boss, Hugh Jenkins, and a few trustees of the pension funds to the United States to see their new investments. As they arrived at the Watergate Hotel, they discovered the bar had been demolished at Salgo's direction. She knew nothing about his planned changes and was unaware the bar, which of course provided significant income to the hotel, would be closed until renovations were completed. She prided herself on having a hands-on management style and was distressed to be caught flat-footed, especially in front of Hugh Jenkins and the pension fund trustees. Salgo, she decided, would from now on need closer supervision.

From that point forward, Luscombe checked in with Salgo regularly, questioning every aspect of Watergate operations and insisting on approving major expenditures and contracts, as befitting a fifty-fifty partner. After a few months of this, Salgo was fed up. He reached out to a friend, a lawyer in New York, to rant.

"Did you tell me you had a crazy contract with Continental Illinois?" the friend asked.

"Yeah," Salgo replied.

"Read your contract," the friend said. "If it has in it what you were telling me, you had better get yourself a lawyer—a real smart one, a young one." He gave Salgo the name and number of Sidney Dickstein, the founding partner of Dickstein, Shapiro & Morin, one of Washington's powerhouse law firms. Dickstein was both a tough litigator and a smooth behind-the-scenes consigliere to the firm's corporate clients. "He was equally comfortable in the courtroom and in the boardroom," recalled Michael Nannes, a young lawyer who would eventually become chairman of the firm.

Salgo met Dickstein in Washington and together the men reviewed the partnership agreement with Continental Illinois Properties, which had been absorbed into Pan-American Holdings, the U.S. real estate arm of the National Coal Board pension funds.

Salgo had not agreed in advance to allow Continental to transfer their Watergate shares to Wendy Luscombe and Pan-American. In fact, he originally heard about Luscombe's takeover plans only by reading about them in the *Wall Street Journal*.

"They are doing exactly what the contract says neither of us should do," Salgo said.

Sidney looked up from the contract. "I think you have a point."

Dickstein directed Nannes and a first-year associate with the firm, Mark Packman, to dig around for cases which could persuade a court that the acquisition of Continental Illinois Properties amounted to a "transfer" of the Watergate assets, and was therefore subject to the terms of Salgo's original agreement. If a court agreed with that interpretation, then Luscombe's half-ownership of the Watergate was a violation of the original agreement. If a court disagreed, Salgo was stuck with his new partners. Nannes and Packman turned up a single case, *PPG Industries, Inc. v. Guardian Industries Corp.*, that seemed to fit the situation. It was a narrow opportunity, "a very long putt," Nannes advised, using a golf analogy. "We're going with it," said Dickstein.

Dickstein filed a motion for summary judgment, essentially agreeing in advance to all facts in the case, and asked for a ruling. Judge Thomas Aquinas Flannery ruled the purchase of Continental Illinois Properties was indeed a "transfer." Because it had taken place without his permission, Salgo was owed damages. Lawyers for Luscombe and Pan-American Holdings appealed the ruling.

"We were lucky," Dickstein told Salgo. "I can't guarantee you that will happen on the appeal. My recommendation is to settle now."

Under the terms of the settlement, Pan-American made a $100,000 payment to Salgo and agreed to new partnership terms. Both parties were now free to sell their interest in the Watergate at any time, and to whomever they wished.

IN APRIL 1980, ANNA CHENNAULT TOLD A REPORTER FOR *W* magazine that Ronald Reagan and George Bush were "equally qualified" to become president. She didn't care at all for Illinois Congressman John Anderson. "He thinks he can sometimes be a Democrat and sometimes be a Republican," she said, "and that doesn't work." Bush withdrew from the race at the end of May. Reagan accepted his party's nomination in July and on November 4, 1980, Ronald Reagan defeated Jimmy Carter.

Three days after the election, Chennault launched a vigorous campaign to land a job with the new Republican administration. "No words can express my joy and satisfaction on our overwhelming victory," she wrote to three Reagan aides, E. Pendleton "Pen" James, Edwin Meese and William Casey on November 7, "particularly as I am among the first few supporters of Ronald Reagan's candidacy for the presidency. I am proud to say I was right." She recited her activities on behalf of the Reagan-Bush ticket, stating "without modesty" she had been "a very effective spokesman for our cause," raising funds and addressing women's groups and the Asian-American community. She had been offered positions in both the Nixon and

Ford administrations, she added, "but it seemed tokenish to me and I was not in a position to accept." Now, however, she was available.

At the crossroads of my career, I am responsible to many of my own people and the people who have helped the Republican Party because of me. Each election, after we either win or lose, we have always been cast aside or given some token recognition. Governor Reagan, coming from California, I don't think this will be his policy. I know he has lots of appreciation and sympathy for the people who have helped him from the beginning.

. . . If I do not get any recognition, it will be difficult for me to respond to all those people who have worked so hard with me with confidence and dedication.

"I am not particularly interested in any paid job in the White House," she wrote, "but I do think a title of Director of Special Projects, or Counsellor or Advisor to the President on Special Projects," would be appropriate—with a portfolio that included looking after "the problems and interests of Americans Abroad" and advising the president on "Ethnic Affairs."

The same day, Tommy Corcoran wrote to Pen James, who was in charge of appointments for the incoming Reagan administration. Corcoran was not seeking an appointment for himself, he wrote, but was reaching out to recommend Anna Chennault. "I am not sure if she would be interested in a job in the administration," but "her talent and knowledge should be fully utilized in your new Administration." Corcoran said he was forced to write because "Anna Chennault is not the kind of person who will blow her own horn."

Anna, meanwhile, told a reporter she would not accept an appointment in the new Republican administration, despite "rumors circulating around Washington" that a cabinet post was about to be offered to her. "I want to be free and independent," she said, "and I believe I will have the most influence in that capacity."

On December 1, William Casey, the chairman of the Reagan-Bush campaign and Reagan's nominee for director of the Central Intelligence Agency, sent a note to Pen James and passed along his "high opinion" of Chennault's "capabilities." Casey followed up with another note three weeks later. "Anna did everything from the very beginning," Casey wrote. She "worked, raised money, contributed money, stood up to people on many ideas, and, more importantly, she does that with talent and ability and we should find a way to use her talents."

On December 22, 1980, Chennault wrote to Bill Timmons, a lobbyist in the Reagan-Bush transition office, her tone now beginning to verge on despondent. "So many Senators and others have called on my behalf," she wrote, "and I just feel a little disappointed that nothing has been done to recognize my effort and all the minorities who have helped."

> *I just want to make it clear that I am not begging for a job—I have my pride and dignity.*
>
> *I certainly hope something happens very soon before our President-elect takes office. I have calls from the people who worked so hard for us during the campaign and I don't have any answer.*

As Washington geared up to welcome the Reagan administration, Anna Chennault co-hosted a reception at the Capitol Hill Club to welcome the sixteen new Republican senators. "After four years of being about as fashionable as a hula hoop," the *Washington Post* reported, Anna Chennault was back in style. One headline in the *Washington Star* said it all: CHENNAULT'S COMEBACK.

She bristled, however, when *People* magazine referred to her as a skilled hostess on the Washington social circuit. "I am not a hostess," she snapped. "For years I have despised that description."

Chennault was also eager to shed the nickname that had haunted her since 1968. "Don't call her Dragon Lady ever again," the *Washington Post* reported. "Politicians have been using Anna Chennault for years. Using her to entertain them, to introduce them to important people, to raise money for them, to carry their messages, even—say some of her critics—to do their dirty work."

"If people like this ask me to do something again," Chennault said, "I'm going to make them put it in writing. I was younger, and maybe I was also naïve."

Corcoran predicted Anna would never run for office, or take a high-profile job in the Reagan administration, other than perhaps as a "roving ambassador." He offered another prediction: She would never marry him, or anyone else. "Anna is afraid that if she remarries she cannot be buried in that lovely place in Arlington Cemetery where her husband is buried," he said.

"As long as I was the young widow of Chennault, good-looking, it was all right," she told the *Chicago Tribune.* "A woman is all right as long as she sits at home, doing nothing but eating candies." In aviation, for example, "the only women they recognized 20 years ago were what? Stewardesses, that's all. . . .

> Yes, if there's one thing you learn in the man's world, it's that if you are a woman who is successful, you will be kicked out. If you are not a doer, no one will say anything. But once you show some capability, the attack begins.
>
> There are lots of insecure men in this world. When they see that a woman is charming, intelligent, and capable, they say, "Be careful, your brain is showing." And women are no better. "I never experienced discrimination in my life," they say. Well you know they are only saying this to please the men.

When asked whether she might be heading into the government, she deflected the question. "I haven't had time to think about that," she said.

In the hallway of the Reagan-Bush inaugural committee offices, Chennault bumped into a colleague from the U.S. Chamber of Commerce and told him she was headed to Taiwan over the holidays and was planning to deliver something very valuable: five invitations to attend the Reagan inaugural festivities. The invitations delighted Taipei, but when word reached China's ambassador to the United States, Chai Zemin, he threatened to boycott the events if Taiwanese officials attended. Five days before Inauguration Day, Reagan's foreign policy team disinvited Tsiang Yien-si, the secretary of Taiwan's ruling Nationalist Party, who heard the bad news just as he was arriving in Washington. He dutifully came down with a "diplomatic illness" and checked himself into Jefferson Memorial Hospital. A Taiwanese spokesman said he was too ill to attend the inauguration.

The Chinese ambassador attended, along with the rest of the diplomatic corps. Three Taiwanese—members of the group invited by Chennault and subsequently disinvited by the committee— managed to get in anyway, using tickets provided by individual members of Congress. A reporter for the *Christian Science Monitor* said the episode revealed that despite China's harsh rhetoric, the country "is prepared to be flexible on the Taiwan question," provided U.S.–Taiwanese ties "are not flaunted too openly" by the U.S. government. The *Christian Science Monitor* also hinted the scuffle had damaged Anna Chennault's reputation with the Reagan crowd.

"WE'VE NEVER HAD SO MANY ESTABLISHED CONGRESSMEN lose their jobs," said a Washington real estate agent in early December 1980. Republicans netted 34 seats in the House and 12 seats in the Senate, enough to become the majority for the first time in 28 years. A total of 44 Democrats in Congress—32 in the House and 12 in the Senate—lost their reelection campaigns in the 1980 Reagan landslide.

Watergate sellers started raising prices on their apartments within days of the election. A two-bedroom duplex that had been on the market for nearly a year at $325,000 was relisted at $350,000. James Brockett, president of First Commercial Bank in Virginia, raised the asking price of his three-bedroom apartment in Watergate East from $450,000 to $485,000. The owner of a one-bedroom apartment put his unit up for sale five days after the election at $300,000. "That's about $100,000 more than one-bedrooms sell for," scoffed a real estate agent. "He's just trying to make a killing." A two-bedroom apartment sold for $750,000—about double what it would have fetched a year earlier.

Local real estate observers believed the Reagan appointees, coming to town from expensive Southern California, would not be deterred by 15 percent mortgage interest rates. "Prices don't scare them," said one agent.

Just days after the election, Charles Wick, co-chairman of the Reagan inaugural, moved into Watergate South, renting an apartment for $1,800 a month. "We just *love* it," said his wife, Mary Jane. "There is nothing in Washington that has the amenities this place has. The shops, the beauty salon, the dentist, they're all here. And we all have homes in California, so you don't want the responsibility of that here."

Betsy and Alfred Bloomingdale, longtime friends of the Reagans, rented an eleventh-floor apartment in Watergate South. "They treat us very well," said Alfred. "And we can put people up at the hotel." "It's safe," Betsy added. "You don't get mugged."

William Wilson, another member of Reagan's "kitchen cabinet," which had helped finance Reagan's political rise, and who would become U.S. ambassador to the Holy See, rented an apartment with his wife, Betty, in Watergate South. Drew Lewis, Reagan's secretary of transportation, moved into Watergate East. Supreme Court nominee Sandra Day O'Connor took up temporary residence at the Watergate as she prepared for her confirmation hearings before the Senate Judiciary Committee.

Before the election, the Watergate Hotel prepared two budgets:

the Carter budget and the Reagan budget. The Reagan budget was considerably higher. In the first five months of 1981, the hotel spent nearly $1 million to accommodate its new Republican guests. There were fresh raspberries from Chile, chocolate truffles, orchids, copies of the *Los Angeles Times* on doorsteps in the morning and marzipan elephants placed on pillows every night. "Their whole lifestyle is so unlike anything in Washington," gushed Diane Sappenfield, an assistant to Salgo. "They're our royalty."

Publishing magnate Walter Annenberg and his wife, Leonore, known as Lee, along with a maid and butler, moved into a three-bedroom suite on the tenth floor of the Watergate Hotel. Their suite, redecorated at the Watergate's expense in Mrs. Annenberg's favorite colors—beige, pink and green—normally rented for $750 a night, but was offered to them at a special rate a hotel staffer described as "several thousand dollars a week." The Annenbergs considered buying the penthouse apartment of Senator and Mrs. Javits in Watergate West, but it didn't have a river view.

Whenever Carol and Charles Price visited Washington, they rented a suite in the Watergate Hotel next door to the Annenbergs. Carol Price was the Swanson's frozen food heiress; Charles was the new nominee for U.S. ambassador to Belgium. The morning of Lee Annenberg's swearing-in ceremony as chief of protocol at the State Department, Jerry Zipkin—a Manhattan real estate agent and bon vivant, once labeled a "Social Moth" by *Women's Wear Daily*—stood in the lobby of the Watergate Hotel. He tilted his head back and shouted: "Where's *Carol*?!?!"

Carol's mother looked up from a couch in the lobby. "She's in the safety deposit box, getting her jewelry."

Jane and Justin Dart—he was a former drugstore magnate, chairman of Dart & Kraft, Inc., the food and consumer products conglomerate, and also a member of Reagan's "kitchen cabinet"—rented a one-bedroom suite in the Watergate Hotel whenever they visited Washington, staying on the same floor as the Annenbergs and the Prices. Zipkin rented a suite down the hall. "He likes to have everybody on the same floor," observed the hotel's general manager. "If I got an apartment in Washington, it would *definitely* be at the Watergate," Zipkin drawled. "It's so *private.*"

Nancy Reagan and her California girlfriends referred to themselves simply as "the Group." They traveled in a pack. They threw parties for each other. They dined regularly at Jean-Louis, as often as three times a week. "They're the Gucci coochi cost too moochi group," said Watergate South resident Victor Lasky, a former speechwriter for Richard Nixon and Martha Mitchell.

At the Watergate Salon, Antonio Buttaro reported business was up 25 percent since the Reagan crowd arrived. Regulars called it the "Gossip Salon," a place where the women shouted above the din of blow dryers and traded notes about who was leaving the Reagan administration, who was coming in and who they saw at an embassy the night before. Lee Annenberg summoned a hairdresser to her suite every morning at eight. Other customers tinted their eyebrows to match their hair, or indulged in a "bio-peel" treatment to reverse damage caused by the California sun. "Most of 'em don't even have a bottle of shampoo at home," said Tom Gerhart, a Watergate Salon stylist. "I like the California people," added George Ozturk, another stylist. "I don't feel like a hairdresser. I feel like a *sculptor.*" After four years of the Carter administration—when women boasted in the newspapers they did their own hair—Buttaro was elated. "The business has changed completely," he said. "Before it was peanuts. Now it's different."

SHORTLY AFTER MOVING INTO THE WHITE HOUSE, PRESIdent Reagan appointed Elizabeth Hanford Dole as assistant to the president for public liaison, with a portfolio that included reaching out to interest groups across the nation, including ethnic and religious minorities. "What does she know about minorities?" an irritated Chennault told the *Washington Post*. "How does she understand how we feel?"

Chennault fired off another letter to Pen James. "Being among the first few to come out in support of Ronald Reagan," she wrote, "I hoped we would be given special consideration." She asked for a personal meeting with James to discuss her future.

"Anna Chennault has probably done as much for the Republican Party as any woman I know in America," Senator Barry Goldwater wrote James the next day. "I cannot understand why the President hasn't at least called her, talked with her, and better than that, given her something to do in recognition of her long years of service." Goldwater hoped his letter would do some good. "I have used every other track I know and none of them has worked," he wrote, "including a direct communication" with Reagan. "These people need to be kept in the Party," Goldwater concluded, "even though some of them are getting on in years."

On February 10, Chennault wrote again to Ed Meese. "I have not heard from you and I wondered if anything has been done on my assignment. Will you please phone!"

Tommy Corcoran sent a personal letter to President Reagan on February 11. Corcoran and Reagan had something in common: They were Irishmen with a gift for storytelling. Corcoran began his letter with a story.

Corcoran and President Franklin D. Roosevelt were at Hyde Park working on an important speech. Two secretaries were there as well, Marguerite "Missy" LeHand and Peggy Dowd, but the first lady and her mother had gone out and were not expected to return until the afternoon. Roosevelt received "glorious news"—a friend had sent him a pheasant!—and ordered it cooked immediately for lunch. "Thereafter," Corcoran wrote, "we talked more about the pheasant than the speech."

Just before lunch, however, Eleanor Roosevelt returned with her mother and a female cousin. "Four for lunch is a lot for one pheasant," Corcoran wrote. Now the pheasant would have to feed seven.

Roosevelt smiled. "Tommy," the president said, "you are now going to witness an exercise in the highest Presidential diplomacy. I will carve this pheasant so that each lady will appreciate there is no distinction in their rank in my affection. But as a necessary consequence, unhappily for you, nothing can be left but the Pope's nose!"

Corcoran suggested to Reagan that, having been raised in Iowa, he would know what "the Pope's nose" was—the heart-shaped flap covering the bird's posterior.

"For my Anna," Corcoran begged, "please not just the 'Pope's nose.'"

ON SATURDAY, FEBRUARY 7, 1981, PRESIDENT REAGAN POSED for his official portrait in the East Room of the White House and for a second portrait, with Mrs. Reagan, in the Red Room. At 8:05 that night, the Reagans left the White House and headed to the Watergate Hotel for a private dinner at Jean-Louis, hosted by Mary Jane and Charles Wick, in celebration of Reagan's seventieth birthday. Before dinner, the Reagans popped into the Annenbergs' suite in the Watergate Hotel. Peter Buse was introduced to the president as the vice president of the hotel. Reagan shook his hand and smiled: "You must be the youngest vice president in Washington."

The scene was "frantic," recalled Regine Palladin, who helped out in the kitchen for the evening. "Secret Service was everywhere." When she had to use the bathroom off the kitchen, an agent banged on the door. "Please step out immediately," he ordered.

Jean-Louis Palladin served dinner that night to the Reagans and forty-two guests, including Gloria and Jimmy Stewart, CIA director William Casey and his wife, Sophia, and Ted Graber, Mrs. Reagan's interior designer. Watergate residents at the dinner included the Annenbergs, the Bloomingdales, and Attorney General William

French Smith and his wife, Jean. Reagan's entire Southern California "kitchen cabinet" flew in for the event, including Jane and Justin Dart; Virginia and Holmes Tuttle, an automobile dealer; and Marion and Earle Jorgensen, a steel magnate.

"If it weren't for the efforts of this group," Reagan joked during his toast, "I'd be making this speech before the Chamber of Commerce."

Jean-Louis prepared an eight-course meal, including foie gras on toast; scallops with truffle butter and salmon; veal and California asparagus; and ravioli stuffed with wild mushrooms. "It took five hours to do the ravioli," Jean-Louis said. "We made 150 of them—by hand." After the final two courses—a salad, followed by a pastry with raspberries and black currant sherbet—a guest pushed herself away from the table. "I'm going on a grapefruit diet for the next week," she said, sighing.

As much as the staff enjoyed having the president of the United States dine at their restaurant, Palladin's chef de cuisine Larbi Dahrouch considered another night at the Watergate to be even more memorable. Salgo asked Palladin to prepare a late-night dinner for Leonard Bernstein and fifteen guests—at three in the morning. A piano was rolled through the underground parking lot into the restaurant and Bernstein gave an impromptu concert for his friends and the entire restaurant staff.

FINALLY, IN MARCH, CHENNAULT GOT HER MEETING WITH PEN James, who asked her to consider serving on "some commission." She was clearly disappointed. "My first preference is still to serve as Ambassador at Large," she wrote Ed Meese after the meeting, but she was willing to consider something else. "I just hope we will not have to wait too long for appointments for people like ourselves who have made very substantial contributions, not only in time, money and effort, but have been loyal and dedicated Republicans over two decades."

NICOLAS SALGO RELIED CLOSELY ON TWO PEOPLE TO RUN the Watergate Hotel: Gabor Olah de Garab, the hotel's general manager, and Bettye Bradley, the concierge.

Gabor Olah de Garab—everyone on the staff called him Mr. Olah—was born in Pásztó, Hungary, in 1924. After the war, he escaped the Soviet occupation and settled in Italy. He studied hotel management at the École hôtelière de Lausanne in Switzerland and worked at some of the grandest hotels in Italy, including the Excelsior Hotel Gallia in Milan, the Hotel Splendido in Portofino and the Cavalieri in Rome. Giuseppe Cecchi recruited him in 1967 to become the first general manager of the Watergate Hotel.

Bettye Bradley was a high school dropout from Atlanta, Georgia. She was seventeen years old when she married a soldier who had served under General Patton in Europe. It was not a happy marriage. After her son Lee Bradley went off to Emory University, Bettye filed for divorce. She moved to Arlington, Virginia, and found work at the Watergate Hotel reception desk. She quickly made herself indispensable, advising guests where to eat, where to shop, even where to rent a helicopter. Within a year, Salgo promoted her to concierge—one of only fifteen certified concierges working in an American hotel, one of only three women concierges nationwide and the first woman concierge at the Watergate Hotel.

When Salgo took over the Watergate Hotel, in partnership with Continental Illinois Properties, he personally supervised the refurbishing of the hotel's presidential suites. Antique furniture—"very old stuff," one hotel staffer recalled—arrived from Europe. But if Mr. Olah wanted to spend money on something, Salgo would often balk. "Two Hungarians," Bettye said.

"Mr. Olah was old school," Bettye recalled years later. "The guest comes first."

He was also a bit of a "rapscallion," she said. While he never overruled Salgo directly, he sometimes found a way to work around him. "We might have to do some hanky panky," he would tell a staff member who came forward with a request to spend money to satisfy a guest.

Bettye always carried two black leather address books with the phone numbers and addresses of her contacts—for restaurant reservations, theater tickets, masseuses or masseurs, or anything else a guest might need. She resisted converting her files to a computer. "I think you lose contact with your guest when you stare at an electronic screen," she said. "It feels good to thumb through my worn pages to find a secret source."

She knew when guests awoke (from their wake-up calls), what they liked to eat (from room-service orders) and who visited them. "I wasn't nosy," she said, "it was just second nature." Many famous entertainers made the Watergate Hotel their home while they performed at the Kennedy Center next door—just a six-minute walk, although some entertainers insisted on using a hotel limousine. Many years after Bettye had moved on from the Watergate, she shared stories about her tenure at the concierge desk:

Bette Davis walked through the lobby, clutching a paper bag. As she waited for the elevator, the bag slipped from her hands and fell to the floor, with the sound of shattering glass. Bettye smelled alcohol. The bag was full of miniature liquor bottles, perhaps from her most recent airplane flight.

Pearl Bailey came down to the lobby one morning to pick up her newspaper. When a tourist snapped her picture, Bailey screamed at the man, and chased him out the front door and down the sidewalk. She used the large kitchen in her suite one night to cook a roast for Henry Fonda.

Shelley Winters liked to eat breakfast in the hotel dining room, wearing a bathrobe and slippers.

The playwright Tennessee Williams had fallen asleep one night while working on his play *Clothes for a Summer Hotel*. He called from National Airport in a panic: the only copy of the play was missing. Hotel staff retrieved it from behind a headboard.

When Katharine Hepburn arrived one day, fans sent more than fifty flower arrangements for delivery to her suite. She cooked her own breakfast—brown eggs with a New York strip steak, sourced by Bettye from the Watergate Safeway. Her suite never seemed to be cold enough: She kept her balcony doors open and demanded hotel engineers disconnect the room's heater.

Bea Arthur tried to order room service, but the waiter, who was from Korea, couldn't understand her. After many minutes repeating her order, she gave up. "Fuck off!" she shouted, and hung up.

The ballet dancer Rudolf Nureyev called room service at 2:00 A.M. and asked for a bottle of olive oil to be sent up to his room.

Composer Leonard Bernstein told Bettye he needed a Sony Dream Machine to help him get to sleep. When she couldn't locate one in Washington, she put a hotel staffer on a train to New York to purchase one and bring it back before Bernstein returned that night from the Kennedy Center.

Lauren Bacall "chewed out" a hotel operator over the plastic hangers in her suite. Bettye rushed home, pulled her own clothes out of her closet and installed her personal wooden hangers in Bacall's suite. When Bacall checked out at the end of her stay, she took the hangers with her.

After Keith Moon trashed his suite, Mr. Olah threatened to lock him out of the hotel. Moon's manager personally delivered $5,000 to prevent eviction.

"Service separates great hotels from mediocre hotels," Bettye said.

The Watergate attracted foreign diplomats. And at least in one instance, according to Bettye, the diplomats attracted the FBI.

Three guests from North Korea checked into the Watergate. They appeared to be enjoying themselves—they ordered lobster off the room-service menu, Bettye recalled. One night during their visit, the FBI rushed into the lobby. The North Koreans were missing, an agent explained, before rushing out again onto Virginia Avenue. The North Koreans were actually sitting in a corner of the lobby. When the FBI agents returned, Bettye whispered to one of them, "If you'll just look around the corner, you'll find what you're looking for."

The prime minister of Rhodesia, Ian Smith, held a "top secret" meeting in a suite borrowed for the night from a defense contractor. When he returned to the hotel a few months later for a lunch, the hotel was surrounded by protesters.

Visitors from Saudi Arabia, Bettye recalled years later, liked to show pornographic movies in their suites.

Tourists—including an "unbelievable number of Japanese"—came by the Watergate Hotel in droves, she later recalled, to see the home of the famous scandal—unaware, of course, that the break-in had taken place at the Watergate Office Building next door. "They were acting like there was a burglary still in progress," she said. One day, a woman walked into the lobby and asked to be put on "the tour." She said a tour bus had just dropped her off and told her to go inside and see where the Watergate burglars stayed the night of the break-in.

"There's no tour," replied Bettye with a smile.

DECEMBER 6, 1981, TOMMY CORCORAN DIED OF A PULMO-nary blood clot at the Washington Hospital Center. He was eighty years old. Anna spoke at his funeral. "He made the most humble person feel important and many presidents have cherished his friendship," she said. "And what a great teacher he was!"

Anna lost more than a close friend. She lost a business advisor, a fellow movie buff, a press spokesman and a tireless advocate within the political circles of the capital.

"He made us laugh, he taught us to sing," she said. "Wherever he went, there was always music."

When Tommy died, she lost her favorite piano player.

THE REAGAN RENAISSANCE AT THE WATERGATE LASTED
about a year. Lee Annenberg was the first member of "the Group" to
leave. After only seven months on the job as chief of protocol, living
in the Watergate Hotel during the week while Walter managed his
media empire from Philadelphia, she submitted her resignation. "I
adore my job," she said, "but my husband comes first." Betsy and
Alfred Bloomingdale left shortly thereafter.

Mary Jane and Charles Wick kept a long-standing tradition and
celebrated Christmas Eve in 1981 with the Reagans in their Watergate South apartment, then moved to a house in northwest Washington. The Reagans would not return to the Watergate for three
years.

In the fall of 1981, the hottest-selling postcard around Washington depicted First Lady Nancy Reagan wearing a gold crown studded
with jewels and an ermine cape. The caption: *Queen Nancy*. Shortly
after moving into the White House, Mrs. Reagan spent $800,000 in
donated funds on renovations and another $300,000 in donations
to buy new china. Johnny Carson joked her favorite food was caviar.
In July, in London for the wedding of Charles and Diana, she was
booed, and mocked by the notoriously snarky British press. Michael
Deaver, the White House aide overseeing the First Couple's public
image, was relieved when the Watergate crowd started to disperse.
Lunches at Jean-Louis, and the constant round of cocktail parties,
were undermining the Reagans' purpose in Washington, said the
first lady's press secretary, Sheila Tate.

From the perspective of the battered Watergate, it didn't matter.
According to Peter Buse, a page had been turned. "We are no longer
the Nixon Watergate."

There is no other place in the world quite like Watergate, and everyone who lives and breathes there knows it.

Town & Country, June 1982

REPUBLICAN JOHN WARNER WAS FIRST ELECTED TO THE United States Senate in 1978, but after the Reagan landslide of 1980, in which the Republicans took over the Senate majority, Warner decided it was time to ditch his row house in Washington's Dupont Circle neighborhood and move into Watergate South, upstairs from his good friends Elizabeth and Bob Dole. When Warner suggested the move to his wife, the actress Elizabeth Taylor, she replied, "You've got to be fucking kidding me."

Each of the three Watergate apartment buildings had its own rules and regulations governing pets. Depending on the building, you could have a pet if you owned your apartment, but not if you were a renter. If you combined two apartments, you could have two pets. In one building, concerns about the rising pet population resulted in a temporary rule: If your pet died, you were not allowed to replace it. In Watergate South, each resident was allowed no more than two pets.

Elizabeth Taylor owned a succession of cats, dogs and birds. She called them her babies.

In December 1981, a few days before Christmas, Elizabeth Taylor and Senator John Warner announced their breakup. They divorced on November 7, 1982. "What precipitated the separation," according to a Taylor biographer, "was not an act of infidelity, but rather one of thoughtlessness." Faced with the choice—her husband or her "babies"—Elizabeth Taylor dumped her husband.

IN JUNE 1982, *TOWN & COUNTRY* MAGAZINE PUBLISHED AN eleven-page feature story on the Watergate, Washington's "next-best power address"—second only to 1600 Pennsylvania Avenue—and home to "the chicest deli south of Zabar's"; "the best French restaurant in Washington"; a pastry shop "riddled with Sacher torte and other such sins"; four psychiatrists; and a beauty salon that doubled as "the scene of the best daily gossipfest in town." "Privacy is rampant if so desired; security is on a soothing par with that of Buckingham Palace." The only downside: "There is no disco, no golf course and no tennis courts—not even an itty-bitty private one."

"The world of Watergate is an intricate intaglio of personalities where no lines are drawn." Democrats lived across the hall from Republicans. Residents included "presidents of large and small corporations," lawyers, doctors and "merry widows." Ambassadors and other diplomats from Europe (Sweden), the Middle East (Yemen, Qatar and the United Arab Emirates), South America (Brazil and Suriname), Asia (Japan and Korea) and Africa (Somalia) were "supremely content" with their Watergate offices.

The article was accompanied by portraits of twenty-five Watergate residents, posing in their Watergate apartments or offices, or shopping at the Les Champs arcade. "Smiling like a proud father," Nicolas Salgo posed on the terrace of the Kennedy Center as the Watergate loomed behind him. Ambassador Randolph Kidder and his wife, Dorothy—although he was sworn in as President Johnson's ambassador to Cambodia, his credentials were rejected by Prince Sihanouk and he returned home in October 1964—posed in the living room of their duplex, surrounded by the "eclectic ambiance" of contemporary art and Louis XV antiques. Stephane Groueff, director of information for the embassy of Oman, posed with his wife, Lil, who decorated their apartment with wicker furniture in order to give it the feel of a beach house. Sargent Shriver, the founder of the

U.S. Peace Corps and vice presidential nominee on the Democrats' 1972 ticket, was "thriving" in his sixth-floor office in Watergate 600. Elizabeth and Bob Dole posed in their living room, enjoying "the early American ambiance of their Watergate digs." Robert Strauss, who had moved the Democratic National Committee out of the Watergate in 1973, posed with his wife, Helen, in their Watergate penthouse. Decorated primarily in blues and beiges, their apartment contained "an assemblage of objet d'art collected through the couple's extensive travels," including vases he picked up in China while serving as U.S. trade representative during the Carter presidency. "One of Washington's most indefatigable hostesses, Anna Chennault," posed in her Watergate penthouse, "lavishly furnished with Chinese and Japanese antiques, many from her grandfather's home in Hong Kong."

For her photo shoot, the Countess of Romanones wore a "romantically alluring" evening gown by Pedro del Hierro and a "selection of family jewels." A ceramic leopard stood guard in her mirrored duplex apartment in Watergate South, decorated by her friend Duarte Pinto Coelho. "Madrid might be her home base," the caption read, "but the Countess Romanones, an American beauty, enjoys her periodic visits to Washington and New York." The countess, *Town & Country* noted, "is presently writing a new book."

Aline Griffith was born in Pearl River, New York, in 1923, the eldest of six children. Her father was an insurance salesman. She graduated from college in 1943 with "classic features, a college knowledge of French and Spanish and a lot of what was called then 'get up and go.'"

On a blind date in Manhattan, she mentioned an interest in espionage; her date, she wrote later, turned out to be a recruiter for the OSS. He placed her in a three-month stay at "the Farm"—the first OSS training school—from which she was dispatched to Spain. On her first day in Madrid, a handsome young man carried her bags to her room and turned down a tip. In 1947, at age twenty-six, Griffith married him: Luis Figueroa y Pérez de Guzmán el Bueno, the Count of Quintanilla. The handsome twenty-eight-year-old was a painter, and one of the richest men in Spain. The couple's wedding made the "Milestones" column in *Time* magazine, which reported the couple met while the bride "was a wartime employee of the U.S. embassy."

After Luis's grandfather passed away, he inherited the family title and Aline became the Countess of Romanones. She became a familiar name on international best-dressed lists, rode horses daily and restored her husband's seven-hundred-year-old estate in Pascualete, 170 miles southwest of Madrid.

The count and countess rented and later purchased a Watergate South penthouse, Apartment 1517, with a sweeping view of the Potomac and a large terrace on the top floor. She threw dinner parties for members of the White House staff and the cabinet, including William French Smith. There is no record of either the president or Mrs. Reagan joining the countess at her Watergate South apartment, but Mrs. Reagan did come for dinner in the countess's New York apartment in June 1985. Earlier that day, a fire had broken out in the basement, leaving the building without power. The countess refused to cancel the dinner; her private secretary called Donald Trump, one of the dinner guests, to see if he could lend her a generator, and the dinner went on almost as planned—the meal was served by candlelight.

"Having an apartment in Watergate and being so close to members of the government," the countess recalled years later, "made my espionage more effective and constant."

As part of her "espionage," the countess formed a company to place "favorable information about the Argentinian government" in the American press. Rampant corruption, economic depression stemming from the 1981–82 financial collapse (and a resulting $43 billion in foreign debt), and the military defeat in the Falklands War, forced the Argentinian junta to call for democratic elections in October 1983, at which Raúl Alfonsín was elected president. The countess enlisted in the venture her brother William and her brother-in-law Kenneth Crosby, who had worked for the FBI in Argentina during World War II, collecting information on pro-Nazi groups, and later opened an office of Merrill Lynch in Havana, Cuba. "I think neither of them made any money from this," she recalled, "but they were very enthusiastic."

Shortly after William Casey was sworn in as director of the CIA, the countess sent him a list of thirty "influential" European and South African conservatives she said would "gratefully assist in any endeavor to improve relationships," including Brian Crozier, a British author and founder of "the 61," a private spy network.

She wrote to White House aides Michael Deaver and Richard Allen, requesting a meeting between Manuel Fraga—whom she described as the leader of Spain's "most important right party"—and President Reagan. A five-minute meeting and a photograph with Reagan, she explained, "would give psychological strength to the people of the right in Spain." National Security Council aide James M. Rentschler took up her request with the Spanish Desk at the Department of State, which recommended the president not meet with a Spanish political leader until he had first met with Prime Minister Leopoldo Calvo-Sotelo, head of the coalition government. "The main question is timing," Rentschler informed Allen, while noting the Countess of Romanones was a "delicious name!" Her request for a meeting was declined.

In 1985, the countess launched a campaign to land an ambassadorship. She suggested to Casey it "might create a problem" if she were to become the ambassador to Spain, because of her royal title, and offered instead to be sent to El Salvador. Casey called the White House on her behalf. A White House aide vetted her application and, in a memo to Robert M. Kimmitt, the National Security Council's top lawyer, reported the countess was "an enthusiastic supporter" of Roberto D'Aubuisson, a far-right politician linked to death squads in El Salvador and who had recently lost an election to rival José

Napoleón Duarte. "She may be eminently qualified for some other position," the Reagan White House aide wrote, "but we do not need a fan of Major Bob as our Ambassador to San Salvador."

In 1987, the countess released a memoir, *The Spy Wore Red: My Adventures as an Undercover Agent in World War II*, detailing her exploits, which included delivering secret documents around Europe and transmitting messages in Morse code. She organized groups of female agents to cross into Germany and "investigate Gestapo and SS activities." Late in the war, she attempted to cross the border with a small suitcase full of microfilm and radio equipment, narrowly escaping detection, imprisonment and, almost certainly, execution. She confessed to falling in love with a double agent for the Nazis (identified only as "Pierre") and revealed she had committed a murder. Her code name during the war was Butch. Her publisher, Random House, changed it to Tiger, she said, because Butch "had other implications."

Michael Gross, a reporter and fashion columnist for the "Living/ Style" section of the *New York Times*, called her book "breezy and gossipy," "a welcome addition to the espionage genre" and "seedy and sophisticated."

After her husband died in 1987, the countess sold their Watergate apartment. She kept writing, however, and released a second memoir in 1990, *The Spy Went Dancing*, about her hunt for a NATO mole, with the Duchess of Windsor as her accomplice. "Espionage is like a drug," she told a reporter for *People* magazine, as she sipped Diet Coke from a champagne glass. "It makes life very exciting."

A year later, in an article titled "The Spy Stripped Naked," *Women's Wear Daily* declared the countess's books "may be more fiction than fact." Reporter Susan Watters tracked down a declassified file in the National Archives containing eighty pages of "routine reports" from an agent code-named Butch, covering "social life in Madrid and rumors about German agents." The file contained no mentions of the exploits in the countess's book, such as the time she claimed to have "blasted a would-be assassin with her Beretta." The countess was outraged. The files prove nothing, she said. Even if the memos were hers, she would never have written down everything she saw during her service. "You have to keep many things secret," she said.

She acknowledged, however, that her original manuscript had been rejected by a half-dozen publishers, so she made revisions, re-creating dialogue and simplifying the story line while keeping the "core" of the tale authentic. In her author's note at the beginning of *The Spy Wore Silk*, she explained that although some "dramatic moments" had been left out, and various conversations "re-created," her intention throughout "has been to capture the essence and flavor of the places, events, and conversations that actually took place." Her publisher said the countess had invented a new genre: "romantic nonfiction." The countess was simply trying to make the OSS "look good," said Ray Cline, Anna Chennault's lunch companion on June 16, 1972, the day of the Watergate break-in, who was now teaching at Georgetown University. "Espionage is mostly boredom," he said. "Once in a while, about 2 percent of the time, it's very exciting. But 98 percent is drudgery. In order to get her books published, she decided to glamorize."

The countess went on to write two more books: *The Well-Mannered Assassin* (1994) and *El Fin de Una Era* (2010 in Spanish, 2015 in English). A selection of her jewels was auctioned off by Sotheby's Geneva in 2011, including the ruby and diamond demi parure—a matching necklace and earring set—she wore in the *Town & Country* photo shoot at the Watergate nearly two decades earlier, which sold for $409,230, and a 1936 diamond bracelet watch, given to her by the Duchess of Windsor, which sold for nearly six times its high estimate.

RICHARD KIND, A "SLENDER, HAUGHTY BACHELOR," OPER-ated a million-dollar gay prostitution service named Friendly Models out of a townhouse in Georgetown. Kind answered six incoming telephone lines as escorts hung around shooting pool or played video games as they waited for appointments. He provided callers with detailed physical descriptions of his stable of thirty escorts, some as young as eighteen, most of them "clean-cut and collegiate." For diplomats and other international clients, Friendly Models offered escorts who could speak French, Spanish, German and Italian. One call boy, identified only as "Ken" in a *Miami Herald* report, said Friendly Models got the "carriage trade of the gay out-call business" in Washington—serving only the well-to-do market. Prices varied from $60 to $200 a night, payable by Visa or Master Charge, with receipts marked "R.S.K. Associates"—Richard Kind's initials. "Ken" told *Herald* investigate reporter Frank Greve he regularly serviced clients on Washington's Embassy Row, in the hunt country of Virginia and at the Watergate Hotel and apartments.

Leroy Williams was a straight-A student from the only black family in the Sixth and Izard Church of Christ in Little Rock, Arkansas. At the suggestion of congregation member Bob Scott, Williams applied for a position as a congressional page and was accepted. The congregation's Bible study class raised the money to send Williams to Washington. He started as a page in late June 1981 and was elevated to page supervisor by the end of summer. In January 1982, however, Leroy Williams resigned abruptly from the page program and returned to Little Rock.

Six months later, on the *CBS Evening News* broadcast the night of June 30, 1982, a young man was interviewed—on camera, but only in profile, to shield his identity—by correspondent John Ferrugia. According to the report, a congressman had approached the young man, who was at the time a "page overseer," and asked him to come to his office later that evening. "We just sat and talked casually about what had gone on that day," the young man said. "And then he kind of made a pass at me. He told me that he thought I was real nice looking and I was just sitting there trying to soak all this in, because it was really kind of a shock. Then he just started coming on to me and then one thing just happened after another. We did have a sexual relationship at that time." The young man said he had sex with the congressman a total of three times, including once at the Watergate.

"What's the compensation here?" the reporter asked.

"I never saw any money and I don't know anybody who ever has," the young man said. "But the way that 'The Hill' works is that you climb the ladder, so one favor deserves another."

Back in Little Rock, Bob Scott recognized the voice of the CBS informant. Without question, he said to himself, it was Leroy Williams.

The story picked up momentum quickly. The *Miami Herald* reported "a 16-year-old Congressional page" had revealed members of Congress attended "drug parties" and made "homosexual advances." Federal investigators suggested as many as six congressmen could be homosexuals. CBS and NBC reported as many as twelve members of Congress were under investigation for cocaine use. Representative Larry E. Craig, a Republican from Idaho first elected to Congress in the 1980 Reagan landslide, issued a statement saying reports linking him to any homosexual activities were false and "despicable." The FBI contacted Williams and asked him to share his story. Williams reached out to Scott, who agreed to represent him.

On Tuesday, July 6, in the *Arkansas Gazette*, Leroy Williams was identified by name for the first time in connection with the unfolding scandal. Williams said he had arranged appointments with male prostitutes for a Capitol Hill staff member, a Government Printing Office employee and a U.S. senator. He told the *New York Times* the sexual encounter between the senator and a male prostitute—identified only as "Roger"—took place at the Watergate. Williams appeared on Little Rock television station KARK-TV and described in detail what happened at the Watergate:

We at first sat down. We all had a drink and . . . [they] moved to the master bedroom. About an hour later [they] came out and [the Senator] thanked me for making a call for him and expressed the fact that if there was anything he could do for me to get in touch with his office.

Williams said he did not enjoy making the arrangements. "It was something that I just accepted as part of the way you survive while you're in DC," he said. He admitted drug use and homosexual encounters, both before and after going to Washington. He named three congressmen and one senator, but the names were deleted from the broadcast when it aired. Rumors circulated on Capitol Hill that at least seven members of Congress, including two members of the House leadership, had engaged in homosexual activities. But Jack Russ, the deputy doorkeeper in the U.S. House of Representatives, called Williams "a pathological liar."

With Scott by his side, Williams met with FBI agents in Little Rock for about six hours. He took—and failed—a lie-detector test. Scott and Williams flew to Washington, and Williams testified before the House Ethics Committee. He shared with them the names of three congressmen with whom he said he had sex, and the name of the U.S. senator whose Friendly Models encounter he said he had arranged. "Despite the fact that he failed his polygraph test and despite charges by Capitol Hill officials that he's a pathological liar, Leroy Williams maintains he is telling the truth," reported ABC News congressional correspondent Carole Simpson.

Over the next forty-eight hours, Williams began to change his story. He said he did not have sex with three different congressmen "at least seven" times, but only four times. CBS News tracked down "Roger," the Friendly Models escort who had allegedly serviced an unnamed senator at the Watergate. "Roger" said he did not have sex at the Watergate with a senator; he had sex there with Leroy Williams.

On July 10, the *Washington Post* reported Williams admitted lying about arranging a sexual encounter at the Watergate. Williams told the *Post* he had met a "congressman" once for a drink at the Peacock Lounge at the Watergate Hotel, but they did not have sex. (Curiously, the *Post* reporter did not catch Williams's error: the Peacock Lounge was located in the Les Champs arcade, at the other end of the Watergate complex, and not at the hotel.) "You associate congressmen with big things; the Watergate's something big in DC, any way you look at it," Williams said. "And so I guess I was just . . . the evil part of me saying, hey, here's something that sounds good, you know. If you can stick him at the Watergate and make it sound like you know something went on at the Watergate, then that'll make the story sound twice as good."

Leroy Williams returned to Little Rock. In mid-August, he was arrested and fined $77 for public intoxication at a local theater showing *The Rocky Horror Picture Show*. A week later, he was interviewed by two congressional investigators at DeGray Lake, near Arkadelphia. The following day, at a press conference in Little Rock, Williams said his entire story was a fabrication.

"For the past few months I have made some very serious accusations," he said. "These accusations are not true. I have lied. I regret that I have lied. Words can never express the remorse I feel for the pain and the trauma that I've caused." Williams said he did not have sex with any members of Congress and did not arrange a homosexual liaison between a senator and a male prostitute. When asked if he knew of any homosexual relationships involving elected officials, he said, "There may be, but not to my personal knowledge."

"It was my original intention to help the page system, not to hurt it," Williams said. The pages, he said, worked long hours with little adult supervision. Williams said he had been pressured by other pages into abusing drugs and alcohol, and had left the program because he feared he was at risk of becoming an alcoholic.

Richard Kind, the owner of Friendly Models, was charged with conspiracy to pander. He jumped a $2,500 bond and disappeared, according to police and his lawyer. He left behind an IRS lien for $1,028,902.16 for unpaid personal and business taxes on his earnings from 1978 to 1982.

Williams returned to Washington and met with the House Ethics Committee one more time. Over a three-hour session, he recanted his earlier allegations. As Williams left the Capitol, Scott, his pro bono attorney, waved reporters away, telling them his client would not talk to anyone again on the matter. Williams never gave another interview on the controversy. He left Arkansas and moved to Florida, where he now lives with his sister.

In 2007, Scott told the *Idaho Statesman* that "Congressman C" in the 1982 House Ethics Committee report was then-congressman Larry Craig. "I am positive he named Larry Craig in 1982," Scott said. In his 1982 interview with CBS News, Williams said he had sex with Congressman C on three occasions; he then told the FBI he had "sexual relations" with Congressman C on two occasions. According to the House Ethics Committee report, Williams's testimony to congressional investigators about these encounters contained "details" that were different from what he told the FBI. "Congressman C has denied ever propositioning or having sexual relations with Williams. He has said that he never met alone under any circumstances with Williams and does not know him."

In the aftermath of the congressional page scandal, some editors and reporters asked themselves how this false story had spiraled out of control. "He was everybody's exclusive," acknowledged CBS News president Howard Stringer. "I think we should have found that out sooner." On CBS, Williams was identified only as a "former page overseer." On another network, he was a "former page." In the *Arkansas Gazette*, the charges were from "an unidentified former page from Little Rock."

According to a postmortem by the Associated Press, the fierce competitiveness of the news business in the post-Watergate era played a role in feeding the scandal. Since Watergate, more than twenty-five members of Congress had been convicted of various criminal charges. Journalists were now willing to listen to allegations they might have dismissed as preposterous before the night of June 16, 1972.

GUESTS WOULD APPROACH THE FRONT DOOR OF JEAN-Louis at the Watergate through a long, subterranean hallway; along one side, behind glass, were racks of wine and champagne. What guests did not know, however, was that the bulk of Palladin's wine inventory was scattered all over the Watergate behind unmarked doors, in racks and storage bins. The staff spoke about these "undisclosed locations" only in code, in order to deter break-ins.

With the support of Nicolas Salgo, Jean-Louis Palladin built one of the great wine cellars in the United States, recalled Mark Slater, who worked as a bartender, cellar master and, finally, as maître d' for Jean-Louis. Salgo's family owned vineyards, which supplied house wines for the hotel. Salgo attended wine auctions in France, and the hotel had an import license. Shortly after Slater arrived, he heard rumors of the secret wine storage room and tracked it down to a location in the garage. To open the door, he needed two keys—from the hotel's general manager and the chief accountant. When they finally opened the door, Slater said he felt "like Howard Carter gazing into King Tut's tomb." Cases of the finest wines in the world—all acquired by Nicolas Salgo—were stacked throughout the room. When Slater completed his inventory, he discovered the cellar included all the iconic wines of the 1920s through the 1940s, including the 1945 Château Moutone Rothschild, the "wine of the century."

Salgo also knew how to spot a bargain. He bought fifty cases of 1982 Lynch-Bages from Bordeaux, at eight dollars a bottle. For years, it was the Jean-Louis house wine, sold by the glass. "People were flabbergasted we could do this," Slater recalled. As of 2017, the same vintage was available online at nearly $300 a bottle.

ON JULY 23, 1984, SYNDICATED COLUMNIST JACK ANDERSON revealed that Senator Mark O. Hatfield, a Republican from Oregon, was assisting a Greek financier win approval for an oil pipeline across Africa, at the same time the man paid Hatfield's wife, a real estate agent, $40,000 in "real estate fees."

Basil Tsakos, a powerfully built Greek in his sixties, described himself as an "international businessman." Federal investigators later determined his international business experience included arranging the sale of 120 West German tanks to Morocco. He was enormously wealthy, with apartments in Paris, London and Geneva, and a yacht on the French Riviera. In 1980, Tsakos moved to Washington to advance his plan for constructing a 2,200-mile pipeline that would carry Middle Eastern crude oil across sub-Saharan Africa from the Red Sea to the Atlantic Ocean, thereby avoiding the Strait of Hormuz. He incorporated TAPCO, the Trans-Africa Pipeline Company, and set up offices at the Watergate 600 office building on New Hampshire Avenue. According to the FBI, Tsakos was an "imperious, arrogant and obnoxious man who manages to offend most everyone he meets." But he could also be "quite charming or generous to those in a position to help him."

Antoinette Hatfield met Laura Tsakos, Basil's wife and an heiress to a Greek banking fortune, through a mutual friend over lunch in July 1981. Mrs. Hatfield showed the Tsakoses several potential residences, including some at the Watergate. On August 23, 1982, Basil Tsakos had dinner with Senator Hatfield to discuss the $15 billion trans-African pipeline project. Senator Hatfield told investigators this was his first exposure to the idea, and he became interested in it as an alternative to increasing the U.S. presence in the Middle East. The pipeline could allow the United States to import oil from Saudi Arabia even if the Persian Gulf closed. "This appealed to me from a geopolitical point of view," Hatfield said. The senator became an energetic booster of the trans-African pipeline: He hosted a meeting in the Senate dining room to introduce Tsakos to U.S. energy secretary Donald Hodel, mentioned the project to defense secretary Caspar W. Weinberger after a meeting at the White House, arranged for Tsakos to meet with Exxon Corporation president Howard Kauffmann and discussed the proposed pipeline with President Jaafar Nimeiri of Sudan.

After Jack Anderson's column broke, Senator Hatfield asked the Senate Ethics Committee to review the controversy and turned over his files to Senate investigators. He changed his story, telling the *Washington Post* his wife was paid a fee of $15,000 for showing the Tsakoses several apartments, including some at the Watergate, although not the apartment eventually purchased by the Greek couple. "I don't believe that I intended to say it was that particular apartment she introduced them to," Hatfield said. "She had introduced them to the Watergate as part of her duties." He said his wife did not keep records of her time and he could not explain why the payments, in several different checks, totaled $40,000. "There was no rhyme or reason as to when they sent a check," he said. When the *Washington Post* interviewed Basil Tsakos in his Watergate office, the matter became further confused. Tsakos, contradicting Senator Hatfield, said he paid Mrs. Hatfield a $30,000 finder's fee for locating the apartment and $10,000 for help with the decorating.

The FBI and the Senate Ethics Committee opened separate investigations in August 1984. Hatfield was up for election that fall, and as Election Day approached, he and his wife revised the total value of payments received to $55,000 and said they would donate the same amount to charity.

FBI agents interviewed an employee of Tsakos's firm over three days, who told investigators he had overheard Tsakos tell Senator Hatfield in a telephone call: "We'll take a long walk in the woods . . . talk about nature, the animals and lots of things." According to the FBI, the employee said these comments were "very strange inasmuch as Tsakos had no interest in walking or in nature." The employee also said Tsakos had directed a TAPCO accountant to record a $10,000 expenditure marked "A.H."—the initials of Antoinette Hatfield—as a "business expense."

As the FBI investigation got under way, Laura and Basil Tsakos left the country. On August 20, their attorney informed the FBI that Basil was in Greece and Laura was in Switzerland, under the care of doctors for "heart spasms." The lawyer said he could not provide a date by which either of them would be available for an interview by the FBI.

Hatfield skipped the Republican National Convention that year to campaign in his home state at county fairs, ice cream socials and Lions Club luncheons. He won a fourth term by the biggest margin in his Senate career. The justice department investigation, however, kept going.

According to documents released in 2012, under a Freedom of Information Act request filed by Jeff Mapes, a reporter for the *Oregonian*, Tsakos was ready to plead guilty—in exchange for an assurance he would serve no time in jail—and admit paying Antoinette Hatfield $55,000 to gain her husband's support for the trans-Africa pipeline. According to FBI investigators, Hatfield was "the only American official to go out on a limb and support a questionable project." The FBI concluded Antoinette Hatfield "performed literally no work" for three of the four payments she received from Tsakos. Senator Hatfield was never indicted.

After they fled the country, the Tsakoses stopped paying their monthly cooperative fee to Watergate West. That triggered a vote by the co-op board to terminate the Tsakoses' interest in Apartment 602, which the board then rented out for $1,700 a month to Dr. and Mrs. Ahmad Esfandiary. After the Esfandiarys decided to purchase a different apartment in Watergate West and moved out, the Tsakoses' former apartment was used by Watergate West as storage until it was sold in 1994.

In November 1985, a federal grand jury indicted Tsakos for brib-

ery. His attorney informed federal officials his client was in a Paris
hospital undergoing treatment for a heart condition and was too ill
to travel. The justice department decided not to extradite Tsakos
and a federal judge dismissed the grand jury indictment against him
in April 1989. Tsakos eventually recovered, left the hospital—and
disappeared.

ALTHOUGH SHE HAD BRISTLED AT BEING LABELED A "HOST-
ess," Anna Chennault continued throughout the Reagan years to
throw dinner parties at the Watergate, mixing top White House
aides and cabinet members with defense contractors, foreign diplomats, and U.S. and foreign military officials.

In March 1984, White House aide Michael Deaver came for dinner, along with Ambassador Zhang Wen-jin of China, one month
before Reagan's visit to China. In May 1984, she hosted a buffet
reception for the deputy secretary of defense, the commandant of
the Marine Corps, the ambassadors of Thailand and Singapore,
and several members of Taiwan's army and navy. In June 1984, she
hosted a dinner for the ambassadors of South Korea and Malaysia;
Under Secretary of State for Political Affairs Michael Armacost; Vice
Chief of Staff of the U.S. Air Force General Lawrence Skantze; and
executives from defense contractors Northrop, Loral and Grum-
man. In October 1986, she hosted a dinner at the Watergate Hotel
in honor of General Chiang Chung-ling, the commander in chief
of the Taiwanese army. And in October 1987, she hosted a dinner
at the hotel for General Hau Pei-tsun, the Taiwanese army chief of
staff, inviting Watergate neighbors Audrey Mars and Senator and
Mrs. Larry Pressler of South Dakota.

Anna also kept pressing for a presidential appointment, even after
Reagan named her vice chairman, in April 1981, of a commission
tasked with promoting U.S. exports. She asked Edwin Meese to assist in getting her reinstated as a member of the Kennedy Center
Advisory Committee "and the privilege of using the Presidential

Boxes as we had the privilege during the other Republican Administrations." In late 1984, Senator Strom Thurmond wrote President Reagan and White House chief of staff Donald T. Regan to recommend Chennault as "Ambassador-at-Large" or "a similar position of ambassadorial rank." In 1985 and again in 1988, she asked to be appointed to the president's Foreign Intelligence Advisory Board. None of these appointments came through. She was a guest of the Reagans, however, at the July 1985 state dinner for Chinese president Li Xiannian and Madame Lin.

"WATERGATE: A WASHINGTON NEST FOR HIGH-FLYERS" READ the headline in the February 1982 issue of *Washington Dossier* magazine. "An architectural landmark of Washington's cityscape as familiar as the Capitol dome and the fountains of the White House," wrote Mickey Palmer, "its riverside mooring carries with it an exclusivity that's as ultimate a status symbol as the capital city offers." Nicolas and Josseline Salgo posed next to a buffet table in their Watergate South apartment, groaning with dishes prepared by the Watergate Terrace Restaurant and a massive pair of Hungarian silver candlesticks. The walls of their apartment—one of their six homes—were filled with miniature rugs from Persia, Tibet, Arabia and China, giving it the atmosphere of a Middle Eastern bazaar. Elsewhere in the apartment, Salgo displayed a rack of Chinese swords, his collection of old Hungarian silver and artifacts covered in shagreen, a material typically made from sharkskin.

Nicolas Salgo was downsizing. He sold his 1.3-million-acre ZX Ranch in Oregon, the largest cattle ranch in the Pacific Northwest, which was also where he parked Elizabeth Taylor's trailer from the Italian location of her 1963 movie *Cleopatra*, which he had purchased as a souvenir in 1966. Despite his intermittent irritation with his partners, Wendy Luscombe and the National Coal Board pension funds, the Watergate was operating smoothly. Yet, at age sixty-seven, he was restless.

With a Republican in the White House, Salgo thought it might be a good time to try for a federal appointment. He called Bob Page—who had steered him to Continental Illinois in 1977, when Salgo was trying to find a loan to help him purchase the Watergate from Banca di Roma—for advice. Page was from Wichita, Kansas, and recommended Salgo talk to Bob Dole, who lived in Watergate South. Senator Dole in turn connected Salgo with Elizabeth Dole at the White House, who in turn introduced him to Bill Clark, Reagan's national security advisor. Clark invited Salgo to stop by the West Wing and "discuss a few options."

Keith C. Smith, who served under Salgo as the deputy chief of mission in Budapest, later offered a different chronology. He said Salgo had contributed $550,000 to the first Reagan campaign and "gave a discount on the sale of a Watergate apartment to Charles Wick," the head of the U.S. Information Agency. Keith said Salgo wanted to become the U.S. ambassador to France—Josseline was French—but settled for Hungary.

Salgo noticed Clark's cowboy boots and mentioned he was selling the ZX Ranch in Oregon. Clark laughed. "Here are my souvenirs from the ZX Ranch," he said, pointing to his leg. "Two pieces of silver." During the Great Depression, Clark and his father had worked as "buckaroos" at the ZX Ranch. Clark's job was to tame wild horses, one of which tossed him, breaking his leg. It was put back together with pins.

Salgo raised the possibility of becoming U.S. ambassador to Argentina. He had recently visited the Falkland Islands, where he observed lingering bitterness over America's support for Britain during the 1982 Falklands War. Several months later, Salgo's FBI background investigation was complete. The Argentinian ambassador to the United States tipped him off that he had been informed by the U.S. State Department that Salgo was about to be nominated. Clark called Salgo and asked him to come back to the West Wing for another conversation.

Salgo assumed the purpose of the meeting was to discuss the timing of his departure for Buenos Aires, but Clark said he wanted to send him to Budapest instead. Salgo, a native-born Hungarian who had become a U.S. citizen in 1953, worried he would be a target of the Soviet Union, as Hungary was now part of the Eastern Bloc. "I'm not worried about that," quipped Clark. "I know a cowboy when I see one. You're a cowboy. You'll do alright." On September 20, 1983, President Reagan nominated Nicolas M. Salgo to be the U.S. ambassador to Hungary, the first native-born Hungarian to represent America in Budapest. Wendy Luscombe attended his swearing-in ceremony at the State Department.

Salgo placed all of his assets in a blind trust under the management of Bob Page, including his half-interest in the Watergate. "Frankly, I couldn't have cared less," said Salgo. "I enjoyed my new work as ambassador very much. When I quit Watergate, I quit."

Almost immediately, however, Page and Luscombe locked horns. According to Salgo, Luscombe proposed "updating" the hotel, at a cost of $8 million. Page considered the expense unnecessary, but Luscombe persisted. "You want to go ahead?" Page asked. "You will have to do it on your own because we are invoking the clause."

Under the "Salgo formula" in their renegotiated partnership agreement, Luscombe now had to respond by naming a price for Salgo's share of the Watergate. If her offer was high enough, Page could accept it. But if she came in too low, Page had the option of buying the National Coal Board's stake in the Watergate at that price. The British, Salgo wrote later, "changed their underwear, asked for an extension and then named a price which was incredibly high."

Although Salgo's assets were placed in a blind trust, Page sent a message to the U.S. embassy in Budapest containing a password that meant Salgo was to contact him immediately. Salgo got in a car, drove to Vienna and called Page.

Page explained the situation and presented Luscombe's offer, which was about 20 percent above what he thought the Watergate was worth. Salgo suspected the British came in with a strong bid because they thought Page, who managed the finances of Willard Garvey, a wealthy Midwesterner, could easily arrange financing and buy their half of the Watergate.

"You have two options," Page told Salgo.

"What are they?" Salgo asked.

"For the first option, I found a most desirable, elegant, well-run lunatic asylum and reserved a suite for you there."

"And the second option?"

"Let me sell the Watergate to the British."

"My whole fortune comes from there," Salgo recalled years later. The Watergate was by far his most valuable asset, but it was not liquid in any sense of the word. Nor were most of his other investments. In fact, Salgo was cash-poor.

He instructed Page to accept Luscombe's offer. He put part of the proceeds into trusts for members of his family. "Each one of us is on easy street because of that sale," he said later. "For the first time in my life, I had cash."

IN 1984, HER MAJESTY'S HIGH COURT OF JUSTICE IN EN-gland turned down a petition by National United Mineworkers chief Arthur Scargill that pension funds make no further investments overseas or in any energy-producing concerns other than coal. The effect of this ruling, according to a London real estate journal, meant pension fund managers were freed "from the strangle-hold placed on them by the miners' trustees" and could make investments as they saw fit. Luscombe promptly bought another American real estate trust, with prime buildings in downtown Los Angeles and San Francisco, making the pension funds by far the largest British investor in the United States. At age thirty-five, she was on a roll: In August, she reported to the joint boards of the pension funds that operating cash flow for U.S. real estate assets was running $426,000 ahead of budget. Occupancy rates across her American portfolio was 99 percent. By 1986, she and her team of twenty-five were managing more than seventy properties, including an almond orchard in California.

With 100 percent ownership of the Watergate, Luscombe focused on every dollar coming in or going out. The Watergate Office Building was home to several embassies, including one which decided not to pay its rent. When the managers of the building launched eviction proceedings, the embassy claimed "diplomatic immunity" and protested to the U.S. State Department. It was a steamy August in Washington. Luscombe ordered their air-conditioning turned off. Within twenty-four hours, she received a rent check.

In 1985, Hugh Jenkins left his position as investment director for the National Coal Board. His replacement, David Prosser, interviewed firms in New York about the possibility of taking over the management of the coal board's entire U.S. real estate portfolio, then valued at 600 million pounds, or about $1.4 billion. Prosser's maneuvers inevitably appeared in the business press, perhaps intentionally—he was, after all, planning to put Luscombe and her entire team out of a job. His idea went nowhere, but Luscombe knew she could not count on Prosser to give her the support she had enjoyed from Jenkins.

In spring of 1986, the Watergate Hotel occupancy rate was an unimpressive 68 percent—just below the citywide occupancy rate of 69 percent. The outlook was grim: There was a glut of hotel rooms in Washington, and experts predicted the city's vacancy rate could drop to 50 percent. Luscombe solicited proposals from various hotel management companies to take over the hotel from Watergate Companies, Inc., the current management firm, which had previously been headed up by Nicolas Salgo. An industry insider said the Watergate Hotel needed refurbishing and should look abroad for help. "Europeans would put the charm back into it," the source said.

The *Wall Street Journal* reported the Watergate Hotel was losing money on its flagship restaurant, Jean-Louis. Although the cheapest meal was $40, the restaurant was running in the red, due to its high cost of ingredients, $25,000 of Limoges china and $5,000 in tablecloths. "Fear is drifting through the corridors of the Watergate Hotel," Ann Mariano and Phyllis Richman wrote in the *Washington Post*. "Word that a change in management is imminent has touched off speculation that the hotel may shed its panache in the process—not to mention one of its most celebrated attractions, chef Jean-Louis Palladin."

"The future is really uncertain here," said Palladin. "It is totally a black hole." He wanted to stay in Washington—"my kids are American now," he said—but was seriously considering an offer to return to France to run a restaurant on the Château Margaux estate, which could potentially fulfill his dream of getting a third Michelin star. If he were to remain at the Watergate, he told the *Post*, his kitchen would need new equipment and the dining room would need new decorations, including new tables and chairs, at a total cost of about a half-million dollars.

The new managers were "pushing" Palladin to turn a bigger profit, Larbi Dahrouch later recalled. Salgo supported Palladin, but the new owners of the Watergate "only looked at the numbers."

Palladin sat in his office adjacent to the kitchen every day, smoking cigarettes and writing up his menus. "He would have loved to have been profitable," said his sous chef Jimmy Sneed, "but he didn't know how."

Jean-Louis was a "loss leader" for Salgo, who recognized the prestige that accrued to the Watergate for having arguably the best restaurant in the country. "Every chef was in awe of Jean-Louis Palladin," Sneed recalled.

"With Salgo, everything was easy," recalled Regine Palladin. "He let Jean-Louis do whatever." But the new owners "wanted more and more."

Despite the uncertainty surrounding his future, Palladin contin-ued to astonish Washington diners. He served one meal with truffles in every dish—including the ice cream. At a spring luncheon for Washington's elite chefs, Palladin served a *feuillantine* of raspber-ries layered with green basil sprigs. "The chefs were shocked," wrote food journalist Joan Nathan. "Basil's cousin, aromatic mint, would have been delicious. But basil with raspberries?"

After tasting crab soup in Maine, Jean-Louis decided to "do something in my way." He used crab shells in the stock—"there should be the powerful taste of the fresh crab," he said—and added lumps of crab at the last minute. His soup became a favorite dish of Mstislav Rostropovich, musical director of the National Symphony Orchestra.

Luscombe reviewed several proposals to manage the Watergate Hotel, including one from Cunard Line, which managed the *Queen Elizabeth II* ocean liner and owned the Ritz hotel in London. She selected Cunard, giving the firm a seven-year contract to manage the shops and restaurants throughout the Watergate, as well as the hotel, which it planned to turn into a five-star facility. It was Cunard's first venture into the American market, but the company was pur-suing contracts to manage luxury hotels in New York, Boston and Miami—all cities served by Cunard cruise ships.

Cunard turned to Sarah Tomerlin Lee, seventy-six, an imposing woman rarely seen in public without her pearls, whom the *Washington Post* called "the acknowledged empress of hotel interior designers," to launch a two-year renovation of the hotel. Lee's design amounted to a British conquest of the Watergate. "Presidential" suites became "royal" suites. A portrait of Queen Elizabeth II was installed in the "royal promenade" on the hotel's garden level. (When an Ar-gentinian delegation arrived, the hotel's director of sales, Lynda Clugston Webster—who was married to Judge William Webster, former head of both the FBI and CIA—recalled, "the staff had to scramble to hide it somewhere." Nerves were still raw, even years after the Falklands War.) The Watergate Terrace became the Brighton Restaurant. The Saddle Bar—named for Nicolas Salgo's collection of antique saddles—became the Bath Royal Crescent Bar (where guests could order Pimms or Bass Ale and admire a giant birdcage). Banquets and meetings took place in the Trafalgar Conference Room.

In April 1986, the Watergate Hotel issued a twenty-page publicity kit, heralding its new managers, the Cunard Line, and providing details about the Watergate, from a history of its construction to a list of flowers in its gardens (daffodils, tulips, petunias, begonias and marigolds). The packet, wrote the *New York Times*, contained "almost everything anyone ever wanted to know about the Watergate. Almost."

Nowhere in the package was any mention of the events that took place in the early-morning hours of June 17, 1972, when five men were arrested in the offices of the Democratic National Committee.

CLARE BOOTHE LUCE PACKED SEVERAL LIFETIMES OF AC-complishments into her eighty-four years. She was a successful novelist, playwright, politician and diplomat. During the 1952 presidential campaign, Luce campaigned aggressively for the Eisenhower-Nixon ticket, and President Eisenhower later sent her to Rome as the U.S. ambassador, the first woman to serve as an envoy to a major country. Nixon appointed her to the President's Foreign Intelligence Advisory Board, known by its acronym, PFIAB, the civilian board initially created by Eisenhower to provide candid advice to presidents on the quality of the nation's intelligence-gathering activities. After she completed her term, she returned to her home in Hawaii, but kept her apartment on the eleventh floor of Watergate South, across the hall from Jimmy Carter's attorney general Griffin Bell.

Reagan reappointed Luce to the President's Foreign Intelligence Advisory Board in 1981. MRS. LUCE IS BACK, PEPPERY AS EVER, the

New York Times reported. "I've been coming to Washington since the days of Harding; that's almost 60 years," she said. "I don't remember ever getting here and not being told everything is a mess, that the President is not doing as well as he should and he's got all the wrong advisers around him. That's part of the Washington game."

She was slowing down a bit, after nearly a half-century of globe-trotting, but doubted she would remarry. (Her husband, Henry Luce, the former publisher of *Time* magazine, died in 1967.) She was in the market for "a good friend and companion" who could serve as a movie pal and an escort around town. "But most of the intelligent men who would interest me are married to other women," she lamented.

Luce purchased and combined two adjoining apartments in Watergate South, 906 and 907, for $850,000. But the new apartment, she soon discovered, did not meet her needs. It lacked room for her library, photographs and other memorabilia. "And worse," she wrote the president of the Watergate South co-op board, Thomas Bernard Green, "there is no quiet room in which to write and edit my memoirs." She tried to purchase the adjoining apartment—905—but the owners were not interested in selling. Then apartment 903, across the hall, became available for rent. "This quiet apartment which has the advantage to a writer of having no distracting view would admirably suit the purposes of a personal library-study for me," she wrote Green. At a special meeting of the executive committee of the Watergate South board of directors, her request to use Apartment 903 as an office was approved—for her use alone, and not for any "stenographic or clerical staff"—provided she not use any noisy electric typewriters or copy machines.

On the morning of Thursday, May 24, 1984, construction workers accidentally cut two of three cables serving power to Watergate South. That night, at seven-thirty, the president and Mrs. Reagan left the White House for dinner at Watergate South in Luce's apartment, joining FBI director William H. Webster, secretary of the interior Bill Clark and syndicated columnist George Will. At around ten-fifteen, a fuse connected to the remaining power cable blew, plunging Watergate South into darkness. Building staff were able to turn on auxiliary electric power, but there was not enough power to restore elevator service or light the stairwells. Secret Service agents knocked on the doors of Mrs. Luce's neighbors seeking spare candles. As the agents and Watergate employees held candles, the Reagans walked down nine flights of stairs, returned to their car and sped away to the White House.

FOR THE SECOND REAGAN INAUGURAL IN JANUARY 1985, THE Watergate Hotel prepared special gift baskets for its guests, including a marzipan elephant; a "President's Lunch Bar," made with rolled oats and bee pollen, said to be a Reagan favorite; and an assortment of fresh fruit.

That weekend, arctic winds brought nine-degree weather to Washington; Reagan's swearing-in was moved indoors and his inaugural parade canceled entirely. A few weeks later, when the snow melted in a brief thaw, the words "I Love You" and a signature, "Kimberly," appeared as a burned-in message on the lawn facing the Watergate Hotel. Sherry Arnstein, a longtime resident, speculated this "destructive" act of vandalism might have come from an out-of-town guest at the inaugural. "Graffiti is all over the world, and sooner or later it had to come to the Watergate," lamented another resident. The culprit eventually confessed: a fourteen-year-old girl named Kimberly, who lived with her parents in Watergate South.

ON THE MORNING OF JULY 23, 1985, U.S. MARSHALS PLACED Edith Berman's upright piano, lamps, suitcases, a mattress and other belongings on the sidewalk in front of the Watergate West lobby. "It's a disgrace," Berman said. "I've lived here 16 years and I have no trouble with people. They have no complaint against me." She stood in the lobby, dressed in a red housecoat and slippers, leaning on a cane, and said she would camp out on the doorstep. "If they don't like it they can lump it."

Edith Berman was one of the original owners in Watergate West. She often walked home from her office at the Red Cross headquarters near the White House, even on warm summer evenings. Like many other single women living at the Watergate—and many women in Washington at the time—she was intelligent, somewhat underemployed and fiercely self-reliant.

Shortly after moving into her one-bedroom apartment in January 1969, she reported several issues with the appliances to Riverview Realty. Most problematic was the air-conditioning system, which created so much humidity she had to sleep on the living room couch, keeping her bedroom door closed. Her wool rug and pad, parquet floors and the wall in her bedroom were seriously damaged by the moisture. After two years of sleeping on the couch, Edith Berman had enough.

Acting as her own attorney, she filed a lawsuit claiming "breach of express and implied warranties" against Watergate West, Inc., the owners' cooperative association; Riverview Realty Corporation, the sales agent for the building; and Watergate Improvements Associates, the developer. Her lawsuit charged these entities had delivered an apartment "containing numerous defective appliances."

Four years later, she finally had her day in court. On the witness stand, Berman described her travails with the defective air conditioner. Another witness, a member of the co-op board, corroborated her testimony. The lawyer for the Watergate West cooperative said it could not be held legally responsible for the defects reported in January 1969, because the cooperative had not been formed until five months later, long after the defects had been discovered and reported. A lawyer for Riverview Realty said sales agreements showed they acted only as a "managing and sales agent" for Watergate West and any warranties made to Edith Berman would have come only from the developer of the project or the manufacturer of the equipment itself, not the real estate agents.

A jury was selected to hear Berman's case, but the judge stepped in and ruled Riverview Realty acted only as an agent in the sale of Watergate West apartments, and was therefore not "contractually liable to the person who buys the apartment or any condition in the apartment." The judge also ruled in favor of a motion by the Watergate West co-op board to dismiss Ms. Berman's suit and ordered her to pay the board's legal fees, as well as those of Riverview Realty. Edith Berman immediately filed an appeal.

On September 6, 1978, nearly nine years after Edith Berman first moved into her living room at Watergate West to avoid her defective air-conditioning system, the District of Columbia Court of Appeals, in a two-to-one ruling, held Riverview Realty financially responsible for the defects in Watergate West's heating and cooling system. The majority opinion held that the sponsor of the Watergate project was accountable under product liability law for any units that proved defective. While there was no contract between Ms. Berman and either Watergate Improvement Associates or Watergate Construction Corporation, each of those entities was "an integral part of the overall producing and marketing enterprise" and therefore "each one of them can be held accountable to the ultimate consumer for the damage caused by the defective product." For the next five years, *Berman v. Watergate West* was the nation's leading case in the area of "implied warranties" to homebuyers. In 1983, the District of Columbia Court of Appeals extended the protections of *Berman* to condominiums.

For two years, starting in 1979, Edith Berman paid a $40 monthly assessment for her share of improvements to Watergate West's central heating and air-conditioning systems—costs which were not covered by the $600,000 settlement reached with developers in 1977. But the repairs, she said, failed to resolve the problems in her unit. In 1981, she started to deduct $40 each month from her association dues. Within three years, she had held back a total of $1,441.44 and Watergate West successfully petitioned to have her evicted for nonpayment. Berman—acting as her own attorney—appealed the eviction order, but her appeal was dismissed when she failed to file any briefs.

A city truck arrived to take her belongings to a storage facility, but Berman wouldn't allow them to load up. "That's for people who have no money," she said. She called a private moving firm. A neighbor invited Berman to spend the night in her apartment, but she declined. At least two people offered to pay Berman's past-due co-op fees, including Florida senator Paula Hawkins, a Republican, who lived in the Watergate. "Based on her withholding payments since 1975," said a Watergate West lawyer, "we would be leery of letting her back in."

In early 1986, an attorney for Watergate West sold Berman's apartment for $125,000, deducted the outstanding mortgage and $11,910 in attorney's fees, and sent her a check for the balance.

RESTAURANT CORPORATION OF AMERICA, KNOWN BY ITS initials, RCA, ran food service at the Watergate Hotel, the Watergate Terrace Restaurant and the Peacock Lounge in the Les Champs arcade. The hotel kitchen staff was unionized, like that of every other major hotel in Washington at the time, with the exception of that at the Four Seasons in Georgetown. RCA, however, was a non-union employer and hoped to keep it that way, as evidenced by the notice they placed on employee bulletin boards at the Watergate:

SOLICITATION OF ANY KIND, INCLUDING SOLICITATION FOR CLUBS,

ORGANIZATIONS, POLITICAL PARTIES, CHARITIES, ETC. IS NOT PERMITTED

ON WORKING TIME OR IN CUSTOMER AREAS. DISTRIBUTION OF

LITERATURE OF ANY KIND IS NOT PERMITTED ON WORKING TIME OR IN

WORKING AREAS. OFF-SHIFT EMPLOYEES ARE NOT ALLOWED

ON THE PREMISES.

Roxie Herbekian graduated from the University of California, Berkeley, and headed to Washington, hoping to work for a progressive cause, but the best she could land was an unpaid internship. To earn extra money and pay her rent, she answered a help-wanted ad in the *Washington Post* and took a job as a room-service operator at the Watergate Hotel. She started working the morning shift— six-thirty to ten-thirty—from a small desk in the corner of the kitchen. A couple of months later, she picked up a second shift as a waitress in the Peacock Lounge and worked there most days until 4:00 P.M.

A few months after she started working at the Watergate, a waiter invited her to an organizing meeting sponsored by the Hotel and Restaurant Employees Union, Local 25. At that meeting, Roxie and a handful of other employees were given lists of coworkers to contact, along with authorization cards for employees to sign. "It was really exciting," Roxie recalled later. "I was great at getting people to sign up." Sherwood Dameron, a young African-American waiter from Richmond, Virginia, attended the meeting too. He took a list of employees and a stack of authorization cards as well.

A week later, Gene Flick, general manager of the Watergate restaurants, asked Roxie to stop by his office. She remembered him as pale and puffy, a fifty-something version of the Pillsbury Dough-boy. Flick asked her if she was aware of RCA's no-solicitation rule. She said she knew nothing about it, and Flick informed her he was suspending her for three days, pending an investigation. When she returned to work the following Monday, she had been replaced. Flick confirmed she had been fired for violating the no-solicitation rule, but refused to put it in writing. He handed Roxie her severance check. Sherwood Dameron was fired later that day. Roxie took a job with the union, earning $100 a week to organize hotel and restaurant workers in the District. Sherwood also worked a short time for the union, then took a job with another hotel and eventually moved home to Richmond.

An administrative law judge ruled RCA had violated two sections of the National Labor Relations Act by "disparately enforcing" its no-solicitation rule against Herbekian and Dameron by allowing six separate instances of other "solicitations" by employees, including raising funds to buy a going-away cake for a Les Champs waiter, a birthday cake for a Les Champs bartender and a sterling baby spoon for the pregnant wife of a Les Champs chef. On August 21, 1984, the full National Labor Relations Board ordered RCA to offer Herbekian and Dameron their old jobs back and remove from their employment files any records of their firing. The board also demanded RCA post a notice which read in part:

> The National Labor Relations Board has found that we violated the National Labor Relations Act and has ordered us to post and abide by this notice.
>
> WE WILL NOT coercively question you about your union support or activities and the union support or activities of your fellow employees . . .
> WE WILL NOT suspend, discharge, or otherwise discriminate against any of you for engaging in protected concerted or union activity . . .
> WE WILL offer Roxie Herbekian and Sherwood Dameron immediate and full reinstatement to their former jobs or, if those jobs no longer exist, to substantially equivalent positions, without prejudice to their seniority . . . and WE WILL make them whole for any loss of earnings and other benefits resulting from their discharge, less any net interim earnings, with interest.

The Restaurant Corporation of America immediately filed suit to overturn the NLRB ruling and in 1986, a three-judge panel of the District of Columbia Court of Appeals, a federal court second in power only to the Supreme Court, issued a ruling in *Restaurant Corporation of America v. National Labor Relations Board*. By a vote of two to one, the NLRB decision was reversed and the firings of

Roxie Herbekian and Sherwood Dameron were reinstated. According to the majority opinion, written by Judge Robert H. Bork and joined by Judge Antonin Scalia, the other examples of workplace solicitations—for baby spoons and going-away cakes—were simply "instances of intra-employee generosity." While somewhat disruptive within the workplace, these events were "counter-balanced by an accompanying increase in employee morale and cohesion."

When Roxie heard the National Labor Relations Board ruling had been overturned, she was working full-time organizing hotel workers. She saw the decision as simply another in a long list of setbacks for unions during the Reagan era. "Just par for the course," she lamented.

IN MARCH 1989, THE NATIONAL COAL BOARD PENSION FUNDS announced plans to sell their entire portfolio of U.S. property, including the Watergate. "They want to get liquid and go into something else," Wendy Luscombe said. The funds "had been given a good run for their money" and have "not been burned by their investment," she said. "And they are not dumping it."

After Hugh Jenkins left the National Coal Board pension funds in 1985, Luscombe received no new funding to enlarge her U.S. real estate portfolio. It was clear to Luscombe that the U.S. market was simply not a priority for her new boss back in London, David Prosser. She did not want to sit around and watch the unwinding of the $1 billion real estate portfolio she had assembled over the past ten years, and in July 1989, she resigned from both Pan-American and Buckingham Holdings and took a job managing U.S. real estate operations for the Carroll Group, a private real estate company owned by one of the wealthiest families in Great Britain.

The National Coal Board retained Morgan Stanley Realty to handle the sale of its entire U.S. real estate portfolio. News reports estimated the Watergate complex would fetch between $28 million to $71 million—which meant, at the low end, a loss of more than

$20 million or, at the high end, a profit of about the same amount. "I think it's tired," said a Washington real estate investor. "I think it needs some work." A commercial real estate report estimated the Watergate Office Building on Virginia Avenue was 30.6 percent vacant and the 600 New Hampshire Avenue building was 11.6 percent vacant—far above the downtown Washington office vacancy rate of 5.3 percent. The hotel's average occupancy rate was 62 percent, below the citywide average of 69 percent.

"The Cunard people were running the place like a cruise ship," recalled Lynda Clugston Webster, a former marketing director for the hotel, "posting menus in light boxes and bringing in the tourists in tennis shoes."

Complicating a potential sale, Cunard Hotels and Resorts, the Cunard Line subsidiary managing the Watergate Hotel, had a contract giving it the right to continue operating the hotel, even after a sale. Retail tenants in the Watergate shopping mall had options to renew leases at below-market rates. Although the National Coal Board pension funds owned the land underneath the three co-op apartment buildings, each co-op had rights to purchase their land at any time. Further complicating the transaction, John Hancock Life Insurance Company owned the land underneath the Watergate Office Building.

On Friday, March 23, 1990, Cunard Hotels and Resorts agreed to suspend its management contract. The following Monday, the National Coal Board announced the sale of the Watergate Hotel to Trusthouse Forte LLC, a British catering and hotel conglomerate.

Charles Forte immigrated to London from Italy at the age of four with his family and started his first venture, a milk bar on Regent Street, at the age of twenty-six. Two decades later, his company was the largest hotelier in the United Kingdom. His catering division had the contract for London's Heathrow Airport. Charles was knighted by the Queen Mother in 1970 and became Baron Forte of

Ripley in 1982. The same year, his son, Rocco Forte, became the CEO of the company, while Lord Forte remained as chairman.

Trusthouse Forte paid $50 million for the Watergate Hotel. A spokesman said the company would spend up to $8 million renovating the hotel's elevators, health club, entrance, and laundry and banquet facilities. The sale did not include the adjacent Watergate Office Building, or the Watergate Mall nearby, both of which remained on the market for another two years.

As a legal entity, the Watergate was breaking apart. For its first decade and a half, the Watergate had been owned by Società Generale Immobiliare back in Rome and managed by Giuseppe Cecchi or Nicolas Salgo, who had been with the project since its inception. After Salgo left for Hungary, Wendy Luscombe watched the Watergate closely, perhaps with a closer eye to the bottom line than Salgo, but with the same level of dedication. Twenty-five years after the Watergate first broke ground, there was effectively no one in charge of the entire complex. A succession of owners would go on to manage—or mismanage—their parts of the Watergate, including the hotel, the office buildings, the shopping mall, as they saw fit.

From its beginnings, the Watergate brand meant two things: privacy and luxury. The 1972 break-in and its aftermath undermined its privacy. As ownership fell into new hands, the Watergate's reputation for luxury would suffer.

Trusthouse Forte brought in a new general manager for the Watergate Hotel, Ibrahim Fahmy. As part of his orientation, the hotel staff informed him he had access to a white Jaguar sedan that had been left behind by the previous general manager, a flamboyant homosexual in his fifties with a penchant for young Asian men.

One day, shortly after he started at the Watergate Hotel, Fahmy took the Jaguar out to run an errand. He returned a few hours later, visibly shaken. He had driven through Washington's Dupont Circle neighborhood, which at the time was the center of the District's gay community. Young Asian men had thronged around the car, waving and smiling, and knocking on the windows. "What is going on?" he asked his staff. "Why is this happening to me?"

A hotel employee pulled him aside and, in a whisper, explained the situation.

Fahmy ordered a new car.

SHORTLY AFTER TRUSTHOUSE FORTE TOOK OVER THE WA-tergate, an executive summoned Jean-Louis Palladin for a meeting. Palladin declined, and sent his sous chef Jimmy Sneed to represent him. When Sneed entered the office, he recalled, the Trusthouse executive was clearly perturbed.

Palladin's $90,000-a-year salary, the executive said, was excessive and needed to be cut back.

"Absolutely not," replied Sneed. "He needs a raise."

The executive was astonished.

If you don't increase Jean-Louis to $110,000 a year, Sneed warned, "he's gonna walk."

Sneed returned to the restaurant and delivered the news to Palladin. "I got you a raise," Sneed said, smiling broadly.

WASHINGTON LAWYER PAUL ZANECKI HAD WANTED TO LIVE in the Watergate since 1968, when he saw a listing for a two-bedroom apartment for $35,000. Still just a law student, he could not buy it, but many years later he rented a duplex apartment on the first floor of Watergate South, next door to Elizabeth and Bob Dole. In the mornings, Paul would sometimes look out of his second-floor master bedroom window to a surreal scene: Bob Dole in his "tighty whities" on the terrace below, chasing the Doles' dog Leader. At night, when Paul returned home from a long day at a land-use law firm, he would sometimes pass by the Doles' apartment and a small patch of "thank you" bouquets stacked outside their front door. Occasionally, when there was no one around to observe him, Paul requisitioned a floral arrangement, discarded the note and presented it to his wife with a grin.

One morning, after a late night at the Sea Catch restaurant in Georgetown, Paul awoke to the sound of loud banging. Still groggy, he got out of bed, wrapped a towel around his naked waist, walked downstairs and opened the door to the hallway. He recognized the real estate agent he had retained to find someone who could sublet the apartment, so he could take a brief assignment overseas. But he had forgotten all about the appointment to show the apartment that morning. He apologized for his appearance.

The agent introduced the prospective tenants: Marcia Lewis, a writer from Los Angeles, and her daughter, Monica Lewinsky.

CHAPTER NINE: MONICALAND

One of the reasons so many people love hotels so much is the joy of feeling so pampered that all they need to do is lift a finger, push a button on the phone and someone will bring them a five-course meal, a bottle of champagne or maybe just a soda and a handful of peanuts.

Whatever you want, it can be provided. If you need a shirt cleaned and pressed for your meeting, someone will do it. If your air conditioning isn't working, you just call downstairs, and someone will fix it.

Savvy Washingtonians know there is a place just like this, but even better: You can buy a cooperative apartment there and live as if you're on vacation full time. Where is this paragon of pampering? The Watergate, of course.

Washington Times, April 25, 1997

FOR CHRISTMAS 1993, THE WATERGATE HOTEL PRESENTED Jean-Louis Palladin with a custom-made La Cornue stove, in azulejo-blue porcelain with brass trim. He designed it himself. It formed its own ten-and-a-half-foot-long island, so cooks could pass dishes from one side to the other, and generated 23,500 BTUs—60 percent more than a typical restaurant stove. Four of its ovens were electric, for pastry; four were gas, providing moist heat for meats and poultry in a vaulted shape that eliminated the need for basting. The price tag: $88,000.

Washington Post food critic Phyllis Richman described Palladin's new toy with a string of superlatives: the power of a Lear jet, the roominess of a Rolls-Royce, the durability of a sable coat and the efficiency of a Rolex watch. "Like a teenager making a case for a new car," she wrote, "Palladin has promised to be ever more creative and productive." In addition to sixteen powerful gas burners, the new oven came with strings: Palladin agreed to take over food service for the entire hotel.

His duties now included, in addition to Jean-Louis, the River-view restaurant in the hotel, which was transformed into a brasserie, the hotel room service and all banquet catering. He told Richman he planned to make the best breakfast in Washington, with his own preserves, create new recipes for egg dishes, and work with Marvel-ous Market, a local bakery, to create "croissants of beautiful quality" and not mere "little packets." "My job?" he said, laughing. "Every-thing, A to Z, to take care of the entire hotel. I will be in the back, I will be upstairs, I will be everywhere."

"The banquets were hard on him," recalled the hotel's catering manager, Cathy Arevian. "It just wasn't the way he wanted to do things." His kitchen was still small—the walk-in refrigerators were around a corner—and whenever there was a large banquet upstairs at the hotel, he was forced to set up an entire food preparation line in an adjacent room. His dissatisfaction with these makeshift facilities sometimes drove him to unleash profanity-laced tirades, which were audible in the adjoining banquet room. And it wasn't easy to adapt Palladin's inventive recipes to large-scale events at the Watergate Hotel. One day, Arevian planned a menu for two hundred guests, including one dish with a fava bean puree. She had seen fava beans on the menu at Jean-Louis. Palladin was furious. He gave her a seat in the kitchen and pointed to a mountain of fava beans. "Get to work!" he shouted, and stomped away. "I shelled fava beans until I felt as if my fingernails would fall off," Arevian recalled.

Lynda Webster brought groups of VIPs in for special luncheons. Palladin found these events annoying. One day, Webster booked a group of congressional wives. Palladin prepared a first course of Pacific geoduck clams, which were known for being flavorful and crunchy—and shaped like a large, uncircumcised penis. Palladin burst through the kitchen door and paraded a steaming plate of phallic clams around the restaurant, grinning as he presented the dish to each table of mortified women.

For Jean-Louis Palladin's fiftieth birthday in 1996, friends and

colleagues, including food writers Phyllis Richman and Joan Nathan and all the top chefs of Washington, surprised him with a party
aboard an Odyssey cruise ship. As they sailed past the Watergate,
Jean-Louis released balloons into the air. Across the water, in the
Riverview restaurant of the hotel, lights flashed in response.

Jean-Louis's contract with the hotel expired in April 1996. He
chose not to renew it, he said, because Trusthouse Forte, the hotel's
new owners, had refused to invest $250,000 in renovations. "After
17 years, it looks a little tired." Instead, he had been told he could
lease the space from the hotel, in exchange for 5 percent of gross
sales. "New people bought the hotel," he told a reporter, "and we
don't have the same view."

Philip Wood, vice president of operations for Exclusive Brand,
the luxury hotel division of Trusthouse Forte, said the decision was
Palladin's alone. "Jean-Louis didn't want to negotiate," Wood said.
"He didn't respond to our initial offer to lease the premises. He
was looking for someone to set him up in business, and that is not
our market." Wood also suggested Palladin was distracted by other
ventures. "He has a lot of external interests," Wood said, "and we
wanted a chef who would be dedicated to us."

On June 15, 1996, Jean-Louis Palladin served his last meal at
the Watergate. The restaurant was originally scheduled to close
on June 30, 1996, but the hotel ordered him to close two weeks
earlier. More than five hundred reservations had to be canceled.

Phyllis Richman described one of the last evenings at the famed
restaurant for her readers at the *Washington Post*. A magnificent
flower arrangement greeted diners as they arrived. Maurice Mony,
the maître d', escorted guests to their table. Daniel Nicolas, a captain
who had been with Palladin during the restaurant's entire run, offered drinks and explained the menu: five courses at $85, six courses
at $95 and a truffle menu at $150, not including tax and tip.

Vincent Feraud, the young sommelier, explained the wine list.
When he arrived six years earlier, the cellar held sixty thousand

bottles. But the hotel cut off Jean-Louis's wine budget in 1993. By Feraud's estimate, they would be down to about two thousand bottles when it came time to close.

Nicolas took the order in triplicate—one for the kitchen, one for the cold station (soups, salads and desserts) and one for himself. The chef sent out "a little treat"—Jean-Louis's rings of tempura squid. "They're famous," Richman wrote, "these incomparable rings of squid with an airy puff of batter made only of flour, baking soda and ice water, fried in grape-seed oil at exactly the right temperature to make the outside crisp and the inside silky."

Back in the kitchen, Palladin tasted a strip of bacon. He called out for the mushroom soup.

Palladin and his sous chef, Jose Hernandez, stirred and tasted. "At Jean-Louis, soup is art," Richman wrote.

For the main courses, Palladin roasted small racks of lamb with sage. He sliced a pan of duck breast "with the concentration of a surgeon."

The pace didn't slow down until ten-thirty, when the second seating started to wind down. "The last diners are growing louder with each new pouring of wine," Richman wrote. "And now that it's almost over, the staff is getting a little gregarious, too. Almost a family, this group, about to be broken up."

"Where do you go from Jean-Louis?" asked Kathy Dinardo, a captain since day one.

Feraud looked around the room.

"This is a haunted house now," he lamented.

Jean-Louis opened restaurants in Las Vegas and New York, but never again achieved the same level of notoriety he enjoyed at the Watergate. Unlike other celebrity chefs, he never made money from cookbooks or television shows, and after he was diagnosed with lung cancer, his friends—including chefs he had nurtured, and customers for whom he had cooked—held fund-raisers around the country to cover some of his medical costs. He died in 2001 at the age of fifty-five.

"No matter what, Washington will never again see a restaurant like Jean-Louis at the Watergate," Richman wrote. "Palladin didn't come to show us French food, he came to reinvent American food."

PLÁCIDO DOMINGO FREQUENTLY STAYED AT THE WATERGATE Hotel, out of gratitude to the owner, Trusthouse Forte, which had underwritten one of his concerts with a $1 million contribution. On February 12, 1996, Domingo walked from the Watergate Hotel to the Kennedy Center. Patricia Mossel, the Kennedy Center's executive director, introduced him at a press conference as the new artistic director of the Washington National Opera and proclaimed a new beginning for the company: "the Domingo Era." At Giants Stadium in July, Domingo and two other opera superstars, Luciano Pavarotti and José Carreras, performed the final show of their "Three Tenors in Concert" worldwide tour. The top ticket cost $1,500. A recording of their Rome concert was the best-selling classical album ever; their concert video was the best-selling classical movie video; and 1.3 billion people in seventy-one countries tuned in to watch their Los Angeles show live. At the end of 1996, Carol Publishing and Birch Lane Press released *The Private Lives of the Three Tenors: Behind the Scenes with Plácido Domingo, Luciano Pavarotti and José Carreras*. The author was Marcia Lewis, a writer for the *Hollywood Reporter*.

Following a bitter divorce, Marcia Lewis remained in Los Angeles in order to provide some stability to her children, Monica and Michael. When Monica left for Lewis & Clark College in Oregon in 1993, Marcia decided it was time to try out someplace new. In order to be near her sister, Debra Finerman, Marcia rented an apartment on the first floor of Watergate South. Debra and her husband, Bill, lived in Virginia but kept a pied-à-terre at the Watergate. Bronia

Vilensky, Monica's grandmother, had an apartment upstairs in Watergate South.

After she moved in, Marcia had a conversation with Walter Kaye, a prominent Democratic donor, whose grandson had recently been a summer intern at the White House. She suggested her daughter apply for an internship, and Monica embraced the idea. She submitted an application and was accepted, starting as an unpaid intern in the office of White House chief of staff Leon Panetta in July 1995. During the November 1995 government shutdown, President Clinton stopped by the chief of staff's office for a birthday party, where he struck up a conversation with the young intern. At one moment during the party, she playfully showed Clinton her thong underwear. Later that evening, in an empty West Wing office of a staff member, Lewinsky and Clinton had the first of several sexual encounters.

Lewinsky took a full-time job at the White House Office of Legislative Affairs, processing congressional correspondence, but was transferred to a public affairs position in the office of Pentagon spokesman Kenneth Bacon in April 1996. She called President Clinton on Easter Sunday to tell him she had been transferred, and he promised to bring her back to the White House after the election.

Monica commuted to the defense department and made a life for herself at the Watergate. She worked out in the Watergate Hotel gym and shopped for groceries at the Watergate Safeway. She brought a photograph into the Watergate Gallery to be framed—a picture of her and the president, smiling at an official function, not unlike scores of similar photographs the gallery framed over the years for other Watergate residents. "I remember she was very concerned about leaving it here," recalled Dale Johnson, the gallery owner. "It was priceless to her." Monica was a regular at the Watergate Salon, recommending it to her friend Linda Tripp, who sometimes stayed overnight in the spare bedroom at Watergate South.

In September 1997, Monica's world began to unwind. Her mother moved to New York, to be closer to her new boyfriend, Peter Straus, whom she had met at the launch of her book *The Private Lives of the Three Tenors*. Monica remained behind at the Watergate. White House aide Marsha Scott gave Lewinsky some bad news: the White House position she was seeking had been eliminated. And, unknown to Monica, her coworker at the Pentagon, Linda Tripp, began secretly recording their conversations about Monica's affair with the president.

In October, an anonymous woman called The Rutherford Institute, which was funding the Paula Jones civil lawsuit against Bill Clinton, and told them about the Lewinsky-Clinton affair. Linda Tripp met with *Newsweek* reporter Michael Isikoff and disclosed her tapes of conversations with Lewinsky. At the request of Clinton's personal secretary Betty Currie, White House deputy chief of staff John Podesta contacted U.N. ambassador Bill Richardson and asked him to interview Lewinsky for a job in New York. Richardson's office scheduled a meeting in a Watergate Hotel suite for October 31, 1997. "Over my dead body will you go to that hotel room," Tripp said. "They are trying to set you up." Tripp suggested Lewinsky ask to be interviewed in the hotel's dining room in order to avoid a "compromising situation." In fact, Michael Isikoff had arranged for another *Newsweek* reporter to be in the dining room, so he could observe Lewinsky and Richardson together.

On December 15, attorneys for Paula Jones served Clinton with a request to produce "documents related to communications between the President and Monica Lewinsky." On December 19, Jones's lawyers served Lewinsky with a subpoena. Lewinsky called Betty Currie and told her she was "concerned" about possibly being asked to turn over gifts the president had given her. Currie drove to the Watergate and picked up "a box of stuff" from Lewinsky's apartment. Currie took the box home and put it under her bed. She planned to store the box, she testified later, until Lewinsky "wanted it back."

On January 12, 1998, Linda Tripp delivered her tapes to independent counsel Kenneth Starr. Three days later, Starr asked the justice department for authority to investigate the Lewinsky matter, and a three-judge panel approved the request on January 16. That day, at the request of Starr's deputies, Linda Tripp lured Monica Lewinsky to the Pentagon City Ritz-Carlton. Federal authorities intercepted Lewinsky, and Michael Emmick, a member of Starr's team of prosecutors, told her she could be indicted for perjury, witness tampering and obstruction of justice. Prosecutors offered her immunity, but only if she accepted before midnight. Monica called her mother in New York, reaching Lewis at her Manhattan apartment, while her sister and mother were in town visiting. Monica explained the situation. "Where are you? Where are you?" her mother shouted into the phone. Marcia Lewis knew this day would come. She and Debra had both been aware of Monica's affair with the president, almost from the start. The three women raced to Penn Station to catch the next train to Washington. Debra and Bronia went directly to the Watergate; Marcia went to the Ritz-Carlton to join Monica.

Later that night, back in Watergate South, Marcia and Monica became convinced their duplex was bugged. They spoke only in whispers—in the bathroom, with the water running. "This was not how we should be living in America in this century," Monica told her biographer Andrew Morton. "It reminded me of *The Diary of Anne Frank.*" They moved temporarily into the apartment of Monica's grandmother on the sixth floor.

Just before midnight on January 17, 1998, the "Drudge Report" posted a "world exclusive": "At the last minute, at 6 P.M. on Saturday evening, NEWSWEEK magazine killed a story that was destined to shake official Washington to its foundation: A White House intern had carried on a sexual affair with the President of the United States!" The next day, "Drudge" identified the White House intern as Monica Lewinsky.

On Monday, January 19, 1998—Martin Luther King Day—
Starr's investigators arrived with a subpoena to search Apartment
114 in Watergate South.

IN THE SUMMER OF 1994, YAH LIN "CHARLIE" TRIE SIGNED A
one-year lease on Apartment 121 Watergate South, just down the
hall from Elizabeth and Bob Dole. Although the $3,500 a month
rent on the three-bedroom townhouse was more than he could afford, according to congressional investigators, "appearance was important to Trie" and he believed "a Watergate address gave him a
certain stature as a businessman." He presented to the leasing agent
a letter of reference signed by an official at the Democratic National
Committee.

Charlie Trie grew up in a poor military family that had escaped the
1949 Communist revolution and settled in Taiwan. He immigrated
to the United States in 1974, arriving in Little Rock, Arkansas,
where his older sister operated several Chinese restaurants. In 1984,
Charlie took over one of the restaurants, called Fu Lin, which under
his management became popular with local politicians, including
Bill Clinton, the young governor of Arkansas. The two men became
friends: Trie called Clinton Lao Ke—Chinese for "old Clinton"—
and the governor helped Trie when he ran into trouble with the local
health department.

Trie told Clinton he was tired of the restaurant business and
wanted to try something new, perhaps open some sort of trading
firm focused on China. Clinton encouraged the idea, telling his
friend that China was "evolving politically" and would soon be expanding its global trading relationships. Trie took the governor's
advice, sold the restaurant and in October 1992 started Daihatsu
International Trading Corporation—sharing a name, but nothing
else, with Daihatsu Motor Company of Japan, exporters of a "large
compact" automobile, the Daihatsu Charade. Trie's venture got off
to a rocky start. He lost most of the profits from the sale of his

restaurant when he tried, without success, to market a Chinese-made wrench to Walmart and other U.S. chain stores. After another failed attempt in early 1994 to buy and refurbish the Camelot Hotel in downtown Little Rock, Trie decided to follow his friend, the former governor of Arkansas and now the president of the United States, to Washington.

Trie used his Watergate apartment to host delegations of visiting Chinese and Taiwanese businessmen for receptions and parties. Ng Lap Seng, chairman of a commercial and residential real estate firm based in Macau, and Antonio Pan, a Taiwanese-born businessman, worked out of Trie's Watergate apartment whenever they were in town.

Between May and June 1994, Trie and his wife donated $100,000 to the Democratic National Committee, which qualified him as a member of the DNC's finance board of directors. Trie was seated at the head table of a fund-raising dinner for Asian donors to the Clinton-Gore reelection campaign on May 13, 1995. During his welcoming remarks, President Clinton turned to Charlie and said, "It's been 20 years since I had my first meal with Charlie Trie. At the time, neither of us could afford a ticket to this dinner."

Trie sought a White House appointment to the newly created Presidential Commission on U.S. Trade and Investment Policy, but was told the fifteen-member commission was already full. He kept pushing. He lined up endorsements from the Democratic National Committee and Ernest Green, a Lehman Brothers banker, longtime fund-raiser for the Democratic Party and another friend of Clinton from Arkansas. Despite concerns within the administration that Trie, who just four years earlier was running a Chinese restaurant in Little Rock, lacked the stature to join a panel whose members included the CEO of American Express, the former chairman of the Export-Import Bank and the CEO of the Recording Industry Association of America, White House aides made it clear to staff at the office of the U.S. Trade Representative that Trie was "a must person." In January 1996, President Clinton signed an executive order adding a few more slots to the commission, one of which was set aside for his friend Charlie Trie.

On March 20, 1996, Charlie Trie called Michael Cardozo, a banker and the executive director of the Presidential Legal Expense Trust, which was established in June 1984 to fund the personal legal bills of the Clintons arising from the Whitewater and other investigations and various lawsuits. Cardozo, who had never heard of Trie, suggested they talk over the phone, but Trie insisted on meeting in person. The next day, in Cardozo's conference room, Trie opened the conversation by explaining his history with President Clinton, tracing their friendship back to Little Rock. Trie then asked if Cardozo's merchant banking firm could assist in finding a U.S. distributor for a Chinese-made novelty item—a small package that, when punched with a fist, as Trie demonstrated personally, inflated to become the shape of an immediately recognizable product, like a bottle or can of Coca-Cola. Perplexed by the demonstration, Cardozo said he could not be of assistance. Trie then said he was aware of the Clintons' mounting legal bills and wanted to help. He emptied a manila envelope onto the conference table. According to Cardozo, "out came a mound of checks and money orders" totaling $460,000. As he looked at the pile on his table, Cardozo flashed back to Watergate and Maurice Stans, the ill-fated finance chairman of the Nixon reelection campaign. "When people drop large sums of money off in manila envelopes in Washington, DC," Cardozo said later, "you've got to be really careful about how you handle those funds."

Trie excused himself to attend a lunch next door at the Palm Restaurant. Cardozo and his assistant, Sally Schwartz, studied the checks and money orders closely and immediately flagged about $70,000 as problematic—missing names or addresses, or made out to an amount above the $1,000 limits in the trust's guidelines. The trust had received other "bundled" contributions, but the $460,000 sitting on their table was as much as half the total contributions received to date, and the average contribution was nearly five times higher than a typical contribution. When Trie returned from lunch, Cardozo returned $70,000 in "problematic" contributions to Trie, who assured him he could "cure" any problems. With respect to the remaining contributions, Trie said he was about to be appointed to a federal commission and could not have his name connected to them.

Over the next two weeks, Schwartz inspected Trie's checks and money orders closely. She discovered some of the money orders were sequentially numbered, which meant they were purchased at the same location, but were filled out by people scattered around the country. A number of checks from different accounts had the same misspelling of the word "presidential"—spelled instead as "presidencial." The trust retained Investigative Group, Inc., known as IGI, a private investigative firm, to dig further. IGI determined that Trie likely laundered some or all of the funds through members of the Suma Ching Hai Buddhist sect based in Taiwan, a controversial organization described by some as a cult. Beginning in June 1996, the trust began mailing contributions back to the donors, enclosing a cover letter instructing them they could resubmit their contributions if they met the trust's guidelines. Because the donations were received and returned during the first half of 1996, they were not included in the next report from the trust, released on August 14, 1996, which listed only "contributions accepted." At a press conference on the trust's mid-year financial disclosure, Cardozo was specifically asked by a reporter whether any contributions were returned because they came from someone who was "unsavory or anything like that."

"No," Cardozo responded.

Bill Clinton was reelected to a second term on November 5, 1996. Three days later, he signed a copy of his campaign book, *Between Hope and History: Meeting America's Challenges for the 21st Century*, "To Charlie Trie with thanks." A Clinton aide mailed the signed book to Trie at his Watergate South apartment.

On December 2, 1996, NBC investigative reporter John Mattes called Michael Cardozo and said he was working on a story about a large number of contributions by Asian-Americans to the trust that had been returned. Cardozo met twice with Clinton White House aides to review the history of the Trie-related contributions, none of which had yet been disclosed to the public. White House aides decided to release details about the contributions at a press conference, and Cardozo called Mark Fabiani, a former White House counsel who had handled press inquiries related to the Whitewater controversy, to manage the logistics. On December 16, Cardozo announced the trust was returning approximately $600,000 in donations Trie had delivered to their offices, after an internal investigation had raised "significant concerns" about the true sources of the money. "Just a few years ago, Trie, a Taiwan-born U.S. citizen, was serving up Chinese food in a shabby section of downtown Little Rock, Ark.," the *Los Angeles Times* reported. "Today he is known as an international deal-maker and Democratic high roller who maintains an address at the luxury Watergate apartments in Washington and has access to the White House."

White House spokesman Lanny Davis told CNN's Wolf Blitzer the Presidential Legal Expense Trust had "done the right thing" by returning $600,000 in contributions at a time when the Clintons still faced over $2 million in legal fees. "As soon as anyone in the White House learned that Mr. Trie had some fundraising problems, which wasn't until October when it got some publicity," Davis added, "immediately there was a heads up to the DNC to check this individual out regarding contributions and fundraising practices."

"This is a very positive story from our standpoint," Davis added.

Trie fled the country in January 1997, three months after investigators searched his Watergate South apartment. He did not return to the United States until 1998, when he pleaded guilty to one felony count of causing the Democratic National Committee to make a false report to the Federal Elections Commission and to a misdemeanor charge of making $5,000 in contributions in the names of others. He was fined $5,000, sentenced to four months' home detention—in Little Rock—and three years' probation, and ordered to perform two hundred hours of community service. The DNC and the Presidential Legal Expense Trust returned a total of $1.3 million in contributions raised by Charlie Trie.

In March 1998, the Senate Governmental Affairs Committee concluded its investigation into the Clinton-Gore presidential campaign fund-raising controversies. The investigation, which lasted a year and included thirty-two "often vituperative and partisan public hearings," cost taxpayers $3.5 million. Democrats on the committee refused to endorse the Republican majority's findings and issued their own conclusions. "I thought I could pull everybody together," lamented committee chairman Fred D. Thompson, the Tennessee Republican. "But I couldn't do it."

Republicans concluded the Chinese government "fashioned a plan before the 1996 elections . . . to influence our political process, ostensibly through stepped-up lobbying efforts and also funding from Beijing. Over time, the plan evolved and the PRC engaged in much more than simply 'lobbying.'" According to the Democrats on the committee, however, the investigation turned up "no evidence that funds from a foreign government influenced the outcome of any 1996 election, altered U.S. domestic or foreign policy, or damaged our national security."

Charlie Trie, Republicans concluded, had "raised and laundered contributions for the benefit of the President and First Lady. . . . The evidence also reveals that senior members of the White House staff were informed of this disturbing fact. . . . Rather than publicly disclosing Trie's involvement with the Trust, however, the White House sought to keep the matter secret until after the presidential election."

The Democrats disagreed, saying any delay in disclosing the return of the checks Trie delivered to Michael Cardozo was driven by legitimate concerns "about protecting the privacy" of other donors who were making perfectly legal contributions. Furthermore, the Democratic National Committee had "no reason" to suspect Trie of any wrongdoing at the time, in part because he had "prospered in the restaurant business in Arkansas" and also because he "maintained offices at an expensive location"—his apartment at the Watergate.

According to the *Washington Post*, Republicans failed to uncover evidence that put any Democratic operative or donor in jail. Democrats in turn failed to construct a credible defense of the Clinton campaign fund-raising machine, and were able to move the controversy to the back burner "only when it was replaced by the fresher, and far easier to understand, controversy involving former White House intern Monica S. Lewinsky."

Conservative columnists, including Michelle Malkin and Morton Kondracke, gave the Clinton-Gore 1996 campaign scandal a name: Chinagate.

AFTER LEAVING HIS PARENTS' WATERGATE WEST APARTment, David Bradley bought the Lee House on Capitol Hill as the new home of Research Counsel of Washington. It was a four-story walk-up with no central air-conditioning. Each night during the summer, the windows were left open to cool down the building. In the morning, there was a thin layer of ash on the windowsills and sometimes on the desks. Their next-door neighbor was Lee Crematorium. When the new summer interns figured out the real source of the ash, David recalled, "we suffered H.R. problems."

In the summer of 1983, Princeton undergraduate Katherine Brittain started an internship at the Research Counsel. She was tall and blond, with blue eyes and a beautiful smile. David, thirty, was smitten. He wanted to know more about her. He owned a research company, after all. His findings were not promising: She was already in a serious relationship.

David asked her to return the following summer, luring her with a new research project. But his real agenda was personal: Were she ever to become single again, he hoped to work up the courage to ask her out on a date. They had lunches in the office, then went out for lunch. They met for dinner at restaurants around town. They went for horseback rides on weekends. "Either he's the nicest man in the world," Katherine confided to her mother one day on the phone, "or he's interested in me."

Katherine broke up with her boyfriend and delivered the good news to David in person. He asked her out on a date. "We could talk all night," she recalled with a smile. "He was kind, interesting, and had an engine inside to change the world." She thought they could be real partners, in love and work. "I don't think that combination happens very often." Within a year, they were engaged.

David by now owned a one-bedroom apartment on the third floor of Watergate East, with a large terrace overlooking the Potomac River. "It was the best bachelor pad in the District," Katherine recalled years later with a laugh. But as a twenty-two-year-old recent college graduate in a building filled with older women, she was self-conscious. She channeled her frustration into a gift for David: a book of collages, inspired by another young woman who felt like a fish out of water—Eloise, the girl on the "tippy-top floor" of New York's Plaza Hotel, made famous in a series of books written by Kay Thompson and illustrated by Hilary Knight. She titled her book: *Katherine at the Watergate*.

David and Katherine married in 1986. After a dozen years on Capitol Hill, their company, the Advisory Board—they had renamed it in 1986—needed a new home. Employees were scattered among several townhouses on Capitol Hill. Interoffice mail was delivered between buildings in a red wagon.

Katherine, pregnant with their first child, took charge of the move. She toured potential offices around Washington while David attempted to nudge her toward the Watergate. She was skeptical but willing to listen. He presented his case: The Watergate, with its mix of buildings and open spaces, felt like a campus—an updated version of the "city within a city" marketed by developers of the complex decades ago. Watergate 600 had a space for a large conference room to host briefings and other events for their expanding client list of health care executives. Out-of-town clients could be put up easily in the Watergate Hotel. "The Watergate is perfect," he told her. Katherine, however, thought the complex was "too old" for their young workforce.

After their son Carter was born, Katherine went on maternity leave and David saw his window of opportunity. He began negotiating with the owners of the Watergate office building at 600 New Hampshire Avenue and signed a lease for four floors, plus half of the lobby level.

ON NEW YEAR'S DAY 1995, ROCCO FORTE, THE CHAIRMAN OF Trusthouse Forte, the British catering and hotel giant whose holdings included the Watergate Hotel, became Sir Rocco. Queen Elizabeth II named him a knight bachelor for "services to tourism," joining Sir Ian Maurice Gray Prosser ("For services to the Brewing Industry") and Sir Robert Graham Stephens, the voice of Aragorn on a BBC Radio serialization of *Lord of the Rings* ("For services to Drama") on the New Year Honours list.

Rocco's father, Lord Forte, had surrendered the company chairmanship three years earlier, but remained on the board. Now that Rocco was finally in charge, he was intent on transforming the family business into "a modern company." He sold off the contract catering business in order to concentrate on hotels and roadside restaurants. Profits were up sharply in London and Trusthouse Forte—known as THF, once mocked as "Truly Horrible Food"—appeared to have weathered the worst of the recession.

At 7:45 A.M. on November 22, 1995, Gerry Robinson, CEO of Granada Group, a conglomerate with a range of interests from television and theme parks to catering and bingo, called Rocco at his London home. A butler answered the phone and informed Robinson the master of the house was away at the moment—"on the Yorkshire moors, shooting." Sir Rocco, Robinson thought, should be at his desk managing his company.

Robinson was the ninth of ten children born to an Irish father and a Scottish mother. He considered becoming a Catholic priest, but switched to accounting, beginning his career as a clerk with Matchbox Toys at age seventeen. He joined Granada as CEO in 1991 and became chairman the following year. He had a reputation in some circles as a vicious cost-cutter. Monty Python's John Cleese dismissed him as "an upstart caterer." But under Robinson's leadership, Granada's stock price soared 444 percent in just five years.

Robinson wanted to expand Granada's catering business by purchasing the catering division of Trusthouse Forte, but Rocco refused to let him even submit a bid. "We simply couldn't get a look in," Robinson said. Rocco dismissed Granada for thinking "too short term" and sold the division to its senior managers. Robinson believed Sir Rocco was acting out of emotion, not in the interests of shareholders, and launched a "covert operation" to investigate the entire Trusthouse Forte empire. He sent teams into the field to investigate every asset, from the Travelodge budget hotel chain in the United States to the Savoy Hotel in London. Based on these reports, Robinson concluded, the shareholders of Trusthouse Forte would benefit from a new owner.

When Rocco got back from the moors and returned Robinson's call, he was informed Granada Group had launched a takeover bid. "I was quite taken aback," Rocco recalled.

According to Robinson's presentation to shareholders, Trusthouse Forte's management had repeatedly failed to deliver profits, earnings and dividends. As a result, over the past five years, the value of Granada Group shares soared, while Trusthouse Forte's stock price was flat. Robinson also gleefully leaked to the press that he had tried to reach Sir Rocco at home, but was informed he was out hunting grouse. "It was a good talking point," sniffed Olga Polizzi, Rocco's sister.

"Robinson doesn't have one quality business in his portfolio," Rocco declared. "He doesn't talk about style or service—he doesn't believe in them—which is why he's such an inappropriate person to run this business."

The battle lasted nine weeks. On January 23, 1996, Robinson announced a majority of Trusthouse Forte shareholders had accepted his $5.9 billion bid for the company. It was the worst day of Rocco's life, said one of his close friends. "He has effectively lost everything his father built."

Rocco tried to buy the Watergate and sixteen other luxury hotels back from Granada. His offer—which some sources said was 30 percent below the value Granada placed on them—was rejected.

Rocco and his sister formed a new hotel company and started over. Gerry Robinson became Sir Gerrard Jude Robinson, knighted by the queen for "services to the Arts" on the 2004 New Year Honours list.

AS THE TWENTY-FIFTH ANNIVERSARY OF THE WATERGATE break-in approached, Jim Herrald decided the time had come to part with a piece of history.

A year after the break-in, in 1973, he had started work at the Watergate as the building superintendent. One day, he called in a locksmith to do some work and listened intently as the man reminisced about changing the locks after the break-in at the Democratic National Committee. The man, James Rednowers, still had the old lock.

"A little light went on in my head," Herrald recalled. He badgered the locksmith and finally got him to part with the lock and to sign a notarized statement that the lock was taken from Suite 600 of the Watergate Office Building.

Herrald visited a Smithsonian curator in the early 1980s to see if there was interest in purchasing the lock, but the curator said only that the museum could accept the lock as a charitable donation. "Thanks, but no thanks," Herrald said.

After her husband passed away, and her children grew up and left for college, Gail Wolpin grew increasingly lonely and bored. She played tennis and opened a designer store for children, which caught fire the first day and burned to the ground. She rebuilt, but the clothing business was not a fit. She wrote herself a letter, which read in part: "I'm doing nothing with my life." She decided to become an auctioneer—to this day, she says she is not sure why—and attended the Mendenhall School of Auctioneering in High Point, North Carolina, "America's Top Quality Auction School since 1962." She found an old building in the nearby town of Phoebus, Virginia, and opened the Phoebus Auction Gallery in 1992. Auctioneering, Gail became fond of saying, was the world's second-oldest profession. Unlike the oldest profession, however, about 90 percent of the auctioneers at the time were men.

Herrald had sold other items from the Watergate through another auction house and was unhappy with the results. He called Wolpin, explained how the lock had come into his possession and asked her if she might be interested. She arranged to meet him at the food court of a nearby shopping mall. He brought along his wife, who was also in her seventies and very frail. He opened his briefcase and took out the four-pound brass lock. Wolpin inspected it and suggested the lock could fetch as much as $25,000.

Phoebus Auction Gallery scheduled the sale for May 26, 1997. A few days before, the *Wall Street Journal* picked up the story, and it instantly became worldwide news. The day of the auction, ABC, CBS and CNN arrived. More than three hundred bidders and Watergate buffs crammed into the room—probably the biggest turnout, employees said, since the "erotic art" auction held there the previous October. Wolpin opened the bidding at $1,000 so a "whole lot of people" could get a shot at history. Pete Peterson, an antiques dealer and insurance salesman from Yorktown, Virginia, had the highest bid in the room, at $10,000. "You know, it brings you immortality if you give it as a gift to the Smithsonian," Peterson said.

Wolpin had an absentee bid of $13,000, from a man in Boston who did not wish to be identified. She turned to Herrald and advised him to hold out for a better offer. "There are a million bells, but there's one Liberty Bell," she said. "There are a million locks, but there's one Watergate lock, the one that was taped." (Actually, the *Washington Post* reported from the auction, the Watergate burglars taped open the locks to three doors. Herrald said the other doors were long gone. "They could be in a junk pile, for all I know," he told the *Post.*)

Herrald took Wolpin's advice and rejected the absentee bid. THINGS JUST DIDN'T CLICK AT SALE OF HISTORIC LOCK, read the *Washington Post* headline.

Five years later, according to Bill Welch, the information officer for Phoebus Auction Gallery, Jim Herrald's lock was sold for more than $20,000. Welch delivered it to a lawyer's office and agreed to terms of sale that protected the sales price, as well as the identity of the buyer, who identified himself only as "a former manager at the Watergate."

ON THE MORNING OF JANUARY 21, 1998, THE LOBBY CLERK IN Watergate South made his rounds through the building, distributing the morning's edition of the *Washington Post*. On the front page—in a story headlined CLINTON ACCUSED OF URGING AIDE TO LIE—the *Post* reported Whitewater independent counsel Kenneth W. Starr had expanded his investigation of the president "to examine whether Clinton and his close friend Vernon Jordan encouraged a 24-year-old former White House intern to lie to lawyers for Paula Jones about whether the intern had an affair with the president."

From that moment forward, Monica said, "it just went crazy."

Photographers, camera crews and reporters camped out on the New Hampshire Avenue sidewalk near the entrance to the Watergate South lobby in an around-the-clock "Monica Watch." A building manager warned Monica and Marcia against venturing outside, because reporters and film crews had taken positions on balconies overlooking their terrace.

According to one cameraman, whenever Lewinsky appeared, "It's like a Chinese fire drill." According to Phil Rascona, who managed the Watergate Barber Shop, "This place was surrounded by photographers. It was like the old Westerns, when the Indians went around the covered wagons."

On January 26, speaking from the Roosevelt Room in the West Wing, President Clinton addressed the matter for the first time, famously saying: "I did not have sexual relations with that woman, Miss Lewinsky. I never told anybody to lie, not a single time; never. These allegations are false." That day, Lewinsky was seen in public for the first time since the story broke, as she left the Watergate underground parking lot in a black car, seated next to her lawyer, William Ginsburg.

Lewinsky stayed mostly indoors, curtains drawn, writing letters, knitting and watching movies. "She might as well be in jail," said Ginsburg. "The isolation for her is very tough." The curtains shut out photographers—and sunshine. The *Baltimore Sun* called the Watergate her "Gucci prison."

"More than 25 years after it first gained infamy," one wire service reported, "the Watergate complex is again at the center of a firestorm that could bring down a president. . . . The free world's axis of power no longer runs along Pennsylvania Avenue, from the Capitol to the White House. For the next few days or weeks, it runs from the office of Independent Counsel Kenneth Starr . . . across town to the Watergate."

"The ghost of Watergate has been rattling through the Lewinsky scandal like some chain-dragging Dickensian spirit," the *San Jose Mercury News* reported.

Watergate residents and shopkeepers alike banded together to protect what remained of Lewinsky's privacy. Watergate Pastry delivered her favorite chocolate mousse cake. Friends and relatives became "surrogate shoppers" at the Watergate Safeway. Jose Capestany, the owner of Watergate Florist, refused to speak to the press. "Monica's mother is a customer of ours," he said.

Lewinsky's next-door neighbor, Senator Bob Dole, just two years after his stinging presidential defeat, greeted the mob of reporters outside the lobby of Watergate South. "Look, I won! I'm back!" He sent reporters boxes of Dunkin' Donuts, for which he was employed as a spokesman. Dole said he had not engaged his famous neighbor in conversation—because he did not want to be subpoenaed. "Where was Gordon Liddy when I needed him?" Dole wisecracked. The scandal, however, gave Dole an idea. If Monica and her mother ever moved out, he told the *New York Times*, he was interested in buying their apartment and merging it with his own.

Monica eventually stopped working out at the Watergate Hotel gym, fearful other guests might surreptitiously take her photograph. She did not attend her mother's wedding that summer to New York businessman Peter Straus.

On September 11, 1998, Kenneth Starr reported to Congress, listing eleven impeachable offenses, including perjury, obstruction of justice, witness tampering and abuse of power, in a 445-page document forever known as the Starr Report. The report contained graphic details of the sexual relationship between the president and the former White House intern. Internet traffic doubled from the previous day; 20 million people read the report online over forty-eight hours.

In mid-October, Lewinsky moved out of the Watergate. She sent her neighbors a printed, hand-signed farewell note:

As I depart 700 New Hampshire, I wanted to apologize for the inconveniences of the past nine months. To those of you who have passed along your kind words, I greatly appreciated your support during this difficult time; and I thank you. I hope you all know how very sorry I am that so much attention was brought to this building.

The Doles bought Apartment 114 from the owner—Giuseppe Cecchi, who had acquired it as part of another transaction. When Bob Dole first saw the unit shortly after Monica's departure, he thought it was "not too well-kept." Monica had taped to her bedroom wall a photograph of a man—Dole would never identify him by name. Someone had written a "vulgar word" across the bottom of the image. "We probably should have kept the picture," Dole said with a shrug years later, "and showed it off."

After the remodel, Senator Dole gave a tour of their expanded apartment. He gestured toward the kitchen and dining room, where the former Lewinsky apartment once began. "See all that back there?" he asked with a smile. "That's all 'Monicaland.'"

The impact of the Watergate scandal has been so significant that it made a permanent imprint on the American psyche and earned "Watergate" a place in the American lexicon as synonymous with scandal and corruption.

Nomination of the Watergate for listing
on the National Register of Historic Places, August 2005

IN THE SUMMER OF 2000, EDWIN "E.C." SCHROEDER, WHO managed acquisitions for the Beinecke Rare Book & Manuscript Library at Yale, arrived at Walter Pforzheimer's duplex apartment on the seventh floor of Watergate East, accompanied by a half-dozen colleagues.

Walter had suffered a stroke a few years earlier and was in a wheelchair. He was as sharp and quick-witted as ever, but tired easily and could no longer climb the stairs to check on the books stored on the upper level of his apartment. He did not allow a stroke to interfere with the standing orders he had with a number of rare book dealers, so books continued to arrive at the Watergate every week. They were stacked in corners or against walls, waiting for the day he would be well enough to catalog them and place them exactly where they needed to be. That day never came.

As Walter watched from his wheelchair at the foot of the stairs, E.C. poked around the upstairs sitting area. It was filled with rows of shelves that reached nearly to the ceiling, completely filled with books. Between the shelves, books were stacked knee-high on the floor. A leak had sprung in the ceiling many years ago—long after Walter made his last climb up the flight of stairs before his stroke—and the piles of books stacked on his desk were now covered with mold.

Incredible, E.C. said to himself as he surveyed the apartment. There were fifteen shelves of "French Royal Bindings"—450 volumes from the seventeenth and eighteenth centuries, bound in red leather. Another fifteen or sixteen shelves held the world's finest collection of the writings of Frank Stockton, an American author of adventure and fairy tales that were wildly popular in the late-nineteenth century. There were twenty-eight shelves of Molière and another forty-seven shelves of books inspired by Molière, totaling 2,200 volumes—the most extensive collection of its kind outside France. Walter's seventh-floor duplex also held twenty-five shelves of rare first editions of English and American literature, known as "high spots" among librarians. Another eight shelves of various books were downstairs, in his fourth-floor studio apartment. The two apartments contained 133 feet of speeches and correspondence and 100 volumes of newspaper clippings. Walter's library of espionage-related books included 9,746 volumes—including three books by Aline, the Countess of Romanones.

It took E.C. and his team a full week to pack up the collection as Walter watched from his wheelchair, issuing instructions and snapping at them whenever some task seemed at risk of being performed incorrectly. Every evening, E.C. and Walter would have dinner at the Watergate Hotel, along with Walter's nurse and a neighbor in the Watergate, Alice Deangelo, Walter's longtime friend and confidante.

When the seventh-floor apartment was finally empty, E.C. looked around. It was larger than he originally thought, now that it was no longer the home of nearly four decades of voracious collecting. Walter appeared to be relieved. In his declining health, maintaining the collection had become a burden.

On Friday afternoon, at the end of a long week, two large trucks pulled out of the garage underneath the Watergate and headed north to New Haven, Connecticut. The collection of Walter Pforzheimer was on its way to a new home.

NIKKO SECURITIES, WHICH HAD HELPED FINANCE TRUST-house Forte's purchase of the Watergate Hotel in 1989, emerged from the Granada takeover battle as the new owner of the hotel in 1996. Just two years later, however, buffeted by a weak economy in Japan, Nikko decided it was time to sell the Watergate Hotel and hired Blackstone Real Estate Advisors in New York to find a buyer. Blackstone reviewed the hotel's financial performance and concluded the local market was solid and the Watergate was simply not getting its fair share. Blackstone purchased the hotel for its own portfolio—paying $39 million, or more than $168,000 per room—and announced Swissotel, a hotel management company in which Blackstone was also an investor, would operate the property under a new name: Swissotel Washington—the Watergate.

In a press release, Swissotel described its new role as manager of the "prestigious landmark" as a "major step" in the company's efforts to expand in key business centers around the world. Blackstone and Swissotel also announced plans to give the property an $11 million "makeover" as part of a strategy to revamp not just the thirty-one-year-old building, but its clientele. "We're going to depend a little less on transient volume business and more on the upscale individual travelers," said the hotel's new general manager, Alfred Matter.

Blackstone and Swissotel invested a total of $13 million in renovations, but the Watergate now faced serious competition from new luxury hotels, including the renovated Willard Hotel on Pennsylvania Avenue and new hotels in the West End neighborhood, near Georgetown. In total, more than two thousand new hotel rooms came on the market in the District between 1999 and 2003. The Watergate was now considered too far from downtown Washington for business visitors and not convenient to the city's major tourist attractions. Business at the Watergate Hotel dropped 30 percent between 1999 and 2003. After four years of disappointing results, Swissotel walked away.

Blackstone brought in Eastdil Realty to manage the hotel and find a buyer. "We're very encouraged," said Larry Wolfe, an executive with Eastdil. "It's a world-famous complex. Everyone knows the Watergate name." Wolfe soon found a buyer and in May 2003, Blackstone released the name of the next owner of the Watergate Hotel: Monument Realty, one of the most prominent developers in the Washington region.

Michael Darby, Monument's forty-three-year-old president, was fit and trim, with a shaved head and intense blue eyes. More than twenty years earlier, as an engineering student at the University of Melbourne, he took "a practical year" and found a job with a Washington, DC, construction company. He fell in love with Washington—he thought the city was comfortable to live in and clearly on the verge of a construction boom—and decided to come back after graduation. He answered a classified ad in the *Washington Post* for an "assistant project manager" with the Oliver Carr Company. Darby was one of two hundred candidates for the position and the only applicant who didn't blink during the interview when informed the project was renovating and expanding the Willard, one of the most famous hotels in America. "You were the most confident," the hiring manager told him. Darby had just gotten off the plane and had never heard of the Willard. "Maybe I got the job falsely," he quipped years later.

Darby cofounded Monument Realty in 1998 and, with Lehman Brothers as an equity partner, developed 2.7 million square feet of offices and apartments throughout the region. "We were prolific," Darby recalled. "It seemed like everything we touched turned to gold."

Eastdil presented the Watergate Hotel to Darby and his team for consideration. As a hotel, Darby thought the location was "a little problematic." The hotel was "off the beaten track" and the entrance to the hotel from Virginia Avenue was "hidden" and "kind of strange." Although each suite had water views, the rooms were "a little big" and had not been renovated for a very long time. There wasn't a ballroom. The number of meeting rooms was insufficient for a hotel of its size. "It seemed like a very good buy," he said—as an apartment building, or perhaps as a mixed-use building, with a boutique hotel on the lower floors and residences above. There were already three apartment buildings in the complex, with "high-profile owners."

Darby announced plans to spend $70 million to buy the hotel and convert its suites to 150 luxury condominiums. He promised a new restaurant, a renovated fitness center and another 150 parking spaces. Efficiency apartments would sell for $600,000, three-bedroom apartments for more than $2 million. "It's a terrific address already," said Darby. "We hope to benefit from that with a very high-end product that is some of the best real estate in Washington." The purchase from Blackstone, however, was contingent upon modifications to the original Planned Unit Development permit for the site, allowing Darby to convert the hotel to apartments.

Darby brought in a team of architects to study the Watergate Hotel and draw up plans for converting it to residences. According to Frank Durkin, a longtime architect at the firm Hickock Cole, if Darby had described his vision to them before purchasing the building, they would have responded simply, "You're crazy."

"Washington has this thing about buildings that aren't 'explainable,'" Darby said years later. "Washington's not a great city for doing very different things, which is a shame." Because of the District's height limits on all buildings, developers were restricted to rectangular structures with traditional designs and very little open space. The Watergate was "a very unusual building in Washington, with its curves and everything," but seemed to Darby "a little bit dated." He only got comfortable with the building's design when he did some research and unearthed Luigi Moretti's description of the exteriors of the buildings as representing "notes on a sheet of music." Darby stood on one of the balconies on the hotel's upper floor and looked around him. None of the balustrades lined up. *It's all moving and flowing*, he thought to himself—*like music*.

If the Watergate's form was outstanding, however, its function left much to be desired.

Over time, renovations to the building had focused only on aesthetics and failed to address deeper problems. The original single-pane windows were prone to leaks and needed to be replaced with modern, double-pane windows. The garage was falling apart in places, with exposed rebar in some areas. The contract with Washington Gas, which owned and operated on-site the plant to heat and cool each of the Watergate's buildings, was costly to keep and, with its cancellation penalty, expensive to terminate. The hotel's health club and indoor saltwater pool needed an overhaul. The subterranean former home of Jean-Louis at the Watergate was cramped and dark. "It was the smallest kitchen I had ever seen in my life," Darby said later. "I don't know how he did it."

The building was heated and cooled through a three-pipe mechanical system—"the worst type of system you can have for a hotel," Darby explained. There were separate pipes into the building for hot and cold air, but only one pipe going out. That meant a guest in one room could not have the air-conditioning on while a guest in another room wanted heat. The entire building had to be heated or cooled at the same time. This was especially problematic in late spring and early fall, when Washington could be cold one day, and hot and humid the next. On top of that, the original copper pipes were "decrepit" and leaky. Fixing the problem required taking out the entire heating and cooling system and starting over. Within each unit, hot and cold air flowed through fan-coil units under windows. "It eliminated the need for ducts," Durkin observed, "which was fine in a hotel room. But not so fine in a luxury condominium."

Load-bearing columns throughout the building were sixteen feet apart, which provided fine dimensions for hotel rooms, but was "lousy" for apartments—bedrooms that were too big and living rooms that were too small. Because apartments on upper floors were larger than the ones on lower floors, kitchens would be in different places on different floors. That meant kitchen exhaust from a lower floor would have to come up through an upstairs neighbor's living room or bedroom. Every floor in the Watergate Hotel was different, which meant balconies were located off living rooms in some apartments, but not in others. Balcony floors were raised slightly, which meant residents had to step up when they went outside, which created "tripping issues" to be addressed. At one end of the building, the balconies sagged.

The biggest problem, Darby and his architects agreed, was ceiling heights. Measured from "slab to slab"—from concrete floor to concrete ceiling—the floors were only eight feet apart. Ideally, there would be another two feet of space in which to place electrical, plumbing and other systems.

As Durkin conducted his own research on the building and read more about Luigi Moretti, he came to appreciate the care with which Moretti had designed the building to take advantage of its location. Light streamed into every apartment. Every apartment had a view of the water.

Despite its flaws, the Watergate was unique and Darby had buyers who wanted to live there. He built a sales center on the sixth floor to give prospective buyers a feel for what the building would soon become. All ducts for heating, cooling, electrical and plumbing were kept to the interior walls or to the sides of the rooms, opening up the views, which he planned to enhance with new floor-to-ceiling windows.

"It was the Watergate name and the water views were right there," Darby recalled years later. New, modern apartments would "set the stage" for a new era at the Watergate, raising property values in the other three Watergate apartment buildings.

"We thought everyone would be happy," he said.

MICHAEL DARBY AND BILL STEIN, A MANAGER FROM BLACK-stone's New York office, met privately with five members of the Watergate East co-op board, including Lewis Herring, the president. Stein and Darby explained they had discovered that seventy-five underground parking spaces and common areas, including the lower levels containing the Watergate fitness center and the former location of Jean-Louis Palladin's restaurant, were in fact owned by Watergate East and leased to the hotel at very favorable terms—$1 per month over sixty years. It was originally some sort of accounting device, likely concocted by Giuseppe Cecchi or Nicolas Salgo in the 1960s, that essentially provided a subsidy from Watergate East, the first building in the complex, to the hotel. The leases would expire in twenty-five years and Lehman Brothers, Darby's equity partner in the hotel, was insisting the hotel own the parking spaces outright, and therefore be in a position to sell them as deeded parking to purchasers of new apartments, or renegotiate the leases to new terms of ninety-nine years. It was the first time anyone on the Watergate East board had heard about the leases. If their predecessors on the board had known anything about the matter, they had not passed the information along. Darby and Stein put an offer of $900,000 on the table. The board asked Bill Wolf, a lawyer who lived in Watergate East with his wife, Audrey, a literary agent, to represent the association in the negotiations with Darby and Monument Realty.

Darby's offer set in motion a chain of events that would divide parts of the Watergate community into warring factions for the next five years.

IN LATE MAY, THE *WASHINGTON POST* REPORTED ON DARBY'S plans to close the hotel and reopen the building as condominiums. The sluggish economy, and the sharp decline in travel following the September 11, 2001, attacks, had hit all local hotels very hard. The Watergate, because of its location—"blocks from the core of downtown and not near a Metro station," the *Post* reported—drove Blackstone and Monument to conclude the hotel had more value as condominiums than as a hotel.

As soon as the threat of conversion appeared in print, several parts of the Watergate community rose in opposition. Barbara Spillinger, a Watergate West resident, said she and her neighbors feared the condos could become housing for nearby George Washington University students. The developer could sell condominiums to anyone, and owners could resell their apartments at any time. A cooperative apartment, however, can require every owner to be approved by the board of directors, which can consider financial and other factors in making their decisions. "Co-ops give us more control over who buys," Spillinger said. Ron Cocome, president of the Foggy Bottom Association and a resident of the Watergate, opposed converting the hotels to condos, but if Darby reopened the hotel as a cooperative—mirroring the ownership structure in each of the three residential buildings in the Watergate complex—that might be acceptable.

On June 2, 2003, the *Washington Post* ran a letter from Peter Ehrenhaft with the headline WARY AT THE WATERGATE. Ehrenhaft, a Watergate West resident, was a former partner with Fried, Frank, Harris, Shriver & Kampelman, the first tenant in the Watergate 600 office building. He argued for retaining the hotel, blaming the drop-off in business not on the hotel's location, but on "shortsighted" managers who had driven away Jean-Louis Palladin; a revolving door of owners who had failed to invest in the hotel, including its health club, which had become a "run-down relic"; and "an attitude of separation and aloofness from the Watergate community and the neighborhood." If each of these issues was addressed, he suggested, the hotel could thrive once again.

Darby reached out to the boards of each of the three Watergate apartment buildings to present his plans and, he hoped, gain their endorsements. Watergate South, the building farthest from the hotel, supported the proposal without much prodding. Dorothy Miller, president of the Watergate West co-op board, described the initial discussions with Darby as "constructive," but said several issues needed to be addressed, including an ongoing shortage of parking at Watergate West, which might be exacerbated by conversion of the hotel to residences; chimneys and other rooftop structures

Darby proposed for the new penthouses, which might spoil views from the upper floors of Watergate West; and his plans to place surface parking outside the lobby, which was inconsistent with the original design of Luigi Moretti, who placed all Watergate parking belowground.

To address at least one of the initial objections some Watergate residents were raising, Darby agreed the new residences in the hotel would be cooperative apartments, not condominiums. Local real estate experts, however, questioned the timing, noting that another 8,300 new condos were expected to be built in the District over the next two years. Darby waived away any concerns. "There haven't been many high-end residential units," he said.

That left the issue of the parking spaces and the common areas. According to Darby, the Watergate East board had not set aside sufficient reserves "for many, many years." The building was in constant need of repairs and improvements, and was looking "run-down." The residents were older—he thought the average age must be close to seventy—and therefore possibly reluctant to set aside an appropriate level of reserves "because they didn't expect to be there much longer." This worked to his advantage, he thought. The owners might look at the sale of the parking spaces as a way to build up the building's reserve funds, painlessly.

In September 2003, Darby agreed to pay $4.25 million for the parking spaces and common areas, totaling 46,000 square feet. But when Wolf presented the deal to the board, they voted six to five against approving the transaction. He was stunned.

Some members of the board did not want any part of Watergate East to be sold to Monument Realty, fearing a sale would simply clear a path for Darby to close the Watergate Hotel. "Looking back," said Audrey Wolf, who later followed her husband on the Watergate East board, "I don't remember why they wanted so fiercely for the hotel to remain, but they did." Others thought the issue was too important to decide without a vote of the owners. As a compromise, the board voted to bring the issue to the entire membership of Watergate East in January and sent a letter to the District Zoning Commission, going on record as opposed to the conversion of the hotel to apartments until a full vote of the residents could be conducted.

On January 22, by a vote of 54 to 46 percent, a majority of the Watergate East co-op shareholders voted to approve the sale. The vote was measured in shares, allocated based on the square footage of apartments, with 33,428 votes for the sale and 28,535 votes against. Measured by the number of apartments, however, 100 owners voted in favor of the sale, but 101 voted against it.

On January 29, at 6:30 P.M., the District Zoning Commission took up the petition from Blackstone Real Estate Advisors to modify the original permits for the Watergate in order to replace the hotel with another apartment building. The first witness was Benjamin Kass, a lawyer for Watergate East, who dropped a bombshell: He revealed that four dissenting board members had just filed suit in the Delaware Court of Chancery challenging the January 22 vote. Kass explained that the Watergate East board, by a vote of six to five, had determined that 75 percent of the membership was required to approve the sale of the parking spaces and common areas—a threshold had not been met at the vote on January 22. Members of the board supporting the sale, however, had taken the position that approval only required a majority of those present or by proxy. Until the question was resolved by the Court of Chancery, Kass said, it was impossible to say whether Watergate East supported converting the Watergate Hotel into apartments.

On February 25, 2004, Chancellor William B. Chandler III, a Yale-trained lawyer serving his second term on the Delaware Court of Chancery, acknowledged the proposed sale of the parking spaces and common areas to Monument was divisive and could "hasten the demise of the famed Watergate Hotel." But the proposed transaction, he said, did not require approval by 75 percent of the Watergate

East membership. The sale needed approval of a super-majority only if it involved "substantially all" of the assets of the association, and 75 parking spaces and a ballroom were at best "an insubstantial portion of Watergate East's overall assets." Residents of Watergate East had in fact been misled by their own board not only on the votes needed to approve the sale, but on the necessity of voting at all. No provision of law or the Watergate East's own governing documents, he concluded, required members of Watergate East to vote on the sale of either the parking spaces or the common areas.

Chandler expressed grave doubt about the ability of the Watergate East board of directors to evaluate the matter. Members of the board were dug in on opposing sides of the question and, "to be generous, fractious." Because residents had been led to believe they would be given the opportunity to vote on the sale, he ordered a new vote of the membership, at which a simple majority of those present, or represented by proxy, would be required to approve the sale. The vote was scheduled for April 12, 2004, the next annual meeting of the Watergate East membership.

A GROUP OF WATERGATE RESIDENTS OPENED ANOTHER front in the war against the conversion of the Watergate Hotel into residences. Calling themselves the Committee to Preserve the Watergate Heritage, they filed an application with the District's Historic Preservation Office to designate the Watergate a historic landmark.

Because of its location, adjacent to Rock Creek Park and the Kennedy Center, most changes to the Watergate were subject to review by the Commission of Fine Arts. Designation of the Watergate as a historic landmark would require a second level of review, by the Historic Preservation Review Board. Designation as a federal landmark would also mean the Watergate would qualify for certain tax deductions, and would be eligible for historic preservation grants.

Whether landmark status would prevent the conversion of the Watergate Hotel to apartments, however, was an open question. The landmark application specifically noted the complex was unique because it included a mix of offices, residences and a hotel. "We don't designate use," said a District preservation official. "We try to protect the physical characteristics."

The driving force behind this historic designation campaign was Judge Pauline Newman, a resident of Watergate West who had distinguished herself as a patent attorney before Reagan appointed her to the Court of Appeals for the Federal Circuit in 1984. Like many of the Watergate's early residents, she was a single, professional woman. She did not like to cook and ordered meals sent up from the Watergate Hotel or ate in the hotel's restaurant whenever she worked late, which was often.

At the first hearing before the District Historic Preservation Review Board, Watergate South resident Dorothy Olsen testified against the historic designation. She objected to the use of historic designation "to control what an owner does" with his or her property, she said, and "a bungled political robbery" did not merit landmark status. "I'd hope people would be ashamed, not proud," she said.

Judge Newman and her committee had hired Emily Eig and her firm Traceries, specialists in architectural history and historic preservation, to help guide them through the designation process. As Eig watched the first hearing of the District Historic Preservation Review Board to consider the Watergate's application, she detected skepticism. Some board members could not quite wrap their brains around designating the Watergate, which was not even fifty years old, "historic." Tersh Boasberg, the board's chair, said he needed more information on Luigi Moretti before he could make an informed judgment. Someone had sent him "Google information" on Moretti, he said, but it was in Italian: "It would be helpful if we had it in English." The board postponed a decision, pending more documentation on the Watergate's history and architecture. Boasberg, chairman of the preservation review board, also asked that any reference to hotel conversion be dropped from the landmark application.

Eig and her team of architectural historians went to work. To be registered as a historic building, it was necessary that the Watergate convince the board that it was an outstanding example of American architecture; a masterwork of its creative team, principally Luigi Moretti and the landscape architect Boris Timchenko; and a site of exceptional national political significance. Eig prepared a detailed, sixty-page application, hitting each of the three points hard, and sent it over to the Watergate West committee for review and comment. A lawyer for the committee called Eig with a suggestion: Would it be possible, he asked, to delete any reference to the break-in at the Democratic National Committee and the fate of Richard Nixon?

Absolutely not, Eig replied. If the residents wanted the Watergate to be listed as historic, its notorious political history would carry the application across the finish line. Without a mention of the Watergate scandal, the application was doomed to fail. "Leave it in," the lawyer conceded.

THE DISTRICT ZONING COMMISSION RECONVENED THE night of March 1 to consider the conversion of the Watergate Hotel to apartments. To accommodate an overflowing crowd, chairs and a television screen were set up in a hallway. "You could feel the angst in the room," Chairman Carol Mitten later recalled.

In addition to BRE/Watergate, LLC—the Blackstone entity selling the Watergate Hotel to Monument Realty—a number of groups petitioned to participate in the hearing, including the Committee of Concerned Owners in Watergate East (in support), Watergate East (opposed), Watergate East Committee Against Hotel Conversion to Co-op Apartments (opposed) and a handful of individual residents. The zoning commission accepted the petitions of two groups:

the Committee of Concerned Owners in Watergate East and the Watergate East Committee Against the Hotel Conversion to Co-op Apartments.

The Committee of Concerned Owners in Watergate East was organized by Bill Wolf, who had earlier negotiated the $4.25 million deal with Michael Darby. A lawyer, Wolf had lived in the Watergate since the 1960s; after he and Audrey married in 1980, they combined two duplexes on the seventh floor of the building, leaving in place the two original staircases. At the top of one staircase, Audrey kept an office; at the top of the staircase at the other end of their apartment, Bill kept a study. The couple enjoyed having a hotel in the complex, because they could order food and have it sent up. "Not that we did it very often," Audrey recalled. "But it was an option." They had deep concerns about living next door to a condominium, but when Darby agreed to sell his new units as cooperative apartments, they decided to support the hotel conversion.

Jack Olender represented the Watergate East Committee Against Hotel Conversion to Co-op Apartments. As a young man, he turned down Harvard Law School to attend the University of Pittsburgh so he could help his father, a Jewish refugee from Russia, manage the family's fruit and vegetable store in McKeesport, Pennsylvania. In his last year at law school, he met a man who changed the course of his life: Melvin Belli, the renowned plaintiffs' lawyer known as the King of Torts. After graduation, Jack moved to Washington and took a teaching fellowship at George Washington University Law School, at the suggestion of one of his favorite professors, to learn more about the field of personal injury law. He started his own firm, specializing in medical malpractice, and was the first lawyer to win more than $1 million in a settlement for brain damage at birth.

When Jack and his wife, Lovell, decided it was time to buy an apartment, in the early 1980s, Jack had one requirement: The apartment needed to be within walking distance of his office, which was near GWU, because walking was good for his health, and long drives from the Washington suburbs were a waste of valuable time. Their first apartment, in Watergate West, was "fine, but a little cramped." When their neighbors moved out and offered to sell their water-facing apartment, Jack and Lovell leaped at the opportunity to expand. Two members of the Watergate West board of directors, however, for reasons Jack never quite figured out, opposed the sale and lined up votes on the board against it. "I thought they were insane," Jack recalled. "And I said, 'to Hell with that.'" They sold their Watergate West apartment and bought a three-bedroom apartment with a den—formerly owned by Kathy and Maurice Stans—on the twelfth floor of Watergate East.

When news of the proposed hotel conversion first surfaced, Jack's neighbors recruited him to lead the opposition. He was reluctant to get involved at first. He had avoided serving on the Watergate East board, but had served on a number of building committees, which he found to be "generally dysfunctional." Residents seemed to like chairing committees in order to appear important to their neighbors, he observed, but did not accomplish much. He also noted something disturbing about the building's governance, at all levels: Watergate East residents seem to have divided themselves into factions. But Lovell kept badgering her husband to step up. She was confined to a wheelchair and used the Watergate Hotel indoor swimming pool regularly. She wanted to keep using it.

"It was as though it was his pool," Darby recalled with irritation years later.

Darby and his team met with Olender to hear him out and attempt to resolve the impasse. Darby explained that Monument was expecting to replace the pool, and that Watergate residents would be able to purchase memberships. "It didn't matter to him," Darby recalled.

What finally tipped the scales against the conversion, Jack said, was his sense of "social justice." Watergate East was the oldest building in the complex. If a wave of residents dumped their apartments and moved across the way into a new building, they would never look back. Their replacements would be unlikely to support needed investments in Watergate East going forward and the community would unravel. *We would be abandoned*, he thought. He agreed to manage the fight to save the Watergate Hotel.

Every two weeks, the residents committed to saving the hotel gathered in Jack's wood-paneled study—the same "Africana" room which had formerly displayed Maurice Stans's collection of safari souvenirs. The key members of the group included retired Virginia judge Lester E. Schlitz; Ellen Cooper, a businesswoman from New York; Carol Radin, an artist with a rooftop studio and another regular in the Watergate Hotel swimming pool; and a doctor whom Olender recalled years later was a former Israeli soldier and, therefore, someone who "wasn't afraid of anything."

Just before the zoning commission hearing, the land-use attorney they had hired suddenly backed out. Jack was a malpractice lawyer. He knew he was in over his head, but there was no one else who could take the case.

Olender asked the zoning commission for a postponement until after the April 12 vote of the Watergate East owners. Norman Glasgow, a lawyer representing the Blackstone team, objected. The hotel conversion, he said, had been under discussion since November 2003. An "unbelievable number" of community meetings had been held. "Anyone that could take the position that they have not had an opportunity to be involved in this," he added, has "been out of the country for the last six months." Richard Aguglia, representing Watergate West, said he was "sympathetic" to Olender's circumstances, but was ready to proceed. Chairman Mitten suggested a compromise: The hearing would be split over two days, with the first day dedicated to the proponents and the second day dedicated to the opposition, in order to give opponents time to collect themselves and collaborate on an effective presentation.

Michael Darby stepped up to the microphone. "When the current owners of the Watergate Hotel announced that the hotel was for sale and I first toured it last March," he began, "I immediately thought: 'Wouldn't this be great—if we can convert the hotel to high-quality residences.' With the Watergate's name, 654 high-quality residences already are here and those wonderful views up and down the Potomac River, these new units would be some of the finest in the city."

Darby walked the zoning commission through his key arguments for closing the hotel and converting the building to apartments. Demand for residential housing in the District of Columbia had picked up. Each year, more than 7,500 high-income households in the Washington metropolitan area looked for new homes, but only six new urban luxury projects—representing just 284 units—had been constructed the previous year to meet this demand. He described protections in place that would prevent GWU students from renting apartments. He agreed to make the renovated health club available to residents of Watergate West, Watergate East and Watergate South, and give residents of each of the three existing buildings access to "community rooms" adjacent to the new restaurant area and overlooking the outdoor pool. To address concerns of Watergate West over a parking shortage, Darby would provide 146 new parking spaces for residents, nearly double the original plan.

Finally, to address some residents' concerns about Monument's ability to finance the conversion, Darby provided a letter of support from his investment partner: the real estate arm of Lehman Brothers.

Darby raised the possibility that the hotel might continue to deteriorate and fall into the hands of a "low-quality hotel operator." Bill Stein, representing Blackstone, explained that the hotel, despite more than $13 million in renovations, had "not met our expectations." Two different management companies had been unable to improve the hotel's performance. Stein expected some residents to come forward and say they used the existing Watergate Hotel services. "I wish that was the case," he said, "but unfortunately it's not." In 2003, only about $150,000, amounting to less than 1 percent of the total revenues of the Watergate Hotel, came from residents of the Watergate complex.

The final presentation in support of Monument's plan came from economist Jim Prost, who walked the commissioners through an economic and fiscal impact analysis that showed a net positive economic impact of $6 million, additional sales tax revenues to the District totaling about $460,000, and a 30 percent increase in direct and indirect jobs compared to the existing use of the property as a hotel.

"The simple fact is the hotel is more valuable as residential units," Darby concluded.

"Why do you still have opposition?" zoning commissioner Anthony J. Hood asked Darby.

"Unfortunately you can't please everybody," Darby replied.

Daniel Sheehan, a resident of Watergate East, followed the Monument team and endorsed the conversion as an alternative to seeing the hotel continue to decline and perhaps turn into "Motel 6 at the Watergate." Barbara Spillinger, a resident of Watergate West, endorsed the conversion on behalf of the Foggy Bottom Association, which supported it. "Those of us who live in the Watergate complex do not live on an island," testified William Dakin, a resident of Watergate East. "When you go beyond our little complex into the larger community," he continued, conversion of the hotel expanded the property tax base for the city and pushed back against the encroachment of GWU, which threatened to turn all of Foggy Bottom into a "vast dormitory."

Outside the hearing room, supporters of the hotel conversion hinted Secretary of State Condoleezza Rice, a resident of Watergate South, agreed with them, but her spokesman swatted down the idea, telling a reporter who asked for comment, "I don't think we're going to have anything on this one." A spokesman for another Watergate

South resident, Supreme Court Justice Ruth Bader Ginsburg, also declined to comment.

After a short break, the meeting resumed at 8:46 P.M., and Jack Olender, representing the committee of Watergate East owners opposed to the conversion, stepped forward. He decided not to focus on the merits of the conversion, but on the credibility of Monument Realty and its president, Michael Darby.

"How many projects do you have going at this time with Monument Residential LLC?" Olender asked.

"I don't know exactly," Darby replied.

"Do you have any?"

"Different projects have different entities. I don't understand the question."

"Mr. Olender, what's the relevance of this?" asked Carol Mitten, the zoning commission chair.

"I'll show this in a few minutes, Your Honor," Olender replied.

Mitten pressed him. "I want you to tell me—"

"Can I approach the bench?" Olender interrupted.

"No," she replied, "you have to tell me now in front of everyone."

"The thing is, Your Honor—"

"And I'm not 'Your Honor.' This is not a court and so we're a little less formal, but still respectful. So I appreciate your deference, but I just want to keep it in perspective."

Olender paused and smiled. He reminded Mitten he was a malpractice lawyer, not a zoning lawyer. "I'm doing the best I can."

He turned back to Darby.

"Why did you finance the lawsuit against Watergate East?" Olender asked. Monument Realty had underwritten the challenge supporters of the hotel conversion had filed with the Delaware Court of Chancery.

"I object," interrupted Norman Glasgow, Darby's attorney.

Mitten turned to Olender. "I would ask you again, what's the relevance of that?"

"The relevance, Your Honor," Olender explained, "is they are so desperate to get this land that Watergate East has, and that they need for their project, that they have gone to the extent of ripping asunder the residents of Watergate East!"

The audience erupted in cheers and boos.

"No! No! No!" Mitten shouted from the dais, banging her gavel. "There will be no expressions from the audience!"

She turned back to Olender.

"I just want you to understand what we do here, okay?" She sighed. "Some of these legal machinations that go on, they go on outside this hearing room. What we're interested in is the zoning case that's before us, which is what we do the testimony about, and that's where I'd like you to focus your attention in the cross-examination."

"Yes." Olender nodded.

"And desperation or no desperation, or whatever goes on to convince people to support something or to not support something, is really not relevant for us. As long as people are making arguments that are relevant for us, that's what we want to hear."

Olender suggested Mitten and her fellow commissioners should be interested in the character of Michael Darby.

"You're not going to get Mr. Darby to admit that he's some sort of, you know, a bad guy," replied Mitten.

"I don't want him to, "said Olender. "I just want him to give the facts. The facts are that he put—he and his company paid for six board members to be sued."

"I renew my objection, Madam Chair," said Glasgow.

"Mr. Olender," said Mitten, "you're just going to have to move on to another subject."

Opponents of the hotel conversion introduced into the record a letter from Plácido Domingo, general director of the Washington Opera, opposing the plan. "The elimination of the Hotel would not only diminish the lifestyle of the residents, but would adversely affect the position of the Watergate Complex in the District as an acclaimed example of urban living," he wrote. If the hotel conversion were to proceed, Watergate East resident Sol S. Shalit wrote the zoning commission, "there will *never again be a Watergate Hotel.* This may not sound like much, if you think of it merely as a sum of physical entities like square footage, people, restaurant, health club, etc. But you will have eliminated not just a hotel, but a *mental concept*. You will have wiped out forever from our vocabulary a living cultural icon, part of history, and part of the *nation's cultural landscape.* It's like making the Plaza Hotel in NYC *disappear* forever into just another hi-rise apartment building. These are cultural *monuments*—and you can see the irony—they have a *history*, and you will have turned it into *archaeology.*"

Mitten invited everyone back in three days to hear from the opposition.

"Hope it's a little cooler in here," she sighed.

On March 4, 2004, the District Zoning Commission resumed its hearing on the conversion. Richard Aguglia, the attorney representing Watergate West, led off the roster of witnesses against the proposal and zeroed in immediately on an assertion made repeatedly during the first session: that the Watergate Hotel was losing money. Under the District's zoning laws, Aguglia said, "economic hardship is not a standard of evaluation." In other words, the Watergate Hotel's financial condition was irrelevant. Even if it were relevant, he continued, the owners of the hotel—Blackstone's real estate arm—had failed to produce anything in support of their claims and had failed to demonstrate that no other entity, other than Darby's Monument Realty, was interested in purchasing the hotel, or operating the property as a hotel.

Geoffrey Fritzger, a Watergate West resident, testified it was "absolutely incomprehensible" for the owners to suggest the hotel was losing money. Every night, he said, "I almost get blinded by all the TV sets that are still open at 11:30 and 12:00 o'clock."

Alvin R. McNeal, a planning consultant, testified the Watergate complex was a "cultural institution" and "part of the folklore of the District of Columbia." The hotel, he said, was an important "branding element" of the complex and provided "vitality" to the development twenty-four hours a day. George Oberlander, another planning consultant, advised the zoning commission that Foggy Bottom had already lost four hundred hotel rooms near the Kennedy Center when GWU was granted permission to convert the Howard Johnson Motor Lodge, directly across the street from the Watergate Office Building, to student housing.

Liz Thorne, president of the Hotel and Restaurant Employees Local 25 union from the AFL-CIO—the same union to which Roxie Herbekian and Sherwood Dameron had belonged—also testified against the conversion. Thorne dismissed the "ludicrous and heartless" claims made during the first zoning commission hearing that employees of the Watergate Hotel could find work elsewhere in the District. "These workers and the others at the Watergate will not be absorbed," she said. "They will be unemployed and, candidly, because of their age, they will likely never work again."

Dr. Maurizio Ragazzi, a resident of Watergate West, quoted from the writings of Luigi Moretti: "To seek clearly and then be lost means to be enchanted." That may be true for art and architecture, Ragazzi said, but not for real estate development. His wife followed him to the podium, demanding preservation of the Watergate intact as a "world class monument throughout the world." She denounced proposed changes to the hotel's exterior, especially the "awful, awful carports."

Clarence Booker, an employee at the Watergate for thirty-seven years, including twenty years as a resident and manager of Watergate West, said the average age of residents in the building was "about 70." Many of them, he said, were lonely and had nothing to do each day but walk over to the hotel.

"Watergate represents more than just a roof over our heads,

which is why we are so personally offended by the prospect of it being altered," testified another self-described "very content resident," Ellen Cooper, a member of the group that met regularly in Jack Olender's study. "We regard it as a landmark which has not yet been given its due."

Jack Olender rose from his seat. Rather than present his arguments from a witness table, he walked across the room to where a podium was standing in a corner. He slowly wheeled the podium into place in the middle of the hearing room.

Darby shook his head in disbelief. He knew Olender's style wouldn't work with Mitten and her colleagues. "It was just silly," he recalled thinking. "This wasn't a case of law."

Olender asked Darby whether Monument Residential LLC was legally registered to do business in the District of Columbia.

"Everything we do is completely aboveboard," Darby snapped. "If you're implying that it isn't, I resent that."

"I'm trying to get the facts, sir," Olender replied.

Mitten interrupted from the dais. "What's the relevance?" she asked Olender.

"Because he tells three and four different things on different occasions, that's the relevance," Olender replied, "and I think you're entitled—and I would think *required*—to assess the veracity of these witnesses."

"I'd like you to pick another subject," Mitten responded.

"That's all I have." Olender smiled, and sat down.

Mitten asked Darby and his colleagues if they had a closing statement—Norman Glasgow said they would submit a written statement for the record—and announced comments could continue to be received until April 29 at 3:00 P.M., in order to allow for the results of the April 12, 2004, vote by the owners of Watergate East to be included in the record.

At 9:39 P.M., the meeting was adjourned.

AS THE WATERGATE EAST VOTE ON THE CONVERSION neared, each side campaigned furiously. A flyer in favor of the sale listed the names and phone numbers of the "six antidemocratic and recalcitrant Directors" who opposed the sale and urged residents: "Call them and insist on democracy. This is America, under the rule of law. It is not Afghanistan, under the rule of the Taliban."

Opponents of the conversion responded with a flyer titled "THE CHOICE IS SIMPLE" which warned against "accepting 155 new luxury hi-rise co-ops next door directly competing with our own apartments, depressing our market values, and turning us into the 'has been' 'Old Watergate.'"

"This issue has been so emotional," said Audrey Wolf. "You see people in the lobbies and you don't want to get in the same elevator with them. . . . They give the cold shoulder. They won't speak."

"There was definitely ill will," Olender later recalled. "The climate in the building turned very nasty."

On April 12, the Watergate Hotel's Monticello Room was packed with Watergate East residents. Bruce B. Drury, a partner with a prominent accounting firm, was on hand to audit the vote. As residents handed in their paper ballots, Drury and an assistant used the building manager's laptop computer to count the votes and assign them an appropriate weight, based on their shares in the cooperative—which in turn reflected the size of their apartments.

The first item issue on the ballot was an election to fill the expired terms of three members of the Watergate East board of directors. Drury reported that three pro-sale directors had been elected, tipping the balance of the board from six to five against the hotel conversion to six to five in favor.

The next vote was on Monument's offer to purchase the parking spaces and other property beneath the Watergate Hotel for $4.25 million.

Drury announced the result. The proposed sale was approved by a narrow margin: 35,040 shares in favor and 34,548 against—a margin of just 492 voting shares.

The new Watergate East board—which was now narrowly dominated by a pro-conversion majority—cheered the result. But the matter was far from settled.

Over the next two days, many residents—primarily those opposed to the conversion—pressured Drury for more detail about the ballots, including the votes of individual owners. On April 14, 2004, Jack Olender wrote Bill Condrell, the outgoing president of Watergate East, and asked how many apartments voted each way. Drury turned to Kioumars Aghazadeh, the general manager of Watergate East, for advice. Aghazadeh, known in the building as "Mr. Que," deleted from his laptop the electronic copy of the April 12 vote. Drury later testified he had been instructed to destroy paper copies of the ballots and proxy instructions, but refused to name the person who gave the order. By April 15, all records of the vote had been destroyed.

On April 19, Olender wrote to Daniel Sheehan, the newly elected president of Watergate East, demanding the number of owners and apartments who voted for and against the sale, so he could include that information in his submission to the District Zoning Commission. "If you do not provide it timely [sic]," Olender wrote, "I will reference it in my file and argue the inference that the majority of apartments and individuals voting against the sale was considerably larger than the majority who voted against the sale at the previous meeting." That night, board members heard rumors the ballots had been destroyed. Bill Condrell immediately called Dan Sheehan, who denied it. The next morning, Dr. Judith Eaton, a Watergate East resident, asked Drury for additional information about the membership vote. Drury replied that he had destroyed all paper ballots and proxies, and had deleted the software program from the laptop "at the direction of the board." She asked

Drury who exactly had ordered the destruction of the records. Drury replied that he had been ordered by Sheehan and Mr. Que, and he did so despite his personal "angst and fear" about doing it. Drury also told Dr. Eaton he was "muzzled" by the board and building management. Neither Bill Wolf nor Dan Sheehan said they ordered the destruction of the ballots and proxies.

"Why would anyone want to destroy the ballots, proxies and software program for one of the most important votes that WEI has ever held and a vote that was decided by fewer than 1% of total shares?" asked Eaton, in a memorandum circulated to owners.

"It's a second Watergate cover-up," Olender fumed.

On April 22, owners of Watergate East found a two-page letter in their mailboxes headlined: AN OUTRAGE HAS BEEN COMMITTED— OUR VOTING RECORDS DESTROYED! "We're shocked to hear," wrote six owners of Watergate East, "that the first action of our new [Watergate East] President was to order the destruction of our April 12 voting records." Preserving records of the election, they wrote, constituted "elementary considerations of fairness and respect" for the owners of Watergate East as well as the voting process itself.

The destruction of the paper and computer record of the vote has raised serious doubts on the very outcome of the vote. In light of these new circumstances, as the April 12 vote record has been irremediably destroyed, we have no other option than to request that a new vote be taken, without delay, at a special meeting of [Watergate East] members. We trust that you will join us in this request, irrespective of your vote on the sale of [Watergate East's] properties, because we all have a common interest in preserving the integrity of the deliberation process by the [Watergate East] membership.

On April 22, former board president William Condrell, in an open letter to residents of Watergate East, made note of the "disturbing" development. "Apparently," Condrell wrote, "within a few days after the vote, the auditor, who had kept the voting records in his possession, destroyed them and did so in spite of questions being raised at the time from members concerned about the recording of their vote." Condrell promised to seek a special meeting of the Watergate East board "to determine the full circumstances."

The next day, Dan Sheehan wrote to the owners of Watergate East. He had hoped that his first message to them would be "focused on reconciliation, reconstruction, and moving forward." Instead, he was writing to them about the destruction of records. Sheehan declared "categorically and unequivocally" he did not order the destruction of the ballots. Nor did he order anyone else to tell Drury to destroy any ballots. Sheehan said his instructions were limited to declining requests to know "how certain apartments voted." Sheehan wrote there was "no question" in his mind that the results of the April 12 election were final. He called the controversy around the destruction of ballot and other records a "red herring" and expressed his hope that Watergate residents could move on. "I know that this will not be the end of the issue," Sheehan wrote, "and truly the only folks happy about this continuing are the owners of the small copy shop down on the plaza."

In response to Jack Olender's pending request for the number of owners and apartments on each side of the Monument sale, Sheehan replied the board no longer had those records, and in any event the only relevant results of the April 12 membership vote were based on the number of shares, not on the number of apartments.

Residents opposed to the conversion immediately began collecting signatures to demand another vote. One resident hung out in the lobby of Watergate East to corner neighbors as they returned from work. "Sour grapes," sniffed Michael Darby. Enough signatures were gathered to force yet another vote, which the board scheduled for early June. To make sure there would be no accusations of ballot fraud, the board paid the League of Women Voters more than $1,500 to monitor the election.

On April 29, 2004, the final day allowed for submitting comments to the District Zoning Commission, the Watergate East Committee Against Hotel Conversion to Co-op Apartments filed an eleven-page "rebuttal, closing remarks and submission" and a three-page "findings of fact," each signed by Jack Olender, which argued that the destruction of the April 12 ballots required a "re-vote" by the owners, and that Bill Stein, representing Blackstone, had misled the zoning commission when he said no other luxury hotel operators were interested in the property. In response to an assertion by Monument that the Watergate Hotel was originally conceived as "an apartment-style hotel, contemplating stays of a month or more," Olender argued that was irrelevant—the equivalent of asserting the hotel was conceived as "a rest and recreation stop for visiting Martians."

On May 10, 2004, at 6:30 P.M., Carol Mitten called the zoning commission to order. The commission, she said, must balance the impact of preserving existing amenities at the hotel against the changes sought by the developers. She said the developers, by offering to retain access to a restaurant and the Watergate Hotel health club, had retained two aspects of the property that seemed to be most important to current residents of the complex.

Vice Chairman Anthony J. Hood said he was "perplexed" by the case. Opponents of the conversion to apartments, he said, had raised issues that made him "stop and think." But the developer's offer to provide $300,000 in affordable housing elsewhere in the District—in exchange for permission to build and sell $3 million apartments—was unacceptable. The developers should be forced to include affordable housing at the Watergate as a condition for converting the hotel.

"I think we have to look at Washington in a broad context," said Commissioner Kevin Hildebrand. "We are a tourist city and we want to attract the tourist market to Washington." Hildebrand appeared to be leaning against the conversion.

Commissioner John G. Parsons echoed Mitten's observation about retaining access to the health club and restaurant. The fifth and final commissioner, Gregory Jeffries, remained silent.

Mitten called for a vote.

Hood voted against revising the Watergate's original zoning to allow for the hotel conversion. Jeffries abstained. Hildebrand joined Mitten and Parsons in support, and the zoning change was approved by a vote of three to one.

AS THE THIRD AND FINAL VOTE OF THE WATERGATE EAST membership on the conversion approached, Dan Sheehan said the $4.25 million offered by Monument could protect residents against future fee increases. But another resident, retired diplomat William S. Diedrich, said the loss of the hotel bar lounge would be tragic. "It's a decent place to go have a $15 hamburger," he said.

Michael Darby was optimistic. The hotel conversion was a "done deal," he told the *Washington Post*. He announced Lehman Brothers had agreed to be a major investor in his deal to buy the Watergate Hotel from Blackstone.

On the night of June 9, hundreds of Watergate East residents once again filled the Monticello Room in the Watergate Hotel to cast their ballots, which were then collected, locked up and transported to the offices of the District of Columbia League of Women Voters. The next day, on June 10, 2004, the League of Women Voters announced the results: The Monument offer was voted down, by a margin of just 0.7 percent.

"We're so pleased," said Diedrich. "It's delightful."

"We won. We won," said Evelyn Y. Davis, a self-described "corporate watchdog" living in Watergate East.

"I'm very, very frustrated," lamented Audrey Wolf.

"I can't believe it," added her husband. "I'm not very happy."

While the votes were being tallied and before the outcome was announced, however, the Watergate East board of directors, which was narrowly in favor of the hotel conversion, called a special meeting. They voted five to four, with two members absent, to sell the parking spaces to Monument Realty. Three weeks later, the board reaffirmed its support for the sale but agreed to wait for a final ruling from the Delaware Court of Chancery.

IN AUGUST, MONUMENT REALTY ANNOUNCED IT HAD COM-pleted the purchase of the Watergate Hotel from Blackstone—the *Washington Post* reported the sale price at around $55 million—and announced the new name for the building: Belles Rives at The Watergate. In the coming months, as the hotel prepared to close, the developer offered charitable organizations discounted rates for the use of public reception areas. Potential buyers of cooperative apartments were invited to spend a free last night in the hotel in the suites where their new homes would soon be located.

Darby approached Thomas Keller, the famed chef and founder of Per Se in New York and The French Laundry in California, to open a new restaurant at the Watergate. As a young man, Keller had begged Jean-Louis Palladin to hire him as an apprentice chef. "I will not teach you," Palladin sneered, and turned him down.

Over dinner, Darby made the case to Keller for returning to Washington in triumph, and working out of the same building where Jean-Louis Palladin had reinvented American cuisine.

"I could see it in his eyes," Darby recalled. "A desire to go back to where he'd been told he can't do something—and then do it."

Darby took some friends to the top floor of the Watergate Hotel late at night and showed them the spectacular views of the Potomac River, Georgetown, the National Cathedral, the Kennedy Center and the Washington Monument. The others went inside, but he stayed on the balcony for a few more minutes.

As he looked around, he found it hard to believe that "a guy like me"—a surfer from Australia—was now an American citizen and the owner of a building that had so much history in the United States.

Wow, he said to himself.

ON OCTOBER 18, 2004, WILLIAM B. CHANDLER III RELEASED his third and final decision on the Watergate controversy from the Delaware Court of Chancery. In light of the "acrimony separating the two membership factions"—those supporting and those opposing the sale—the Watergate East board of directors "had a duty to establish a fair, open, fully informed, and verifiable vote," he wrote. Because the ballots had been destroyed "prior to verification and during a period of increasing inquisition," he added, "the April vote lost any indicia of reliability and fair process." He concluded the April 12, 2004, vote, at which the sale of property to Monument Realty was narrowly approved, was "fatally flawed" and tossed it aside.

He next turned to the vote held on June 9, 2004—which was requested by petition from more than fifty owners and monitored by the League of Women Voters—at which the sale of property to Monument Realty was declined. He praised the board of directors for avoiding another debacle and certified the results as "the only legitimate vote cast on the Monument sale."

That left one open issue: the intervening vote by the Watergate East board of directors, the day after the June vote, to approve the sale to Monument. Chandler referred to his February 25 order, in which he stated the owners of Watergate East had been informed for more than a year that they would have the opportunity for a "fair and meaningful" vote on the sale. While the composition of the Watergate East board had shifted from a six-to-five anti-sale majority to a six-to-five pro-sale majority, he said, that did not change the fact that the owners themselves were promised a vote. Chandler ordered the June 9, 2004, vote against the sale to be counted. The sale was off.

"We feel vindicated," said Jack Olender.

Said another Watergate East resident opposed to the conversion: "It's delightful. It's delicious. It's de-victory."

THE HISTORIC PRESERVATION REVIEW BOARD MET ON FEBruary 23, 2005, to consider the application from the Committee to Preserve the Watergate Heritage to designate the Watergate as a historic landmark. Chairman Boasberg opened the hearing by stating the obvious: The Watergate application, he said, was "an extremely interesting case."

Over the past several months, the board received a number of letters, nearly all in support of landmark status. The DC Preservation League called the Watergate "an exceptional example of modern era design in Washington, DC." The local chapter of Docomomo, an organization founded in 1988 to protect important examples of modern architecture, praised the Watergate as an example of a "brief but exhilarating period" of twentieth-century architecture, and noted that the use of "computer-aided design" was "quite revolutionary at the time." James M. Goode, author of *Best Addresses: A Century of Washington's Distinguished Apartment Houses*, which featured the Watergate, praised "the sweeping, curvilinear building footprints and the 'sawtooth' railings of the numerous balconies that provide both air circulation and privacy to residents." The Watergate, he added, "remains the best example of self-contained living in the city."

Richard Longstreth, a professor at George Washington University and past president of the Society of Architectural Historians, endorsed landmark status. "As a design," he wrote, "Watergate indeed stands alone—not just in Washington, but in North America." The Watergate may seem like a "strange" group of buildings, but that was only because it was "really one-of-a-kind in the United States." The Watergate represented Luigi Moretti's response to a major current in Italian architecture of the 1950s and 1960s, which found inspiration in natural forms. Moretti developed "an equally bold approach to design" by applying mathematical principals to organic forms. "Watergate is famous in Italian architectural circles," Longstreth explained, "not for its political associations, but as Moretti's most ambitious and most fully developed manifestation of this pursuit."

Mario di Valmarana, who worked on the Watergate as a young architect and was now a professor at the University of Virginia, endorsed landmark designation and urged the historic preservation board to protect the "overall look" of the Watergate, as well as its important details, such as signage and canopies. Changes to these elements of the building, he wrote, "if not legislated and controlled, can jeopardize the intrinsic beauty of the complex."

The board of Watergate South supported the designation of the Watergate as a historic landmark. The president of the Watergate South board of directors, Dr. Neil Livingstone, a counterterrorism expert and author of a 1996 book, *Protect Yourself in an Uncertain World: A Comprehensive Handbook for Your Personal and Business Security*, once received a letter in the mail from overseas, addressed simply to "Neil Livingstone, The Watergate, USA." The fact that the letter reached Livingstone, wrote Jason Finch, the general manager of Watergate South, "is a clear indication that the name recognition of The Watergate is worldwide."

The board of directors of Watergate East, however, opposed landmark status. They feared treating Timchenko's landscaping as a historic landmark would be "impractical and confining" in the future, as plants and trees aged and needed to be replaced. Moreover, because the Watergate was built before passage of the Americans with Disabilities Act and before 9/11, security and accessibility upgrades would become "arduous" and "time-consuming" if the property was designated a landmark. But the board's biggest concern was the motivation behind the landmark crusade itself. "In the main," wrote Dan Sheehan, president of the board, "the proponents of this stratagem are among the cohort opposing the change in use of the Watergate Hotel. Our fear is they have been misled into assuming an 'historic' designation would preclude any change in use" from the original Watergate zoning. "It is our intent to preserve Watergate East as the unique property it has become and to strive to enhance its value to the city and our residents," he concluded. "We feel this can best be accomplished without additional regulation and cumbersome oversight."

Emily Eig battled a minor case of laryngitis as she briefed the board on the "exceptional significance" of the Watergate. She showed how the placement of the buildings by Luigi Moretti took advantage of the spectacular view of the Potomac, but did not "turn its back on the city." She noted the office buildings lacked balconies, a treatment chosen by Moretti to differentiate business and residential use within the complex. She compared Watergate West to an ocean liner, and pointed out the "nautical feel" of the rooftop structures, inspired by Gaudí's buildings in Barcelona.

The Watergate, Eig said, was conceived at a time when people were moving to the suburbs in droves, driven in part by the fear of racial violence. The Watergate bucked that trend. It drew people back into the city, giving them urban amenities they thought were lost. And it offered "modernity" at a time when cities seemed old and tired.

She then turned to the Watergate scandal. The break-in at the Watergate "changed the face of politics," she said. "It also changed the face of journalism."

After the board's analyst explained how modifications to the buildings and grounds could be performed over time, Chairman Boasberg signaled his approval. Another commissioner, who said he came into the hearing "a doubter"—"I never warmed up to it architecturally," he said—concluded the Watergate's architecture was "quite wonderful."

By a unanimous vote, the board designated the Watergate a

historic landmark and ordered it to be entered into the District of Columbia Inventory of Historic Sites and listed in the National Register of Historic Places. According to the board, the applicants had made a compelling case for the "special nature" of the Watergate. Moretti's design—"at once urban and anti-urban"—replaced an aging industrial area but did not perpetuate the existing street grid; instead it created a new form on the location, with spaces "more on the scale of an urban square, rather than the immense no-man's-lands of Corbusier." The board also embraced the Watergate's "notorious position in American history," as the site of "a significant, and probably transcendently important event."

"The Watergate made peace with its own history," Eig reflected years later. "And Washington made peace with the Watergate."

KAREN JOHNSON WORKED IN THE FIRST PRESIDENTIAL CAM-paign of George W. Bush. A native Texan, she did not join the administration in 2001 but stayed in Texas as a lobbyist for the association of state public works contractors, which her father headed. Work brought them to Washington frequently and in 2005 they decided to buy a condo, rather than continue to waste money on hotels. Through a real estate agent, Karen learned of a co-op apartment on the tenth floor of Watergate South. The owner had inherited the apartment from his parents, who were among the original buyers in 1971, and was eager to sell.

When Karen and her father first saw the unit, it was ghastly: boxes everywhere, stacks of newspapers and magazines, piles of clothes. The owner had carved out space for a futon in the middle of the living room to sleep. Tom turned to his daughter and said, "We ain't doing this."

But Karen looked out the windows and took in the view of the Potomac River. She could see Georgetown University and Key Bridge. A balcony ran the entire length of the apartment.

"It's got great bones," she said to her father. "And it has potential."
She turned to the real estate agent. "I'll take it."

ONE SUNDAY AFTERNOON IN WATERGATE SOUTH, SECRE-
tary of State Condoleezza Rice sat at her Steinway piano with four
friends who made up her chamber music ensemble: Sohye Kim,
the first violinist, with two degrees from Juilliard; Robert Battey, the
cellist, who taught music at the University of Missouri for twelve
years; Lawrence Wallace, the violist, a former law school professor
who served as deputy solicitor general under eight presidents; and
Joshua Klein, the second violinist and youngest member of the
group, and a former clerk for Supreme Court Justice Sandra Day
O'Connor.

When Rice first arrived in Washington in early 2001 to become
President George W. Bush's national security advisor, she chose this
Watergate South apartment the same way she decided on every other
place she had lived—because it had a good spot for her piano. For
Vogue magazine, Annie Leibovitz photographed Rice running on her
treadmill, watching a baseball game in her study and resting an elbow
on her piano, in a Duchesse-satin strapless evening gown by Richard
Tyler ($2,795). The photos and the accompanying article hit news-
stands just a few days after the 9/11 attacks.

After tuning up, Rice and the other members of the ensemble
played through the first movement of Schumann's Piano Quintet in
E flat major. "We generally like to start off with a nice finger-buster
for the Secretary," Battey, the cellist, joked. After the Schumann,
they turned to the first movement of Shostakovich's Piano Quintet
in G minor, a piece they were still learning, and fell out of sync.
"My tempo is not your tempo," Rice said. They tried again—and
stumbled once more. "I hesitated to turn the page." Rice frowned.
"I'll get that fixed." After Shostakovich, they played Brahms's
Piano Quintet in F minor, which went well. Then they packed

up their instruments and hung around for white wine and cheese before saying goodbye.

Members of the chamber group had become "like my best friends," Rice said. "We are like family."

In addition to regular chamber music sessions, Rice hosted an annual Christmas party at her apartment, inviting colleagues from the White House and the State Department. The first year at the Watergate, Attorney General John Ashcroft, a competent pianist, played Christmas carols. Another year, Yo-Yo Ma played the cello.

Karl Rove, Bush's top political advisor at the White House, knew that his White House colleague Harriet Miers was friends with Nathan Hecht, a justice on the Texas State Supreme Court and a brilliant pianist. Rove persuaded Miers to bring Hecht along as her plus-one the following year, and nudged Hecht to take a turn at the piano. Rice was wowed by his virtuoso performance. "I think that guaranteed me an invitation from then on," Rove later recalled. The party may have had remarkable musicians, but the singers left something to be desired. "It was the worst '12 Days of Christmas' you ever heard in your life," Rove said, laughing.

Years later, another element of Rice's annual Watergate South party was stuck in his memory: "The worst Christmas goodies you've ever seen. We were opening the Triscuit boxes to find something to put the cheese on."

"Thank God," Rove laughed, "the foreign policy of the United States did not depend on Condi Rice having to lay out a lavish set of hors d'oeuvres."

ON APRIL 27, 2006, SCOT J. PALTROW REPORTED IN THE *WALL Street Journal* a new development in the federal investigation of former congressman Randall "Duke" Cunningham, who had resigned from Congress seven months earlier, admitted taking $2.4 million in bribes and pleaded guilty to tax evasion and conspiracy. According to Paltrow's report, federal investigators were expanding their investigation of defense contractor Brent Wilkes to determine whether he had provided Cunningham with prostitutes and the free use of hotel suites, including rooms at the Watergate.

Another contractor, Mitchell Wade, who had already pleaded guilty to charges of bribing Cunningham and was cooperating with prosecutors, said Cunningham occasionally called him to request a prostitute and Wade would then send a limousine to pick up a woman, swing by the congressman's apartment and deliver them both to the Watergate Hotel. According to Wade, Wilkes arranged the transportation, sourced the prostitutes and rented the suites at the hotel.

San Diego Union Tribune reporters Marcus Stern, Jerry Kammer, Dean Calbreath and George E. Condon, Jr., who had earned a Pulitzer Prize for their reporting on the Cunningham scandal the year before, now set their sights on Brent Wilkes. They learned from a confidential source that Wilkes would often come to Washington on a Sunday or Monday and stay in a Watergate suite for several days, before flying back home to San Diego. He would store his suits—and his booze—at the hotel between trips.

New York Times columnist Maureen Dowd wrote that Kyle "Dusty" Foggo, a favorite of CIA director Porter Goss and the third-highest official in the spy agency, was a close friend of Brent Wilkes, who was now "entangled in allegations of louche and lewd behavior involving limos, hookers, a poker player with a missing digit from the CIA named 'Nine Fingers,' and Watergate hospitality suites where more was offered than just Scotch and pretzels."

"Been to the Watergate, haven't done that," Dowd wrote.

The CIA eventually confirmed Foggo had attended poker games at the Watergate Hotel with Brent Wilkes, his "close boyhood friend." On May 5, Foggo's boss, CIA director Porter Goss resigned after just two years on the job.

In November 2007, a jury convicted Brent Wilkes of thirteen counts of bribery, conspiracy and money laundering. According to prosecutors, Wilkes had supplied Cunningham with meals, gifts, trips and prostitutes for over a decade. Wilkes funneled $636,000 in cash bribes to Cunningham, including $535,000 to pay off a mortgage on the congressman's home in Rancho Santa Fe. In exchange, Cunningham used his influence in Congress to place earmarks in the federal budget and then steered up to $87 million in federal contracts to Wilkes.

A year later, Foggo pleaded guilty to one count of fraud. Prosecutors said Foggo helped Wilkes win a $3 million contract to supply bottled water to CIA personnel in Iraq and Afghanistan, in return for the promise of a lucrative job and lavish gifts, including a weeklong stay at a Scottish castle.

Former Reagan campaign manager and White House aide Ed Rollins gave the scandal a name: Hookergate.

AS HUNDREDS OF NEW CONDOMINIUMS FLOODED THE DIS-trict real estate market in 2006, Darby reevaluated his plans for Belles Rives at The Watergate. In January 2007, Monument Realty resurfaced with a new strategy to operate the Watergate Hotel as a hybrid: switching from 100 percent cooperative apartments to a mix of one-third apartments and two-thirds "ultra-luxury" hotel suites. The shift, he argued, would allow the Watergate to compete at the level of the Ritz-Carlton and Four Seasons chains.

Michael Darby and the board of Watergate East eventually settled on a sale price of the parking lots and other property beneath the hotel, at a price of about $250,000—$4 million below his original offer. With a permit in hand from the District Zoning Commission to convert the hotel to residences, he obtained a $69.8 million construction loan from PB Capital, a subsidiary of Deutsche Postbank AG.

Darby announced the Watergate Hotel would close for an eighteen-month, $170 million renovation. Once reopened, he said, the Watergate would be "probably higher-end than any other hotel in Washington." Rooms in the refurbished hotel, he said, would go for up to $2,000 a night. The Watergate name would remain. "It's too good a name to change," Darby said.

Under union rules, the hotel was required to give employees a sixty-day notice before closing. Klaus Peters, the manager of the hotel, later observed there are two "incredibly tough times" in the life of any hotel: when it opens, and when it closes. "Usually the final 60 days is chaos," he said. "But the Watergate Hotel staff was absolutely perfect."

The last guests were served their continental breakfasts and checked out. There was a small, emotional party for the last few members of the staff. A typed note, on hotel stationery, was taped to the front door: "We apologize for the inconvenience. But as of August 1, 2007, the Watergate Hotel is closed for renovation."

The hotel's closure was "devastating" for the other businesses at the Watergate, recalled Anton Obernberger, owner of Watergate Pastry. There was so much media interest in the closing of the hotel, the public thought the entire Watergate was shuttered. Business at Watergate Pastry dropped 50 percent. For years, people would call him up and asked if he was still open for business. "We heard the Watergate was closed," one caller said. "But your website is still up."

"Yes, we're open," he sighed.

Saks Jandel, a family-run clothing store that had operated on the first floor of Watergate East, shut its doors following the closures of Colette of Watergate, a women's clothing store, and a Gucci boutique. The closure in turn reduced business at the Watergate Salon, which was in the hands of Claudia Buttaro, the second generation of the Buttaro family to run the salon. As business dropped off, some of her staff moved on. "The hairdressers wanted to go where it's a hip and happening place," she said, as a stylist nearby trimmed an elderly client's hair under the watchful eye of a caregiver.

"The Watergate is not a destination for shoppers the way it used to be," reported the *Washington Post*. "All you need to do is walk around Watergate to see it needs renovation," said a local real estate agent.

"Forget clothes," said a resident. "One wonders why there aren't bookstores and video rentals. You don't have to be an Einstein to see that."

Business dropped off at the Watergate Safeway, which became known around Washington as the "Senior Safeway." Within a few years, despite a furious signature-gathering effort by Watergate residents, Safeway shut down its Watergate location.

"It's not the same as when I moved in," said one resident. "The mall is like a ghost town. It used to be so elegant."

BentleyForbes, the California-based owner of the Watergate Office Building, sued Monument Realty for failing to maintain its garage, which was above the part of the garage owned by Bentley-Forbes. Slabs of concrete became loose and fell onto the garage floor. Within a few years, BentleyForbes—named by its founder, C. Frederick Wehba, because it "sounded prominent and blue-blooded"—would forfeit the office building to one of its lenders.

Tenants started leaving the Watergate Office Building on Virginia Avenue. The departure of the Saudi Arabian Cultural Mission was difficult for Phil Rascona, the owner of the Watergate Barber Shop—another second-generation Watergate business. The Saudi ambassador, Rascona said, always sent "long-haired students down for grooming." Former senator Bob Dole stopped coming to the Watergate Barber Shop as well, but for another reason. "He colors his hair and goes to a salon now." Rascona shrugged. "He wants to look 70."

NATIONAL CONTENT LIQUIDATORS, ALSO KNOWN AS NCL, specialized in liquidating hotels, prior to their demolition or renovation, including the Willard in Washington, DC, and a number of hotels in Las Vegas, including the Dunes, the Sahara and the Aladdin. Don Hayes got his start in the business at age fifteen, accompanying the president of the company on auctions. By the time he turned forty, Hayes was president of the firm.

Hayes managed the liquidation of the Commodore Hotel in New York in 1978. He met the hotel's new owner, Donald J. Trump, in the former New York New York restaurant to go over plans for the auction. But Trump did not want to discuss the auction: He wanted Hayes's opinion on the glass samples he was considering for the exterior of the building. NCL liquidated several hotels for Trump. There was never a problem getting paid, Hayes recalled. "We paid *him*."

The NCL sales team heard about the Watergate renovation, reached out to the managers there and got the job. The first step was to do an appraisal. Hayes and Klaus Peters, the hotel manager, walked through every room in the hotel, conducting a "head to toe" inspection. Hayes prepared an inventory and began marketing the sale.

As Labor Day weekend approached, NCL turned the Watergate into a department store. In the hotel ballroom, they set up a "boutique" to sell higher-priced items, like paintings, silver and glassware. Some items were staged in the lobby. Suites 214 and 314, where the Watergate burglars stayed the night of the break-in, were staged as sales rooms, with prices attached to mattresses and furnishings.

In total, more than twenty thousand items were for sale, including silver, china, glassware, gold-framed mirrors, a baby grand piano, thirteen "Grecian-style columns" and a fleet of Sony Dream Machines. Martini glasses were priced at $2 each, wooden desks from the suites at $85. Frying pans from the hotel kitchen? Six dollars.

Hayes later recalled there was one big problem with this particular sale: the lack of branded Watergate items. When NCL had liquidated the Plaza Hotel in New York, there was a wealth of Plaza-branded towels, ashtrays and the like. But because the Watergate Hotel had mostly done away with branded items following the 1972 break-in, there was virtually nothing available for sale bearing the name "Watergate." Moreover, because the hotel suites and public areas had been renovated several times since the mid-1970s, there were virtually no relics from the Nixon era.

The ornate *W* on a glass door was priced at $750, while silver teapots with a *W* engraved on the side were $55 apiece.

Michael Darby fielded calls from all over the world about the liquidation sale. Klaus Peters gave interviews as well: His brother heard him on the radio, while hiking in Switzerland. "This must be the most media attention we have had since the scandal," said Peters. "But this time, the coverage is positive."

On the first day of the sale, to discourage sightseers, shoppers were charged a $10 admission fee. The public was let into the lobby fifty at a time. Customers could go into any room and pick out an item, go downstairs to the lobby to pay for it and then return upstairs to carry it out themselves. The baby grand piano sold for $7,500. A nineteenth-century oil painting in the lobby sold for $12,000. David Urso, a former Secret Service agent, bought the sign down the hall from where the burglars camped out in preparation for their foray into the Watergate Office Building next door.

The entire liquidation took about a month. The last unsold items were dispersed to local charities. Broken items went into the Dumpster. The sale was projected to bring in $700,000, but total receipts exceeded $1 million.

As Hayes and his team left the hotel, he recalled years later, "there was nothing left in the building but an echo."

ON JULY 24, 2008, THE DC COURT OF APPEALS RULED MONUment Realty had the legal right to convert the hotel to condominiums, clearing away the final lawsuit filed by Jack Olender and his allies at Watergate East who opposed the conversion. "We recognize that the petitioners feel very strongly about changes to the Watergate complex and that there may be substantial evidence supporting some of their factual arguments," John R. Fisher, an appointee of President George W. Bush, wrote in a unanimous opinion. "However, applying our standard of review to the record at the time of the hearing, we conclude that the Commission's order is clearly supported by substantial evidence."

Darby's victory was a long time coming, but he found no reason to celebrate. "We weren't going to wait forever," he said, "and so we moved in a different direction."

Four weeks later, on Monday, September 15, 2008, Lehman Brothers declared bankruptcy.

"I will remember that day until I die," Darby recalled.

He and his team knew something was wrong at Lehman Brothers, their partners in twenty-six different projects around Washington, a portfolio worth $2.6 billion. "You could feel it," Darby said. As the price of Lehman's shares fell, senior executives worried more about their underwater stock options than real estate projects in the pipeline. Darby's top contact at Lehman Brothers quit and went to work for someone else. A couple of joint projects had to be canceled after Lehman executives balked about committing any more cash to new ventures.

On Sunday night, September 14, 2008, at around ten-thirty, the board of directors of Lehman Brothers called Bryan Marsal, head of the restructuring firm Alvarez & Marsal, and asked him to take responsibility for winding down Lehman Brothers, which would declare bankrupty the next morning.

"How much planning has gone into the bankruptcy?" Marsal asked.

"This phone call is the first planning we've done," said a Lehman Brothers director.

Lehman Brothers declared bankruptcy the next morning. Darby, sitting in his office, answered the phone. It was a friend from Lehman Brothers. "It's over," the caller said.

Alvarez & Marsal took over the management of the Lehman

Brothers assets, including a global real estate portfolio worth $23 billion, with both secured and unsecured loans, and equity investments in a range of projects at various stages of development.

"Since the bankruptcy announcement, Monument has been working closely with Lehman to ensure that its properties are properly funded and managed in order to maintain the value of these assets," Darby said in a statement on September 21. "Monument remains committed to its projects and is ready to move forward with the development of these properties with Lehman or a new partner."

A few days before Christmas 2008, Darby got a tip from a friend who still worked at Lehman Brothers. "They want to shut you down," the friend said. "They want to take every asset away from you and shut you down."

"It was just a nightmare," Darby recalled.

Lenders called Darby day and night, asking him for information he did not have. They couldn't reach anyone at Lehman, so they called Darby. "We couldn't tell them anything," Darby said. "No one knew what was going on."

In the months leading up to its collapse, Lehman had sold loans to various entities around the world, secured by various assets, including Monument Realty projects in which Lehman had taken an equity stake. Darby started getting calls from investors around the world—including banks in Bermuda and Holland—identifying themselves as the new owners of a Monument project and asking to come to Washington to tour their new assets. Darby explained these were not assets that were generating cash, but real estate projects in various stages of development. Several investors threatened to declare the loans in default and seize the projects. Darby patiently sat down with each of them, one by one, and worked out plans to create value out of each project and service their loans.

Darby approached PB Capital, who had backed a construction loan for the Watergate Hotel conversion. "I'd like to keep the Watergate," he told them. "I'd like to put it back and give it another shot."

A year after Lehman Brothers collapsed in the largest bank-ruptcy in U.S. history, Michael Darby told the *Washington Post* he was still committed to the Watergate. Monument was working with PB Capital to restructure the loan and bring in new investors so the renovations could proceed. "At the end of the day, it's a landmark," said a PB Capital banker. "There are investors with an interest."

The new investors never appeared.

On July 16, 2009, PB Capital announced Monument was in default and the Watergate Hotel would be sold at auction.

Darby speculated later that PB Capital was concerned the trustees in charge of liquidating Lehman Brothers' assets would oppose any transaction under which Darby repurchased the Watergate at a steep discount.

"They felt they had no choice," Darby said. "But there's always a choice."

Darby compared the Lehman Brothers bankruptcy to the days he surfed as a young man off the coast of Australia. "It was like be-ing out in the surf," he said, "and you go over the first wave and you look out into the sea and there's a bigger wave. And you go, 'Okay.' Then you go over that bigger wave and you go to the next wave, and it's a bigger wave."

For two years, he said, "the waves never got smaller."

PB Capital retained David Astrove, a lawyer with a Washington firm, to supervise the auction. Astrove reached out to Alex Cooper Auctioneers and its president, Paul Cooper. It was a family business: Paul had been working there since he was twenty, alongside his fa-ther and brothers. The firm was started by Paul's grandfather in 1924. The real estate recession was in full swing and Alex Cooper Auctioneers was handling a steady flow of foreclosures.

The first step was to place a public notice in a local newspaper, the *Washington Times*. Almost immediately, Paul's phone began to ring off the hook. Reporters speculated the Jumeirah Group of Saudi Arabia could become the Watergate's new owners. Robert

Holland, developer of the Washington Harbour waterfront complex in Georgetown, expressed interest. "At the end of the day, I believe this will be the premiere hotel in Washington," said Holland. "Eighty percent of the rooms have water views and they're not great—they're spectacular." Holland told the *Washington Post* he preferred negotiating in private rather than at an auction. He estimated renovations would cost at least $100 million, perhaps as much as $170 million.

Every buyer was flying blind, Darby recalled. "For anybody to understand the complexity of that project" and understand the true cost of renovating the Watergate Hotel "without the information that we had, would have been impossible."

As the sale date approached, Paul Cooper fielded calls from interested bidders and media around the world.

The auction was held on August 21, 2009, at the offices of Alex Cooper Auctioneers on Wisconsin Avenue, near the Maryland border. It was a hot summer day. The room was packed with reporters, bidders, film crews and a few curiosity seekers. The air-conditioning was failing to keep up. Paul worried that his dad would begin to sweat—like Nixon in the televised debate with John F. Kennedy.

The auction drew ten registered bidders, who were required to bring certified checks for $1 million. Some news outlets inaccurately reported bidding would start at that level. Observers of the local real estate market did not expect the sale price to reach $40 million, the amount Monument owed to PB Capital.

Minutes before the auction was to begin, Astrove took Cooper aside and informed him the opening bid would be set at $25 million. Cooper's heart sank. He wanted to get people into the auction spirit, competing against each other. A lower opening bid—perhaps as low as $5 million—might fuel the bidding, get "feverish activity" in the room. But Cooper worked for the seller, and had no choice but to follow Astrove's instructions.

Astrove had another number, known only to him and his client, at which he would stop the bidding and allow the Watergate to be sold. If that number was not reached, PB Capital would step in and submit a pro forma bid and shut down the auction.

At 10:40 A.M., the auction began. There was a sixteen-page terms of sale—thirteen of which were "meets and bounds"—the geographical designation of the property line, all numbers and degrees. As required by law, various members of the Cooper family took turns over the next thirty minutes, reading every word of the terms of sale.

At eleven-thirty, Joseph Cooper, Paul's father, approached the podium and started the auction. He called six times for an opening bid at $25 million.

No one in the room raised a paddle.

"It's a Washington landmark," he pleaded. "It's a national landmark, really."

David Astrove finally stood up and signaled to Paul Cooper and his father to follow him into a glassed-in office, just behind the podium. Astrove informed them PB Capital would submit a pro forma bid of $25 million, take the Watergate Hotel off the market and conclude the auction.

Everyone filed back into the room. Joseph Cooper asked once more for a bid of $25 million. Astrove nodded in response.

"Sold," said Cooper.

The auction was over.

IN THE SUMMER OF 1980, MARGARET TRUMAN, DAUGHTER OF the thirty-third president, released her first novel, *Murder in the White House*. The story took place during the administration of the fictitious Robert Webster, sometime after the presidency of Jimmy Carter. Webster's secretary of state Lansard Blaine was found in the Lincoln Bedroom, strangled by a guitar string. Prior to meeting his demise, Blaine's life "was one long orgy with various women at his apartment in the Watergate."

In Truman's book a character overhears a network news report:

> People who live in the Watergate apartment complex probably wish history would keep its distance. The name of their home became a synonym for political chicanery in 1973 and 1974. Now it seems likely to become a synonym for erotic fun and games—even for harem-keeping—by high ranked public officials.

The book sold well, becoming a Book of the Month Club alternative selection, and inspired a twenty-five-book "Capital Crimes" series, including *Murder at the Watergate*, published in 1998, in which the Watergate became a crime scene from top (a researcher fell to her death from the roof) to bottom (when a union organizer is shot in the basement garage).

Warren Adler closed his Washington public relations firm shortly after he helped launch the Watergate in the 1960s and moved to New York. He wrote more than forty novels, including *War of the Roses*, the epic account of an acrimonious divorce, which was adapted into a film starring Michael Douglas, Kathleen Turner and Danny DeVito in 1989. Adler returned to the Watergate in 1992. In *The Witch of Watergate*, Adler sent his heroine

Fiona Fitzgerald, a homicide detective, to investigate the murder of a lonely and miserable *Washington Post* reporter, whose body was discovered hanging over the balcony of her Watergate apartment from a noose around her neck.

IN HIS THIRD AND FINAL EDITION OF *SAFIRE'S POLITICAL Dictionary*, William Safire listed more than a dozen scandals with the "-*gate* construction," including *Koreagate*, *Lancegate* (involving Jimmy Carter's budget director, Bert Lance), *Applegate* (involving the suppression of a report on the finances of New York City), *Floodgate* (after Daniel Flood, a congressman), *Billygate* (Billy Carter), *Pearlygate* (televangelists), *Irangate* (the Iran-Contra affair), *Iraqgate* (grain credits and rocket technology), *Travelgate* (the White House travel staff dismissed in the early days of the Clinton administration), *Rubbergate* (bounced checks at a bank in the U.S. House of Representatives) and *Scalpgate* (the delay of Air Force One at Los Angeles International Airport while Clinton received a $200 haircut). "Clearly," Safire wrote, "the -*gate* construction is too useful to be slammed shut."

Safire died in 2009, but the "-*gate* construction" lives on.

The 2013 closure of the George Washington Bridge by appointees of former New Jersey governor Chris Christie became *Bridgegate*. There were two *Deflategate* scandals in 2016, one involving the rear tires of British Formula 1 driver Lewis Hamilton, the other involving New England Patriots quarterback Tom Brady. U.S. swimmer Ryan Lochte's fabrication of events that took place late one evening during the Summer Olympics in Rio de Janeiro became *Lochtegate*. In season five of HBO's *Veep*, a newspaper reports a member of President Selina Meyer's staff called her a "c**t." The episode was named "C**tgate." The 2016 release of an audio recording of *Access Hollywood* correspondent Billy Bush and Republican presidential candidate Donald J. Trump became *Pussygate*.

AT THE END OF GEORGE W. BUSH'S SECOND TERM, KAREN Johnson rented out her tenth-floor apartment in Watergate South to a senior member of Hillary Clinton's team at the State Department and returned to Texas. Karen's tenant signed a two-year lease, the maximum allowed under the building's rules.

As the end of the lease approached, Karen caught up with Karl Rove, a friend from the 2000 campaign. Rove had recently divorced his wife and was renting a house in Georgetown that turned out to be an utter disaster. Every time it rained, he heard water cascading inside the walls, and black mold sprouted throughout the house. He told Karen he needed to find a new place—fast.

"Why don't you take my apartment at the Watergate?" Karen offered.

Rove abandoned Georgetown and moved into Watergate South. He made a few changes, turning the dining room into a study and installing bookcases. From the balcony, he watched crew teams glide down the Potomac River in the early-morning hours. Sometimes he would catch a glimpse of one of the presidential helicopters circling overhead on training flights.

Karl and Karen kept in touch and met often for drinks or dinner. He confessed he was absolutely inept at organizing his own social life, so Karen and another mutual friend set him up with one woman after another. "Each date was a disaster," Karl said, laughing.

After a "strikeout" with one woman, whom an exasperated Karen considered her "best and highest offer," there was only one arrow left in her quiver. "Well, Karl," she said, "I guess you're gonna have to take me out."

They married the following year and kept their Watergate apartment until 2016.

Martha and John Mitchell's former duplex apartment, 712-N in Watergate East, went on the market at about the same time. Clark Bason, nephew of Carolyn Bason Long and Senator Russell Long, put the property on the market after his aunt died. Clark removed Martha Mitchell's telephone from the master bathroom before the sale, and displays it in his Palm Springs home.

MONUMENT REALTY AND MICHAEL DARBY BOTH SURVIVED the collapse of Lehman Brothers. The National Association of Broadcasters announced plans to move from downtown Washington to a new ten-story headquarters, to be constructed by Monument Realty, in the District's Capitol Waterfront neighborhood. Monument broke ground in January 2017 on a 171-unit condominium building nearby. Lenders had been leery of financing large condominium projects after the recession, Darby said, but the Washington rental market was oversupplied. "People are looking to buy," he said. "So the logical thing is to build condos."

As he reflected on his recovery from the Lehman Brothers collapse, Darby offered another analogy from his youth in Australia. "It's like if you're a surfer and you're out on the waves, riding six foot waves and having a great time," he said to a reporter, "and all of a sudden a 15-foot wave comes out of nowhere and hits you and smashes you on the head and you say, 'I'm never going back out there again because there may be a 20-foot wave that hits me.' The answer's no, I surf. I'm going to surf again."

Wendy Luscombe lives in New York's Hudson Valley. She retired as an active real estate investor and now serves on a number of corporate boards and trains Fjord horses. She never forgot her years as the owner of the Watergate. "It wasn't a real estate project," she recalled years later. "It lived and breathed." She stays in touch with Hugh Jenkins, who hired her in her twenties to build a U.S. real estate portfolio for the National Coal Board.

Giuseppe Cecchi, now in his nineties, runs his development firm, IDI Group, from the twentieth floor of an office tower in Rosslyn, Virginia, with his three sons, Enrico, Carlos and John. He tried to buy the Watergate Hotel from PB Capital, but they rejected his offer. From his desk, he can look across the Potomac and see the Watergate. In September 2016, Cecchi and his wife, Mercedes, hosted a fund-raiser in their Virginia home for the presidential campaign of another real estate developer: Donald J. Trump.

JACK OLENDER STILL LIVES ON THE TWELFTH FLOOR OF Watergate East. He has no regrets about his fight to stop the conversion of the hotel to apartments. "Some people have good sense and are nice." He smiles. "And then there are other people."

Audrey Wolf lives in the duplex apartment she shared with her late husband. She says the new health club at the Watergate Hotel is "so expensive that nobody can use it." She is working with her neighbors in Watergate East to figure out where to put their own gym somewhere in the building.

For nearly fifty years, Anna Chennault's activities during the final days of the 1968 presidential campaign continued to fascinate historians and other researchers. Six months after LBJ's death in January 1973, his former national security aide Walter W. Rostow sent an envelope to Harry Middleton, the director of the LBJ Library. "Sealed in the attached envelope," Rostow wrote, "is a file President Johnson asked me to hold personally because of its sensitive nature." Known as the "The 'X' envelope," the files contained documents concerning "the activities of Mrs. Chennault and others" in the 1968 election. Rostow recommended the file be sealed for fifty years, but ordered the documents unsealed after twenty-one years, in July 1994.

In 2014, Ken Hughes published *Chasing Shadows: The Nixon Tapes, the Chennault Affair, and the Origins of Watergate*, in which he argued that Nixon was paranoid over the possibility the Chennault affair—a possible violation of the Logan Act, which bars private citizens from conducting foreign policy—might eventually be revealed. Nixon's reaction to the publication of the Pentagon Papers by the *New York Times* in June 1971, one year before the Watergate break-in, was to direct to the creation of the Special Investigations Unit—"the plumbers"—to prevent additional leaks that might reveal the truth of Chennault's activities.

On January 2, 2017, Anna Chennault made the front page of the *New York Times*. While working on a new biography of Nixon, John A. Farrell found notes taken by H.R. Haldeman from a phone call with the Republican candidate on October 22, 1968. Haldeman wrote Nixon's instructions, which included "Keep Anna Chennault working on SVN," or South Vietnam, and "Any other way to monkey wrench it? Anything RN can do."

Timothy Naftali, the former director of the Nixon Presidential Library, said the notes "remove any fig leaf of plausible deniability" of Nixon's involvement in the incident. "This covert action by the Nixon campaign," Naftali told the *Times*, "laid the ground for the skulduggery of his presidency."

In 2015, Anna Chennault celebrated her ninetieth birthday. She has lived on the fourteenth floor of Watergate East for more than fifty years, surrounded by a lifetime of photographs showing her with presidents and other officials from around the world, as well as her extensive collection of Chinese art and artifacts. She sometimes eats her meals facing an easel that holds a large painting of her late husband, General Claire Lee Chennault. She was one of several residents appearing in a 2016 *Wall Street Journal* story about the Watergate. From the day she first appeared in the American press, initially on the arm of her husband, and later as a hostess in her Watergate penthouse, she was perfectly coiffed, dressed in furs and evening gowns, or wearing elegant cocktail dresses and business suits, often of her own design. When she appeared in the *Wall Street Journal*, however, she wore an ill-fitting cotton dress. Her hair was in mismatched plastic curlers.

Down the hall from the Doles, Ruth Bader Ginsburg lives in the ground-floor duplex apartment in Watergate South she and her husband, Martin, purchased shortly after she joined the DC Circuit Court of Appeals in 1980. Martin followed her to Washington from New York, taking a position on the faculty of the Georgetown University law school and becoming "of counsel" to Fried, Frank, Harris, Shriver & Jacobson, on the sixth floor of the Watergate 600 office building next door. The Ginsburgs and the Scalias—Supreme Court Justice Antonin Scalia, a Reagan appointee, and his wife, Maureen—celebrated many New Year's Eve dinners at the Ginburgs' Watergate apartment with their families and a few friends, including fellow Supreme Court Justice Elena Kagan and former solicitor general Ted Olson, who represented the presidential campaign of George W. Bush before the United States Supreme Court in *Bush v. Gore*, and his wife Lady Booth, a lifelong Democrat. Until his death in 2010, Martin Ginsburg generally took charge of the cooking. He was very skilled in the kitchen: While stationed in Oklahoma with the U.S. Army, he worked his way through the *Escoffier* guide to French cooking. The main course was often something Scalia had shot on a recent hunting trip, such as elk or wild boar.

Residents at the Watergate's three apartment buildings—Watergate East, Watergate West and Watergate South—share tips and advice via a Google group managed by Patricia Moore, the elegant wife of Arthur Cotton Moore, a prominent Washington architect. Residents suggest doctors or pet-sitters, or sell items they no longer need—"a lot of crap," Patricia laments. She monitors the group closely; she can tell if a Watergate resident might be fading, she said, based on the frequency and tone of their communications.

Patricia and Arthur live in a Watergate South penthouse, with sweeping views of the Potomac River. "Moretti was extremely great," said Arthur, reflecting on the Watergate's original architect, Luigi Moretti. "He gave so many apartments views of the river, which was very unusual for the time. Moretti appreciated the value of the river. He was way ahead of American architects at that time."

"But the teeth," as Arthur called the unusual balconies throughout the Watergate, "the teeth were a mistake."

ACCORDING TO TINA WINSTON, THE WIDOW OF HENRY WIN-
ston, the longtime Watergate manager, a stairwell door that had
been taped open the night of June 16, 1972, disappeared mysteriously
from a locked storage room in the Watergate sometime in the late
1990s. Years later, Mrs. Winston saw the door again—in the
collection of the Newseum in downtown Washington, DC. A
Newseum guide told her the door was donated to the museum.
"Maybe one of the engineers, or somebody working in the building,
took it," she speculated. "I don't think the guy who took it, kept it
for twenty years, gave it away for nothing."

Carrie Christoffersen, the Newseum's chief curator, explained
how the door ended up in their collection. The FBI removed the
door in 1973 and returned it after concluding the investigation
into the break-in, and the door ended up in storage. According
to Stephen Pace, who worked at the Watergate as an engineer, the
maintenance area was about to be moved and he decided to rescue
the door, rather than let it be thrown out. He took it home and
put it in his apartment. When *Washingtonian* magazine ran a small
item about the door, Newseum curators tracked Pace down. He
loaned it to the museum, and it became part of the permanent
exhibition in 2008. The Newseum purchased the door from Pace
in 2012.

JACQUES COHEN, A FRENCH-SPEAKING ORTHODOX JEW
from a Canadian hotel family, attended the 2009 auction in the
offices of Alex Cooper Auctioneers but did not bid. After the Watergate Hotel failed to sell, he negotiated privately with PB Capital,
and a year later, his family firm, Euro Capital Properties, bought the
hotel for $42 million.

On June 14, 2016, the Watergate Hotel reopened after a $125 mil-
lion, four-year renovation. The transformation of the hotel was an
international effort: Austrian craftsmen created the wood-slat walls;

furniture in the lobby came from Italy; rugs were manufactured in Spain.

In 1965, Arturo Pini di San Miniato created colonnades and other devices to disguise the low ceilings in the model apartment for Watergate East. Fifty years later, Israeli designer Ron Arad, facing the same problem as he renovated the Watergate Hotel, gave the ceilings in each room a reflective polish near the walls, transitioning to a matte finish in the center of the rooms. The overall effect meant the walls are reflected on the ceiling, making them look taller. Just as Luigi Moretti had introduced curves to the Watergate, to evoke the waves of the Potomac River, Arad imprinted a ripple effect into the granite floors. In another nod to the water, the fittings and furnishings in the hotel's 336 rooms are similar to those found on a yacht.

Before the 1972 break-in, said Rakel Cohen, Jacques's wife and the director of design for Euro Capital Properties, the Watergate Hotel "was a glamorous place, was a playground for famous people. We're trying to bring that back to life." She set out to address the scandal "in a delicate way and a fun way." Room keys instruct guests "No need to break in." The hotel's media kit included a USB port disguised as a cassette tape. The overall effect, according to one reviewer, was "a theme-park version of *All the President's Men.*"

Because the Watergate is listed in the National Register of Historic Places, the new owners are eligible for a 20 percent tax credit on the renovations, which were approved in advance by the Commission of Fine Arts, the Historic Preservation Review Board and the National Park Service.

Elizabeth and Bob Dole attended the hotel's black-tie opening. The Doles still live in Watergate South, in the apartment Bob purchased more than forty years ago and expanded after Monica Lewinsky and her mother moved out. Elizabeth's office is next door, at Watergate 600.

Michael Santoro, the executive chef at the Watergate Hotel, served a dinner at the hotel's Kingbird restaurant in July 2017, in honor of Jean-Louis Palladin. A team of chefs created a five-course dinner. Robert Wiedmaier, who first met Palladin in 1986 and succeeded him as executive chef of the Watergate Hotel after Palladin's departure, prepared a gauteau of foie gras, with California squab and a bordelaise sauce.

Jimmy Sneed, who worked side by side with Jean-Louis Palladin at the Watergate, now helps his daughter run a vegetarian restaurant in Richmond, Virginia. "I wouldn't have traded those five years of being screamed at for anything," he says, laughing.

THE WATERGATE OFFICE BUILDING WAS IN NEED OF RENOVA- tion when Penzance, a local real estate investor, purchased it for $76 million in 2011. Penzance was drawn to the Watergate by its location—with easy access to northern Virginia, Georgetown and the suburbs of Maryland, without having to fight downtown traffic. "It was also an oasis in the heart of the society," said a sales broker involved in the transaction. "Where else could you find a park like that, right outside your office?

"Penzance saw an opportunity," he added.

The company remodeled the office building, opening up suites to take advantage of the sweeping views of the Potomac. New tenants signed leases, including the National Trust for Historic Preservation and Kipp DC, the nonprofit public charter school network. The sixth floor has been renovated many times since the Democratic National Committee moved out. The current tenant, an academic publishing company, recently installed a small exhibit to commemorate the Watergate break-in and aftermath, including a timeline of the scandal and a commemorative plaque and a copy of the August 7, 1974, *Washington Post*, with the headline NIXON RESIGNS.

Research Counsel of Washington, the company David Bradley started in his mother's den in Watergate West, eventually grew to become two separate, publicly traded companies, which were later acquired for a combined $5 billion. Katherine and David both work out of Watergate 600. From his office on the eighth floor, David runs Atlantic Media Group, which owns *The Atlantic* and *National Journal*, as well as the CityLab news service, which reports on urban innovation. Upstairs, Katherine runs CityBridge Education, a nonprofit she and David founded in 1994 to apply "best practices" research to the nonprofit sector. Carter Bradley, the third generation of entrepreneurs in the family, works downstairs in the offices of the Ivy Research Council, a start-up he created as a Princeton sophomore, with John Plonk and Nicholas van der Vink, to figure out better ways to manage on-campus college recruiting. In 2003, the Bradleys bought the Watergate 600 office building; they sold it in 2017.

At Campono, the Italian restaurant on the ground floor of Watergate 600, young people bring laptops and have lunch or coffee in a booth or at a table on the patio, facing the Kennedy Center. Conversations are more likely to center on social media metrics or venture capital than on the latest political intrigue.

LUIGI MORETTI'S LIFE AND WORK HAS BEEN REDISCOVERED and embraced by architects and architectural historians. A seminar sponsored by the American Academy in Rome and organized by Corey Brennan, a Rutgers professor in classics, brought twenty-five scholars from Italy and the United States together to discuss Moretti's career. In 2010, MAXXI, Italy's national museum of contemporary art, mounted an exhibition of Moretti's life and work, including models that survived from Studio Moretti. The former fencing academy Moretti designed in Foro Mussolini, now known as Foro Italico, was the site of the trials of the Red Brigade terrorists for a number of crimes, including the assassination of Italian prime minister Aldo Moro in 1978. The building's dramatic interiors are now used for fashion shoots.

Tommaso Magnifico, Moretti's nephew, who retrieved his body from the yacht in the Tyrrhenian Sea during the summer of 1973, lives in Rome—a few floors above the apartment Luigi Moretti once shared with his wife, Maria Teresa. Tommaso became an architect, following in the footsteps of Luigi Moretti and his grandfather, Luigi Rolland. "It's in the DNA," Tommaso told a recent visitor. Tommaso keeps in his study a framed political cartoon from the early 1960s, by Joaquín de Alba, in which Luigi Moretti presents his original Watergate designs to the befuddled members of the Commission of Fine Arts. The architect's designs for the Watergate are scattered on the floor. "Well, what would you say to something like this?" Moretti asks, holding up a drawing of the Leaning Tower of Pisa.

Tommaso remembers his uncle as "a poetic and passionate soul" who believed "one should never lose heart, never get bored." He also recalls another piece of advice from Luigi Moretti: "Keep going and know more."

IN 2013, THE *WASHINGTON POST* REPORTED A BABY BOOM was under way in Washington, DC. According to census figures, the number of children under five grew by almost 20 percent since 2010. New parents were largely in their thirties and early forties. As more millennials reach their early and mid-thirties, the *Post* predicted, "the number of babies is expected to soar."

KinderCare, the country's largest provider of child care and early childhood education services, operated four centers in Washington, each completely full. Jeff Slater, who managed real estate operations for the Portland-based company, began looking for another site in Foggy Bottom, where KinderCare already had two centers. His requirements: easy access to freeways, on-site parking so parents can take their time picking up and dropping off their children, and light-filled, ground-floor space. He found a perfect spot and signed a lease in late 2017, for the space once occupied by the Watergate Safeway.

Shortly after Watergate East opened, the *New York Times* reported the building had "more dogs than children."

Anton Obernberger, owner of Watergate Pastry, was especially delighted to learn a day care center would be just a few steps away from his bakery.

"All those birthday parties."

ACKNOWLEDGMENTS

THIS BOOK, LIKE THE UNIQUE BUILDING AT THE CENTER OF the story, would not have come together without the hard work of a small army on two continents.

I am grateful to my principal researchers. Working in Sacramento, California, Kaitlin Bruce tracked down documents and images from around the world, found the least-costly version of dozens of obscure books on Amazon and eBay and managed a voluminous Watergate archive. In Washington, DC, Saman Zomorodi made himself a virtual resident of the National Archives in order to unearth the complex history of the earliest days of the Watergate. And in Rome, Anthony Majanlahti joined me on interviews and took me through the Central State Archives, where together we sifted through the papers of the once-great company Società Generale Immobiliare and pieced together, through the surviving minutes, the tragic end to the Aldo Samaritani era of that legendary firm. Kaitlin, Saman and Anthony share several traits in common—they are brilliant, creative and tireless—and this book would not have come together without them.

Many of the surprises in this book came from remarkable individuals who sat for interviews, answered my questions over the phone or via e-mail and provided documents and photographs whenever I asked. I want to thank the architects, builders and others who brought the Watergate to life, including Warren Adler, Giuseppe Cecchi, Clara and Bill Graff, Sheldon Magazine and Adrian Sheppard. I am especially grateful to Tommaso Magnifico, the nephew of Luigi Moretti, for sharing his recollections about the life and death of his uncle; to John Cecchi, for building upon the information his father shared; to the family of Nicolas Salgo, for making available to me his memoir prior to its publication; and to Regine Palladin, for sharing stories about her late husband, Jean-Louis Palladin, and his legendary restaurant.

I am also grateful to three individuals who steered the Watergate through its compelling and tumultuous history after the 1972 break-in, and shared their stories with me: Michael Darby of Monument Realty; Wendy Luscombe, who added the Watergate to the real estate portfolio of the National Coal Board and worked closely with Nicolas Salgo; and C. Frederick Wehba.

Many current and former residents of the Watergate agreed to be interviewed and shared their memories, documents and photographs, as did their friends and family members. I am grateful to Annelise Anderson, Clark Bason, Noelle Blanchard, Katherine and David Bradley, Shelley and Pat Buchanan, Joaquín de Alba Carmona, Deborah Gore Dean, Senator Bob Dole, Ann Simon Hadley, Marija Hughes, Gayley Knight, Patricia and Arthur Cotton Moore, Jack Olender, Scott O'Connor, Sally Quinn, Carol Radin, Warren Ratner, the Dowager Countess of Romanones, Karl Rove, Fred Schwartz, Doug Wick, Gigi Winston, Tina Winston, Audrey Wolf and Paul Zanecki.

I also want to thank people who worked at the Watergate, at Jean-Louis at the Watergate, or in one of the businesses within the complex: Kioumars "Mr. Que" Aghazadeh, Cathy Arevian, Paula Brenneman, Dean Brenneman, Claudia Buttaro, Bill Caldwell, Larbi Dahrouch, Sara Fabian, Roxie Herbekian, Jean Main, Anton Obernberger, R. Klaus Peters, David Lee Scull, Bobby Shriver, Daniel Singer, Mark Slater, Jimmy Sneed and Lynda Clugston Webster. Two former employees of the Democratic National Committee were especially helpful in describing the events of June 1972: R. Spencer Oliver and Bruce Givner. I also want to thank the family of Bettye Bradley, the Watergate Hotel's first woman concierge, for making available to me the interviews she recorded.

The following scholars of architecture and politics patiently answered my questions and provided important historical context: Corey Brennan; Carrie Christoffersen, curator of collections, the Newseum; Marco Impiglia; Bob Kapsch; Benoît Lecat at Cal Poly, San Luis Obispo; Tim Naftali; professors Salvatore Santuccio and Nicolo Sardo; Edwin "E. C." Schroeder of Yale's Beinecke library; and Peter Waldman of the University of Virginia.

I benefited greatly from interviews with many people who were part of one or more episodes in the Watergate's dramatic story, including David Astrove; Paul Cooper, the third generation of the Alex Cooper Auctioneers family; Len de Pas; the architect Frank Durkin; Emily Eig of Traceries, Inc.; Don Elder, cofounder of the Men's Titanic Society; David Finley Williams, who spoke to me about his grandfather, Commission of Fine Arts chairman David Finley; Frank Greve of the *Miami Herald*, who covered the "Friendly Models" scandal; Don Hayes, president of National Content Liquidators; Justin Kennedy; Jura Koncius at the *Washington Post*; Carol Mitten, former chairman of the District Zoning Commission; Jerry Kammer; the auctioneer Stephanie Kenyon; Michael Nannes; former U.S. solicitor general Ted Olson; Paul Leeper; *Washington Post* food writer Phyllis Richman; James Rosen, the biographer of John Mitchell; James M. Rowe; Bob Scott; Jeff Slater of KinderCare; Sheila Tate, former press secretary to First Lady Nancy Reagan; and Gail Wolpin and Bill Welch from Phoebus Auction Gallery. Special thanks to Clarissa Rowe for tracking down documents from her mother's personal archives, and to the family of William Walton.

Archivists and curators in Washington, DC, were especially important in bringing this book to life. I want to thank William Creech, Robert Ellis and Joetta Grant at the National Archives; Bruce Kirby and Malea Walker at the Library of Congress; Jessica Richardson at the Historical Society of Washington, DC; Leah Richardson at the Gelman library at George Washington University; Susan Raposa at the U.S. Commission of Fine Arts; Marcella Brown at the National Capital Planning Commission; Elaine Booth at the DC Office of Zoning; Bruce Yarnell at the DC Office of Planning; Bryant Johnson at the U.S. District Court for the District of Columbia; Shawn Dickerson at the DC Court of Appeals; Kurt G. F. Helfrich at the National Gallery of Art and Kate Eig Hurwitz at EHT Traceries.

Thirteen presidential libraries provided valuable material on the Watergate and some of its most famous residents. I want to thank Spencer Howard at the Herbert Hoover Presidential Library and Museum; Kendra Lightner and Ken Moody at the Franklin D. Roosevelt Presidential Library and Museum; David Clark at the Harry S. Truman Library; Kevin M. Bailey and David Holbrook at the Dwight D. Eisenhower Presidential Library, Museum and Boyhood Home; Laurie Austin, Dana Bronson, Katherine Crowe, Sara Powell, Katie Rice and Jennifer Roesch at the John F. Kennedy Presidential Library and Museum; Barbara Cline, Kelly Ellis, Allen Fisher, Margaret Harman, Alexis Percle, Ian Frederick-Rothwell, Liza Talbot and John Wilson at the Lyndon Baines Johnson Library and Museum; Carla Braswell, Nicholas Herold, Rachel Johnston, Dorissa Martinez, Jonathan Movroydis, Meghan Lee-Parker, Ryan Pettigrew and Phillip Pham at the Richard Nixon Presidential Library and Museum; Timothy M. Holtz, James Neel and John J. O'Connell at the Gerald R. Ford Presidential Library and Museum; Alan Houke, Sheila Mayo and Mary Ann McSweeney at the Jimmy Carter Library and Museum; Beth Calleros, Joanne Drake, Gina Risetter, Jennifer Mandel, Shelly Williams and Ray Wilson at the Ronald Reagan Presidential Library and the Reagan Foundation; Elizabeth Staats at the George H. W. Bush Presidential Library and Museum; Marshall Yokell at the William J. Clinton Presidential Library and Museum; and Malisa Culpepper, Zachary Roberts and Sarah Quick at the George W. Bush Presidential Library and Museum.

I am also grateful to Sarah D'Antonio at the Robert J. Dole Institute of Politics at the University of Kansas; Lee C. Grady at the Wisconsin Historical Society; Cindy Brightenburg at Brigham Young University; Rob Boston at Americans United for Separation of Church and State; Kathy Correia, Suzanne Grimshaw, Laura Kellen, Karen Paige, Garrett Shields and Lisa Wade at the California State Library in Sacramento; Jenny St. Clair Thomas at the Church History Library in Salt Lake City, Utah; Kathleen Dickson and Kathleen Luckey at the British Film Institute National Archive in London; Katie O'Connell at the New York Public Library; and Michelle Gullion at the National First Ladies' Library.

I am indebted to the following friends who provided insight and advice, or helped connect me to others for interviews: Nicholas Accinelli, Kris Anderson, Joshua Altman, Michael J. Bayer, James H. Burnley, Kyle Butts, Janet Cam, Kevin Chaffee, Gia Colombraro, David Davenport, Juanita Duggan, Franco Impalà, Alan Kaden, Charles Kieffer, Katie and Alex Mathews, Renato Miracco, Colleen Moran, Christyne Nasbe, Alma and John Paty, Carlos Reyes, Teresa Rosenberger, Bob Salladay, Greg Schneiders, Martha Sherrill, Karen Skelton, Ben Stein, Jim Strock, Erik Taylor, John Ulrich, Marion Watkins, Mark Weinberg, Rob Wilcox, Bill Whalen, John Yoo and Zachary Young.

The book benefited from a team of researchers, translators and transcribers, including Monique Archuleta, Rachel Binnington, Barbara Cochran, Madeline Court, Eric DeVilliers, Adam G. Erickson, Jackie Foust, Carol Gould, Randall Hahn, Jason Ince, Gordon Li, Elizabeth A. Novara, Gabriel Ozuna, Dr. W. Raymond Palmer, Neerali Patel, Molly Peters, Olivia Shahloup and Huma Utku.

I want to thank my manager and mentor, Chris George, for encouraging me to tackle this subject as my first book, and for his guidance and support as it took shape. I am grateful to my agent, Flip Brophy at Sterling Lord Literistic, for matching this book to the perfect publisher, and for providing much-needed perspective and advice.

Henry Ferris believed in this book from the start and guided me through its initial steps. I am grateful to him for his encouragement and suggestions. My editor, Nick Amphlett, improved the book dramatically, and I wish to thank him and his colleagues at William Morrow, including Lauren Janiec, Tavia Kowalchuk, Owen Corrigan, Tom Pitoniak, Stephanie Vallejo, Liate Stehlik and Lynn Grady, for bringing this book from proposal to publication.

Finally, I want to thank friends and family who listened patiently while I shared my growing pile of "fun facts" about the Watergate or explored potential characters and story lines at length, hijacking what might otherwise have been more wide-ranging dinner conversations.

NOTES

PROLOGUE

1   On the front page of the *Post*: *Washington Post*, June 16, 1972.

1   "mechanical walkers": *Watergate East Anniversary Issue 1964–1992*, 61.

2   213-suite: Watergate press release, April 12, 1967.

2   fourteen cameras in Watergate East: *Washington Star*, June 25, 1965.

2   wrote in his logbook: Records of the Watergate Special Prosecution Force, National Archives 304970.

2   flirting with ninety degrees: *Washington Post*, June 16, 1972.

3   against her wishes: Winzola McLendon, *Martha: The Life of Martha Mitchell* (New York: Ballantine Books, 1979), 192–193.

3   "She never got to go anyplace": *Washington Post*, June 16, 1974.

4   At 8:07 A.M.: President Richard Nixon's Daily Diary, June 16, 1972, Nixon Presidential Library.

4   Volpe . . . who lived with his wife, Jennie: *Life*, August 8, 1969.

4   At 9:30: Daily calendars, Anna Chennault papers, Harvard University Library.

4   "humane and decent": *Washington Post*, June 16, 1972.

5   boarded a Gulfstream II jet: McLendon, 2.

5   At noon: Chennault daily calendars.

5   "If it only had": *New York Times*, March 12, 1972.

5   arrived at National Airport: Jim Hougan, *Secret Agenda: Watergate, Deep Throat and the CIA* (New York: Random House, 1984), 180.

5   lobster tails: Ibid., 185.

5   It had been a long flight: James Rosen, *The Strong Man: John Mitchell and the Secrets of Watergate* (New York: Doubleday, 2008), 297.

5   Bruce Givner: Hougan, 189.

6   Pausing only to step onto the balcony: Bruce Givner interview, June 20, 2017.

6   Shortly after one in the morning: Hougan, 197.

CHAPTER ONE: THE FOGGY BOTTOM PROJECT

9   was now for sale at $3 million: *Washington Post*, July 23, 1948.

10   "thus adding materially": Ibid.

10   "were it not for those tanks": *Washington Post*, July 24, 1948.

10   Hotelier Conrad Hilton: *Washington Sunday Star*, July 20, 1969.

10   high bidder at $935,000: "$935,000 Top Bid Rejected As Gas Co. Site Sale Fails," *Washington Post*, November 10, 1948

11   formed a syndicate: *Time*, September 28, 1953.

11   "high character": *Washington Post*, September 13, 1953.

11   Harrison & Abramovitz: *Washington Post*, March 9, 1954.

11 extending the option: *Washington Post,* June 15, 1955.

12 "a human computer": *Time,* January 25, 1963.

12 "Many of my colleagues fear": *Fortune,* June 1965.

12 "We once considered Italy's boundaries": Ibid.

14 "Potomac deal": SGI board minutes, February 1, 1960, Central State Archives, Rome.

14 Salgo became a partner: Nicolas Salgo, *Success Begins After 5:00 P.M* (North Charleston, SC: CreateSpace Independent Publishing Platform, 2017), 105.

15 endorsed the design unanimously: National Cultural Center, press release, April 1, 1960.

15 "little short of breath-taking": Roger Meersman, "The Kennedy Center: From Dream to Reality," Records of the Columbia Historical Society, Washington, DC, Vol. 50, 1980, 543.

15 "beautiful but grandiose": *New York Times,* February 4, 1962.

15 top consulting architect: *Washington Post,* February 19, 1963.

15 like a Renaissance prince: Adrian Sheppard, "Four Essays on Moretti: Luigi Moretti: A Testimony," April 2, 2008, *Luigi Moretti (1907-1973) Razionalismo e transgressivita tra barocco e informale,* (Electra Editore, 2010).

16 fundamentally an introvert: Tommaso Magnifico interview, November 16, 2016.

16 joined the team: *Newark Star-Ledger,* November 15, 2009.

16 walked the site: Federico Bucci and Marco Mulazzani, *Luigi Moretti: Works and Writings* (New York: Princeton Architectural Press, 2002), 213.

16 San Vittore Prison in Milan: Ibid.

16 Studio Moretti: Sheppard, 2008.

17 "the connection": Salvatore Santuccio and Nicolo Sardo interview, November 17, 2016.

17 "extreme modernism": Mario Valmarana interview, 2009

17 He drew inspiration: Adrian Sheppard, "The Watergate Project: A Contrapuntal Multi-Use Urban Complex in Washington, DC," *Luigi Moretti (1907-1973) Razionalismo e transgressivita tra barocco e informale,*(Electra Editore, 2010), 7.

17 "the Roman way": "Moretti—a lecture," Mario di Valmarana, December 8, 2005, summarized by George Arnstein. www.watergate50.com.

17 leaving his mark: Sheppard, 2008.

18 "sing": Ibid.

18 "angry thumb": Ibid.

18 "considered satisfactory": Milton Fischer memorandum to Giuseppe Cecchi, March 10, 1961, Central State Archives, Rome.

18 "mediocre": Antonio Cecchi correspondence, March 24, 1961, Central State Archives, Rome.

20 "I need a real Washingtonian": Elizabeth Ulman Rowe, Oral History interview, June 16, 1975, LBJ Presidential Library.

20   Harvard philosophy graduate: *New York Times*, February 1, 1973.

20   Rowe was elevated to vice chairman: NCPC meeting transcript, June 8, 1961.

21   "harmonious": Giuseppe Cecchi memorandum, June 8, 1961, Central State Archives, Rome.

21   He recommended: Warren Adler interview.

22   in capital letters: Donald H. Drayer Archive, Library of Congress.

22   "That's how the Watergate name came over to us": Salgo, 108.

22    $650,000: Meersman, 568.

23   "the community will gain a great deal": National Capital Planning Commission (NCPC), "Proposed Watergate Towne Development," September 6, 1961.

23   "attract people to Washington": NCPC Transcript of Proceedings, September 14, 1961.

24   Mrs. Rowe had no questions: Ibid.

25   commissioners met privately: Commission of Fine Arts (CFA), meeting minutes, September 20, 1961.

25   "an impression of openness": Ibid.

25   "until such a time": William Finley memorandum, annotated, October 2, 1961, SGI archives.

25   *"Molto bene!"*: Ibid.

26   He suggested the entire parcel: NCPC transcript, November 9, 1961.

26   PLANNING COMMISSION IS TRYING: Giuseppe Cecchi cable, December 4, 1961, SGI archives.

27   "put up a strong fight": Giuseppe Cecchi memorandum, December 5, 1961, SGI archives.

27   "informing them of our frustration": Royce Ward memorandum, December 5, 1961, SGI archives.

27   "Mrs. Rowe's visionary dream": Cecchi memorandum, December 5, 1961, SGI archives.

27   "I believe now is not the time": Aldo Samaritani memorandum, December 18, 1961, SGI archives.

27   "reserved for public purposes": *Washington Post*, December 24, 1961.

27   "fuzzy thinking": *Washington Star*, December 27, 1961.

28   Over the holidays: *Washington Post*, December 26, 1961.

28   "The Church of the Catholic candidate": Presidential Campaign Files, 1960, Kennedy Presidential Library.

29   "a company owned by the Vatican": Protestants and Other Americans United, *Church and State*, January 1962.

29   He told Cecchi not to "surrender": Giuseppe Cecchi memorandum, January 17, 1962, SGI archives.

29   "good design quality": National Capital Planning Commission, "Watergate Towne—Design Analysis," January 30, 1962.

29   "It is costing these people a lot of money": NCPC meeting transcript, February 1, 1962.

30   "so many lumps of sugar": Ibid.

30   The motion passed: "Watergate Towne Chronology," February 17, 1962.

30   "a turning point": Foa correspondence, February 2, 1962, SGI Archives, Rome.

32   James C. Wilkes, Jr., a land-use attorney: District of Columbia Zoning Commission, Public Hearing, April 13, 1962.

32   "It is going to be a Trojan Wall": Ibid.

32   "disappointment with the preliminary plans": "Statement of the Commission of Fine Arts before a Hearing of the Zoning Commission," April 13, 1962.

32   The CFA was "greatly concerned": "Watergate Project Foes Present Views to Zoners," *Washington Star*, April 14, 1962.

32   "overpowering": Statement of the Commission of the Fine Arts Before a Hearing of the Zoning Commission, April 13, 1962, attached as Exhibit K to Minutes of the Commission of Fine Arts, April 17, 1962.

32   "neither fine nor artful": *Washington Post*, April 19, 1962.

33   The following week: Charles H. Atherton, "Memorandum for the Board Re: Watergate Development Meeting, New York City," April 24, 1962.

33   "To those who oppose the project": *New York Times*, April 29, 1962.

33   WHITE HOUSE ACTS: *Washington Post,* May 5, 1962.

34   WEAK IN THE KNEES: *Washington Star*, May 6, 1962.

35   "White House concerns": *Washington Post*, May 11, 1962.

35   Moretti, through an interpreter: *Washington Post*, May 16, 1962.

36   Moretti said he had studied Washington: Ibid.

36   "depend on Moretti's judgment": *Washington Post*, May 19, 1962.

36   issued a joint statement: CFA, "Joint Press Release," May 18, 1962; also in CFA meeting transcript, September 18, 1963, 119.

37   "there would seem to be no reason": *Washington Post*, July 20, 1962.

37   in the spring of 1963: *Washington Post*, July 14, 1962.

37   Finley would step down: Columbia Association website, accessed January 5, 2017. See also James W. Rouse & Company, Inc., press release, October 30, 1963.

37   In mid-July, Drew Pearson: *San Bernardino Sun-Telegram*, July 4, 1962.

38   Lowell, assistant director of the organization: *Washington Post*, November 11, 1962.

38   urged supporters to protest the Watergate: Ibid.

38   Stone presented his revised plans: National Cultural Center, press release, September 11, 1962.

39   More than fifteen hundred letters: *Washington Post*, November 17, 1962.

39   Horsky sent Kennedy a three-page memo: Charles Horsky memorandum, January 23, 1963, Kennedy Presidential Library.

39   "I propose to continue to respond this way": Ibid.

39   Kennedy instructed Horsky: Charles Horsky, Second Oral History Interview, August 13, 1964, Kennedy Presidential Library.

40   "monumental dullness": Paul Rudolph, "A View of Washington as a Capital—Or What Is Civic Design?," *Architectural Forum*, January 1963.

40   Horsky reported that: Charles Horsky memorandum, January 25, 1963, Kennedy Presidential Library.

40   "like a rugged representative of the New Frontier": *Washington Post*, June 21, 1963.

41   Walton suggested five more candidates: William Walton memorandum, undated, Kennedy Presidential Library.

41   "If you can't lick them, join them": President Kennedy to Bill Walton, March 30, 1963, Kennedy Presidential Library.

41   "I don't blame you": Mary Hackett, *William "Bill" Walton: A Charmed Life* (Boston, MA: Braden Books, 2013), 157.

42   "I hope we can influence good design": *Washington Post*, June 21, 1963.

42   "too sharp": Finley correspondence, April 17, 1963.

42   "overpowering mass": CFA minutes, April 16, 1963.

42   "Fine Arts Commission is favorable": SGI board minutes, May 28, 1963, SGI Archives.

42   "a touch of Rome": *Washington Post*, August 6, 1963.

43   "It's pretty bad": CFA transcript, September 18, 1963.

44   "a substantial reduction": Walton to Green, CFA meeting transcript, September 18, 1963.

44   "like spaghetti": *Washington Post*, October 18, 1963.

44   "The Watergate architects originally cooperated": *Washington Post*, October 21, 1963.

45   "will soon start": SGI board minutes, November 11, 1963, SGI Archives.

45   met in closed session: CFA transcript, November 19, 1963.

45   "do credit to the standing": Ibid.

45   "We tried very hard": Ibid.

45   "we are not going to be handled": Ibid.

47   "a marvelous facility": Walton to Clark, November 20, 1963.

47   The meeting was originally suggested: Stanton to Jenkins, December 30, 1963, LBJ Presidential Library.

48   "very deeply sympathetic": CFA transcript, January 8, 1964.

49   "I feel the project can be saved": Ibid.

49   "Thank you for coming": Ibid.

49   "so-called Watergate development": Arthur M. Schlesinger, Jr., memorandum to the President, January 9, 1964, LBJ Presidential Library.

49 "full support": *Washington Post*, January 10, 1964.

50 "entirely frank with you": Samaritani correspondence, January 10, 1964, CFA files.

50 "would look favorably": *Washington Post*, January 25, 1964.

50 Congress officially changed the name: Meersman, 556–557.

50 The next morning: *Washington Post*, January 25, 1964.

CHAPTER TWO: CITY WITHIN A CITY

51 "might be too much": Royce Ward memorandum, October 10, 1962, SGI archives, Central State Archives, Rome.

52 "there would be resistance": Ibid.

52 As excavation began: *Washington Post*, March 14, 1962.

52 "no continuous straight lines anywhere": *Washington Post*, November 14, 1964.

53 Roberts turned to Engineering Physics Co.: "Computer Lends Individuality to Vast Watergate Project," IBM press release, December 21, 1965.

53 He later estimated: *Washington Post*, November 14, 1964.

54 "the atmosphere of a formal Renaissance-style garden": *Washington Star*, December 18, 1964.

54 He threw his hat on the floor: Giuseppe Cecchi interview, March 2, 2016.

54 "marble hair": *Washington Post*, May 30, 1964.

54 displayed on a cyclorama: *Washington Evening Star*, January 22, 1965.

54 The ad showed the floor plan for Apartment 403-N: *Washington Post*, November 14, 1964.

55 "the ultimate in aural privacy": Watergate East marketing brochure, GWU archives.

55 Prices ranged from: *Washington Star,* April 10, 1964.

55 Lewis said women were the key to his marketing strategy: *Washington Star*, January 8, 1965.

56 It offered three things they wanted: Emily Eig interview, February 27, 2017.

56 "What all of this means": *Washington Star*, June 25, 1965.

56 By mid-February: *Washington Daily News*, February 19, 1965.

56 He stepped out of a champagne reception: *Washington Post*, February 19, 1965.

57 Guests at the reception: *Washington Business Journal*, June 17, 2002.

57 One guest: Chennault daily calendars, Harvard University Library.

57 in love: Anna Chennault, *A Thousand Springs: The Biography of a Marriage* (New York: Paul S. Eriksson, 1962), 110–111.

58 A Chinese wife knows: Ibid., 20.

58 He left her $225,500: Catherine Forslund, *Anna Chennault: Informal Diplomacy and Asian Relations* (Wilmington, DE: Scholarly Resources, Inc., 2002), 41.

58 He was an advocate: David McKean, *Tommy the Cork: Washington's Ultimate Insider from Roosevelt to Reagan* (South Royalton, VT: Steerforth Press, 2004), 167–168.

59 "intoxicating": Forslund, 42.

59 "a popular watering hole for ranking Republicans": Ibid., 45.

59 "sales room": *Washington Examiner*, July 17–19, 1969.

60 "It will be necessary to vigorously oppose": Kennedy Center meeting minutes, December 2, 1964, Kennedy Presidential Library.

60 Becker reviewed the Watergate's "height problem": Arthur M. Schlesinger Personal Papers. Alphabetical Subject File, 1960–1965. Kennedy Center for the Performing Arts: Executive Committee summary of actions, 1965. AM-SPP-P05–012, John F. Kennedy Presidential Library and Museum.

60 "woefully crowding in": *Washington Post*, April 18, 1965.

61 "relevant official body": Becker correspondence, March 2, 1975.

61 "My client has tried": *Washington Post*, June 17, 1965.

61 That weekend, the model apartment: *Washington Post*, June 19, 1965.

61 "where he inherited the family title of duke": *Washington Star*, June 11, 1964.

62 According to a report: *New York Times*, May 11, 1969.

62 "I'm the only American citizen": New York Public Library, New York Times Company records. Clifton Daniel papers 1955–1979.

62 An internal *Times* investigation: Ibid.

62 "restrained but vibrant tone": *Better Homes & Gardens*, September 1964.

62 "Oriental Opulence and Italian Grandeur": *Washington Post*, June 6, 1965.

62 "Well, it's different": *Washington Post*, October 23, 1965.

63 "squeezed down": *Evening Star*, June 11, 1965.

64 Samaritani thanked: Watergate East Dedication Program, October 1965.

64 Clara sat with him: Clara Graff interview, January 24, 2017.

64 The first Watergate East apartment was sold: Watergate East, *Anniversary Issue, 1964–1992*, 72.

64 George Arnstein had recently accepted: George Arnstein oral history, GWU, April 12, 2013.

65 "Where do we eat?": Watergate East, 72.

65 They employed a full-time gardener: Jan Pottker, *Crisis in Candyland: Melting the Chocolate Shell of the Mars Family Empire* (Bethesda, MD: National Press Books, 1995), 88.

65 "in any sense of the word": Ibid.

65 "investing in the stock market": *New York Times*, June 25, 1966.

65 "the paintings were hung": Watergate East, 73.

65 "so it wouldn't make a splash": *New York Times*, June 25, 1966.

65 "bought on sale at Bloomingdale's": Ibid.

66   "Your future happiness is assured here": William Simon correspondence, June 19, 1968.

66   All new residents also received: Watergate East, 35–38.

66   He reported back to her: Koubek correspondence, December 20, 1965, Chennault papers, Harvard University Library.

67   She persuaded them: *Washingtonian*, June 1967.

68   "I knew right away": Hayden B. Peake and Samuel Halpern, *In the Name of Intelligence: Essays in Honor of Walter Pforzheimer* (Washington, DC: NIBC Press, 1994), 25–26.

68   The collection was in part a resource: *New York Times*, December 28, 2003.

68   Pforzheimer also used the collection: Tim Naftali interview, March 2, 2017.

68   three thousand volumes: *Life*, August 8, 1969.

69   SGI executives in Rome ordered: Unsigned memorandum, February 18, 1966, SGI archives.

70   "patience and understanding": Watergate East, Inc., "Report From Management," March 28, 1966.

70   "with alacrity": SGI board minutes, SGI Archives.

70   "popular tunes": *Georgetowner*, November 10, 1966.

71   called "apartments" in the press release: "The Watergate Adds Elegance and Grace to Washington's Hotel Scene," press release, April 12, 1967.

71   "presidential suites": *Washington Post*, April 1, 1967.

72   "awful": Samaritani correspondence, November 8, 1967, SGI archives.

72   "more restrained in its design": Press release, April 12, 1967.

73   "closest friends": *Washingtonian*, June 1967.

73   She invited FBI director J. Edgar Hoover: Hoover correspondence, March 28, 1967, Chennault papers, Harvard University Library.

73   Chennault's guests admired her "oriental" living room: *Washington Star*, April 11, 1967.

73   Lady Bird Johnson admired the view: *Washington Star*, August 6, 1967.

73   "Nothing's too good for the party of the people": *Washington Star*, July 21, 1967.

73   "The music is soft and piped": *Miami Herald*, August 12, 1967.

74   "plush": *Washington Post*, July 20, 1967.

74   "quite inexpensive": *Washington Star*, July 21, 1967.

74   "smooth start": *Columbus Dispatch*, July 6, 1967.

74   The Johnson organization reserved space: R. Spencer Oliver interview, September 25, 2016.

74   Now they wanted the building nixed entirely: *Washington Star*, September 28, 1967.

75   the "unattractive arrogance": *Washington Post*, October 13, 1967.

76   The fate of the final Watergate building was now in the hands: *Washington Star*, October 19, 1967.

76   The board voted: *Washington Post*, December 1, 1967.

76   $500,000 to stop construction: *New York Times*, January 16, 1964.

76   The interior department told: William Simon correspondence, June 19, 1968.

76   "didn't have final Commission approval": NCPC transcript, December 7, 1967.

77   "We could see the fires": Arnstein oral history, April 12, 2013.

77   stood at the windows: Oliver interview, September 25, 2016.

77   Udall announced a compromise: Meersman, 570.

77   "bright fluorescent lights": *Washington Post*, April 23, 1968.

78   "promise": Simon correspondence, June 19, 1968.

78   "the controlling stockholder in SGI": Ibid.

78   "In my view": Ibid.

79   Carl Bernstein: *Washington Post*, October 31, 1968.

79   "The developers took our money": *Washington Post*, June 27, 1968.

80   "NO! NO!": Chennault correspondence, June 28, 1968, Richard V. Allen papers, Hoover Institution Archives, Stanford University.

82   LBJ told them: Forslund, 62.

83   Johnson was warning Nixon: Ibid., 67.

83   "It's very important that our Vietnamese friends understand": Rosen, 54.

83   The call was reported: "X File," LBJ Presidential Library.

85   ABC projected a Nixon victory: Rosen, 55–56.

85   "Put that with the other stuff": LBJ note, November 8, 1968, "X File," LBJ Presidential Library.

85   She had "very real psychological problems": Rosen, 66.

85   the same facility where Zelda Fitzgerald: Luke J. Spencer, "Zelda Fitzgerald's Abandoned Sanitorium," Atlas Obscura, https://www.atlasobscura.com /places/zelda-fitzgerald-s-abandoned-sanatorium.

85   "holding up the selection of Nixon's cabinet": Rosen, 67.

85   According to Chennault, John Mitchell had been to her penthouse: Anna Chennault, *The Education of Anna* (New York: Times Books, 1980), 179–180.

86   $325,000: *Washington Post*, January 17, 1968.

86   $1,000 per month: Ibid.

86   "You've heard me talk about her": Chennault, 179.

CHAPTER THREE: *TITANIC* ON THE POTOMAC

87   Edith and Lee Burchinal received: *Washington Daily News*, January 31, 1969.

87   "It takes a heap of selling": *Washington Post*, January 11, 1969.

88   "All of us in this office": Ibid.

88   "construction gripes": Ibid.

88   members of the local chapter: *Washington Star*, October 11, 1968.

88   "create a restful mood": *Washington Post*, October 19, 1968.

88   Sixteen design students: *Washington Star*, May 19, 1968.

88   until noise: *Washington Post*, August 1, 1965.

89   "some real 'guts'": McAfee correspondence, February 14, 1969, Pietro Lazzari papers, 1878–1998, Archives of American Art, Smithsonian Institution.

89   "To go forward at all": *Washington Post*, February 25, 1969.

89   "I bring a lot of paperwork home on weekends": Ibid.

90   Hanford . . . recommended: Shelley Buchanan interview, December 2, 2016.

90   "It's easier for the White House limousine": *Washington Star*, July 20, 1969.

91   "Isn't it mad": *Washington Post*, February 25, 1969.

91   "They were rather snobbish": Annelise Anderson interview, October 18, 2016.

92   Martin purchased a used car: *Wall Street Journal*, March 25, 1969.

92   "I like my old things": *Washington Post*, February 25, 1969.

92   "more traditional": McLendon, 80.

92   "I'll just have to paint": *Washington Post*, February 25, 1969.

93   proudly showed off her bulging closets: McLendon, 78.

93   "progressive party": *Wall Street Journal*, March 25, 1969.

93   "a smattering of unofficial Republican heavyweights": *Washington Star*, July 20, 1969.

93   "the icing on the cake": *Newsweek*, February 16, 1970.

94   "Mr. A. Chennault": Office of the President-Elect, December 2, 1968, Chennault archives.

94   NEXT PERLE MESTA?: *Washington Post*, January 29, 1969.

94   "hostess with the mostess" and a "Party Queen": *Cleveland Plain Dealer*, January 26, 1969.

94   "The Tiger Lady": *Washington Sunday News*, February 23, 1969.

94   "Madame Chennault": *Palm Beach Life*, March 1969.

94   "Who told you that?": *St. Louis Post-Dispatch*, January 2, 1969.

95   "no comment": *Washington Post*, January 29, 1969.

95   "manifestly untrue": *Washington Evening Star*, February 11, 1969.

95   Dragon Lady: Ibid.

95   The FBI was called in to investigate: *Washington Daily News*, March 4, 1969.

95   "It's really a tragic thing": Ibid.

95   "What a way to live": Knight Ridder, January 4, 1970.

96   "Because of your friendship": Moretti correspondence, June 18, 1969, SGI archives.

96   "the biggest tax evader in postwar Italy": Gerald Posner, *God's Bankers: A History of Money and Power at the Vatican* (New York: Simon & Schuster, 2015), 185.

97   "sufficiently uncomfortable": *Fortune*, August 1973.

97   "Only one light was burning": Luigi DiFonzo, *St. Peter's Banker: Michele Sindona* (New York: Franklin Watts, 1983), 11.

98   "Rockefeller interests in New York": *Washington Post,* June 19, 1969.

98   "Our policy is to avoid maintaining control of companies as in the past": *Fortune,* August 1973.

99   "an advisor-diplomatic messenger": Chennault correspondence, December 10, 1968, Chennault archives.

100   "Stay out of it": McClendon, 71–72.

101   "The public must wait for my book": *Washington Sunday Star,* July 13, 1969.

101   "If I tell all": *China Post,* August 28, 1969.

101   A Humphrey aide confirmed: *Washington Post,* July 10, 1969.

102   "an insult": *China News,* July 22, 1969; *New York Times,* July 23, 1969.

102   "Mr. White is an excellent writer": *Chicago Tribune,* July 23, 1969.

102   "The Mysterious Anna Chennault": *Washington Examiner,* July 17–19, 1969.

102   "For whom does Anna Chennault work?": Ibid.

102   "She is down here a lot": Ibid.

102   "I deny the accusations as false": *Washington Post,* July 29, 1969; *China News,* July 30, 1969.

103   She referred all further inquiries: Ibid.

103   "Anna, in rapturous prose": *Washingtonian,* September 1969.

104   a woman "of fierce ambition": *Seattle Times,* April 6, 1969.

104   Mr. Fixit: *New York Times,* July 31, 2013.

105   "Since you had the liaison": Rosen, 69.

105   President Nixon hosted a state dinner: *Washington Post,* November 20, 1969.

105   "high-level title": Rosen, 60.

107   More than a dozen Watergate residents: Contested Material Collection, Box 51, Folder Number 16, Nixon Presidential Library.

107   "was diplomatically out of town": *Washington Post,* June 13, 1971.

107   The General Services Administration reduced its standard rate: Jesse Smith memorandum, September 24, 1971, SGI archives.

108   stepped up marketing efforts: Ibid.

108   To capitalize on the excitement surrounding the Kennedy Center: Ibid.

109   "We are trying everything": Ibid.

110   "most receptive": Villarosa correspondence, October 9, 1970, SGI archives.

110   Sweden opened a new chancery: *Washington Post,* October 31, 1971.

111   for a $14,000 profit: Knight Ridder, January 4, 1970.

111   now started at $32,000: Ibid.

111   On the tenth floor: *Washington Post,* July 23, 1970.

111   optimism permeated SGI headquarters: SGI board minutes, August 27, 1973, SGI archives.

112   "Watergate-type": *Washington Post,* July 22, 1970.

112   Henry Winston became president: *Washington Evening Star,* April 25, 1972.

112 "In little more than a year": *Newsweek*, February 16, 1970.

113 "overtones of racism": Arnstein oral history, April 12, 2013.

113 A waiter from the Watergate Hotel: *Globe and Mail*, July 25, 2009.

113 "so I don't feel left out": Chennault, *The Education of Anna*, 199.

114 "and really swung it": *Washington Evening Star*, January 30, 1970.

114 "to discuss an issue": Chennault, *Education of Anna*, 180.

114 "I love it": Knight Ridder, January 4, 1970.

114 "a glittering Potomac Titanic": *Washington Post*, May 3, 1970.

CHAPTER FOUR: NOT QUITE PERFECT

115 "You bring the dollars": *Washington Post*, May 3, 1970.

115 "You have a new boss": Salgo, 111.

116 "Republican Bastille": *Washington Post*, May 3, 1970.

116 "in charge of this thing": *Washington Post*, February 20, 1970.

116 "in case they threw firebombs": Ibid.

117 "I sure wish": Ibid.

117 "say hello": *Washington Post*, February 21, 1970.

117 The next day was peaceful: Ibid.

117 "absurd": *Washington Evening Star*, February 25, 1970.

117 inscribed a copy: *Washington Post*, May 3, 1970.

117 "Hello, gorgeous!": *Washington Sunday Star*, October 12, 1969.

118 "Holy Hell broke loose": McLendon, 108.

118 "That letter is what gave me the courage": Ibid., 109.

118 "a national celebrity": Ibid., 104.

118 "hordes of reporters": Rosen, 118.

119 "My family worked for everything": Ibid., 118–119.

119 "His answer infuriated me": McLendon, 174.

120 "and heard the sound of his world turning upside down": Rosen, 123.

120 "What else can I do": McLendon, 123.

120 "I love her, that's all I have to say": Rosen, 123.

120 "command post": McLendon, 123.

120 to a stint at the U.S. Post Office: *Washington Evening Star*, April 15, 1970.

120 "the darling of the press": Madeleine Edmondson and Alden Duer Cohen, *The Women of Watergate* (Scarborough House, Briarcliff Manor, NY: Stein and Day/Publishers, 1975), 36.

120 "I love the Democrats": McLendon, 124.

120 "totally unprepared": *Detroit Free Press*, July 2, 1972

121 "like others react to hard liquor": Ibid.

121 "Those two months": McLendon, 137.

121 "The Silent Majority embraced her as its own": Ibid., 127.

122   "It was obvious": Ibid., 117–118.

122   "She has to be watched": Ibid., 200.

122   Sprinkled throughout: *Life*, August 8, 1969.

123   "It's a disgrace": *Washington Sunday Star*, February 1, 1970.

123   "The noise is terrible": *Newsweek*, February 16, 1970.

123   "It's not a good place to live": Knight Ridder, January 4, 1970.

124   "Once we noticed": *Wall Street Journal*, March 25, 1969.

124   Additional leaks appeared: *Evening Star*, June 25, 1969.

124   "We couldn't breathe at all": Knight Ridder, January 4, 1970.

124   "I thought I had seen a lot of water in the submarine service": Ibid.

124   "went berserk": Ibid.

124   "It's computerized": Annelise Anderson interview, October 18, 2016.

125   "There used to be hotel policemen": *Washington Daily News*, March 4, 1969.

125   "elevator scenes": *Wall Street Journal*, March 25, 1969.

125   "somebody on the inside with a key": *Washington Star*, July 20, 1969.

125   "inside jobs": Knight Ridder, January 4, 1970.

126   Carolyn Blount, wife of the postmaster general: Ibid.

126   "Usually at dinner parties": *Washington Post*, August 16, 1970.

126   The occasion was a farewell dinner: Ibid.

126   Sally's parents: Sally Quinn interview, February 1, 2017.

127   "They all wanted their parties covered": Ibid.

127   "She was extremely aggressive": Ibid.

127   "I loved watching her": Ibid.

127   "Richard Nixon missed a good party": *Washington Post*, November 10, 1969.

128   "the Watergate is where it's happening": *Milwaukee Journal*, March 10, 1970.

128   "Your apartment is lovely": Nancy Reagan correspondence, undated (post-marked March 17, 1972), Chennault archives.

129   "Miss Woods, please": Nixon Presidential Library Materials Staff, Tape Subject Log (rev. 10/06), Conversation No. 15–126.

130   "personally telephoned": *Washington Post*, November 24, 1971.

130   "Anna Chennault has beauty": *Los Angeles Times*, October 11, 1970.

130   "Anna Chennault is like a woman with a small bosom": *Palm Beach Post*, September 27, 1970.

130   "If the war in Vietnam were to end tomorrow": reprinted in *Milwaukee Journal*, March 10, 1970.

131   "She still relishes": *Life*, October 2, 1970.

131   "a lonely, frustrated woman": Edmondson and Duer Cohen, 44.

131   One night at dinner in Anna Chennault's penthouse: Chennault, *The Education of Anna*, 181.

131 "vastly inadequate": Miedzinski correspondence, November 1, 1971, Maurice M. Stans papers, Minnesota Historical Society.

132 Residents were outraged: Robert M. Caldwell correspondence, August 4, 1972, Stans papers.

132 "a practice followed for the past six years": Ibid.

133 When word leaked out: Maurice Stans, *The Terrors of Justice: The Untold Side of Watergate* (New York: Everest House, 1978), 147.

133 "They can't do this": McLendon, 193.

133 "Pat and Adele cut them off of every list": Ibid., 192.

134 "corrective work": Brief for Appellees, U.S. District Court of Appeals for the District of Columbia Circuit, *Watergate West, Inc., et al., v. Watergate Improvement Associates, LTD., et al.*, March 1, 1976.

134 "temporary and basically ineffective": Ibid.

134 The board then retained new engineers: Ibid.

135 Cecchi could not recall: Cecchi interview, March 2, 2016.

136 "They weren't able to document anything": *Washington Post*, March 9, 1972.

136 why did Watergate values keep rising?: *Washington Evening Star*, March 3, 1972.

136 Three weeks later, the developers fired back: *Washington Evening Star*, March 24, 1972.

137 "Are you crazy?": Cecchi interview, March 2, 2016.

137 A check for $2,500: National Archives RG 460: Records of the Watergate special prosecution force—campaign contributions task force, Box 14, National Archives, College Park, Maryland.

137 On Monday, May 22: Hougan, 139.

139 He wrote in his logbook: Ibid., 146.

139 Johnnie Walker Red: E. Howard Hunt, *American Spy: My Secret History in the CIA, Watergate & Beyond* (Hoboken, NJ: John Wiley & Sons, Inc., 2007), 215.

139 They emerged at six: Hougan, 146.

139 The next night: Ibid., 151.

139 On Monday: Ibid., 152.

140 "delighted": Ibid.

140 The firm identified fifteen different problems: Alice De Angelo, Watergate East Inter-Office Memo, March 9, 1973, Stans papers.

141 "hippie clothes": *Washington Times*, June 16, 1992.

CHAPTER FIVE: THE MAELSTROM

143 "a sensation": Patrick J. Buchanan, *Nixon's White House Wars* (New York: Crown Forum, 2017), 400.

143 "His voice was low": Ibid., 270.

144 "Holy crap!": Givner interview, June 20, 2016.

144 A waiter brought a telephone: Rosen, 297.

144 "That is just incredible": Ibid., 300.

144 "I thought that was strange": Robert Parry, consortiumnews.com, March 20, 2014.

145 like any other Sunday: Stans, 80–81.

146 "Jesus Christ!": Rosen, 303–305.

146 "Those bastards": Ibid., 304.

146 Liddy asked LaRue to turn up the radio: Ibid., 311.

146 "I'm not going to stand for all those dirty things that go on": Ibid., 106.

146 "He feels she's suicidal": Ibid., 322.

146 "I wondered if you could tell me": Chennault, *Education of Anna*, 217.

147 "I did not know": Stans, 193–194.

147 whom Chennault had feted: *Washington Evening Star*, May 2, 1969.

148 "I really oughta get going to all these nice parties": Tape Subject Log, Conversation No. 744–1, June 30, 1972, Nixon Presidential Library.

148 "aborted": Stans, 369–370.

148 "I played right into their hands": McLendon, 207–208.

148 admired a blue corduroy sofa: Deborah Gore Dean interview, September 6, 2016.

149 "may have been too much": *Detroit Free Press*, July 2, 1972.

149 "My bride was tired of traveling": *McCall's*, July 1973.

150 "plush, spacious duplex": *Washington Daily News*, August 7, 1972.

150 "ridiculously low": McLendon, 211.

150 "Everybody's taste is different": *Washington Daily News*, August 7, 1972.

150 "Goodie, goodie": McLendon, 217.

150 "We'll have to vote": *Washington Evening Star and Daily News*, September 21, 1972.

151 twentieth-largest bank: *Forbes*, December 1972.

151 "You must believe me": Ibid.

151 "Sindona's reasons": *Fortune*, October 1974.

151 "In Italy I would go to jail": *Forbes*, December 1972.

151 "financial gangster": *Business Week*, April 29, 1972.

151 "final touch": *Washington Evening Star and Daily News,* September 15, 1972.

152 "airport bazaar flavor": *Washington Post*, August 6, 1972.

152 "The serious financial and structural correction problems": Caldwell correspondence, Stans papers.

153 added two requests: Stans correspondence, August 8, 1972, Stans papers.

154 "It was the first time I met Bob": Bob and Elizabeth Dole, *The Doles: Unlimited Partners* (New York: Simon & Schuster, 1988), 148–149.

155   "poor reputation": Joan E. Spero, *The Failure of Franklin National Bank* (Washington, DC: Beard Books, 1999), 79.

155   Sindona recruited Peter Shaddick: Ibid., 76.

155   All Cecchi could do: Cecchi interview, March 2, 2016.

155   Watergate didn't need the publicity: Salgo, 113.

156   $4,000 per month: Bettye Bradley oral history, 1983.

156   "We had to go with anonymous towels": Cecchi interview, March 2, 2016.

156   "These are private people": *New York Times Magazine*, October 15, 1972.

156   Tourists gaped: *New York Times,* June 17, 1973.

156   "The Watergate Tour": Ibid.

157   "All of a sudden": *Grand Rapids Press,* January 19, 1975.

157   Sindona later revealed: Sindona correspondence, September 7, 1981, Reagan Presidential Library.

157   "I just turned down a million dollars": Stans, 186–187.

158   "certainly not by me": Sindona correspondence, September 7, 1981, Reagan Presidential Library.

158   Chennault asked to be named: Chennault correspondence, January 4, 1973, Chennault archives.

158   "And then he'll just brush it off": Ken Hughes, *Chasing Shadows: The Nixon Tapes, the Chennault Affair, and the Origins of Watergate* (Charlottesville, VA: University of Virginia Press, 2014), 158.

159   a three-year term: *Washington Evening Star and Daily News,* January 31, 1973.

159   "You know, I have a protégé": Hughes, 157–158.

159   Anna Chennault never got her private meeting: Ibid.

160   "a constant reminder": R. Spencer Oliver interview, September 25, 2016.

160   Committee moved out: *Washington Daily News,* March 24, 1974.

160   "less than we have": Kathryn J. McGarr, *The Whole Damn Deal: Robert Strauss and the Art of Politics* (New York: Public Affairs, 2011), 144.

160   "is also its most valuable": *Washington Post,* May 14, 1973.

160   "a premier place to live": *Washington Post,* May 19, 1973.

160   "it isn't evident": *San Antonio Light,* February 19, 1974.

161   "We're down to the more solid stores": *Washington Post,* February 17, 1974.

161   "Don't be bugged with the commonplace": *Washington Star-News,* March 28, 1973.

162   failed to generate: *Sunday News,* March 24, 1974.

162   "Everybody tells me": *Jet,* March 17, 1973.

163   died of a brain tumor: *The Guardian,* October 9, 2000.

163   "might show up stoned": Buchanan interview, December 2, 2016.

163   swimming laps in the hotel pool: *Rolling Stone,* September 27, 1973.

163   "had bounded out of bed": Buchanan, *Nixon's White House Wars,* 311.

164 "But I was the only one who wasn't under indictment": George Arnstein oral history, April 12, 2013.

164 "very aggressive": Adrian Sheppard interview, January 23, 2017.

165 "one of the most horrible experiences": Tommaso Magnifico interview, November 17, 2016.

165 Back in Canada: Adrian Sheppard interview, January 23, 2017.

165 "a cruel joke of destiny": Tommaso Magnifico interview, November 17, 2016.

166 "Why live next door": *Washington Post*, July 28, 1974.

166 "tight": *Washington Post*, September 8, 1973.

166 "spang in the middle of Watergate": Ben Bradlee, *A Good Life: Newspapering and Other Adventures* (New York: Simon & Schuster, 1995), 390–391.

167 "are you into *that*?": Sally Quinn interview, February 1, 2017.

167 "the butler": *Washington Star News*, October 18, 1973.

167 "queen of the Watergate": *Washington Post*, October 18, 1973.

167 "a Republican has been welcomed back": Ibid.

169 a long, deep scratch: Edward W. Brooke, *Bridging the Divide: My Life* (New Brunswick, NJ: Rutgers University Press, 2007), 210.

169 That Christmas: Buchanan, *Nixon's White House Wars*, 363.

169 Shaddick and Bordoni concealed: Spero, 79–82.

170 "In rejecting the bid": *Business Week*, May, 18, 1974.

170 since the Depression: *Time*, May 27, 1974.

170 Shaddick resigned: *Business Week*, May 18, 1974.

170 "nervous": *Newsweek*, June 3, 1974.

170 less than $9 million: *Fortune*, June 1974.

170 Banca di Roma extended: *Business Week*, July 13, 1974.

171 22,000 volumes: "The Historical Intelligence Collection," CIA, https://www.cia.gov/news-information/featured-story-archive/2011-featured-story-archive/walter-pforzheimer.html.

172 "She's living one day at a time": *McCall's*, June 1975.

173 In the steam room: *People*, March 3, 1975.

174 Italy's Watergate: *Business Week*, March 3, 1975.

176 Stans pleaded guilty: Stans, pp. 368–372.

176 about $86 million: Based on an exchange rate of .001495 lira to the U.S. dollar, Monday, October 21, 1974.

177 "a huge feast": *La Repubblica*, August 30, 1995.

177 "The unexpected cyclone": SGI board minutes, March 8, 1975, SGI archives.

177 "with profound bitterness and disappointment": Ibid.

178 "They have poisoned me": *New York Times*, March 23, 1986.

178 dissolved: acs.beniculturali.it.

178 "The maelstrom was over": Stans, 384–385.

CHAPTER SIX: A LITTLE BLOOD

181 "The wine trade is to France": *New York Times*, October 26, 1974.

181 a wide range of charges: *New York Times*, September 13, 1973.

182 "little more than wrist-slapping": *New York Times*, December 19, 1974.

182 "I will be the Nixon of Bordeaux": *New York Times*, October 26, 1974.

182 "Winegate": *New York Times*, December 21, 1974.

183 the first post-Nixon scandal: William Safire, *Safire's New Political Dictionary* (New York: Random House, 1993), 278.

183 "May I talk to you?": Salgo, 113.

184 Mark Felt: watergateatlandmark.com, retrieved August 1, 2017.

184 Bob Dole faced: Bob and Elizabeth Dole, 154.

185 Anna Chennault's friendship with Gerald Ford: Forslund, 96.

185 "I always resent it": Ibid., 88.

186 "Anna has 'wondered'": Corcoran letter, August 22, 1975, Chennault archives.

187 "The President requested": Robert T. Hartmann memorandum, September 3, 1975, Ford Presidential Library.

188 "unallowable": *Washington Star*, September 15, 1975.

188 "the taxpayer shares the cost of these parties": Ibid.

188 Gruenstein's discovery made: *Washington Post*, September 16, 1975.

188 "You probably read that Northrop": *Washington Star*, September 22, 1975.

188 "so tiny and sweet-looking": *Washington Post*, October 3, 1975.

189 She brought Tommy Corcoran: State Dinner guest list, October 2, 1975, Ford Presidential Library.

189 Northrop had paid Chennault: *Washington Post*, October 6, 1975.

189 "Nobody pays for my parties": *Philadelphia Inquirer*, October 12, 1975.

189 "There is a distinct possibility": *Washington Post* news service, reprinted in the *Waukesha Freeman*, October 16, 1975.

190 "widespread, systematic": *Milwaukee Journal*, October 16, 1975.

190 The Pentagon launched audits: Associated Press story, 1976, undated, Chennault archives.

190 Chennault told investigators: Forslund, 110.

190 "not known": *Philadelphia Inquirer*, October 12, 1975.

190 Chennault continued as a Northrop consultant: Monthly consultant reports, Chennault archives.

190 "Unless your services are fully described and accurately recorded": John R. Alison memorandum, August 29, 1980, Chennault archives.

190 A pistachio pudding shortage: *Washington Post*, February 26, 1976.

191 the popularity of Watergate Cake: Ibid.

191 "cover-up icing": *St. Joseph News-Press*, July 30, 1975.

191 One version: *Deseret News,* May 5, 2010.

191   "but we can't substantiate": "The History of the Watergate Salad" Kraft Foods, kraftbrands.com.

191   "Perhaps to alleviate": *Washington Post*, November 13, 1975.

191   "We haven't invented anything": *Washington Post*, February 2, 1976.

192   "rather unappealing": Camille Stagg correspondence, February 4, 2017.

192   a reader sent the recipe: *Evening Independent*, March 15, 1977.

192   "to create something for the buffet": Stephanie Frazier, "Watergate Salad of Jake's Tyler," WSMV Channel 4, November 14, 2014, www.wsmv.com.

192   "which doesn't always contain real pistachios": *Richmond Times-Dispatch*, August 4, 1999.

192   "We tell them we had nothing to do with it": Anton Obernberger interview, July 11, 2017.

193   The recipe: "The History of Watergate Salad," Kraft Foods.

194   "We had much in common": Chennault, *The Education of Anna*, 222.

194   "It all sounded very wholesome": Ibid., 223–224.

195   "I'm his piano player": *New York Times*, August 16, 1977.

195   Suter's tavern: ghostsofdc.org and *Foggy Bottom News*, February 1964.

195   now occupied by the Watergate: Ibid.

196   "The name Tongsun Park meant a good party": *People*, March 6, 1978.

197   "I wasn't terribly surprised": Chennault, *The Education of Anna*, 224.

196   "South Korea is a friendly power": *New York Times*, September 7, 1977.

197   "Washington is a marvelous city": *New York Times*, April 15, 2005.

197   "It's a high, hard one": *Washington Post*, July 24, 1977.

198   Anna was trying out a new look: *Honolulu Star-Bulletin*, November 24, 1976.

200   "In retrospect": Martin Berkeley Hickman, *David Matthew Kennedy: Banker, Statesman, Churchman* (Provo, UT: Desert Book Company, 1987), 170.

201   "What they really wanted": Salgo, 117.

202   Continental Illinois spokesman: *Wall Street Journal*, November 4, 1977.

202   His new title: "Nomination of Nicolas M. Salgo to Be United States Ambassador to Hungary," White House Press Release, September 20, 1983.

202   625,000: *Wall Street Journal*, September 1, 1981.

202   assets of $5 billion: *Forbes*, November 26, 1979.

202   When she graduated: *Forbes*, October 12, 1981.

202   He tracked her down: *Daily Mail*, January 23, 1987.

203   thirty-hour day: *Management Review*, November 1986.

203   "Mr. Luscombe's secretary": *Forbes*, October 12, 1981.

204   I. M. Pei: Regine Palladin interview, August 21, 2017.

204   "When can you start?" Jimmy Sneed interview, August 10, 2017.

204   "I was fed up with problems": *Washington Post*, December 2, 1979.

205   "a good moment": Ibid.

205 "mischievous": Palladin interview, August 21, 2017.

205 Salgo also agreed to hire: Larbi Dahrouch interview, September 3, 2017.

205 "a little strange": Palladin interview, August 21, 2017.

206 "an orange cave": *Washingtonian*, October 2015.

206 "Americans like to chew things": *Washington Post*, December 2, 1979.

207 "Never before": Ibid.

207 The offer came: *New York Times*, March 28, 1979.

207 "We demand a little blood": *Washington Business Journal*, June 12, 1989.

208 A *New York Times* analysis concluded: *New York Times*, May 16, 1976.

208 "Ronald Reagan has an unusual tax problem": *Washington Star*, May 18, 1976.

209 "a private matter": *Washington Post*, August 1, 1980.

209 The tax return showed: Ronald Reagan Presidential Campaign Papers, 1964–1980, Box 45, Reagan Presidential Library.

209 "because it was good from an investment standpoint": *Washington Post*, August 1, 1980.

209 By far the best-performing: Reagans' 1979 joint federal tax return, Reagan Library campaign files 1980, Reagan Presidential Library.

209 "Operationally there is no change here": *Washington Post*, October 16, 1979.

CHAPTER SEVEN: THE REAGAN RENAISSANCE

211 "The Watergate is to Washington": *Washingtonian*, September 1983.

211 "The only good thing about them": Fred J. Maroon, *Jean-Louis: Cooking with the Seasons* (Charlottesville, VA: Thomasson-Grant, 1989), 17.

211 Carter White House: "Raising the Stakes," *Edible DC*, Summer 2012.

211 "less pleased with chicken": *Washington Post*, December 2, 1979.

211 Palladin and his team: Larbi Dahrouch interview, September 4, 2017.

212 Ober managed: *Washington Post*, February 11, 1975.

212 ten thousand Americans: *New York Times*, January 16, 1975.

212 Her reasoning: Deborah Davis, *Katharine the Great: Katharine Graham and the Washington Post* (Bethesda, MD: National Press, Inc., 1979), 276.

212 "Did God send you to me?": Maroon, 82.

213 "From Exotic Peking": Undated newspaper advertisement, Chennault archives.

213 "Please write your book": Chennault, *The Education of Anna*, 230–31.

213 She was still upset with Nixon: *Washington Star*, August 20, 1979.

213 had made her bitter: Ibid.

214 "Politics is a very cruel game": Ibid.

214 "If I were not an Asian," *W*, April 25–May 2, 1980.

214 "What Anna fails to realize": Ibid.

214 "Mitchell was quick to the point": Chennault, *The Education of Anna*, 193.

215 "high-handed secrecy and unnecessary haste": Ibid., 239–242.

215 Senator Barry Goldwater praised the book: Ibid.

215   "a great contribution": Goldwater correspondence, October 4, 1979, Chennault archives.

215   "the strange riverfront structure": Chennault, *The Education of Anna*, 217–218.

216   "readable but rather shallow": *New York Times*, February 3, 1980.

216   "That was an enticing prospect": Bùi Diem, *In the Jaws of History* (Boston: Houghton Mifflin Company, 1987), 236–245.

217   "I don't think anyone really has the knowledge": Chennault correspondence, January 7, 1985, Chennault archives.

218   and studied whether: *Washingtonian*, October 1, 2000.

219   Who makes uniforms: Ibid.

220   "We had it coming": David Bradley correspondence, February 2, 2017.

221   "He was equally comfortable": Michael Nannes interview, February 17, 2017.

222   "equally qualified": *W*, April 25–May 2, 1980.

222   "No words can express my joy": Chennault correspondence, November 7, 1980, Hoover Institution archives.

223   "I am not particularly interested": Ibid.

223   "I am not sure": Corcoran correspondence, November 7, 1980, Hoover Institution archives.

223   "I want to be free and independent": *Argus Leader*, November 7, 1980.

224   "After four years": *Washington Post*, January 14, 1981.

224   CHENNAULT'S COMEBACK: *Washington Star*, undated, Chennault archives.

224   "I am not a hostess": *People*, January 26, 1981.

225   "Anna is afraid that if she remarries": *Washington Post*, February 15, 1981.

225   "There are lots of insecure men": *Chicago Tribune*, January 11, 1981.

225   "I haven't had time to think about that": *People*, January 26, 1981.

226   The invitations delighted Taipei: *Christian Science Monitor*, January 29, 1981.

226   "We've never had so many": *Washington Post*, December 4, 1980.

226   Watergate sellers started raising prices: Ibid.

227    $750,000—about double: *Washington Post*, May 28, 1981.

227   "Prices don't scare them": *Washington Post*, December 4, 1980.

227   Watergate Hotel prepared two budgets: *Washington Post*, May 28, 1981.

228   "They're our royalty": Ibid.

229   Regulars called it the "Gossip Salon": "Watergate Beauty Salon has a Rodeo Drive Tint," *New York Times*, February 27, 1982.

229   "Before it was peanuts": *Washington Post*, May 28, 2001.

230   "What does she know about minorities?": *Washington Post*, February 11, 1981.

230   "I cannot understand": Goldwater letter to Pen James, February 4, 1981, Hoover Institution archives.

231   "the Pope's nose": Corcoran correspondence, Chennault archives.

231   "You must be": *Washington Post*, May 28, 1981.

231   "Please step out immediately": Palladin interview, August 21, 2017.

232 Jean-Louis prepared: *Washington Post*, February 9, 1981.

232 Salgo asked Palladin: Dahrouch interview, September 4, 2017.

233 Giuseppe Cecchi recruited him: "Gabor Olah de Garab Watergate Hotel Manager, 1967–1985," Watergate East Online, www.watergate50.com.

236 "And what a great teacher": Eulogy prepared by Anna Chennault, undated, Chennault archives.

237 "I adore my job": Associated Press, November 16, 1981.

237 "We are no longer the Nixon Watergate": *Washington Post*, May 28, 1981.

CHAPTER EIGHT: A NEST FOR HIGH-FLYERS

239 "You've got to be fucking kidding me": FoxNews.com, March 23, 2011.

239 Depending on the building: *Washington Post*, May 28, 1981.

239 "What precipitated the separation": David Bret, *Elizabeth Taylor: The Lady, The Lover, The Legend, 1932–2011* (New York: Greystone Books, 2011), 232.

241 "classic features": *Washington Post*, April 27, 1991.

242 "was a wartime employee": *Time*, July 7, 1947.

242 Mrs. Reagan did come for dinner: Jennifer Egan, "The Countess's Private Secretary," *New Yorker*, June 5 and 12, 2017.

242 As part of her "espionage": Romanones correspondence with the author, June 9, 2016.

243 She wrote to White House aides: Romanones correspondence, May 19, 1981, Reagan Presidential Library.

243 "The main question is timing": James M. Rentschler memorandum, November 1981, Reagan Presidential Library.

243 "might create a problem": Romanones correspondence, November 5, 1981, Hoover Institution archives.

244 "a fan of Major Bob": Burghardt memorandum, March 22, 1985, Reagan Presidential Library.

244 "had other implications": *Newsweek*, March 24, 1991.

244 "seedy and sophisticated": *New York Times*, June 21, 1987.

244 "Espionage is like a drug": *People*, May 7, 1990.

245 "You have to keep many things secret": *Newsweek*, March 24, 1991.

245 "romantic nonfiction": Ibid.

245 "Espionage is mostly boredom": Ibid.

245 auctioned off by Sotheby's Geneva: ArtKabinet, May 24, 2011.

247 "Then he just started coming on to me": *CBS News with Dan Rather*, June 30, 1982.

247 Representative Larry E. Craig: *New York Times*, July 8, 1982.

247 Williams was identified by name: Associated Press, July 7, 1982.

247 at the Watergate: *New York Times*, July 8, 1982.

248 "We at first sat down": United Press International, July 9, 1982.

248 "It was something that I just accepted": Ibid.

248   "a pathological liar": Associated Press, July 7, 1982.

248   "Leroy Williams maintains": ABC News transcript, July 9, 1982.

248   he did not have sex: United Press International, July 9, 1982.

248   CBS News tracked down "Roger": *Washington Post*, July 10, 1982.

249   Peacock Lounge: Ibid.

249   "If you can stick him": Ibid.

249   "I have lied": Associated Press, August 27, 1982.

249   Richard Kind, the owner of Friendly Models: *Miami Herald*, July 16, 1982.

250   "I am positive he named Larry Craig": *Idaho Statesman*, December 2, 2007.

250   According to a postmortem: Associated Press, September 19, 1982.

251   "undisclosed locations": Ibid.

251   "like Howard Carter": Mark Slater interview, August 8, 2017.

252   "real estate fees": *Washington Post*, July 23, 1984.

252   "This appealed to me": *New York Times*, July 24, 1984.

253   He changed his story: *Washington Post*, August 8, 1984.

253   the matter became further confused: Ibid.

253   he and his wife revised: *New York Times*, August 16, 1984.

254   "performed literally no work": *Oregonian*, June 2, 2012.

254   That triggered a vote: District of Columbia Court of Appeals, *Watergate West Inc. v. Barclays Bank, S.A.*, September 14, 2000.

256   WATERGATE: A WASHINGTON NEST FOR HIGH-FLYERS: *Dossier*, February 1982.

257   With a Republican in the White House: Salgo, 163.

257   "gave a discount": "A Conversation with Ambassador Keith C. Smith," Library of Congress, 2004.

258   Salgo placed all of his assets in a blind trust: Salgo, 119.

259   "My whole fortune comes from there": Ibid., 121.

259   Her Majesty's High Court of Justice: *Estates Times*, September 21, 1984.

260   including an almond orchard: *Management Review*, November 1986.

260   Luscombe ordered their air-conditioning turned off: Wendy Luscombe interview, June 8, 2016.

260   Luscombe solicited proposals: *Washington Post*, March 18, 1986.

260   "Europeans would put the charm back into it": Ibid.

261   the Watergate Hotel was losing money: *Christian Science Monitor*, March 7, 1984.

261   "Fear is drifting through the corridors": *Washington Post*, March 18, 1986.

261   If he were to remain: Ibid.

261   "only looked at the numbers": Dahrouch interview, September 4, 2017.

261   "but he didn't know how": Sneed interview, August 10, 2017.

261   "With Salgo, everything was easy": Palladin interview, August 21, 2017.

262   "But basil with raspberries?": *Washington Post*, August 29, 1982.

262   "do something in my way": *New York Times*, March 22, 1987.

262   Cunard Line: *Washington Post*, April 17, 1986.

262 Cunard's first venture: *The Times*, March 16, 1986, Trafalgar House press clippings copy.

262 "the acknowledged empress of hotel interior designers": *Washington Post*, July 31, 1988.

262 "the staff had to scramble": Lynda Clugston Webster interview, July 21, 2017.

262 Lee's design amounted to a British conquest: *The Guardian*, August 2, 1988.

263 "Almost": *New York Times*, April 24, 1986.

263 Watergate South, across the hall: *People*, July 25, 1977.

263 MRS. LUCE IS BACK, PEPPERY AS EVER: *New York Times*, November 13, 1981.

264 "I've been coming to Washington since the days of Harding": Ibid.

264 "stenographic or clerical staff": Green correspondence, July 28, 1982, Clare Boothe Luce papers, Library of Congress.

264 That night: *Washington Post*, May 26, 1984.

265 "President's Lunch Bar": Watergate Hotel news release, January 11, 1985.

265 "Graffiti is all over the world": *Washington Post*, February 14, 1985.

265 "It's a disgrace": *Washington Post*, July 24, 1985.

267 For the next five years: *Washington Post*, May 14, 1983.

268 "That's for people who have no money": *Washington Post*, July 24, 1985.

268 "we would be leery": Ibid.

269 "It was really exciting": Roxie Herbekian interview, February 24, 2017.

271 "They want to get liquid": *Australian Financial Review*, March 10, 1989.

271 "not been burned": *Washington Post*, August 6, 1989.

271 received no new funding: *Financial Times*, March 9, 1989.

272 "I think it needs some work": *Washington Post*, July 6, 1989.

272 "The Cunard people were running the place": Webster interview, July 21, 2017.

272 Complicating a potential sale: *Washington Post*, December 22, 1989.

272 Cunard Hotels and Resorts agreed: *Washington Post*, March 26, 1990.

272 National Coal Board announced: *Washington Post*, March 27, 1990.

273 Trusthouse Forte brought in a new general manager: Cathy Arevian interview, May 2, 2016.

274 "Absolutely not": Sneed interview, August 10, 2017.

274 Zanecki had wanted to live in the Watergate: Paul Zanecki interview, October 25, 2016.

CHAPTER NINE: MONICALAND

277 For Christmas: *Washington Post*, December 18, 1993.

278 "The banquets were hard on him": Arevian interview, May 2, 2016.

278 Pacific geoduck clams: Ibid.

279 Lights flashed in response: *Nation's Restaurant News*, May 20, 1996.

279 "New people bought the hotel": Ibid.

279   "Jean-Louis didn't want to negotiate": Ibid.

279   More than five hundred reservations: *Washington Post*, June 15, 1996.

280   Unlike other celebrity chefs: *New York Times*, November 26, 2001.

281   "No matter what": *Washington Post*, June 15, 1996.

281   $1 million contribution: Marcia Lewis, *The Private Lives of the Three Tenors* (New York: Boulevard Books, 1998), 81.

281   Following a bitter divorce: Andrew Morton, *Monica's Story* (New York: St. Martin's Press, 1999), 53.

282   Marcia had a conversation with Walter Kaye: Ibid.

282   Later that evening: "Time Line: Clinton Accused," *Washington Post*, September 13, 1998, https://www.washingtonpost.com/wp-srv/politics/special/clinton/timeline.htm.

282   She brought a photograph: *Baltimore Sun*, February 3, 1998.

283   "They are trying to set you up": Morton, 140.

284   Monica called her mother: Ibid., 182.

284   Later that night, back in Watergate South: Ibid., 191.

284   "It reminded me": Ibid., 250.

285   Starr's investigators arrived: Ibid., 196.

285   $3,500 a month: Exhibit 19–12, "Investigation of Illegal or Improper Activities in Connection with the 1996 Federal Elections Campaigns," U.S. Senate Governmental Affairs Committee, March 5, 1998, 2563.

285   a letter of reference: *Newsweek*, February 16, 1998.

286   "It's been 20 years": *Washington Post*, January 29, 1998.

286   "a must person": *Los Angeles Times*, July 20, 1997.

287   Cardozo flashed back to . . . Maurice Stans: CNN transcript, July 30, 2017.

288   "To Charlie Trie with thanks": Photocopy, stamped "THE PRESIDENT HAS SEEN" and dated November 8, 1996, FOIA Number 2008-0825-F, Clinton Presidential Library.

289   "significant concerns": *Los Angeles Times*, December 18, 1996.

289   "a very positive story": CNN transcript, December 18, 1996.

289   three months after: *Washington Post*, January 30, 1998.

291   "only when it was replaced": *Washington Post*, March 6, 1998.

291   and Morton Kondracke: "GOP must launch a new probe of Chinagate," *Jewish World Review*, August 9, 1999.

291   "we suffered H.R. problems": David Bradley correspondence, July 16, 2017.

292   "Either he's the nicest man in the world": Katherine Bradley interview, December 6, 2016.

293   "The Watergate is perfect": David Bradley interview, December 6, 2016.

294   should be at his desk: *Blood on the Carpet*, episode one, BBC 2, September 13, 1993.

294 "an upstart caterer": *Telegraph*, August 30, 2006.

294 "We simply couldn't get a look in": *Blood on the Carpet* episode one, BBC 2, September 13, 1993.

294 "I was quite taken aback": Ibid.

295 "It was a good talking point": Ibid.

295 "Robinson doesn't have one quality business": *Independent Online*, retrieved February 25, 2017.

295 The battle lasted nine weeks: *Los Angeles Times*, January 24, 1996.

295 Rocco tried to buy the Watergate: *Independent Online*, retrieved February 25, 2017.

297 "There are a million locks": *Washington Post*, May 27, 1997.

297 "They could be in a junk pile": Ibid.

297 Herrald's lock was sold for more than $20,000: Bill Welch interview, July 12, 2016. The lock was sold by Nate D. Sanders Auctions on December 14, 2017, for $62,500. The consignor's identity was not disclosed.

297 "a former manager at the Watergate": Ibid.

297 On the front page: *Washington Post*, January 21, 1998.

297 "it just went crazy": Morton, 199.

298 building manager warned: Ibid., 200.

298 "Chinese fire drill": States News Service, January 29, 1998.

298 "This place was surrounded": Phil Rascona oral history interview, GWU, 2014.

298 Lewinsky was seen in public for the first time: Examiner News Service, January 26, 1998.

298 "She might as well be in jail": *USA Today*, January 29, 1998.

298 The curtains shut out photographers: Morton, 200.

298 "Gucci prison": *Baltimore Sun*, February 3, 1998.

298 "More than 25 years after it first gained infamy": States News Service, January 29, 1998.

298 "the ghost of Watergate": *San Jose Mercury News*, December 7, 1998.

299 Dole, just two years after: *New York Times*, March 29, 1998.

299 20 million people: *Wired*, September 11, 2009.

300 "As I depart 700 New Hampshire": *Chicago Tribune*, October 14, 1998.

300 Giuseppe Cecchi, who had acquired it: John Cecchi interview.

300 "not too well-kept": Robert Dole interview, March 2, 2016.

300 "See all that back there?": *Wall Street Journal*, September 1, 2016.

CHAPTER TEN: DONE DEAL

301 *Incredible*: E. C. Schroeder interview, March 22, 2017.

303 "prestigious landmark": *Washington Business Journal*, December 7, 1998.

304 "a little problematic": Michael Darby interview, June 19, 2016.

305   "You're crazy": Frank Durkin interview, December 5, 2016.

305   "Washington has this thing": Darby interview.

306   "It was the smallest kitchen I had ever seen": Ibid.

308   "blocks from the core of downtown": *Washington Post*, May 31, 2003.

309   "Co-ops give us more control over who buys": "Watergate owners seek condo conversion," *Northwest Current*, May 14, 2003.

309   WARY AT THE WATERGATE: *Washington Post*, June 2, 2003.

310   "There haven't been many": *Washington Post*, January 26, 2004.

310   "for many, many years": Darby interview, June 13, 2017.

310   "Looking back": Audrey Wolf interview, December 2, 2016.

311   by a vote of 54 to 46 percent: District Zoning Commission, hearing transcript, January 29, 2004, 16–17.

313   "We don't designate use": *Northwest Current*, September 22, 2004.

313   The driving force: Eig interview, February 17, 2017.

313   "a bungled political robbery": *Northwest Current*, September 29, 2004.

313   Someone had sent him "Google information" on Moretti: "Preservation board puts off decision on Watergate complex designation," Ibid.

314   Would it be possible?: Eig interview.

314   "You could feel the angst in the room": Carol Mitten interview, February 17, 2017.

315   "Not that we did it very often": Wolf interview.

315   As a young man: Jack Olender interview, February 27, 2017.

316   "fine, but a little cramped": Ibid.

316   "generally dysfunctional": Ibid.

316   "It was as though": Darby interview.

316   "It didn't matter to him": Ibid.

316   "social justice": Olender interview.

317   "wasn't afraid of anything": Ibid.

317   He knew he was in over his head: Ibid.

319   Outside the hearing room: *Washington Post*, June 8, 2004.

325   "six antidemocratic and recalcitrant": Ibid.

325   "THE CHOICE IS SIMPLE": Ibid.

325   "This issue has been so emotional": Ibid.

325   "There was definitely ill will": Olender interview.

326   The proposed sale was approved by a narrow margin: Bill Condrell memorandum to the Membership of Watergate East, April 22, 2004.

326   "at the direction of the board": Judith Eaton memorandum, April 22, 2004.

327   "angst and fear": Ibid.

327   "muzzled": Ibid.

327   "It's a second Watergate cover-up": *Washington Post*, May 9, 2004.

328   "Sour grapes": Ibid.

329 League of Women Voters: *Washington Post,* June 8, 2004.

330 "It's a decent place": Ibid.

330 "done deal": Ibid.

331 Three weeks later: Memorandum of Opinion, Court of Chancery, State of Delaware, *Baring et al. v. Watergate East, Inc., et al.,* October 18, 2004, 8.

331 In August, Monument Realty announced: *Commercial Real Estate News,* August 20, 2004.

331 Darby approached Thomas Keller: Darby interview.

331 "I could see it in his eyes": Ibid.

331 As he looked around: Ibid.

333 "We feel vindicated": *Washington Post,* October 19, 2004.

333 "It's de-victory": Ibid.

334 "the name recognition of The Watergate is worldwide": Finch correspondence, September 22, 2004.

336 "The Watergate made peace": Eig interview.

337 "I'll take it": Karl Rove interview, December 16, 2017.

337 One Sunday afternoon: *New York Times,* April 9, 2006.

337 Annie Leibovitz photographed: *Vogue,* October 2001.

338 "like family": Ibid.

338 "The worst Christmas goodies you've ever seen": Rove interview.

339 "Been to the Watergate": Reprinted in *Arizona Republic,* May 2, 2006.

339 a jury convicted Brent Wilkes: *San Diego Union-Tribune,* February 20, 2008.

340 A year later: *Los Angeles Times,* September 30, 2008.

340 Hookergate: CNN transcript, May 5, 2006.

340 Darby reevaluated his plans: Bisnow.com, January 11, 2007.

340 $69.8 million construction loan: *Real Estate Finance and Investment,* January 14, 2005.

341 "It's too good a name to change": Associated Press, August 6, 2007.

341 "incredibly tough times": Klaus Peters interview, October 20, 2016.

341 "We apologize for the inconvenience": *Washington Post,* August 6, 2007.

341 closure was "devastating": Anton Obernberger interview, July 11, 2017.

341 "The hairdressers wanted to go": *Washington Post,* November 26, 2011.

341 "The Watergate is not a destination": *Washington Post,* January 25, 1993.

342 "Forget clothes": Ibid.

342 "Senior Safeway": *Washington Post,* November 2, 2011.

342 "It's not the same": *Washington Post,* November 26, 2011.

342 BentleyForbes, the California-based: *Washington Business Journal,* November 17, 2008.

342 "He wants to look 70": *Washington Post,* January 25, 1993.

343 "We paid *him*": Don Hayes interview, February 21, 2017.

344 virtually no relics from the Nixon era: Ibid.

344    $750: *Washington Post*, September 4, 2007.

344   "This must be the most media attention": ABC (Australian Broadcasting Company) News, September 7, 2007.

344   David Urso, a former Secret Service agent: Getty Images.

344   "there was nothing left in the building but an echo": Hughes interview.

345   "We weren't going to wait forever": *Northwest Current*, August 6, 2008.

345   "I will remember that day": Darby interview.

345   "How much planning": *Spiegel Online*, March 13, 2009.

345   "It's over": Darby interview.

346   "Since the bankruptcy announcement": *Washington Post*, September 22, 2008.

346   Darby approached PB Capital: Darby interview.

347   "There are investors with an interest": *Washington Post*, July 2, 2009.

347   "They felt they had no choice": Darby interview.

348   He estimated renovations would cost at least $100 million: *Washington Post*, July 19, 2009.

348   "For anybody to understand": Darby interview.

348   Cooper's heart sank: Paul Cooper interview, February 20, 2017.

349   "It's a Washington landmark": McClatchy wire report, July 21, 2009.

349   "Sold": Cooper interview.

EPILOGUE

351   Blaine's life "was one long orgy": *Globe and Mail*, June 26, 1980.

351   "People who live in the Watergate apartment complex": Margaret Truman, *Murder in the White House* (New York: Arbor House, 1980), 59.

353   "Well, Karl": Rove interview.

354   "People are looking to buy": Bisnow.com, July 21, 2017.

354   "It's like if you're a surfer": *Washington Business Journal*, September 13, 2013.

354   "It wasn't a real estate project": Luscombe interview.

354   He tried to buy: Cecchi interview.

355   "Some people have good sense": Olender interview.

355   "so expensive": Wolf interview.

355   but ordered the documents unsealed: Hughes, 214.

356   "remove any fig leaf": *New York Times*, January 2, 2017.

357   While stationed in Oklahoma: *New Yorker*, March 11, 2013.

357   The main course: *USA Today*, December 25, 2007.

357   "But the teeth": Patricia and Arthur Cotton Moore interview, June 13, 2017.

358   "Maybe one of the engineers": Tina Winston interview, June 16, 2016.

358   Carrie Christoffersen, the Newseum's chief curator, explained: Carrie Christoffersen interview, September 15, 2016.

358    $42 million: *Property Week*, June 11, 2010.

359   "was a glamorous place": *Los Angeles Times*, April 14, 2015.

359   20 percent tax credit: Eig correspondence, August 21, 2017.

360   A team of chefs: *Georgetown Dish*, July 18, 2017.

362   "a poetic and passionate soul": Magnifico interview.

363   "more dogs than children": *New York Times*, June 25, 1966.

363   "All those birthday parties": Obernberger interview.

INDEX

31901064530092